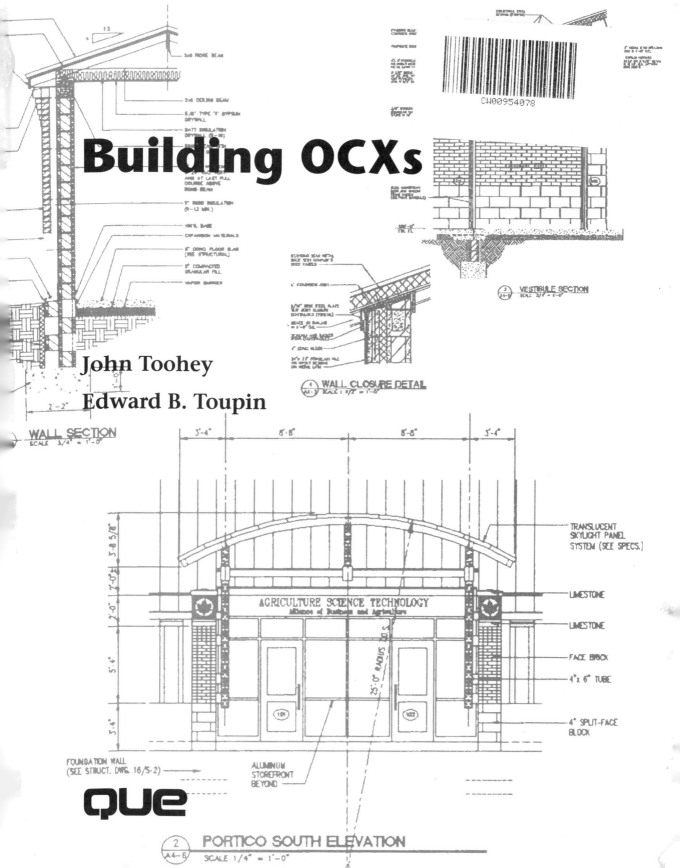

Building OCXs

John Toohey

Edward B. Toupin

que

Building OCXs

Copyright© 1995 by Que® Corporation

Library of Congress Catalog No.: 95-67835

ISBN: 0-7987-0138-3

97 96 95   6 5 4 3 2 1

Interpretation of the printing code: the rightmost double-digit number is the year of the book's printing; the rightmost single-digit number, the number of the book's printing. For example, a printing code of 95-1 shows that the first printing of the book occurred in 1995.

Publisher: Roland Elgey

Associate Publisher: Joseph B. Wikert

Director of Product Series: Charles O. Stewart III

Managing Editor: Kelli Widdifield

Director of Marketing: Lynn E. Zingraf

Credits

Product Director
Bryan Gambrel

Acquisitions Editor
Fred Slone

Production Editor
Maureen A. Schneeberger

Copy Editors
Lori Cates
Patrick Kanouse

Assistant Product Marketing Manager
Kim Margolius

Technical Editor
Steve Potts

Acquisitions Assistant
Angela C. Kozlowski

Operations Coordinator
Patricia J. Brooks

Editorial Assistant
Michelle Williams

Book Designer
Sandra Schroeder

Cover Designer
Karen Ruggles

Production Team
Claudia Bell
Amy Cornwell
Brad Dixon
Chad Dressler
DiMonique Ford
Dennis Clay Hager
Jason C. Hand
John Hulse
Daryl Kessler
Clinton Lahnen
Bob LaRoche
Elizabeth Lewis
Darcy Meyers
Steph Mineart
Dennis Sheehan
Kris Simmons
Mike Thomas
Scott Tullis
Suzanne Tully

Indexer
Michael Hughes

Composed in *Stone Serif* and *MCPdigital* by Que Corporation.

Dedication

For Alexander, Selma, and Daniel

John Toohey

Acknowledgments

First, I would like to thank Joe Wikert at Que Corporation for getting me involved in this project.

To Fred Slone, my acquisitions editor, for all his help and assistance.

To Maureen Schneeberger and Bryan Gambrel for editing the manuscript.

To all the other people at Que—Patty Brooks, Angie, and those whose names I do not know.

And finally, my coauthor Ed Toupin.

About the Authors

John Toohey is currently employed as the development manager at Traffic Software Inc. and is the chief developer of Object-Fax, a network fax solution for Windows and DOS. Object-Fax was used by Microsoft to demonstrate OLE 2.0 at its first public showing in Seattle in May of 1993. He has been working as a software developer for ten years since leaving the Irish Armed Forces. John has been working with Windows since version 1.0 and was one of the first beta testers of OLE version 1.0.

John is married to Hafdis and they have three children, a son Alexander, a daughter Selma Drofn, and another son Daniel. They currently live in Reykajavik, Iceland.

Edward B. Toupin is degreed in mathematics, computer science, and electronics technology, and is an automation engineer for a Denver-based engineering firm. Edward designs and develops applications under various platforms for industrial control, expert system applications, database management, GIS, mobile satellite applications, integration solutions, and network management and communications. Some of his network research is outlined in his book *Network Programming under VMS/DECnet Phases IV and V* by QED/ John Wiley & Sons. Edward's publications with Que include *Easy Programming with C, Visual Basic 4.0 Expert Solutions*, and *Special Edition Using Turbo C++ for Windows*.

Trademarks

All terms mentioned in this book and enclosed CD that are known to be trademarks or service marks have been appropriately capitalized. Que cannot attest to the accuracy of this information. Use of a term in this book should not be regarded as affecting the validity of any trademark or service mark.

We'd Like to Hear from You!

As part of our continuing effort to produce books of the highest possible quality, Que would like to hear your comments. To stay competitive, we *really* want you, as a computer book reader and user, to let us know what you like or dislike most about this book or other Que products.

You can mail comments, ideas, or suggestions for improving future editions to the address below, or send us a fax at (317) 581-4663. For the on-line inclined, Macmillan Computer Publishing has a forum on CompuServe (type **GO QUEBOOKS** at any prompt) through which our staff and authors are available for questions and comments. The address of our Internet site is **http://www.mcp.com** (World Wide Web).

In addition to exploring our forum, please feel free to contact me personally to discuss your opinions of this book: on CompuServe, I'm at 75230,1556; and on the Internet, I'm **bgambrel@que.mcp.com**.

Thanks in advance—your comments will help us to continue publishing the best books available on computer topics in today's market.

Bryan Gambrel
Product Development Specialist
Que Corporation
201 W. 103rd Street
Indianapolis, Indiana 46290
USA

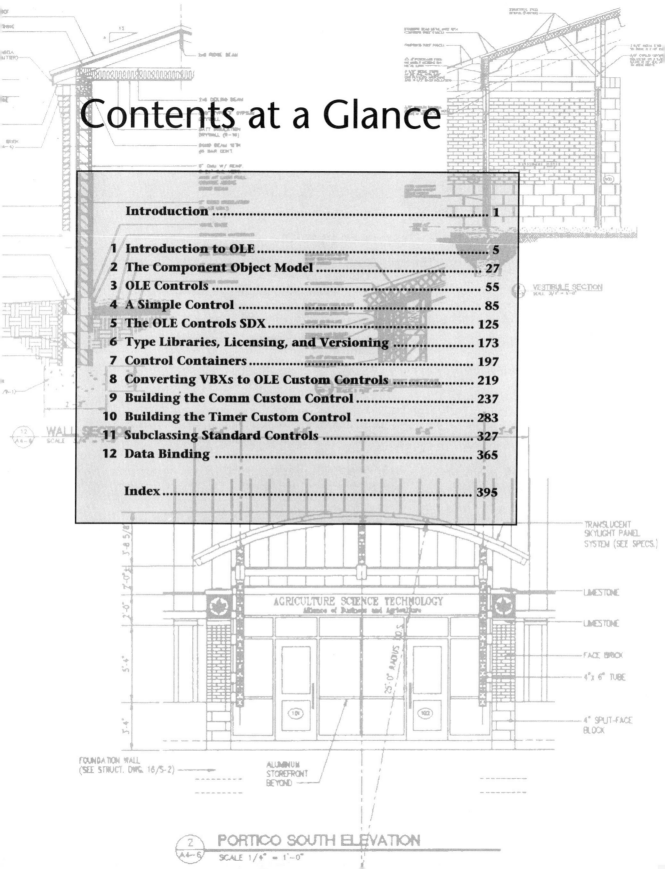

Contents at a Glance

Table of Contents

Chapter 3   OLE Controls   55

Chapter 6   Type Libraries, Licensing, and Versioning   173

Chapter 7   Control Containers   197

Introduction

Without a doubt, the next revolution in software will be component software. These software building blocks will be used to build the next generation of application software. At the heart of this component software revolution are OLE controls.

By combining OLE automation, Visual Editing, and a component software architecture, OLE controls provide developers and users with the best features of OLE and Visual Basic controls (VBXs). A huge industry already exists in the development of VBX controls for Visual Basic. With the release of OLE controls, this industry is set to explode. OLE controls provide a significant number of the advantages of VBXs. The most important advantages include the fact that OLE controls are designed from the ground up. They are extensible, portable (they are available in 16-bit and 32-bit implementations), they are not dependent on the Visual Basic environment, and, as you will see in this book, are relatively easy to implement. This next section takes you on a quick tour of what this book covers.

Roadmap

The goal of this book is to provide you with the necessary background information to understand OLE. It provides a step-by-step guide to actually developing OLE controls and a reference that you can refer to as you begin to develop your own controls. The following is a breakdown of the chapters in this book.

Chapter 1—Introduction to OLE

In this chapter, you are introduced to OLE and its technologies. OLE is a complex system that consists of many separate technologies. This chapter also provides an overview of each of the technologies and the history behind OLE.

Chapter 2—The Component Object Model

The heart of OLE is the object model upon which it is built. The model is called the Component Object Model (COM) and provides the infrastructure for OLE. An understanding of COM is vital for every OLE developer.

Chapter 3—OLE Controls

Microsoft provided significant advancements to OLE in order to provide support for OLE controls. In this chapter, you will examine the architecture of OLE controls in depth.

Chapter 4—A Simple Control

Chapter 4 provides a look at what is required to actually develop an OLE control. In this chapter, you will use MFC and Visual C++ 2.0 to create a 32-bit OLE control. The OLE ControlWizard provided with the Control SDK is used to help you build the control.

Chapter 5—The OLE Controls SDK

A number of new classes and extensions to MFC were added to provide support for OLE controls. This chapter examines these new classes in detail and also the utilities provided with the OLE Controls SDK.

Chapter 6—Type Libraries, Licensing, and Versioning

A detailed examination of OLE type libraries is provided in this chapter. Type libraries contain descriptions of properties and methods that a control or OLE automation server wants to expose. The chapter continues with a discussion of licensing and versioning issues as they pertain to OLE controls.

Chapter 7—Control Containers

OLE control containers are standard OLE in-place containers that have been enhanced to support the insertion of OLE controls. This chapter introduces you to the extensions required for a container to support controls.

Chapter 8—Converting VBXs to OLE Custom Controls

This chapter leads you through the steps required to convert a VBX control to a OLE control. The basics of control migration are covered, as is the use of the ControlWizard as an aid in porting.

Chapter 9—Building the Comm Custom Control

A small communication control is developed in this chapter. Each step involved in creating a control is covered, from using the ControlWizard to using the Test Container for final testing.

Chapter 10—Building the Timer Custom Control

The focus in this chapter is the building of an OLE control that has no interface. The timer control developed here is used to notify an application of preprogrammed events.

Chapter 11—Subclassing Standard Controls

Using standard Windows controls as base classes for your own custom OLE controls is the subject of this chapter. Subclassing is a technique familiar to most Windows programmers, but the techniques shown in this chapter will raise that to new heights.

Chapter 12—Data Binding

The ability to bind an OLE control to a data source such as a SQL server is a powerful feature. This chapter examines what is required to support bound controls.

Conventions Used in This Book

To enhance the usability of this book, the following typographical conventions have been utilized:

- Words or phrases defined for the first time appear in *italic*. Words or phrases that you are asked to type appear in **bold**. Screen displays and on-screen messages appear in a `special typeface`.

- Names of classes, functions, variables, messages, macros, and so on also appear in a `special typeface`.

- A code continuation character (➥) has been used in a code when a code line is too long to fit within the margins of this book. This symbol indicates that due to page constraints, a code line has been broken that normally would appear in a single line. In your programs, you should type the two lines as one.

Chapter 1

Introduction to OLE

by John Toohey

Although this book is concerned with teaching you how to create OLE controls (sometimes incorrectly called OCXs—OCX is the usual file extension for OLE controls), an understanding of OLE technologies is very important.

This chapter looks at the following topics:

- The history of OLE and the motivation for its development
- The document-oriented paradigm
- The promise of component software
- The major OLE technologies

The Story Behind OLE

An important feature of OLE is *application integration*. This idea is not new. It was first introduced in Microsoft Windows through dynamic data exchange (DDE).

DDE was not actually a feature of Windows; rather, it was a protocol that defined how two applications could communicate and exchange data with each other. DDE was originally developed for Microsoft Excel, the application that developers always used to test against their own DDE applications. It was always a case of doing what Excel did and not what the protocol said. DDE was built around a client-server model and was difficult and idiosyncratic for both users and developers.

OLE 1.0, which Microsoft introduced in June 1991, was Microsoft's first attempt to deliver an object-oriented model for Windows (see fig. 1.1). OLE 1.0 was built on top of DDE and introduced the concept of compound documents.

Fig. 1.1
The history of OLE from its beginnings to the present day.

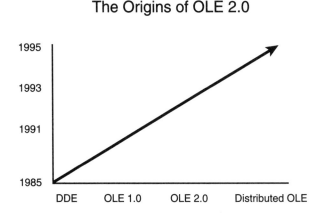

The Origins of OLE 2.0

Like DDE, OLE was originally developed to solve a problem for a Microsoft application. The developers of Microsoft PowerPoint wanted a way to use Microsoft Graph as a presentation element in their application, so they developed a protocol called the Microsoft PowerPoint Graph. In Microsoft PowerPoint, a graph is embedded in a presentation as an object. The protocols used to develop the original specification for Microsoft PowerPoint formed the basis for OLE 1.0; and the concept of an application being used as a container for an object forms the core concepts for OLE 2.0.

The concepts of *linked* and *embedded* objects were first introduced through compound documents. A *compound document* is a document that consists of data objects from various applications. You can either embed or link these objects. An embedded object is fully contained within the document. A linked object contains the path to a data source that contains the original data. To edit an embedded or linked object, you simply double-click on the object. The OLE libraries then execute the OLE server associated with that object.

When you are finished editing the data, you quit the server application, and the OLE libraries update the presentation data. The container does not have to display or print the object, because the OLE libraries take care of rendering the object to the printer or display.

The OLE 1.0 libraries, which shipped with Windows 3.1, were intended as a means of integrating applications.

However, programming for OLE 1.0 proved difficult for developers outside Microsoft Corporation. Although this difficulty was partially due to the lack of documentation and example code from Microsoft, a major part of the problem was due to the underlying DDE protocols.

DDE is an *asynchronous protocol*, which means that when you call a function, the function call returns immediately even though the DDE libraries have not completed the requested task. You then have to wait in a message loop, constantly polling a status function.

Because you are passing data between the object and the container, you have to make copies of the data in memory and pass pointers to the data. This works fine for small amounts of data, but if you embed a sound clip or a large graph in a container such as Write, you can bring the entire system to its knees.

Linked objects caused major problems when the user moved the data source. The user would receive an unfriendly broken links error message and had to attempt to restore the link manually.

In May 1993, Microsoft formally released OLE 2.0, after undergoing a series of design previews and extensive beta testing by many independent software vendors (ISVs). The OLE 2.0 architects addressed all the shortcomings of OLE 1.0 and delivered a robust, scaleable object system for Windows. OLE 2.0 goes far beyond the capabilities of OLE 1.0 and beyond being a mechanism for creating compound files.

The features of OLE 2.0 are powerful and compelling. OLE 2.0 introduces a powerful interapplication drag-and-drop protocol, in-place editing of embedded objects, object programmability, Uniform Data Transfer (UDT), and structured storage for objects.

The object model used in OLE 2.0—the Component Object Model (COM)—defines a binary object standard. Because COM defines a binary model, OLE 2.0 is independent of the applications and programming languages that you use to create your applications. The COM defines a binary standard because it defines how an object is actually laid out in memory. It defines an interface pointer as being a pointer to a table of function or method pointers. This table is known as a *vtable*. Conveniently, this layout scheme is the same scheme as C++ compilers use to define an object in memory.

This independence ensures interoperability between objects created by different vendors. If you write an object in C++, a Visual Basic programmer can use your object in his or her application because the methods of connecting to objects and exchanging data are provided through a common interface.

A Scaleable Object System

OLE 2.0 provides the foundation for future object systems from Microsoft. You can see how the system is designed from the ground up to be extensible and scaleable by examining three major parts of the current release:

- Lightweight remote procedure call (LRPC)

- The structured storage system

- Monikers

The following sections discuss each of these three new features. These features were key elements to the OLE architects. Although the architects knew that some of these features would not be available in the initial release of OLE 2.0, by designing the architecture as they did, they have assured a long future for OLE.

Lightweight Remote Procedure Call (LRPC)

The mechanism by which objects communicate with each other in OLE 2.0 is called *lightweight remote procedure call* (LRPC). LRPC takes care of marshaling parameters and interface calls from one process to another. This mechanism even handles the translation of calls and parameters from a 16-bit environment to a 32-bit one, and vice versa.

At any time, you can change the subsystem for *true remote procedure call* (RPC) to make OLE 2.0 a distributed object system (see fig. 1.2). In fact, this is what Microsoft has done with distributed OLE, in which the LRPC system is replaced with an RPC system. The RPC system used by Microsoft is compatible with the standard defined by the Open Software Foundation (OSF) in its Distributed Computing Environment (DCE) model. This will help to ensure that OLE will interoperate with other object systems.

Microsoft and Digital have demonstrated such a system. In the demonstration, an OSF/1 server ran a stock quote object that updated an Excel spreadsheet running on a Windows NT machine. Excel was not aware that the data was being sent to it from a remote machine or that the originating object was running on a UNIX machine.

The entire process was transparent to both the user and the application. Every OLE 2.0 compliant application can connect remotely to other objects without requiring any changes to the application's code; in fact, you don't even have to recompile such applications.

Scaleable Components

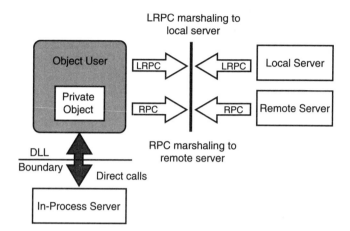

Fig. 1.2
These are scaleable
components—an
in-process object
server, a local
object server,
and a remote
object server.

The Structured Storage System

OLE 2.0 incorporates a structured storage system that provides persistent
storage for objects. All objects, whether they be compound document objects
or OLE controls, need to be able to store and retrieve data. OLE's structured
storage provides a transacted storage architecture and a set of COM interfaces.

Storages and Streams

Compound files (OLE's current implementation of structured storage) provide
a file system within a file system. Compound files are structured similar to
the DOS file system with *streams* (files) and *storages* (directories). Stream
names can be as long as 32 characters. Each stream and storage is, in fact, an
object and can be accessed through COM interfaces.

In structured storage, each component object can have its own stream. During the lifetime of the object, it can read and write to this stream. The object
has full control over the amount of data that is read or written. This solves a
major problem of OLE 1.0, in which an object had to read its entire data into
memory to access the data. Although each object has its own stream, a compound document—such as a word-processing document—that contains
many types of objects is physically stored as a single disk file. Thus Microsoft
uses the phrase "a file system within a file" when referring to compound files.
The internal structure of a compound file is similar to the structure of your
hard disk.

Within any compound file, several storage and stream objects exist (see fig. 1.3). The first storage object, the *root storage*, is the parent of all other storages and streams. You create storages and streams much as you create files and directories. Like the DOS file system, storages can contain other storages and can be nested arbitrarily deep.

Fig. 1.3
OLE structured storage showing streams and substorages.

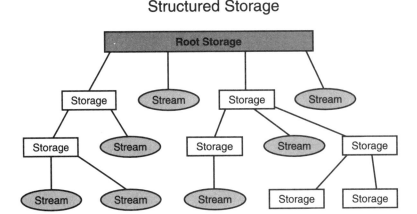

Structured Storage

Access Modes

Normally, when you update and write changes back to a data file, the data is updated immediately on the disk. Even most disk caches will not cache a disk write. It is just too dangerous. However, this makes an "undo" system difficult to implement. The transacted access mode of structured storage attempts to solve this problem.

Structured storage supports two modes of access:

- In *direct* mode, any changes made to the object's data are immediately written to the file.

- In *transacted* mode, the changes are buffered until either a commit or rollback operation is performed.

One of the reasons that transacted mode is so important is because of compound documents. For example, suppose that you have a Word 6.0 document that contains an embedded spreadsheet object from Excel. You decide to change some of the figures in the spreadsheet and activate the object. When you finish, you save the changes and deactivate the object to return to Word. You then decide to exit Word *without* saving the changes that you made to the text. You now have a problem: What should be done to the changes that you made to the spreadsheet object? This is precisely the problem that transacted storage tries to solve. If you open the spreadsheet object in transacted mode, the container (Word, in this case) can simply close the storage without committing the changes. When you re-open the document, the changes that you made to the text and to the spreadsheet figures have been discarded.

Transacted mode has its price. Performance suffers because the mode takes a "snapshot" of the original data and stores it in an unused portion of the file. For large objects, this process can take time. Normally, this performance hit would not be a problem. If you want to take advantage of rollback (undoing changes to your data files) and commit (making those changes permanent) in your application, you use transacted mode access and accept the performance hit; if speed is more important, you open the storage in direct mode.

However, with structured storage, the choice is not that simple. Unfortunately, in the current implementation of compound files, any storage that you open in direct access mode must also be opened exclusively. In other words, no other process can open that storage, not even in read-only mode. While not a problem in a single-user environment, this constraint is a major headache in a network environment. Perhaps future releases of compound files will solve these problems.

Transacted access applies only to storage objects, not to stream objects. All stream objects are opened in direct, and therefore exclusive, mode.

Standard Streams

The OLE specification defines special streams called *property sets* that conform to a standard layout. Any application that can read property sets can extract information from your files. This feature is particularly powerful if the system shell can also read property sets.

In fact, this is the case in Windows 95. One special property set is the Summary Information stream, which can include such information about the document as the author's name, the last time the document was saved, the full name of the document, thumbnails, and keywords. The Windows 95 shell can search through compound files for Summary Information fields. Future versions of the shell will use property sets to perform indexing on objects so that the system can rapidly find objects within any given namespace.

Availability

The current implementation of compound files is implemented on top of the file allocation table (FAT) file system of Windows 3.1 and NTFS (NT File System) under Windows NT. A future version of Windows NT will implement a native OFS (Object File System) that will directly support storage and stream objects. Compound files provide binary compatibility across all platforms on which OLE is implemented. OLE is currently implemented on both the Windows and Macintosh platforms, and compound files created on one platform can be read on the other. The current implementation of compound files even provides automatic conversion between Macintosh PICT formats and Windows BMP formats.

The Future of Structured Storage

How far can Microsoft go with structured storage? One direction in which Microsoft is heading is toward a unified namespace represented by a root storage. Network nodes would be substorages, and the volumes on these nodes would also be substorage objects. In fact, remote and local volumes and their directories and files would be storage and stream objects. If Microsoft accomplishes this goal, you will be able to place the system shell on top of root storage, and then browse or search the entire enterprise namespace—truly information at your fingertips.

Monikers

A new type of object, called a *moniker*, addresses link tracking. In OLE 1.0, the broken links created by moving files were a major annoyance. Links were so easily broken because they were stored as absolute pathnames. OLE 2.0 partially solves this problem by providing object monikers, which enable you to store relative pathnames with the absolute pathnames. The operating system (OS) actually moves the files, so the problem of broken links will be completely solved only when support from the OS is implemented. Microsoft promises this support in the OFS of a future release of Windows NT. Current OLE applications, when running on this release of Windows NT, will automatically receive this support through the system's implementation of object monikers. Again, no changes to the application's code will be required.

Component Software

A major problem facing every software vendor today is the increasing complexity of modern applications. In order to stay ahead of the race, you need to constantly add more and more features to your application. This constant pressure for more features bloats your application, making it more and more difficult to debug and develop. The end result is applications that over-promise, under-deliver, and are late.

The idea of software components as building blocks is not new. The standard libraries shipped with your compiler are collections of components. However, because of their granularity, they are not very useful on their own.

One much touted solution, which many of you are no doubt familiar with, is Object Oriented Programming (OOP). Even after struggling with C++ for a year or two, many programmers never realized the promise of object reuse. Part of the problem is that to gain the maximum benefit from using a class library, you must have access to the source code. The source code is important for fully understanding the workings of the base classes that you are using. An additional problem occurs when the vendor of the class library releases a new version of its product. This dependence on source code for object reuse is not viable.

What is needed is a means to seamlessly integrate third-party products into your applications. These products must provide a clean and well-defined interface and must totally isolate you from internal changes to the code. What is needed is binary reusable objects.

Software reuse and plug-and-play components have been promised by OOP vendors for years. However, it was only with the initial release of VBX (Visual Basic controls) technology from Microsoft that we first truly saw plug-and-play components. An entire industry has since developed around this technology.

Visual Basic Extensions
The initial release of Visual Basic (VB) shipped with 16 controls. These controls were designed to assist the developer in quickly creating VB applications by allowing the developer to concentrate on the actual application that was being developed. These controls allow the developer to provide the application with a 3D look or add additional functionality, such as rich text edit controls or hierarchy list boxes.

A Control Development Kit (CDK) was then released, enabling commercial developers to develop Visual Basic controls or VBXs for the growing market of corporate developers. Over the years, almost every type of utility has been encapsulated into a VBX. Examples of controls range from spreadsheet type grid controls to communication controls. Why did VBXs achieve a success rate that has thus far eluded traditional OOP methods? The answer is probably because VBXs are delivered in binary form with a clearly defined standard interface.

VBXs could be used out of the box with little or no problems.

OLE Controls

Unfortunately, the VBX architecture is closely tied to the Windows 16-bit platform. VBXs' dependencies on things such as based pointers has made it extremely difficult to port VBXs to a 32-bit platform such as Windows 95 or Windows NT. These dependencies also mean that VBXs could never run on a MIPS or Alpha platform.

Another problem was that it was not possible to extend VBXs. In other words, if I have a VBX that performs, say 90% of the work that I require, there is no way for me to inherit that 90% and add the additional 10% of functionality myself.

Finally, hosting VBXs proved to be a difficult task. Apart from Microsoft's Visual Basic, very few other environments supported VBXs. Even Visual C++ could only support the 1.0 release of VBX. This was due to the proprietary nature of the interfaces between VBXs and their host environment.

Obviously, something needed to be done. Microsoft's solution is the OLE controls specification. OLE controls do not build on the current VBX architecture; nor do they extend it. They are built around the current OLE architecture. They use the same object model—COM—as standard OLE objects.

The fact that OLE controls are based on OLE means that they are available in both 16-bit and 32-bit environments. They are also available to any application that supports OLE. OLE controls will be the centerpiece of the component software revolution (see fig. 1.4).

Fig. 1.4
Types of OLE controls.

OLE Controls

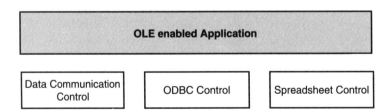

Because OLE is an open specification, OLE controls will undoubtedly be supported by far more host vendors than VBXs. OLE controls will be available for use in any OLE container that support controls. Future versions of Microsoft Word and Microsoft Excel will support OLE controls.

As you will see in later chapters, Microsoft is also providing tools to assist developers in porting existing VBXs to OLE controls. This process is quite simple and should ensure that the thousands of VBXs available today will soon be available as OLE controls.

The OLE Technologies

In many people's minds, OLE is a Microsoft technology for creating compound documents in the Microsoft Windows environment. Actually, OLE is far more than that (see fig 1.5). OLE comprises an object model which is the foundation for all further versions of Windows. OLE is also a technology which extends far beyond compound documents and Windows itself. OLE is available for the Macintosh, and OLE servers have been demonstrated running in a UNIX environment.

OLE Technologies

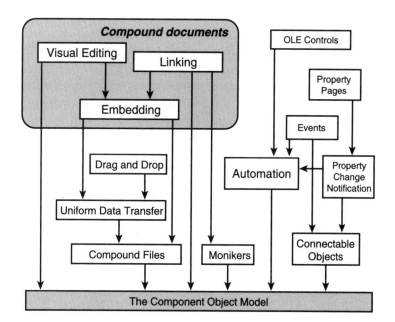

Fig. 1.5
The OLE Technologies: Compound documents to OLE controls.

In order to help people understand the scope of OLE, Microsoft has begun to use a number of terms when discussing OLE. These terms are meant to help people differentiate between the various technologies.

OLE Component Object Model

The *OLE Component Object Model* (COM) is the core object model that serves as the unifying architecture for all of Microsoft's object technologies. The COM describes how objects interact and communicate with each other. COM is destined to be the ubiquitous object model for all future system offerings from Microsoft. The next chapter examines the COM in detail.

OLE Documents

OLE documents are compound documents created using one or more OLE-enabled applications.

In the Document-Oriented Interface (DOI) model, the document itself is the focus of all the user's work. To begin working with a document, the user does not start an application and then choose Open from the File menu; instead, the document is simply opened. The underlying OS or system shell understands how to open a generic container to display the document for viewing or editing. This container is simply a storage place for various types of objects. These objects can be formatted text, graphics, numbers, video clips, or even embedded sound clips.

Objects can be moved around the containers or dragged and dropped to another container. To manipulate these objects, users invoke the object servers that support the objects. In the DOI paradigm, each object contains both the data and the code that can edit or view the data. Clicking any object with the right mouse button usually brings up a pop-up menu that displays the various verbs that the user can invoke on that object.

In fact, the DOI paradigm fundamentally changes the definition of the word *document*. You normally associate the term *document* with a specific type; for example, you might associate a word-processing document with Microsoft Word or a spreadsheet document with Microsoft Excel. A *compound document*, on the other hand, is a collection of parts or objects; the document itself simply keeps all these objects in one place.

OLE documents introduce two technologies, visual editing and object linking, which are now examined in more detail.

Visual Editing

Visual editing, or the in-place editing of embedded objects, is probably the most discussed aspect of OLE 2.0. From a user's perspective, one of the most difficult aspects of OLE 1.0's user interface (UI) is the context switch that occurs when the user double-clicks an object. The object's server is invoked and executed in a separate window. Instead, visual editing does what most users would naturally expect: the data is edited within the container. Visual editing is the first step toward achieving a true document-oriented interface. In visual editing, the application comes to the user, instead of forcing the user to come to the application.

So what actually happens during visual editing? The user first selects the object and double-clicks it. At this stage, the data that the user is viewing is simply a presentation metafile that, with the help of the OLE libraries, the container draws in its client area. By double-clicking the object, the user invokes the object server. The object server then attempts to negotiate with the container for space for its toolbars and other adornments. If this negotiation succeeds, the server creates an editing window and awaits user input.

A major part of this complex series of negotiations involves menus. While the object is in-place active, its menu merges with the container's menu. Each object contains a special set of menus that are used for in-place activation. The rules are simple. The container supplies three submenu groups: the File group, the Container group, and the Window group. The object supplies the Edit group, the Object group, and the Help group. These submenu groups are combined to form the menu for the activated object (see fig. 1.6). The implementation of merged menus is made more complex by having to deal with context-sensitive help and keyboard accelerators. Help or error messages that are normally displayed on the object server's status bar are routed to that container's status bar.

Visual Editing Menu Merging

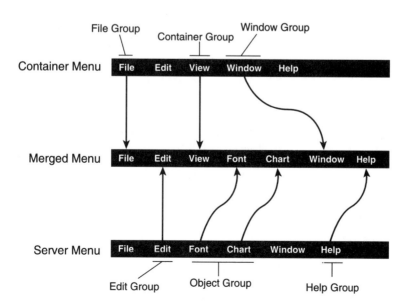

Fig. 1.6
This is an example of menu merging during the in-place activation of an OLE object.

This seamless integration with the container makes the object appear to be part of the container. When finished with the object, the user simply clicks on the client area to deactivate the object. The object removes its frame adornments and floating windows, and removes the merged menu. The server shuts down and the updated data returns to the container for storage.

Like so many software features, visual editing, while making it easy for the user to edit embedded objects, is extremely difficult for the developer to implement.

Visual editing applies only to embedded objects. Because the container stores an embedded object's data, you can edit it. A linked object's data, on the other hand, is stored elsewhere, so you must edit it within the object server.

Visual editing as provided in the initial release of OLE is not perfect. Currently, OLE provides no support for irregularly shaped objects (those that are not rectangular). Likewise, large objects that straddle page boundaries in the container are not supported. For example, when a large spreadsheet object is embedded in a container, the user may want to activate a part of the object that lies on a particular page. This process, known as *extended layout negotiation*, is mentioned in the OLE 2.0 design specification but did not make it into the current release.

Another area of importance for visual editing is toolbar negotiation. Unfortunately, vendors have a long way to go before agreeing on a standard appearance for toolbars. The merging of menus during visual editing is possible only because Microsoft has laid down all standards and guidelines for an application's menus since the first release of Windows. All applications that adhere to the Windows interface guidelines include File, Edit, and, in the case of Multiple Document Interface (MDI) applications, Window menus. This standardization greatly simplifies the process of merging menus. The same standardization has not yet been done for toolbars.

Object Linking

Before you can understand link tracking and management technology, you need to be familiar with the following terms:

- A *link* or *linked object* is an OLE object that contains a reference to a link source.

- A *link source* is an object that provides the source data for the linked object.

- A *moniker* is a handle to a link source that is persistently stored with the linked object.

■ *Moniker binding* is the process of getting a pointer to a running instance of the link source from the linked object's moniker.

These terms often are a source of confusion for developers when they begin to work with OLE.

Object linking (the *L* in OLE) has existed since the inception of DDE. OLE 1.0 introduced two distinct types of compound document objects:

■ *Embedded objects*, the data of which is completely contained by the document.

■ *Linked objects*, the source data of which is stored apart from the document.

OLE 1.0 also had four major restrictions that frustrated both users and developers:

■ The definition of the link source was an object with two parts: the document name and the item name. Therefore, you could not link to embedded objects in the document or use nested links.

■ The document name was stored as an absolute path. This was the source of the `broken links` error messages that users often encountered. If you moved the source document from its original location, you broke the link.

■ Automatic links were a problem. If you linked a chart to your document and opened the chart in a separate application, no automatic updating of the linked chart would take place. To affect automatic linking in OLE 1.0, you had to open the linked chart from within the document.

■ If you opened an OLE 1.0 compound document that contained linked objects, you had no way to determine whether the presentation data was up to date.

OLE 2.0 addresses each of these problems. The release supports linking to embedded objects, arbitrarily deep-nested linking, linking to files with absolute and relative pathnames, and linking to ranges (such as bookmarks or spreadsheet cells).

So, from a container's point of view, what is the difference between a linked and an embedded object? A linked object in a container is actually an embedded object. The major difference (apart from the COM interfaces supported) is that the native data for a linked object is a special OLE object called a *moniker.* (Chapter 2, "The Component Object Model," covers COM interfaces in detail.) The moniker object contains a reference to the actual source object.

A moniker is an object that contains a reference to a link source. The most basic operation that you perform on a moniker is that of binding it to the object that it references. In binding, the linked object is connected to the link source and an interface pointer is returned. You can then use this pointer to retrieve the updated presentation data for an object or to activate the object for editing.

Monikers come in different types, some defined by the user and some pre-defined by OLE. There are five predefined monikers:

- A *composite moniker*, as its name suggests, is composed of other monikers. Each of these simple monikers contains information that enables the containers to access the link source. For example, if your Microsoft Excel spreadsheet contains a quarterly report, the current sales figures are actually an embedded database object. Furthermore, the pie chart on the sheet is actually linked to the figures in the database object. The composite moniker that references the figures would be composed of three monikers (see fig. 1.7). Each moniker within the composite moniker has information that leads to the actual link source.

Fig. 1.7
A composite moniker composed of three simple monikers.

Composite Moniker

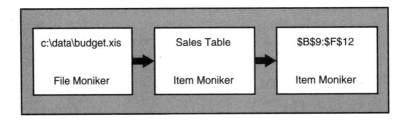

- Although you create monikers from left to right, they are bound from *right to left*. The reason for this right-to-left direction is that binding is a potentially expensive process, and if you are already positioned somewhere on the moniker, the process is much quicker if you begin at the right.

- A *file moniker* is a simple moniker that contains a pathname to a link source. The pathname can be absolute or relative. An absolute path is in the form c:\dev\src\abc.cpp while a relative path is in the form

..\src\abc.cpp. When you bind to a file moniker, the creating application is determined (with `GetClassFile`), executed, and asked to open the file described in the moniker. Opening files can be an expensive process, particularly on busy networks, which is one of the reasons that the composite monikers bind from right to left. If the file is already opened, you do not want to re-open it. Even if you create an absolute file moniker for a particular object, OLE will also create a relative moniker from the absolute one. This relative moniker always takes precedence over the absolute one when binding. The absolute moniker is used only if the relative moniker fails to bind.

- An *item moniker* is actually a generalization of the OLE 1.0 `document`, `item` referencing system. Item monikers are application-defined references to items of data within a particular document. Examples include cell ranges in a spreadsheet and bookmarks in a word-processing program. You can nest item monikers arbitrarily deep, as in the following example:

```
document[,item[,item[,item]]]
```

In this case, the rightmost moniker binds to the moniker on the left, and so on, until the reference is resolved.

- An *antimoniker* removes the moniker that precedes it in a composite moniker. When you create a composite moniker, you constantly append new monikers to it, which are added from left to right. However, no mechanism exists for removing or deleting one of these simple monikers. Instead, you use an antimoniker. These monikers cannot be bound to and perform no other useful function.

- *Pointer monikers,* instead of referencing objects in passive space (on disk), only reference objects in active space (process memory). You cannot serialize pointer monikers, but you can marshal them to a different process.

OLE 2.0 provides relative path link tracking. Therefore, if you have a link to a file that resides in C:\DATA\EXCEL and move the entire tree structure to D:, the relative moniker \EXCEL\BUDGET.XLS may be enough to locate the file. However, if you move the file to D:\REPORTS\BUDGET.XLS, the moniker binding fails.

The current implementation method works in two cases:

- When the link source and the container are moved or copied but retain the same relative directory structure. This happens especially if both documents are in the same directory. In this case, the relative moniker binding always works.

- When the link source remains constant and the document is moved elsewhere. In this case, although the relative moniker fails to bind, the absolute moniker succeeds.

For general link tracking to work, support from the underlying OS is required. This support will probably come with a new type of moniker called a *tracking moniker*. This moniker will be responsible for recording the tracking information for a particular object. Although the new moniker will require changes to the OLE libraries, these changes will not result in the breaking of existing applications.

One problem with OLE 1.0 involves automatic links. If you open a linked source separately from the container that contains the linked object, the presentation data for the link is not updated. The OLE 2.0 architects decided to solve this problem with the Alert Object Table (AOT). This table is basically a list of objects and monikers that must be updated. Unfortunately, the OLE 2.0 architects omitted the alert object table from OLE 2.0, so automatic links remain a problem. If you are curious about the proposed implementation of the alert object table, the OLE 2.0 design specification includes its documentation.

OLE Automation

OLE automation has been described as the universal macro language. It provides a standard means for applications to control each other. Applications can expose various objects through automation, and these object can be manipulated through scripting languages and other automation-enabled applications.

Microsoft originally conceived OLE automation as a means of providing a global macro language for Windows. Ultimately Microsoft decided against this, however, opting instead to let ISVs develop their own macro languages and tools, and thus give the user a greater choice. Microsoft did, however, develop a version of Visual Basic, called Visual Basic for Applications (VBA), which provides this global macro language to Microsoft Office products such as Excel 5.0. OLE automation should replace custom macro languages in applications.

With an OLE automation tool such as Visual Basic 3.0, a user can get a list of all automation servers in the system and the available methods and properties for each. Visual Basic 3.0 then provides the user with the means to access these methods. Microsoft Word 6.0, for example, exposes its entire macro language (WordBasic) through one automation object. This one object enables the user of a Visual Basic program to control Microsoft Word completely from within the Visual Basic application.

This mechanism opens up enormous possibilities for writing custom applications, especially for corporate developers. Excel 5.0 supports over 128 programmable objects. As more developers add OLE automation support to their applications, the boundaries between applications will begin to blur and you will see tighter application integration on the desktop.

Why would you want to expose your application's functionality? Every software developer knows what it is like to deliver a product to a customer only to be asked why certain features and functions were not included in the application. By exposing your application's methods through OLE automation, you enable the user to decide how best to use this functionality. Using an OLE automation tool such as Visual Basic 3.0, your customer can completely customize your application. You no longer have to read your customer's mind, anticipating all of his or her favorite features, and can instead concentrate on delivering a tool set that the customer can use in many ways. In fact, the programming tool that the user uses to drive your application can be any application that supports OLE automation.

One useful feature of OLE automation is National Language Support (NLS). This feature enables you to translate exposed object and property names into the user's native language. In the past, a problem with macros was that they were often dependent on English names in menus and dialog boxes. For example, if you ran the macro on a machine running the German version of Windows, the macro would break. NLS also extends to support such things as data formats and decimal points. Therefore, a spreadsheet object, for example, can interpret a number differently depending the location information given to the object. This interpretation can be critical. For example, the number 500.00 is interpreted as 500 in the United States but 50,000 in Scandinavia.

OLE Controls

The OLE controls specification defines an architecture for software components. The OLE controls architecture replaces the old VBX architecture used by Visual Basic. OLE controls build on and extend the initial release of OLE. Chapter 3, "OLE Controls," examines the OLE controls architecture in detail.

The Common Object Model

One of the design goals for OLE was that it should be available on a number of different platforms. OLE is available today for Windows 3.x, Windows NT, and the Macintosh. It has also been demonstrated running under UNIX.

The Common Object Model (COM) is an open architecture, jointly developed by Microsoft and Digital, that enables interoperation between OLE and Digital's ObjectBroker technology. Built on a core subset of OLE and a communication protocol based on DCE RPC, the Common Object Model is the first step toward making OLE a true multi-platform object system.

COM enables applications that use ObjectBroker to cooperate and communicate with OLE applications. This interoperability is completely transparent to the OLE applications.

ObjectBroker is one of the first fully compliant CORBA applications. Applications that use ObjectBroker are provided with transparent access to objects and resources on a variety of platforms, including OSF/1, OpenVMS, ULTRIX, HP-UX, and SunOS.

NOTE   The Common Object Request Broker Architecture (CORBA) is a specification produced by the Object Management Group (OMG). The OMG, like the OSF, is a consortium of computer vendors including companies such as Microsoft, Hewlett Packard, IBM, Digital, and Sun Microsystems. OMG's purpose is to develop specifications to integrate object technology with distributed computing.

COM allows OLE applications running under Windows NT to access objects—through the ObjectBroker technology—existing anywhere on the enterprise. These links are totally transparent to both the object server and the clients.

At the Win32 Developers Conference held in Anaheim, California in December 1993, Microsoft demonstrated an OSF/1 server running a stock quote server being linked to a copy of Excel running on Windows NT (see fig. 1.8). The Excel application contained a spreadsheet that was being constantly updated by data being sent from the OSF/1 server. Neither Excel nor the OSF/1 application knew anything about each other. This once again demonstrates the strength and scalability of the Common Object Model.

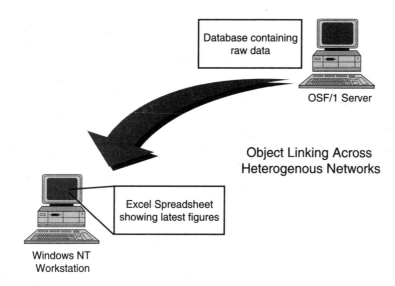

Common Object Model

Fig 1.8
The Common
Object Model can
link objects across
heterogeneous
networks.

From Here...

That concludes your introduction to OLE and its principle technologies. OLE is one of the most important developments undertaken by Microsoft in recent years. Part of the success and acceptance of OLE depends on its openness. Microsoft has from the very beginning invited outside developers to take part in design reviews for OLE. After its initial release, OLE was made a part of WOSA (Windows Open System Architecture), thus ensuring that OLE will become an open standard similar to some of the other WOSA technologies such as ODBC and MAPI.

For more information relating to the topics in this chapter, you may want to review the following chapters in this book:

- Chapter 2, "The Component Object Model," provides more information on the Component Object Model (COM), which is the heart of OLE. An understanding of its features and operation is vital to developing OLE applications.

- Chapter 3, "OLE Controls," describes in more detail information about the OLE Controls architecture.

Chapter 2

The Component Object Model

by Edward B. Toupin

The Component Object Model (COM) is the name given by Microsoft's architects to the underlying object model for OLE. The Component Object Model, while providing the foundation for OLE, also provides the framework for all future object systems from Microsoft. Being an object model, with emphasis on the word model, means that developers could use COM as a framework for any kind of software development.

The COM defines a binary standard for object interaction. This means that it is not dependent on any particular language implementation. It can be implemented in any language that supports double-pointer redirection. Methods in COM objects are invoked by calling the function pointer for that method. The function pointers for a particular object are laid out in virtual function tables. Any language that can support virtual function tables can be used to implement COM applications.

Understanding the principles of COM and its inner workings will provide you with the tools to fully exploit OLE and many other future systems from Microsoft, all of which will be based on COM.

This chapter looks closely at the implementation details of COM, including the following:

- Object interface—both standard and custom—and how it works

- Sharing objects between multiple clients through reference counting

- Locating and loading objects

- The structure of the registration database and how to use it in OLE

■ Object servers

■ Reusing objects with OLE

■ Some miscellaneous features of the COM, including memory management, enumerators, and marshaling

Object Interfaces

In the Component Object Model, objects communicate with each other through *interfaces*. The OLE design specification defines an interface as "a grouping of a set of semantically related functions into a named unit." In other words, an interface is an atomic unit in the COM. The model guarantees that if you receive a pointer to an interface, the object supports all the methods defined for that interface. An interface defines a contract between the object and the object user.

Interfaces are defined in C++ as virtual classes. In other words, interfaces are simply types or templates that describe a virtual function table. The interface definition provides a description of the function table; it does not provide any implementation. It is not possible to create an instance of an interface. A developer of a component object will usually implement all the methods described by an interface.

When you create a component object, you do not receive a pointer to the actual object; rather, a pointer to a COM interface is returned. You then use the pointer to access the method described by the interface. An important point to note here is that you cannot access any data members that an object may have. COM interfaces only describe methods. The interface pointer returned to you is totally opaque. However, the COM does define special data objects that are used to transfer data between processes. This restriction is an important difference between COM objects and traditional C++ objects.

A component object is an object that implements at least one COM interface called IUnknown (by convention, all interfaces are named so that the first letter of their name is *I*). Most component objects support multiple interfaces. Each interface provides a specific set of services.

Interfaces can never be updated or changed. This ensures that conflicts can never occur between object servers and object users when a new version of an object is released. If a developer needs to update an interface, a new interface must be created. A number of examples of this can be seen in the current release of OLE. The COM interface that is responsible for creating objects is called IClassFactory. The original interface is defined as follows:

```
DECLARE_INTERFACE_(IClassFactory, IUnknown)
{
    // IUnknown methods
    STDMETHOD(QueryInterface)(THIS_ REFIID riid,
        LPVOID FAR* ppvObj) PURE;
    STDMETHOD_(ULONG,AddRef)(THIS) PURE;
    STDMETHOD_(ULONG,Release)(THIS) PURE;

    // IClassFactory methods
    STDMETHOD(CreateInstance)(THIS_ LPUNKNOWN pUnkOuter,
        REFIID riid,LPVOID FAR* ppvObject) PURE;
    STDMETHOD(LockServer)(THIS_ BOOL fLock) PURE;
};
```

Here you can see that IClassFactory supports two methods, CreateInstance and LockServer, in addition to the IUnknown methods that are required of all COM objects. When Microsoft needed to add support for licensing of OLE Controls, it needed to add new methods to the IClassFactory interface. The only way for it to do this was to create a new interface called IClassFactory2 with a new interface ID. This new interface is shown here:

```
DECLARE_INTERFACE_(IClassFactory2, IClassFactory)
{
    // IUnknown methods
    STDMETHOD(QueryInterface)(THIS_ REFIID riid,
        LPVOID FAR* ppvObj) PURE;
    STDMETHOD_(ULONG,AddRef)(THIS) PURE;
    STDMETHOD_(ULONG,Release)(THIS) PURE;

    // IClassFactory methods
    STDMETHOD(CreateInstance)(THIS_ LPUNKNOWN pUnkOuter,
        REFIID riid,LPVOID FAR* ppvObject) PURE;
    STDMETHOD(LockServer)(THIS_ BOOL fLock) PURE;

    //  IClassFactory2 methods
    STDMETHOD(GetLicInfo)(THIS_ LPLICINFO pLicInfo) PURE;
    STDMETHOD(RequestLicKey)(THIS_ DWORD dwReserved,
        BSTR FAR* pbstrKey) PURE;
    STDMETHOD(CreateInstanceLic)(THIS_ LPUNKNOWN pUnkOuter,
        LPUNKNOWN pUnkReserved, REFIID riid, BSTR bstrKey,
        LPVOID FAR* ppvObject) PURE;
};
```

Here you can see that the new interface supports all the methods of the original interface in addition to the methods added for licensing support. Applications that support licensing will use this new interface when they create COM objects. Older applications that know nothing about licensing will continue to use the original interface.

This notion of interfaces is a core concept in the COM. When you work with OLE, you constantly work with interfaces. Component objects are similar to C++ objects, with some important differences:

- Component objects do not support traditional inheritance. You reuse objects in OLE by using either aggregation or delegation. You will look closely at both these methods at the end of this chapter, in the section "Object Inheritance, Aggregation, and Delegation."

- The compiler implements interfaces as pointers to virtual function tables, or *vtables*. This implementation is useful, because C++ compilers use the same method to dispatch functions. You don't have to use C++ to implement COM interfaces (remember, such interfaces are binary), but the language does make implementation much easier.

- Each interface is uniquely identified by an interface identifier known as a GUID. This use of a GUID guarantees that no collision can occur when the system is locating objects. You will examine GUIDs in detail later in this chapter.

The Interface *IUnknown*

To qualify as a COM object, an object must support at least one special interface: IUnknown. The OLE headers define this interface as follows:

```
interface IUnknown
{
    virtual HRESULT    QueryInterface(IID& iid, void **ppvObj) = 0;
    virtual ULONG      AddRef() = 0;
    virtual ULONG      Release() = 0;
}

*note interface is defined as struct
```

As you can see, this code defines all the functions as virtual. The code defines an interface, but does not implement it. Only the order of a set of function signatures is defined. Any object that supports the IUnknown interface also implements the IUnknown interface.

Figure 2.1 shows an object that implements IUnknown. You will notice the double-indirection that is used to access the member functions and the fact that data can never be accessed through a COM interface.

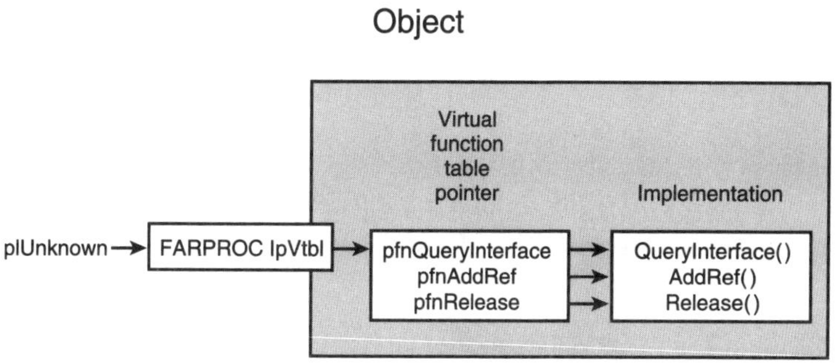

Object

Fig. 2.1
The internal
representation of a
COM object.

```
                              Virtual
                             function
                              table
                             pointer            Implementation

pIUnknown →  FARPROC lpVtbl →  pfnQueryInterface     QueryInterface()
                               pfnAddRef        →    AddRef()
                               pfnRelease       →    Release()
```

COM provides the method QueryInterface, which enables objects to support multiple interfaces. This method enables the user to ask the object whether it supports a particular interface.

For example, suppose that you have a pointer to an OLE object defined as pUnk, and you want to see whether this particular object supports the interface IOleObject. The following code segment demonstrates how you can find out:

```
    {
         LPOLEOBJECT pOle;
         HRESULT hr;
         .
         .
         .
         // Ask the object, through the pointer that you already have,
         // whether it supports the interface IOleObject.
         hr = pUnk->QueryInterface(IID_IOleObject,(void **)&pOle);
         if(SUCCEEDED(hr))
         {
              // The object supports the IOleObject interface.
              // pOle now is the pointer to the object's implementation
              // of IOleObject
         }
    }
```

If the QueryInterface method succeeds, you are returned to a pointer to the interface. The interfaces supported by an object are static; if your QueryInterface method succeeds for a particular interface of an object once, the method will also succeed if you query again. The object may not decide to implement the interface, and then later decline a request for the interface. Object interfaces are static, primarily to allow remote access to the object.

The QueryInterface method also enables you to update an object so that it can support additional interfaces without causing problems for the object's users. The object's user can support new features and still work with older objects. If an object does not support a new interface, the object simply returns E_NOINTERFACE to indicate to the caller that the interface is not supported.

The IUnknown interface supports two functions that are used in reference counting: AddRef() increases an object's reference count, and Release() decreases the reference count.

Reference Counting

After they are loaded into memory, objects can support multiple clients. Then, when all the clients finish using an object, the object is unloaded from memory. But how does the object know when it is no longer needed? How does the object know how many clients are currently using it?

The answer to these questions lies in the COM *reference counting mechanism.* This mechanism ensures that the object is active and available as long as clients are using it. The object itself is responsible for managing the reference count.

However, the object's users must adhere to the reference-counting rules. When you receive a pointer to an interface through QueryInterface, the object has called AddRef() on itself. However, if you copy that pointer, you are responsible for calling AddRef() on the new pointer. When you finish using the object, you call Release(), which decreases the object's reference count. When the reference count reaches zero, the object is free to destroy itself.

These rules sound simple, and they are. However, forgetting to call AddRef() on an interface pointer can result in the object destroying itself while you are using it. Also, forgetting to call Release() on an interface pointer condemns the object to remain forever in memory. Remember, for each *new* copy of an interface pointer you must call AddRef(), and for every destruction of a pointer you must call Release().

These rules have some exceptions. If you have special knowledge about the lifetime of an interface pointer (you wrote all the code or you have access to it), you can skip the reference counting. In the following example, you can see how special knowledge of the nested lifetime of pOle2 enables you to skip calling AddRef for this pointer:

```
{
    LPOLEOBJECT pOle1, pOle2 = NULL;
    HRESULT hr;

    hr = pUnk->QueryInterface(IID_IOleObject,(void **)&pOle1);
```

```
if(SUCCEEDED(hr))
{
    // You now make a copy of this pointer:
    pOle2 = pOle1;
    // You have already locked the object in memory, so you
    // don't have to AddRef() the copied pointer.

    // Use the interfaces
    pOle1->CallSomeMethod();
    pOle2->CallSomeMethod();

    // You are finished with the object, so you release
    // the reference count.
    pOle1->Release();
    // If the reference count reaches zero, the object
    // destroys itself.
    pOle1 = NULL ;     // pointer no longer valid
    pOle2 = NULL ;     // pointer no longer valid
}
    // Using pOle1 or pOle2 here would be incorrect, and
    // could potentially cause a gp-fault.
}
```

As long as you do not release the object's reference count, you can copy the pointer and use it without calling AddRef().

Defining Your Own Interfaces

OLE also allows developers to define their own custom interfaces. This allows you to create applications based on COM that have nothing to do with OLE in particular. For example, you could develop an object whose sole purpose is to access an on-line service and deliver data to your application for processing. In this case, you would define a custom COM object with perhaps an interface called IGetOnLineData. Because of the behind-the-scenes work performed on your behalf when using standard interfaces (such as marshaling of parameters, and so on), creating custom interfaces was not always a straightforward task for developers.

However, Microsoft has now released tools to assist the developer in creating custom interfaces. This section briefly looks at the architecture of custom interfaces.

Custom Interface Architecture

Before you look at the architecture of custom interfaces, the following section quickly examines how you implement standard COM interfaces.

Two terms need to be defined. A *proxy* is a piece of code that is responsible for packaging interface parameters into a message buffer and passing that buffer to a channel (a named pipe or an RPC channel), which is responsible for transferring the data to another process. A *stub* is a piece of code that retrieves data for a channel, unpackages the parameters from the buffer, and calls the client code using the parameters. This process of packaging parameters and unpacking them is known as *marshaling*.

The architecture of proxies and stubs is such that the location of servers and clients is transparent to each other.

Standard Interfaces

When you call `CoGetClassObject` in your code, the default handler in OLE tries to locate the object server by looking up its CLSID in the system registry. (If the server is already running, this step is bypassed.)

The object server's first task is to create and register its class object. The OLE Stub Manager then creates a stub for this class object.

On the client side, the OLE Proxy Manager creates an interface proxy for `IClassFactory` and returns to your application a pointer to this proxy.

When you call `IClassFactory::CreateInstance`, you are actually calling an implementation of `IClassFactory::CreateInstance` in the proxy, which marshals the parameters into the remote procedure call (RPC) channel. The data is then sent across the wire to the object server's class object stub. The stub then unmarshals the parameters and calls the *real* implementation of `IClassFactory::CreateInstance` as implemented by the object server.

The process of creating and using proxies and stubs is used for all COM interfaces except those implemented in in-process handlers. Figure 2.2 shows how the proxies and stubs work together.

Fig. 2.2

Proxies and stubs.

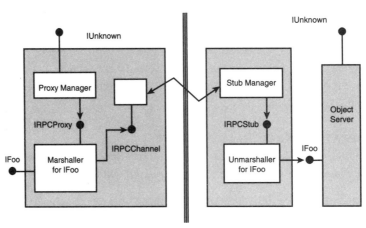

Process Boundary

The main point that you need to understand is that whenever you call a COM interface pointer, you are not actually calling the object server. Instead, you are calling the OLE-generated proxy for that particular interface. This proxy in turn calls a stub (through RPC) that calls the actual server code.

For any particular object, OLE creates an object proxy. This object proxy consists of a Proxy Manager and one or more interface proxies. For each interface that an object supports, OLE creates an interface proxy. The reason that OLE creates a special proxy for each interface is that the interface proxy is responsible for marshaling the interface parameters. This marshaling requires intimate knowledge of the interface definition.

Interfaces are remoted in this manner to enable objects to exist in different processes. (Because interfaces must enable objects to exist in different processes, common function calls cannot work.) The other major benefit of this architecture is transparency. Clients and servers are unaware that they in fact exist in separate processes. This transparency is crucial because it lays the foundation for OLE to add distributed support without requiring changes to the objects.

Marshaling

As mentioned previously, marshaling is the process of packaging data for transmission to a remote process and unpackaging the data at the remote process. As you learned in Chapter 1, one of the design goals of OLE is to make objects accessible to remote processes while keeping the process transparent to both object servers and users. Marshaling is the key technique for achieving this goal.

To implement marshaling support, you create separate functions that support each possible data type. If a pointer to a data buffer is to be marshaled, you must copy the data pointer to another buffer, transmit the buffer, have the receiving stub allocate a new buffer, and finally copy the data into the remote buffer. To marshal a scalar type such as an integer, you simply copy it into the message buffer.

OLE supports two types of marshaling: custom and standard. Standard marshaling of standard COM interfaces is done by proxies and stubs supplied by OLE. Standard marshaling of custom interfaces is done by user-supplied proxies and stubs. These proxies and stubs are supplied as separate DLLs. All proxy and stub components are registered in the system registry under the Interfaces key. Each proxy and stub DLL has an entry in this section (interfaces) named `ProxyStubClsid`.

Custom marshaling, on the other hand, is achieved by proxies and stubs implemented by the object server. One example of custom marshaling is the shared memory mechanism used by compound files in 32-bit Windows. Custom marshaling implements both IStorage and IStream. Developers often use custom marshaling to avoid the context switching of standard marshaling, which adversely affects performance. Custom marshaling is more complex to implement than standard marshaling and requires that the server implement the IMarshal interface.

Custom Interfaces

The OLE libraries provide a set of standard interfaces. These interfaces are defined by the OLE specification. You are free to define your own interfaces; these interfaces are known as *custom interfaces*.

To implement a custom interface, you define and register an *interface ID* (IID). Clients then use this IID when they create objects of that type. This is the easy part of implementing custom interfaces.

As you may have surmised, you must also implement marshaling for your custom interface. The OLE libraries can marshal only the standard COM interfaces.

When OLE 2.0 was first released, developers had to hand-code the proxy and stub for each interface that they wanted to implement. With the release of 32-bit OLE, Microsoft has released a new tool for generating the proxy and stub for a custom interface. This tool is a new version of the Microsoft Interface Description Language (MIDL 2.0) compiler. Instead of writing the code to implement proxies and stubs, you use the Interface Description Language (IDL) to describe the interface. You compile the IDL file with the MIDL compiler. The output from the compiler is the C++ header and implementation files for the proxy and stub. Building the proxy and stub DLL is simply a matter of compiling these files and linking with some libraries supplied with the SDK. After you build the DLL, you must register the new proxy and stub in the system registry.

You can still build custom interfaces for 16-bit OLE, but you must implement the marshaling code manually. Another approach is to use the MIDL compiler to generate the 32-bit proxies and stubs and port them to Win16.

The Service Control Manager

The Service Control Manager (SCM) is a new component of 32-bit OLE. The SCM is responsible for locating and loading OLE servers. Originally, you could simply look up the name of an in-process DLL or local server in the system registry. However, to support OLE's potential capability to locate remote object servers, Microsoft developed the SCM.

You still use the system registry to hold information about each object, and the SCM caches this information. If a client application attempts to create an object from an in-process object server, the SCM passes the request to the OLE libraries. The SCM locates and loads the server, whether it is local or remote. If the server is already running, the SCM connects to it.

The process for locating and connecting to a remote object server consists of the following steps if your application calls BindToObject with a file moniker:

1. The application calls the BindToObject API.

2. BindToObject then invokes the SCM, passing the CLSID for the object.

3. The SCM then connects to or creates the server process.

4. The object server then creates and registers its class object. The object is registered with the SCM.

5. The SCM activates the object. In this case, this activation requires a call to IClassFactory::CreateInstance followed by a call to IPersistFile::Load.

6. The marshaled interface pointer returns to the SCM.

7. SCM returns the marshaled pointer to the client.

8. BindToObject uses this marshaled information to connect directly to the server object.

9. Finally, BindToObject converts the marshaled information into a vtable pointer that is returned to the client application.

The client then uses the vtable pointer to call methods on the object. The process for connecting to remote objects is similar. However, regardless of whether the server is remote, local, or in-process, the client always receives a vtable pointer.

The Proxy

The proxy is the server substitute located on the client side of the process boundary. The proxy is responsible for marshaling the interface parameters and placing them in the RPC channel. This channel is responsible for actually transporting the data. You implement proxies as aggregate objects that consist of a Proxy Manager and an interface proxy for each interface supported.

The Proxy Manager implements the controlling unknown for the aggregate. Each interface proxy supports the IRPCProxyBuffer interface. When you call one of the implemented interfaces, the interface proxy begins by getting a marshaling package from the RPC channel. The IRpcChannel::GetStream method is then used to retrieve the package. The interface proxy then marshals the parameters to the stream by calling IStream::Write for each parameter. After all the parameters are placed in the channel, the proxy calls IRpcChannel::Call to send the data to the remote stub. When this function call returns, the returned parameters are retrieved from the channel and unmarshaled. The proxy then closes the stream and returns the data to the caller. Figure 2.3 shows the structure of the proxy.

Fig. 2.3
The proxy.

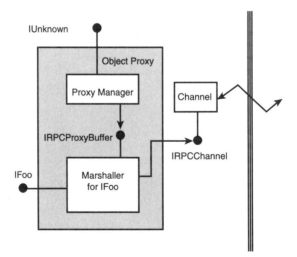

Process Boundary

The RPC run-time library handles the actual transport of the data. The version of RPC developed by Microsoft is fully compatible with the Open Software Foundation's Distributed Computing Environment (OSF DCE). You can configure RPC to use different network transports. Transports are available for NetBIOS, IPX/SPX, and TCP/IP networks. RPC also provides the name service that is used to locate object servers on the network. Finally, RPC provides a security service that restricts the access of objects.

The Stub

After the receiving channel receives the marshaled data, it is passed to the interface stub. The stub then unmarshals the data and makes the actual call on the server interface. Stubs are not implemented as aggregates and each stub supports the IRPCStubBuffer interface.

Both stubs and proxies use the IRPCChannelBuffer to talk to the underlying RPC run-time library.

Figure 2.4 shows the structure of the stub.

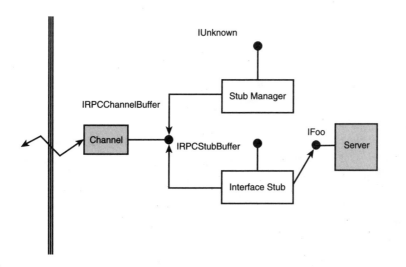

Fig. 2.4
The stub.

How the System Finds Objects

Objects are dynamically loaded into the system whenever users demand the object's services. The objects themselves may already be in memory, on the user's hard disk, or perhaps running remotely on another workstation. How do the OLE libraries know which objects to load and where they are located?

Each object is identified by a special ID, *CLSID* (class ID). A CLSID is a unique, 128-bit number. OLE uses this and several other similar IDs extensively. Besides using a CLSID, OLE uses an *IID* (interface ID) and a *UUID* (universally unique ID), which is sometimes called a *GUID* (globally unique ID). A special program that comes with the OLE SDK, UUIDGEN.EXE, generates these numbers. This utility uses the OLE API function CoCreateGUID to generate the GUIDs. These GUIDs are guaranteed to be statistically unique. This method for naming objects is essential in a distributed environment, which might include millions of objects. Connecting to a wrong object server because of a duplication in object IDs would be disastrous in such an environment.

After obtaining the CLSID for an object, the client calls the OLE API function CoGetClassObject. The following is the function's prototype:

```
HRESULT CoGetClassObject(clsid,grfContext,pReserved,iid,ppv);
```

This function will locate the object, identified by the CLSID in the first parameter, by searching the system registration database for the name of the OLE server associated with that CLSID (see fig. 2.5).

The pointer returned by this function points to the class object for the COM object. If you want to create a COM object in this way, the COM object must implement two objects: a class object and the object that actually implements the functionality of the COM object.

 NOTE After an object is loaded and the client creates an instance of the object, the container cannot determine whether the object was remote or local. The location of the object is completely transparent to the client code.

When the server is located, it is activated and QueryInterface is called for the interface defined in the fourth parameter, iid. As you can see in figure 2.5, the registration database stores much information about the object. In fact, the database is a central repository for all information regarding OLE objects and libraries. The following sections examine each of the database's fields.

The first line is as follows:

```
{00020810-0000-0000-C000-000000000046} = Microsoft Excel 5.0
Worksheet
```

This line describes the CLSID of Microsoft Excel 5.0. This CLSID is the key that the OLE libraries use to locate information about a particular object. The text to the right of the CLSID is the *main user type*. This text usually is presented to users when they select the Paste Special option in an application.

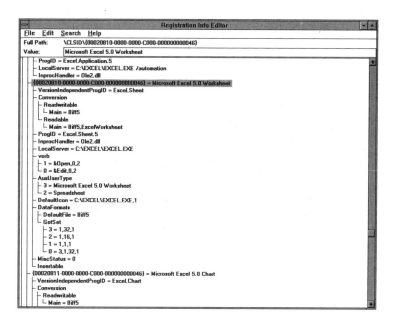

Fig. 2.5
The system
registration
database.

Most of the keys described in the following sections are not required. In fact, only the `LocalServer` and `InProcServer` keys are actually required. Otherwise, the object's purpose determines which keys are necessary. For example, a simple COM object that provides services to a client through a custom interface needs only `InProcServer` or `LocalServer`. However, an OLE compound document that supports conversion and more will require other keys.

VersionIndependentProgID

The `ProgID` field that is used in OLE automation usually contains version information. In figure 2.5, the `ProgID` is `Excel.Sheet.5`. The number 5 indicates version 5.0 of Excel.

However, an object that supports automation should have a `ProgID` that is independent of the product's version, so that users do not have to change their code when a new version of the product is released. In figure 2.5, the `VersionIndependentProgID` is simply `Excel.Sheet`.

Conversion

The `Conversion` field lists the conversion types displayed in the Change Type dialog box. The `Readwritable` key shows types of objects that the object can emulate, and the `Readable` key shows the object types that the application can read and convert.

As Chapter 1 mentioned, the document-centric model of computing enables you to create a compound document with objects of type A and then e-mail the document to another user; that user may not possess server A, but can convert the A object to B-type objects.

These fields show which servers can read objects of a particular type and which servers can read and convert objects of a particular type.

ProgID

The ProgID field is the programmatic identifier for the object. This field is used in automation, which is discussed in more detail in Chapter 4, "A Simple Control." (OLE controls architecture is also discussed in Chapter 4.)

InprocHandler

This field identifies the search path to the in-process handler for this type of object. This handler is usually the default implemented in OLE2.DLL.

LocalServer

The second LocalServer field identifies the name of the object's local server.

InProcServer

This field holds the name of the object's in-process (inproc) server. Local servers typically are implemented in DLLs, and are loaded into the process space of the client. Win32 platforms also have InProcServer32, which points to the 32-bit implementation of the local server.

Verb

This field presents the verbs that the object supports. These verbs are usually displayed on the object's context menu. The field's format is as follows:

```
verb number = name,menu flags,verb flags
```

Verb 0 is always the object's default verb.

AuxUserType

This field contains the auxiliary user types. Type 2 is the application's short name and type 3 is the application's full name. This contrasts to the Main user type which, as you saw earlier, is used in the Paste Special dialog box.

DefaultIcon

This field specifies the default icon that the API call ExtractIcon returns for this object.

ToolbarBitmap

In order to support the insertion of a bitmap on an application's toolbar, a control is encouraged to supply a 16×16 bitmap. The `ToolbarBitmap` key points to a DLL that contains the key. The key contains two parameters. The first is the name of the DLL and the second is the resource number of the bitmap. An application can use the `GetFileResource` API function to extract the bitmap from the DLL.

DataFormats

The `DefaultFile` key shows the default type of objects of this class. The `GetSet` key lists the default data types returned by the default handler during an `EnumFormatEtc` method call. Because these data types are stored in the `DataFormats` field, when a container queries an object, the default handler doesn't have to start the object to retrieve the data formats that the object supports.

MiscStatus

This field contains varied status information about the object. The default handler returns this value during an `IOleObject::GetMiscStatus` call. If the object is running, it gets the status from the running object. In short, these bits are "hints" to containers on how to treat the object (the containers may ignore these hints). Table 2.1 lists all the possible values.

Table 2.1 Miscellaneous Status Information About an Object	
Status Bit	**Description**
`OLEMISC_RECOMPOSEONRESIZE`	If the object's container resizes the space allocated to the object, the object will resize itself.
`OLEMISC_ONLYICONIC`	The object can be displayed only as an icon.
`OLEMISC_INSERTNOTREPLACE`	The object is not to replace the current selection during insertion, particularly if the object is being created as a link to the current selection.
`OLEMISC_STATIC`	The object is static.
`OLEMISC_CANTLINKINSIDE`	The object cannot be a link source for a link. For example, a static object cannot be a link source.
`OLEMISC_CANLINKBYOLE1`	The object can be linked by an OLE 1.0 server.

(continues)

Table 2.1   Continued

Status Bits	Description
OLEMISC_ISLINK	The object is linked, and is being used in OLE 1.0 compatibility code.
OLEMISC_INSIDEOUT	The object can be activated in-place without being UI-active (that is, without activating its menus, toolbars, and so on).
OLEMISC_ACTIVATEWHENVISIBLE	The object should be active whenever it is visible.
OLEMISC_INVISIBLEATRUNTIME	Used by a container that has a distinction between designtime and runtime, as most control containers do, to show the object only when in design mode. A Timer control that fires a Click event at preset intervals might use this bit; it would be visible at designtime (so that the user can set properties on the timer) but not at runtime.
OLEMISC_ALWAYSRUN	Used by a container to always put objects with this bit set into the running state, even when not visible. That is, the container should request that it not be given the standard handler for this object, but that the server be activated instead. This allows the object to fire events and take other proactive action; again, this is useful for timer-like objects. This bit is not normally required for in-process servers.
OLEMISC_ACTSLIKEBUTTON	Used by a container that provides Default/ Cancel buttons. Controls that provide this flag are capable of acting like buttons. In particular, the control's primary event can be triggered in its IOleControl::OnMnemonic method, and the control is prepared to render itself as the default button based on the ambient DisplayAsDefaultButton.
OLEMISC_ACTSLIKELABEL	Used by a container that potentially allows OLE controls to replace the container's native label. The container is responsible for determining what to do with this flag (or ignore it). A container that uses this flag will typically intercept mnemonics or mouse clicks targeted for the label-like control at runtime and reinterpret these messages as attempts to move to the field associated with the label.
OLEMISC_NOUIACTIVATE	Used by a container to determine whether a control doesn't support UI activation. Under OLE 2, such an object was not very useful, because activating it was generally the only way to edit it. With OLE controls, the user can

Status Bits	Description
	program the control using OLE automation or set its properties using property pages; therefore, it can use a non UI-activated control. Note that controls can already indicate that they don't support a separate in-place active state by not including the `OLEMISC_INSIDEOUT` bit.
`OLEMISC_ALIGNABLE`	Used by a container that supports aligned controls. This bit is used by a control that is most useful when aligned on some side of its container. Containers that support such aligned controls can use this bit to decide whether the user should be allowed to align a particular control.
`OLEMISC_IMEMODE`	Marks a control that understands IME Mode. This only makes sense for DBCS versions of Windows. Containers will typically add an IMEMode property to the extended control for controls that mark themselves with this bit.
`OLEMISC_SIMPLEFRAME`	Used by containers to determine whether a control supports the `ISimpleFrameSite` protocol. Containers that also support this interface will use simple frame controls as parents for other controls in the container. In effect, the simple frame control operates as an OLE compound document container, but the frame control's container does almost all the work.
`OLEMISC_SETCLIENTSITEFIRST`	Used by new OLE containers to identify controls that support having `SetClientSite` called first, immediately after being created, and before the control has been completely constructed. Normal OLE compound document containers are written to call `SetClientSite` on embedded objects after calling `IPersistStorage::Load` or `IPersistStorage::InitNew` on the object. Since OLE controls get their persistent state information through their client site and that state information is useful during the load process, they need to have the client site available during `Load` or `InitNew`.

Insertable

If this key is present, the object appears in all Insert Object dialog boxes.

Control

If this key is present, the object is an OLE custom control and appears in Insert Control dialog boxes, as well as in the tool palettes of OLE control container applications.

TypeLib

The TypeLib key is used to register type libraries. Every OLE control will have a type library associated with it. Under the TypeLib key, each type library's CLSID will be stored. The full path to the location of the type library will be found under the appropriate CLSID.

Other Fields

This concludes your tour of the registration database. The database includes many other fields. Some concern OLE 1.0 servers and the shell commands for the Windows Program Manager. Others concern CLSID and server information for all the OLE standard interfaces. However, the most useful and common fields have been covered.

Object Return Codes

As you read the OLE reference manual, you will notice that all interface methods return a new kind of error code called HRESULT (handle to a result code). HRESULT encapsulates both an SCODE (status code) and a handle to some extended error-handling information.

An SCODE type is 32-bits wide and consists of four fields (see fig. 2.6). The topmost bit is the *severity* field. A value of 0 indicates that the function succeeded, and a value of 1 indicates an error. Next is the *context* field. OLE does not implement this field. (In fact, the difference between an SCODE and an HRESULT is that in the HRESULT structure the context field is filled in.)

Fig. 2.6
The structure of an SCODE.

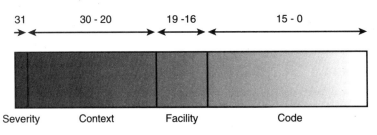

Structure of an SCODE

Next comes the *facility* field, which indicates the category of the error. Microsoft controls the allocation of facilities. Table 2.2 lists the currently defined facilities.

Table 2.2	Currently Defined Facilities
Facility	**Description**
FACILITY_NULL	Common status codes, such as S_OK
FACILITY_RPC	RPC (remote procedure call) error codes
FACILITY_STORAGE	Storage errors (if the lower 16 bits correspond to DOS error codes, the codes' meaning is the same as that of the DOS error codes)
FACILITY_DISPATCH	Automation errors
FACILITY_ITF	Interface-defined error codes

Last is the *code* field, which describes the actual error code.

If you examine the OLE header files, you will see that error codes have the following structure:

```
Facility_Severity_Reason
```

For example, the error code STG_E_MEDIUMFULL (which the GetDataHere method call returns from an IDataObject interface) tells you that the preferred storage medium is not large enough for the requested data. The OLE SDK provides several useful macros for dealing with SCODEs. Table 2.3 lists these macros.

Table 2.3	OLE 2.0 SDK Macros for Handling *SCODEs*	
Macro	**Definition**	**Description**
SCODE_CODE	#define SCODE_CODE(sc)	Extracts the error code from a status code
SCODE_FACILITY	#define SCODE_FACILITY(sc)	Extracts the facility from the SCODE
SCODE_SEVERITY	#define SCODE_SEVERITY(sc)	Extracts the severity field from the SCODE
SUCCEEDED	#define SUCCEEDED(sc)	Returns True if the severity code indicates success

(continues)

Table 2.3 Continued		
Macro	**Definition**	**Description**
FAILED	#define FAILED(sc)	Returns True if the severity code indicates failure
MAKE_SCODE	#define MAKE_SCODE (sev,fac,code)	Makes a new SCODE

The API function HRESULT GetScode(SCODE) returns an SCODE extracted from an HRESULT. The companion to the function is HRESULT ReturnFromScode(SCODE), which generates an HRESULT from an SCODE.

The function HRESULT PropagateResult(HRESULT,SCODE) wraps a previously returned HRESULT with an SCODE and returns the new HRESULT to the caller.

Although Microsoft originally intended to use HRESULTs in a future release of OLE, they have now decided to use SCODEs exclusively. So whenever you see a reference to HRESULT in the OLE documentation, you can treat it as if it were an SCODE.

The COM Memory Allocator

A problem commonly arises when multiple processes use global memory to transfer data. Who should allocate the initial memory block, and who should be responsible for freeing it? Although you can force applications to agree on a convention for managing memory, it is much simpler for the system to provide this memory management.

The OLE solution to this problem is an interface called IMalloc. The interface is defined as follows:

```
interface IMalloc : IUnknown
{
    virtual void * Alloc(cb) = 0;
    virtual void * ReAlloc(pv,cb) = 0;
    virtual void   Free(pv) = 0;
    virtual ULONG GetSize(pv) = 0;
    virtual int DidAlloc(pv) = 0;
    virtual void HeapMinimize() = 0;
}
```

OLE 2.0 defines two types of memory: local and shared. The OLE libraries define and implement two allocator objects to manage memory. The user can define the *local allocator* by passing a pointer to an IMalloc object during a call to `CoInitialize` or `OleInitialize`. The OLE libraries maintain the *shared memory allocator*, which the user cannot modify.

The default implementation uses a subsegment-allocation scheme that is familiar to OS/2 programmers. This scheme, which is based on multiple local heaps, provides efficient access to memory but is constrained by a maximum block size of 64K. This restriction, however, is completely lifted on Win32.

Whenever you need memory, you call the API function `CoGetMalloc()`, specifying the type of memory you want and passing an `IMalloc` interface pointer. The returned pointer gives you access to the allocator object.

As the interface definition indicates, the methods supplied are similar to standard Windows memory-allocation functions.

Enumerators

You probably have already enumerated system objects in Windows. To do this, you call an enumerator function, such as `EnumFonts`, and pass a callback function. The enumerator then uses this callback to communicate with your application.

The COM simplifies this operation by eliminating the need for callbacks. Instead, the COM creates an *enumerator object* for each object that you want to enumerate. Each object that can be enumerated needs a special enumerator defined for it. Therefore, COM defines the *concept* of an enumerator for each object, but not an actual enumerator interface.

Therefore, for each object to be enumerated, a special interface is created: `IEnumString` for strings, `IEnumUnknown` for `IUnknown` pointers, and so on. The interface for a string enumerator is defined as follows:

```
interface IEnumString : IUknown
{
    // Get the next string in the collection
    virtual HRESULT Next(ULONG, LPLPSTR,ULONG *) = 0;
    // Skip n elements
    virtual HRESULT Skip(ULONG) = 0;
    // Reset internal counter
    virtual HRESULT Reset() = 0;
    // Copy a string
    virtual HRESULT Clone(LPLPSTR) = 0;
}
```

A sample function to use this enumerator might look like the following:

```
{
    LPSTR lpStr;
```

```
IEnumString *pEnum;

pEnum = GetEnumSomeWhere();
pEnum->AddRef();
while(S_OK == pEnum->Next(1,&lpStr,NULL))
{
      MessageBox(GetFocus(),lpStr,"String Enumerator",0);
}
pEnum->Release();
}
```

OLE 2.0 uses enumerators extensively, so you will see more of them in upcoming chapters.

Object Inheritance, Aggregation, and Delegation

A familiar feature of object-oriented programming systems (OOPS) is class or object inheritance. The idea is simple. A class implements perhaps 75 percent of the functionality that you need to handle a particular problem; you then create a new object that inherits from the class and adds the missing 25 percent. Although this concept of code reuse works quite well, it has some problems.

The main problem is that you must know the details of the implementation of the base class. You need to know when you must override specific methods and when you can delegate them to the base class. You also must have the source code. (For this reason, all frameworks, including Microsoft Foundation Class and ObjectWindows Library, ship with complete source code.) If you override some of the methods of the base class and make an assumption about the state of the object when you call those methods, the code could break if the base class is revised later. This "fragile base class" problem is always possible when you redefine the base class.

There is also a deeper issue here: the basic difference between Object-Oriented Programming (OOP) and Object-Oriented Systems (OOS). Languages such as C++ and Objective C were designed to enable code reuse between developers and development groups. They were never intended to enable code reuse across multiple development groups or companies.

The Component Object Model helps solve this problem. It provides a binary standard that enables developers to use different languages to create component objects that can be reused by anyone. These objects can even provide reuse across multiple platforms.

The OLE architects chose to use a different method, *aggregation and delegation*, for object reuse.

Aggregation

The aggregation method of object reuse has become quite controversial and the subject of much debate. The object model developed by IBM, SOM (System Object Model), uses traditional inheritance, as does Sun Microsystems' DOE (Distributed Objects Everywhere). In fact, Microsoft is the only developer that does not support inheritance in its object model. Naturally, each camp believes that its method is the best. For developers, the arguments are mostly academic. If you choose to implement OLE in your application, you must use the COM method of object reuse; if you decide to implement SOM, you must use SOM's inheritance.

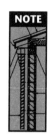

An *aggregate* is like any other object. It implements IUnknown and several other interfaces, and works like any other Windows object. Internally, however, an aggregate is actually a composite object consisting of two or more objects. The object's user is unaware of how the object is implemented. Figure 2.7 shows how the aggregate looks conceptually.

Aggregate Object

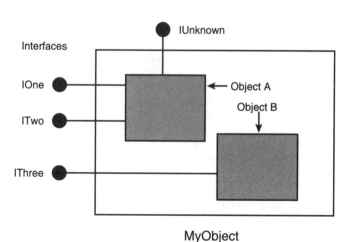

MyObject

Fig. 2.7
An aggregate object.

For this model to work, the two objects must be capable of communicating. A QueryInterface call on interface IThree should be capable of returning an interface pointer to interface IOne or interface ITwo. A Release() call on IThree should release the entire object if IOne or ITwo have no outstanding reference count.

The solution to this problem is a *controlling unknown*, which is a special instance of an IUnknown interface that is responsible for maintaining the reference count for the entire aggregate. The instance is also responsible for exposing the internal interfaces of the composite objects as its own.

To be part of an aggregate, an object must be prepared to forward to the controlling unknown all calls on its IUnknown interface. In other words, if you call the QueryInterface method for an object that is part of an aggregate, the method simply returns a call on the QueryInterface of the controlling unknown. This QueryInterface, in turn, either returns an interface pointer if it supports that interface or directly calls the QueryInterface of the aggregated object.

Figure 2.8 shows an object, MyObject, that supports four interfaces: IOne, ITwo, IThree, and IUnknown. The object is implemented with two internal objects: Object A and Object B. While creating Object B, Object A passed its IUnknown interface pointer to Object B. This interface pointer then became the controlling unknown for that object. If a user has a pointer to interface IThree, a QueryInterface on that pointer for interface IOne would succeed, because the object would delegate the QueryInterface method call to the controlling unknown. The controlling unknown, which is the IUnknown interface for Object A, returns a pointer to interface IOne.

Fig. 2.8
An aggregate object with a controlling unknown.

Aggregate Object with Controlling Unknown

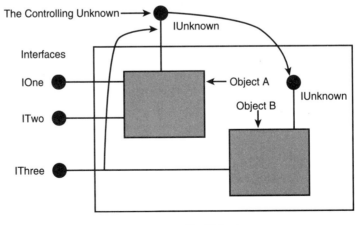

MyObject

How does an object know that it is part of an aggregate, and where does the object get the pointer to the controlling unknown interface? An object knows that it is part of an aggregate only while an instance of the object is being created. The object that wants to create an aggregate passes its IUnknown interface pointer to IClassFactory::CreateInstance when creating a contained object. The object can refuse to become part of an aggregate by failing this call if the punkOuter parameter is not equal to NULL.

Several rules also govern reference counting for an aggregate. These rules are intended to prevent circular references. The OLE programmer's guide provides a full description of each of these rules.

Aggregation is not particularly difficult to implement and incurs little overhead. The main problem is conceptual. Although familiar with object reuse in a C++ world, most programmers have never before seen this type of object reuse. Like all new techniques, aggregation seems strange and difficult at first but, after you overcome your initial resistance, you will find that this method of object reuse is as good as any other.

Delegation

Object reuse using the delegation method involves one object being completely contained by another. If I have an Object RichText—for example a Rich Text Control—that wants to reuse Object TextEdit, a standard edit control, then Object RichText will create an object of type TextEdit when RichText is being created. Object RichText will then expose all of TextEdit's methods by overriding them. When the object user calls a method that is exposed by Object TextEdit, the overridden method will be called and you have the opportunity to change the default implementation of that method. If you do not want to change the default implementation, you simply delegate the method calls to object TextEdit's implementation.

The delegation method is used when you need to change some of the default implementation of a particular object. If you do not intend to change anything, you should use the aggregation method. It can become tiresome implementing stubs for all of an object's method just to delegate to the object for their implementation.

From Here...

That completes your overview of the object model used in OLE. As you saw, COM defines a means by which objects can communicate with each other. It defines a binary standard which is totally independent of the programming language used to implement the objects. It provides a scalable architecture that can be used on a single PC or the largest networks.

For more information about the topics discussed in this chapter, refer to these other chapters in the book:

- Chapter 3, "OLE Controls," delves into more detail about the OLE controls architecture.

- Chapter 4, "A Simple Control," provides information about the actual development of OLE controls.

Chapter 3

OLE Controls

by John Toohey

This chapter provides you with an overview of the OLE controls architecture. You will see what an OLE control is and what extensions were made to OLE in order to support controls.

You will also briefly look at OLE control containers. OLE control containers are standard OLE containers which are aware of and can respond to events generated by controls.

This chapter will also examine the following topics:

- The motivation for OLE controls

- OLE control containers

- OLE automation

- The new COM interfaces that have been added to support OLE controls

The Motivation for OLE Controls

The idea of encapsulating functionality into a self-contained piece of code is not new in Windows. From its earliest days, Windows has been a collection of such units. These units were DLLs. Over time, developers began to provide specific interfaces to access functionality in DLLs. A clear example of this is the Windows File Manager. File Manager can be extended by writing a DLL that conforms to the File Manager Extensions interface. Once the DLL is registered in the File Manager's INI file, it appears as part of File Manager.

However, these types of extensions, as found in the Windows Control Panel and File Manager, were tightly bound to their specific applications. A more generic solution was needed.

The first solution developed by Microsoft was a custom control interface that was aimed at developers using the Windows SDK. The custom control specification defined an interface that could be used by control developers so that their controls would be available to other developers using the dialog editor supplied with the SDK. This approach met with limited success and was soon replaced by the Visual Basic control architecture.

The Visual Basic custom control architecture was developed to provide a common interface for custom controls that were to be used in the Visual Basic environment. These controls became known as VBXs. The popularity of VBXs was such that Microsoft added support for them in Visual C++. Other vendors even added support for VBX to their applications.

The VBX architecture is closely tied to the Windows 16-bit platform. This made it extremely difficult to port VBXs to a 32-bit platform such as Windows 95 or Windows NT. It also meant that VBXs could never run on a MIPS or Alpha platform.

Microsoft's solution is the OLE control specification. OLE controls do not build on and extend the current VBX architecture. They are built around the current OLE architecture. They use the same object model, COM, as standard OLE objects.

The fact that OLE controls are based on OLE means that they are available in both 16-bit and 32-bit environments. They are also available to any application that supports OLE.

What Are OLE Controls?

An OLE control is a standard, embedded OLE object that is capable of being activated in-place as an inside-out object. OLE controls are generally implemented as *in-process object servers*. (In-process servers are object servers that are implemented as DLLs and are loaded directly into the address space of the calling application.) They can also be implemented as local servers, such as EXEs. For performance reasons, they are best implemented as DLLs.

Unlike standard OLE objects, controls can be manipulated programmatically by their container. OLE controls communicate with their container through events, exposed methods, and properties.

In addition to the COM interfaces required of all object servers, OLE controls require a few more. Later in the chapter, you will examine each of these in detail.

Control Containers

OLE control containers are standard OLE containers that support visual editing. In addition to the requirements of an OLE container, a container that supports controls must also support ambient properties and events.

Ambient Properties

The *ambient* properties of a container are those properties that affect the entire container or at least the area in which the control resides. Examples of ambient properties would include the currently selected font, the background and foreground colors, and the current locale (the currently selected nation language and sub-language) in use by the container. The container makes these properties available to its controls at runtime. The controls can use the ambient properties to better integrate with the container.

How does the container communicate these properties to its embedded controls? Each container implements on its site object an `IDispatch` interface that is used by controls to retrieve ambient properties.

The control retrieves a pointer to this `IDispatch` by using `QueryInterface` on the `IOleClientSite` pointer that is received when the control was created. Once the `IDispatch` pointer has been retrieved, the control will then call `IDispatch::Invoke` on each of the standard properties to retrieve its value.

It should be noted, however, that containers are not required to support ambient properties, so a control can expect the call to fail.

Some containers and controls will be written for each other, and thus the container may support a number of custom ambient properties. If this is the case, the control must call `IDispatch::GetIDsofNames` to retrieve the `DISPIDs` of the custom properties. It will then call `IDispatch::Invoke` on each of these `DISPIDs` to get the property values.

Event Handlers

The main difference between a standard OLE container and one that provides support for OLE controls is the container's support for events. Events are generated by controls in response to external events such as the user clicking in the control's client area with the mouse.

Events are handled by another IDispatch interface that is also called the *outgoing* dispatch. Each control has a number of events that it is capable of firing. It is up to the container to implement code to actually handle these events.

Regardless of whether the container provides an implementation for specific events, the control will fire these events. Events for which no handler exists are simply ignored.

Keyboard Handling of Accelerators

The current implementation of OLE provides a mechanism for handling keyboard accelerators. The support is provided through the IOleInPlaceActiveObject interface. The container would normally pass any keystrokes to the active object through IOleInPlaceActiveObject::TranslateAccelerators.

However, this approach is limited to the object that is currently UI-active within the container. Because there is normally only one object that is UI-active at a time, this approach is insufficient for OLE controls.

OLE controls are expected to behave like normal Windows controls when it comes to keyboard handling. So if you have a form that is populated with OLE controls, you would expect to be able to navigate between the controls using the assigned keyboard accelerators.

See the "COM Interfaces" section later in this chapter for more information on keyboard handling.

Loading the Controls

When a container has completed loading all its controls, it can inform each control that the loading process is finished. The container will call the IOleControl::OnContainerFullyLoaded for each of its controls.

OLE Automation

Because much of the interaction between OLE controls and containers takes place through OLE automation, automation is only covered briefly in this section. If you are already familiar with how automation works, you can skip this section entirely.

Background

For many years, application developers have recognized the need to allow users to customize their applications. The first applications to provide user customization were spreadsheets. This was done through macro languages. Gradually over time, these macro languages grew into powerful programming languages. Today, it is possible for the user to create powerful custom applications using products such as Microsoft Excel and Microsoft Word.

However, there are a number of problems with this approach. No two macro languages are the same, not even when the applications come from the same software vendor. Due to the complexity of these languages, it takes a considerable amount of time to become proficient. And because of the lack of a common language, it is not possible to leverage this expertise when moving to another application.

Although today's macro languages allow full control of the application, there is little or no support for controlling one application from within another application. This is important, because although the macro language allows full control of all aspects of the application, it is generally an interpreted language and therefore can be very slow in execution. The lack of development tools is also a major drawback. In some of these applications, laying out a custom dialog box meant the painstaking process of hand coding field coordinates and field lengths. Another problem for people developing vertical applications in these macro languages is the need to ship the source code with the application.

The first attempts to address the cross-application issue was with Dynamic Data Exchange (DDE). DDE allowed you to open a channel between applications and send commands from a client application to a server application. As you know, DDE can be a nightmare to work with—even for experienced developers. It is also slow and provides no support for remote access of servers. Automation allows clients to access server methods as though they were an integral part of the client. OLE automation has made DDE obsolete.

The promise of OLE automation is simply to provide a standard way for applications to expose some or all of their functionality and to allow any other application to access this functionality. Automation opens the door for cross-application macro languages. One of the first examples you have seen of this is Visual Basic for Applications (VBA) that is currently shipping with Microsoft Excel 5.0 and Microsoft Project 4.0. Although this is a proprietary language used solely by Microsoft products, it is nonetheless a cross-application macro language that is driven by automation.

Component objects form the basis of component software. They are the building blocks for tomorrow's applications. OLE automation provides the glue that binds these objects together. Automation provides the means to programmatically control these objects. It should be noted, however, that not all component objects are automation objects and vice versa. In the future, more and more developers will add automation support to their component objects.

Although the main reason for implementing automation in your application would be to allow other applications to exploit your functionality, it is also possible for your application to use automation internally. This feature of automation will allow developers to break down their monolithic applications into smaller, self-contained units and control the interaction between these units through automation.

Before you continue, we should define some of the terminology used when discussing OLE automation.

Term	Definition
Automation Object or Server	Any object that can be programmatically controlled through the IDispatch interface.
Automation Controller	Any application that can control automation objects. Good examples include Visual Basic 3.0 and Visual Basic for Applications.
Method	A function that an automation object exposes and which can be called by an automation controller.
Property	An attribute or variable which can be set or read through automation.

Automation Objects

OLE automation provides developers with a standard means of exposing their application's functionality. It also provides a standard for controlling exposed objects.

So how do you define an automation object? You will remember from Chapter 1 that a component object was defined as being an object that supported at least one interface: IUnknown. An automation object supports IUnknown and a new interface called IDispatch. This interface is the primary means by which applications expose their functionality (see fig. 3.1).

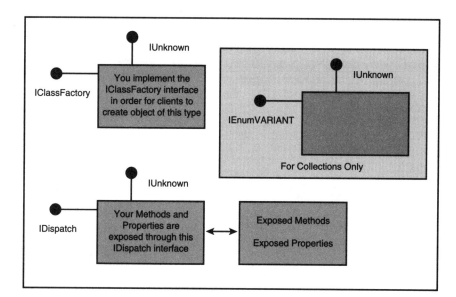

Fig. 3.1
An automation
object.

Because automation objects are COM objects, there must also exist a means of creating it initially. Therefore, every application that supports automation will also implement an object that supports the IClassFactory interface. As usual, the class factory object is responsible for creating the server object.

There are also a number of optional interfaces that an object may support. These include *collections*, which are an interface to access more than one instance of the object. Objects that support collections will expose an interface known as IEnumVARIANT.

Finally, objects need a way to communicate information about the methods and properties they expose. Information is also needed about the number and types of parameters that each method can accept. This information is made available through ITypelib and ITypeInfo.

The *IDispatch* Interface

The IDispatch interface is implemented by all automation objects and is used by all automation controllers when accessing the object. It provides the basic communication channel between the two processes.

The IDispatch interface is defined as follows in listing 3.1:

Listing 3.1   The *IDispatch* Interface

```
DECLARE_INTERFACE_(IDispatch, IUnknown)
{
    BEGIN_INTERFACE

    /* IUnknown methods */
    STDMETHOD(QueryInterface)(THIS_ REFIID riid,
    ➥void FAR* FAR* ppvObj) PURE;
    STDMETHOD_(unsigned long, AddRef)(THIS) PURE;
    STDMETHOD_(unsigned long, Release)(THIS) PURE;

    /* IDispatch methods */
    STDMETHOD(GetTypeInfoCount)(THIS_ unsigned int FAR* pctinfo) PURE;

    STDMETHOD(GetTypeInfo)(
      THIS_
      unsigned int itinfo,
      LCID lcid,
      ITypeInfo FAR* FAR* pptinfo) PURE;

    STDMETHOD(GetIDsOfNames)(
      THIS_
      REFIID riid,
      TCHAR FAR* FAR* rgszNames,
      unsigned int cNames,
      LCID lcid,
      DISPID FAR* rgdispid) PURE;

    STDMETHOD(Invoke)(
      THIS_
      DISPID dispidMember,
      REFIID riid,
      LCID lcid,
      unsigned short wFlags,
      DISPPARAMS FAR* pdispparams,
      VARIANT FAR* pvarResult,
      EXCEPINFO FAR* pexcepinfo,
      unsigned int FAR* puArgErr) PURE;
};
```

OLE automation uses the same object programming model as OLE—the Component Object Model (COM). As with all COM objects, each automation object must support the IUnknown interface. As you can see here, the first three methods in IDispatch are QueryInterface, AddRef, and Release. The interface defines four more virtual methods that need to be implemented.

The first two methods, GetTypeInfoCount and GetTypeInfo, are concerned with retrieving type information from the object. GetTypeInfoCount retrieves the number of type interfaces that an object supports. Currently, this method returns either 1 or 0. A 0 will be returned by objects that do not support any TypeInfo interfaces. These objects can still be controlled through automation; however, an object browser will not be able to extract information about the methods and properties that the object supports. GetTypeInfo is used to retrieve a pointer to an ITypeInfo interface. This interface is used to extract detailed information concerning each method and property exposed by the object. The interface is defined as follows in listing 3.2:

Listing 3.2   The *ITypeInfo* Interface

```
DECLARE_INTERFACE_(ITypeInfo, IUnknown)
{
    BEGIN_INTERFACE

    /* IUnknown methods */
    STDMETHOD(QueryInterface)(THIS_ REFIID riid,
    ➥void FAR* FAR* ppvObj) PURE;
    STDMETHOD_(unsigned long, AddRef)(THIS) PURE;
    STDMETHOD_(unsigned long, Release)(THIS) PURE;

    /* ITypeInfo methods */
    STDMETHOD(GetTypeAttr)(THIS_ TYPEATTR FAR* FAR* pptypeattr)
    ➥PURE;
    STDMETHOD(GetTypeComp)(THIS_ ITypeComp FAR* FAR* pptcomp) PURE;
    STDMETHOD(GetFuncDesc)(THIS_ unsigned int index,
    ➥FUNCDESC FAR* FAR* ppfuncdesc) PURE;

    STDMETHOD(GetVarDesc)(THIS_unsigned int index,
    ➥VARDESC FAR* FAR* ppvardesc) PURE;

    STDMETHOD(GetNames)(THIS_MEMBERID memid,BSTR FAR* rgbstrNames,
    ➥unsigned int cMaxNames, unsigned int FAR* pcNames) PURE;

    STDMETHOD(GetRefTypeOfImplType)(THIS_unsigned int index,
    ➥HREFTYPE FAR* phreftype) PURE;

    STDMETHOD(GetImplTypeFlags)(THIS_unsigned int index,
    ➥int FAR* pimpltypeflags) PURE;

    STDMETHOD(GetIDsOfNames)(THIS_TCHAR FAR* FAR* rgszNames,
    ➥unsigned int cNames, MEMBERID FAR* rgmemid) PURE;

    STDMETHOD(Invoke)(THIS_void FAR* pvInstance, MEMBERID memid,
    ➥unsigned short wFlags, DISPPARAMS FAR *pdispparams,
    ➥VARIANT FAR *pvarResult, EXCEPINFO FAR *pexcepinfo,
    ➥unsigned int FAR *puArgErr) PURE;
```

(continues)

Listing 3.2 Continued

```
        STDMETHOD(GetDocumentation)(THIS_MEMBERID memid,BSTR FAR
    ➥pbstrName,
    ➥BSTR FAR* pbstrDocString,
    ➥unsigned long FAR* pdwHelpContext,
    ➥BSTR FAR* pbstrHelpFile) PURE;

        STDMETHOD(GetDllEntry)(THIS_MEMBERID memid,INVOKEKIND invkind,
    ➥BSTR FAR* pbstrDllName, BSTR FAR* pbstrName,
    ➥unsigned short FAR* pwOrdinal) PURE;

        STDMETHOD(GetRefTypeInfo)(THIS_HREFTYPE hreftype,
    ➥ITypeInfo FAR* FAR* pptinfo) PURE;

        STDMETHOD(AddressOfMember)(THIS_MEMBERID memid, INVOKEKIND
    ➥invkind,
    ➥void FAR* FAR* ppv) PURE;

        STDMETHOD(CreateInstance)(THIS_IUnknown FAR* punkOuter,REFIID
    ➥riid,
    ➥void FAR* FAR* ppvObj) PURE;

        STDMETHOD(GetMops)(THIS_ MEMBERID memid, BSTR FAR* pbstrMops)
    ➥PURE;

        STDMETHOD(GetContainingTypeLib)(THIS_ITypeLib FAR* FAR* pptlib,
    ➥unsigned int FAR* pindex) PURE;

        STDMETHOD_(void, ReleaseTypeAttr)
    ➥(THIS_ TYPEATTR FAR* ptypeattr) PURE;
        STDMETHOD_(void, ReleaseFuncDesc)
    ➥(THIS_ FUNCDESC FAR* pfuncdesc) PURE;
        STDMETHOD_(void, ReleaseVarDesc)(THIS_ VARDESC FAR* pvardesc)
    ➥PURE;
    };
```

As you can see, there are many methods to be implemented to support this interface. Fortunately, you will not normally implement this interface manually. You will usually describe all the methods and properties in a type library and use the ITypeLib::GetTypeInfoOfGuid method to create an ITypeInfo pointer.

Type libraries and the type information interfaces are discussed in greater detail later in this chapter.

The next method defined by IDispatch is GetIDsOFNames. This method is used to map the names of exposed methods and properties to DISPIDs. A DISPID is a 32-bit number that is used to represent a method or property name. The reason you use DISPID is to reduce expensive string table lookup functions. When you access a method or property, you always use its DISPID to identify it. DISPIDs are also used to identify the types of arguments passed to the IDispatch::Invoke method. The following five DISPIDs in table 3.1 have special meanings.

Table 3.1 Types of DISPIDs	
DISPID	**Description**
DISPID_VALUE	The default member for the object. This is the property or method that is invoked if the object name is used from an OLE automation controller without specifying a property or method.
DISPID_NEWENUM	The _NewEnum method. This special, restricted method is required for collection objects. It returns the collection object and should have the flag FUNCFLAG_FRESTRICTED.
DISPID_EVALUATE	Implicitly invoke this method when the OLE automation controller encloses the arguments in square brackets. For example, the following two lines are equivalent: ```\nx.[A1:C1].value = 10\nx.Evaluate("A1:C1").value = 10\n``` In the preceding example, the Evaluate method has the dispatch ID: DISPID_EVALUATE.
DISPID_PROPERTYPUT	Indicates the parameter that receives the value of an assignment in a property put.
DISPID_UNKNOWN	Value returned by IDispatch::GetIDsOfNames to indicate that a member or parameter name was not found.

It is normal practice for applications to call this function, IDispatch::GetIDsOfNames, once for each method or property that it intends to use and cache the DISPIDs returned. This speeds up the process of invoking methods later.

OLE Control Methods

Each OLE control will have a number of custom methods that are exposed to its container. These custom method can be invoked from the container. This is in contrast to the VBX specification, in which only properties could be set by the control's container.

The methods exposed by an OLE control are described in the controls type library. Chapter 6 looks more closely at type libraries and the Object Description Language (ODL) that is used to create them.

OLE Control Properties

Properties are defined by their DISPIDs. Whenever you need to use a control's property in your code, you use its assigned DISPID. A control's properties define the characteristics of a control.

Properties come in four flavors: standard properties, custom properties, extended properties, and ambient properties. The ambient and extended properties are implemented by OLE control containers. Standard and custom properties are implemented by controls.

Ambient Properties Revisited

Ambient properties are used by the container to give a control information about its surroundings. Ambient properties can consist of the background color of a form, the currently selected font, and the locale ID of the container's user interface.

The SDK's documentation defines a set of standard ambient properties. The fact that these properties are predefined means that you can take these properties into account when you are developing your OLE control. These properties are important in order to achieve the effect of total integration between the control and its container.

Table 3.2 shows the standard properties as they are defined by the OLE SDK.

Table 3.2 Standard Ambient Properties			
DISPID	**Name**	**Type**	**Description**
701	BackColor	OLE_COLOR	Specifies the color for the interior of a control (in RGB values).
702	DisplayName	VT_BSTR	Specifies the name the control should display for itself in error messages.
703	Font	OLE_FONT	Font information for the control.
704	ForeColor	OLE_COLOR	Specifies the color for the display of text and graphics in a control (in RGB values).

DISPID	Name	Type	Description
705	LocaleID	VT_I4	Specifies the ID of UI locale.
706	MessageReflect	VT_BOOL	This value is set to TRUE if the container should reflect messages back to the control.
707	ScaleUnits	VT_BSTR	Coordinate unit name being used by container.
708	TextAlign	VT_I2	Specifies how the text should be aligned in a control: 0 is general (numbers to the right, text to the left), 1 is left, 2 is center, 3 is right, and 4 is full justify.
709	UserMode	VT_BOOL	Allows the control to determine how it is being used. If it is being used to design a form (or some other thing), the value is False. If it is being used by an end user interacting with or viewing the control, the value is True. If this property is not present, the control should assume True. Note that this value may change dynamically, because some containers may not distinguish between designing and using a form and may switch without destroying (and reloading) the control.
710	UIDead	VT_BOOL	Allows the control to detect situations in which the container does not want the control to interact with user input. The value of this property can change dynamically. If True, the control behaves normally. If False, the UI is non-responsive; the control shouldn't set the cursor, and should ignore UI input. If this ambient property isn't present, the control should assume a value of False.
711	SupportsMnemonics	VT_BOOL	If True, the container supports mnemonics.
712	ShowGrabHandles	VT_BOOL	If True, the control should not display grab handles when it's UI-active.

(continues)

Table 3.2 Continued			
DISPID	**Name**	**Type**	**Description**
713	ShowHatching	VT_BOOL	If True, the control should not show the normal UI-active hatching feedback when the UI is activated.
714	DisplayAsDefaultButton	VT_BOOL	Exposed only to button-like controls. If True, the button should display itself using default button visuals.

Ambient properties are provided only by containers that have built-in support for OLE controls. Normal OLE containers will not have this support. However, it is important that controls can still function in standard containers. You should also note that containers are not required to support ambient properties. If a container does not support a particular property, it will return DISP_E_MEMBERNOTFOUND to the control.

How does the control retrieve these ambient properties? As you saw earlier in the discussion of OLE control containers, all control containers support a default IDispatch interface on their site objects. (The site object is the COM object implemented by the container that supports IOleControlSite. This interface, coupled with the IOleControl interface implemented by the control, provides communication between the control and its container.) When the control is created, it will have a COM interface pointer (IOleClientSite) to this site. A QueryInterface on this pointer for an IID_Dispatch pointer will return a pointer to the IDispatch interface.

The control can then call the IDispatch::Invoke method using the DISPID of the ambient property that it wants. If the property is not supported, DISP_E_MEMBERNOTFOUND is returned; otherwise, the method will return the ambient property value.

If you need to access non-standard properties, you would simply call IDispatch::GetIDsOfNames to retrieve the DISPID for that property and then call IDispatch::Invoke using the returned DISPID.

When an ambient property changes, the container needs to have some way to inform the control of the changes. Normally, a control retrieves the ambient properties when the control is first initialized. A method in the

`IOleControl` interface, `IOleControl::OnAmbientPropertyChange`, is called to inform the control of the changes. The `DISPID` of the affected property is passed in this method call. The control can then query the container for the new value of the changed property.

Standard Properties

The properties of a control define the characteristics of the control. These characteristics can include the font used in the control, the background color of the control, or its caption. Because so many of these characteristics are common to almost all controls, a standard set of properties has been defined. This greatly simplifies the process of identifying the properties.

Controls are not required to support standard properties; but if they do, they must support them with the names and types as defined in table 3.3.

The following table shows the standard properties and their DISPIDs.

Table 3.3	Standard Properties		
DISPID	**Name**	**Type**	**Description**
501	BackColor	OLE_COLOR	Specifies the color for the interior of the control (in RGB values).
502	BackStyle	VT_I2	Determines whether a control is transparent (0) or opaque (1).
512	Font	OLEFONT	Specifies the current font for the control.
513	ForeColor	OLE_COLOR	Specifies the color for the display of text and graphics in a control (in RGB values).
514	Enabled	VT_BOOL	Indicates whether the control can receive the focus. May also affect the control's appearance.
517	Text	VT_BSTR	Value of a text box, listbox, or combo box.
518	Caption	VT_BSTR	Text displayed in or next to the control.
550	Refresh	None	Forces a repaint of the control synchronously if the control currently has a window, and asynchronously otherwise.

(continues)

Table 3.3 Continued			
DISPID	**Name**	**Type**	**Description**
551	DoClick	None	For button-like controls, simulates the button being clicked by the user. This is used by the support for default and cancel buttons to simulate the button being clicked when the user types Return or Escape.
552	AboutBox	None	Pops up a modal About dialog box for the control.

Standard properties are always identified by a negative DISPID.

Extended Properties

The extended properties of a control are unique in the sense that it is the control container that sets these properties. Although they appear to the user as properties of the control, they are in fact completely managed by the container.

An example of a property that would be an extended control property is the default command button on a data entry form. Obviously, it is the container that would decide what button is the default button. By using the extended property, default, the container will set a particular control to be the default button.

Controls need to be aware of extended properties to avoid the possibility of a conflict between a control's own properties and the extended properties assigned by the container.

Normally, the control need not be aware of the extended properties assigned by the container, but it has access to this information through the IOleControlSite::GetExtendedControl method.

Table 3.4 shows the extended properties currently defined by the OLE SDK.

Table 3.4 Extended Properties			
DISPID	**Name**	**Type**	**Description**
0x00	Name	VT_BSTR	Returns the user-defined name of an object.
0x07	Visible	VT_BOOL	Indicates whether the control is visible on the container.
0x08	Parent	VT_DISPATCH	Always returns the document in which an object is embedded. A control should be able to use this property to enumerate properties of its container, and so on.
0x37	Cancel	VT_BOOL	Returns True if the control is the default Cancel button for the form.
0x38	Default	VT_BOOL	Determines which button on a form is the default button (for example, the default OK button on a dialog box).

A range of DISPIDs is reserved for use by control containers for extended properties. These DISPIDs are in the range 0x80010000 to 0x8001ffff. The values in the preceding table must be called by OR with 0x80010000 in order to get the actual DISPID.

Custom Properties

Custom properties are properties defined by a control that do not belong to the set of predefined standard properties. Custom properties are documented by the control developer so that container developers may use these properties. As you saw earlier, the container will need to call IDispatch::GetIDsofNames to retrieve the DISPIDs of these custom properties.

OLE Control Events

Normal COM objects, such as those found in compound documents, can respond internally to external events such as mouse clicks. They cannot, however, inform their containers or other objects of these events. The ability for a control to generate events is a vital part of the OLE controls architecture.

Every control will have a specific set of events that it is capable of firing. The event set is known as a control's primary event set. The events that a particular control supports are described in the control's type library.

An OLE control will implement an outgoing interface in the form of a single IDispatch interface. This interface is used to fire a control's primary event set. Other interfaces may also be implemented to support other event sets. The control will allow the user to navigate among the different interfaces through QueryInterface.

The important point to remember here is that the container implements the IDispatch interface.

Events are designed and implemented by the control. However, because it is the control container that must respond to the firing of events, a set of standard events must be defined. A convention must also be used that allows control developers to add events. Normally every control will be shipped to the developer with documentation about the events that the control is capable of firing. To assist users of controls, four main types of events have been defined: *request* events, *before* events, *after* events, and *do* events. Developers are encouraged to use these event types.

Request Events

A request event is an event that a control would generate in order to ask the container for permission to perform a certain operation. For example, if a user clicked on a close command button, the control could generate a request event to ask the container whether it was okay to shut down. The last parameter passed by a request event is by reference CancelBoolean type. This type would normally be set to False by the control, and the container may change it to True.

Before Events

Before events, as the name suggests, are fired before something happens. They provide the container with advanced warning that a particular event is about to be generated. Although the container is advised of the forthcoming event, it does not have the power to cancel it.

After Events

After events are fired after an event has occurred. Like before events, these events are merely advising a control container that as event has completed.

Do Events

Do events are by far the most powerful event types. Their power comes from the fact that the user can override the default implementation of the event. Do events can be thought of as virtual functions. The last parameter in a do event is the type EnableDefault. This parameter is set to True by the control before the event is fired. It is then passed by reference to the container.

If the container decides to provide another implementation for the event, it will return False in the EnableDefault parameter. This will cause the control to ignore the event and not call its own implementation. Of course, the control container could do some processing on receipt of the event but return False to allow the control to complete its default implementation also.

Developers are encouraged to use a common convention for naming these events. All before events should be prefixed with the word Before, after events with the word After, request events with the word Request, and finally, do events with the word Do.

Because the firing of events may cause implementation code in the container to manipulate the control's properties, thereby causing another event to be fired, controls should be careful about re-entrancy and race conditions.

The table 3.5 shows the events that have been predefined:

Table 3.5 Predefined Events			
DISPID	**Name**	**Arguments (in order)**	**Description**
-600	Click	None	Occurs when the user presses and then releases a mouse button over a control. For some controls, this event is fired when the value of the control is changed.
-601	DblClick	None	Occurs when the user double-clicks in the control.
-602	KeyDown	KeyCode, Shift	Occurs when the user presses a key when the control has the focus. KeyCode is the key code for the key pressed. The Shift parameter is a bit mask that details the state of the Control, Shift, and Alt keys. KeyCode is passed by reference; changing it sends a different character to the object. Changing KeyCode to 0 cancels the keystroke so that the object receives no character.

(continues)

Table 3.5 Continued			
DISPID	**Name**	**Arguments (in order)**	**Description**
-604	KeyUp	KeyCode, Shift	Occurs when the user releases a key when the control has the focus. See KeyDown for argument details. KeyCode is passed by reference; changing it sends a different character to the object. Changing KeyCode to 0 cancels the keystroke so that the object receives no character.
-605	MouseDown	Button, Shift, X, Y	Occurs when the user presses a mouse button while over an OLE control. The Button Bit mask identifies which mouse button is now down (or up, for MouseUp events). The Shift Bit mask parameter details the state of the Ctrl, Shift, and Alt keys. The X, Y parameters are the current location of mouse over control.
-606	MouseMove	Button, Shift, X, Y	Occurs when the mouse moves over the control. See MouseDown for details on arguments; note that for MouseMove events, Button identifies the set of buttons currently down.
-607	MouseUp	Button, Shift, X, Y	Indicates that the user has released the mouse button over this control. See MouseDown for details on parameters.

A standard Error event is also defined. This event has been assigned the DISPID of -608. This event should be fired from a control when an unexpected error outside the normal use of the control occurs. Normally, controls will return error codes for each method that is called. However, if the control encounters an internal error outside of a method being called, the error event should be used.

The event is defined as follows:

```
Error(short Number, BSTR* Description, SCODE SCode, BSTR Source,
➥BSTR HelpFile, long HelpContext, BOOL* CancelDisplay);
```

The parameters are described in detail in table 3.6:

Table 3.6 Error Event Parameters	
Parameter	**Description**
Number	A local error code.
Description	A short description of the error.
Scode	The OLE error code.
Source	The name of the object causing the error.
HelpFile	The name of the help file associated with the control.
HelpContext	The help file context number.
CancelDisplay	Allows the handler to cancel the event.

Connections

As you saw in Chapter 2, COM defines a way for obtaining pointers to various interfaces through the QueryInterface mechanism. With this mechanism, you can retrieve a pointer from an object. These pointers are known as *incoming interfaces*.

As you saw earlier, controls will fire events that are subsequently handled by event handlers in the control container. These events are transmitted through an IDispatch interface. This interface is known as an *outgoing interface*.

The current release of OLE defines two interfaces that are used to perform notifications between objects. These interfaces, IAdviseSink and IAdviseSink2, are not intended to be extendible, so new interfaces needed to be added to OLE.

These new interfaces are IConnectionPoint and IConnectionPointContainer. IConnectionPoint, which is defined here, provides the connection pointer (that is, the interface pointer) to the object implemented by the container.

```
interface IConnectionPoint : public IUnknown
{
    GetConnectionInterface(IID * pIID);
    GetConnectionPointContainer(IConnectionPointContainer **
    ➥ppCPC);
    Advise(IUnknown * pUnkSink, DWORD * pdwCookie);
    Unadvise(DWORD dwCookie);

    EnumConnections(IEnumConnections * pEnum);
};
```

For each interface that a container supports, it must support one
IConnectionPoint object. The following is an example.

Suppose that a control container wants to implement a specific event handler. The container will implement a sink, which is defined as the actual
implementation of the handler. It will then search the control for the appropriate IConnectionPoint. Once a pointer to an IConnectionPoint has been
located, the container will then call IConnectionPoint::Advise, passing a
pointer to the implemented sink. When an event occurs, the control will
invoke the event handler via the connection pointer.

How does the container locate the connection point for a particular event?
Each control will implement an IConnectionPointContainer interface on
its main object. In other words, you will be able to access this interface
pointer via a QueryInterface on the main object. Once a pointer to an
IConnectionPointContainer has been located, you can use the supplied enumerator to enumerate all the available connection pointers available on that
object.

IConnectionPointerContainer is implemented as follows:

```
interface IConnectionPointContainer : public IUnknown
{
    EnumConnectionPoints(IEnumConnectionPoints * pEnum);
    FindConnectionPointFromIID(REFIID iid, IConnectionPoint **
    ➥ppCP);
}
```

You will see these concepts in action in later chapters, when you begin to
develop your OLE controls.

COM Interfaces

You have already covered the basics of COM interfaces in Chapter 2. You saw
how the Component Object Model provides an object model on which OLE
is built and on which OLE will be extended in the future.

Each OLE control will support the standard interfaces that are required of all COM objects that support Visual Editing. That is, they support the following interfaces:

- IOleObject

- IDataObject

- IViewObject

- IPersistStorage

- IOleInPlaceActiveObject

- IOleCache (optional)

(For a complete description of these interfaces, please refer to the *OLE 2.0 Programmer's Guide.*) They also support IPersistStream and IDispatch. In addition to these interfaces, a number of new interfaces have been defined for the purposes of supporting OLE controls.

IOleControl

The main COM interface for controls is IOleControl and is defined as follows:

```
interface IOleControl : public IUnknown
{
    GetControlInfo(CONTROLINFO * pCI);
    OnMnemonic(LPMSG pMsg);

    OnAmbientPropertyChange(DISPID dispid);
    FreezeEvents(BOOL fFreeze);
};
```

GetControlInfo

The GetControlInfo method is used to return to the container information about the control's keyboard accelerators. It fills in a structure called CONTROLINFO, which contains information about the accelerators. CONTROLINFO is defined as follows:

```
typedef struct tagCONTROLINFO
{
    ULONG  cb;        // Structure size
    HACCEL hAccel;    // Control mnemonics
    USHORT cAccel;    // Number of entries in mnemonics table
    DWORD  dwFlags;   // Flags chosen from below

} CONTROLINFO;
```

The accelerators contained in this table are used only when the control is not UI-active. `IOleInPlaceActiveObject::TranslateAccelerator` takes care of accelerators when the control is UI-active.

OnMnemonic

`OnMnemonic` is the method that the control container will call when it finds an accelerator that matches the accelerator for a particular control.

OnAmbientPropertyChange

If the value of a particular ambient property changes, the control container will use this method to notify the control of the change. The `DISPID` of the property in question is used as a parameter. If more than one property has been updated, the `DISPID DISP_UNKNOWN` is used. In this case, the control should perform an update on all its stored ambient properties.

FreezeEvents

This method is called by the control container to force the control to stop firing events. When it wants to enable the control for firing events, it calls this method with the parameter set to `True`.

IOleControlSite

This is the main COM interface implemented by OLE control containers.

```
interface IOleControlSite : public IUnknown
{
    OnControlInfoChanged(void);

    LockInPlaceActive(BOOL fLock);
    GetExtendedControl(IDispatch ** ppDisp);
    TransformCoords(
        POINTL * pPtlHiMetric,
        POINTF * pPtfContainer,
        DWORD dwFlags);

    TranslateAccelerator(MSG * lpmsg, DWORD grfModifiers);
};
```

OnControlInfoChanged

This method is called by the control to tell the control container to reload its keyboard accelerator information stored in its `CONTROLINFO` array. This can happen if a command button's text changes.

LockInPlaceActive

This method is used to force the control container to keep a control in its active state.

GetExtendedControl

This method is used to retrieve a pointer to the extended control that is being used for a particular control.

TransformCoords

This method is made available to controls so that they can translate their coordinate system into the coordinate system used by the container. It allows the control container to present a uniform coordinate space for all its controls.

TranslateAccelerator

A control will call this method if it does not want to handle a certain keystroke. Calling this method allows the container to handle the keystroke itself or by passing it on to another control.

As you can see from the preceding interface, a great deal of thought has gone into handling keyboard accelerators in these new interfaces. When you see a form populated with OLE controls, you will understand why. Apart from the normal accelerators associated with controls, two special ones deserve a mention.

The handling of the Esc and Return keys is different than for normal accelerators. In a normal Windows dialog box, the Esc key is associated with CANCEL and the Return key with performing a default action.

If a control is a command button type of control and understands either CANCEL or Return, it will be registered in the system registry with the Misc bit OLEMISC_ACTSLIKEBUTTON set. Controls that have this bit set can be assigned with a default or cancel type property. When the user presses Esc, that keystroke is first sent to the control that is UI-active. If the control does process the key because it has the CTRLINFO_EATS_ESCAPE set, it goes no further. However, if it does not process the keystroke, the container will look for the control marked cancel and send the event to that control via OnMnemonic. That control will then perform the cancel operation.

Extended Controls

A problem that arises with controls is that different containers may have different positioning models. In this case, the container would like to implement the positioning properties itself. By doing this, all controls that are embedded in the control container will expose the same coordinate set.

To allow this, the concept of extended controls was introduced. An extended control is a control that aggregates the actual embedded control. You will remember from Chapter 2 that aggregation is OLE's means of providing object inheritance. The extended control that is created by the container will implement the controlling unknown for the embedded control. Any methods or properties not implemented by the extended control will be deferred to the embedded control. The user, however, will see only one control.

Because most controls created with the SDK are in-process objects, they are aggregatable. The container will create the extended control when it creates the embedded control.

Registration Database *MiscStatus* Bits

Various status information about an object can be stored in the system registry. Storing the information here means that the default handle in OLE does not have to activate the object in order to retrieve information from it.

With the introduction of custom controls, Microsoft has extended the fields that are placed in the registry. The values of these fields are obtained by calling IOleObject->GetMiscStatus.

Table 3.7 shows the original fields that are used by OLE Objects. Table 3.8 shows the additional fields added for OLE controls.

Table 3.7 Original *MiscStatus* Fields	
Status Bit	**Description**
OLEMISC_ISLINKOBJECT	This object is a link object. This bit is significant to OLE and is set by the OLE 2 link object; object applications have no need to set this bit.
OLEMISC_INSIDEOUT VISIBLE	This object is capable of activating in-place, without requiring installation of menus and toolbars to run. Several such objects can be active concurrently. Some containers, such as forms, may choose to activate such objects automatically.
OLEMISC_ACTIVATEWHEN	This bit is set only when OLEMISC_INSIDEOUT is set, and indicates that this object prefers to be activated whenever it is visible. Some containers may always ignore this hint.

Status Bit	Description
OLEMISC_RENDERINGIS DEVICEINDEPENDENT	This object does not pay any attention to target devices. Its presentation data will be the same in all cases.
OLEMISC_ONLYICONIC	This object has no useful content view other than its icon. From the user's perspective, the Display As Icon checkbox (in the Paste Special dialog box) for this object should always be checked. Note that such an object should still have a drawable content aspect; it will look the same as its icon view.
OLEMISC_INSERTNOTREPLACE	This object indicates that this kind of object, when inserted into a document, should be inserted beside the selection instead of replacing it. An object that linked itself to the selection with which it was initialized would set this bit. Containers should examine this bit after they have initialized the object with the selection. See IOleObject::InitFromData.
OLEMISC_STATIC	This object indicates that this object is a static object. See OleCreateStaticFromData.
OLEMISC_CANTLINKINSIDE	This bit indicates that this is the kind of object that should not be the link source when its moniker is bound. That is, if when the object is selected its container wants to offer the Link Source format in a data transfer, then the link, when bound, must connect to the outside of the object. The user would see the object selected in its container, not open for editing. Some objects that do not want to implement, being the source of a link when they are embedded, may want to set this bit.
OLEMISC_CANLINKBYOLE1	This object indicates that it can be linked to by OLE 1 containers. This bit is used in the dwStatus field of the OBJECTDESCRIPTOR structure transferred with the Object and Link Source Descriptor formats. An object can be linked by OLE 1 if it is not an embedded object or pseudo object contained within an embedded object.
OLEMISC_RECOMPOSEONRESIZE	If true, this object signifies that when the size that the container allocates to the object changes, the object would like the opportunity to recompose its picture. When resize occurs, the object is likely to do something other than scale its picture. The container should force the object to run so that it can call IOleObject::GetExtent.

Table 3.8   Additional *MiscStatus* Fields

Status Bit	Description
OLEMISC_INSERTNOTREPLACE	The object is not to replace the current selection during insertion, particularly if the object is being created as a link to the current selection.
OLEMISC_STATIC	The object is static.
OLEMISC_CANTLINKINSIDE	The object cannot be a link source for a link. For example, a static object cannot be a link source.
OLEMISC_CANLINKBYOLE1	The object can be linked by an OLE 1.0 server.
OLEMISC_ISLINK	The object is linked and is being used in OLE 1.0 compatibility code.
OLEMISC_INVISIBLEATRUNTIME	Used by a container that has a distinction between designtime and runtime, as most control containers do, to show the object only when in design mode. A Timer control that fires a Click event at preset intervals might use this bit; it would be visible at designtime (so that the user can set properties on the timer) but not at runtime.
OLEMISC_ALWAYSRUN	Used by a container to always put objects with this bit set into the Running state, even when not visible. That is, the container should request that it not be given the standard handler for this object, but that the server be activated instead. This allows the object to fire events and take other proactive action; again, this is useful for Timer-like objects. This bit is not normally required for in-process servers.
OLEMISC_ACTSLIKEBUTTON	Used by a container that provides Default/Cancel buttons. Controls that provide this flag are capable of acting like buttons. In particular, the control's primary event can be triggered in its IOleControl::OnMnemonic method, and the control is prepared to render itself as the default button based on the ambient DisplayAsDefaultButton.
OLEMISC_ACTSLIKELABEL	Used by a container that potentially allows OLE controls to replace the container's native label. The container is responsible for determining what to do with this flag (or ignoring it). A container that uses this flag will typically intercept mnemonics and/or

Status Bit	Description
	mouse clicks targeted for the label-like control at runtime and reinterpret these messages as attempts to move to the field associated with the label.
OLEMISC_NOUIACTIVATE	Used by a container to determine if a control doesn't support UI activation. Under OLE 2, such an object was not very useful, since activating it was generally the only way to edit it. With OLE controls, the user can program the control using OLE automation or set its properties using property pages; therefore, it can use a non UI-activated control. Note that controls can already indicate that they don't support a separate In-Place Active state by not including the OLEMISC_INSIDEOUT bit.
OLEMISC_ALIGNABLE	Used by a container that supports aligned controls. This bit is used by a control that is most useful when aligned on some side of its container. Containers that support such aligned controls can use this bit to decide whether the user should be allowed to align a particular control.
OLEMISC_IMEMODE	Marks a control that understands IME Mode. This makes sense only for DBCS versions of Windows. Containers will typically add an IMEMode property to the extended control for controls that mark themselves with this bit.
OLEMISC_SIMPLEFRAME	Used by containers to determine whether a control supports the ISimpleFrameSite protocol. Containers that also support this interface will use simple frame controls as parents for other controls in the container. In effect, the simple frame control operates as an OLE compound document container, but the frame control's container does almost all the work.
OLEMISC_SETCLIENTSITEFIRST	Used by new OLE containers to identify controls that support having SetClientSite called first, immediately after being created and before the control has been completely constructed. Normal OLE compound document containers are written to call SetClientSite on embedded objects after calling IPersistStorage::Load or IPersistStorage::InitNew on the object. Since OLE controls get stated through their client site and that state is useful during the load process, they need to have the client site available during Load or InitNew.

Registering Controls

A major problem with the current implementation of OLE object servers is the fact that each server must be correctly registered in the system registry in order to function properly. Object servers are usually registered by merging REG files container information about the server with the system registry. If the registry becomes corrupted or if the user neglects to register the server, it will not work.

A new mechanism for registering servers was devised for OLE controls. Each OLE control will contain a string in its version information resource called OleSelfRegister. OLE containers will look for this string in any control that it is asked to use.

Once the container has determined that the control is capable of registering itself in the registry, it will then call CoLoadLibary to load the control into memory and call GetProcAddress to retrieve the function address for DllRegisterServer. When the address has been retrieved, the function will be called and the control will update the system registry with the necessary information.

An additional function, DllUnregisterServer, is also available to allow controls to remove information for the system registry.

From Here...

If you require more detailed information, see the OLE controls documentation supplied with the SDK. As you can see, the addition of OLE controls builds on and extends the current COM architecture. The fact that Microsoft could do this further proves the viability of the COM model for building and extending new object systems.

Refer to the following chapters for more information on the topics discussed in this chapter:

- Chapter 2, "The Component Object Model," provides a detailed look at the Component Object Model and its relationship with OLE controls.

- Chapter 4, "A Simple Control," teaches you how to develop a simple control and see some of these technologies in action.

Chapter 4

A Simple Control

by Edward B. Toupin

In this chapter, you will create your first OLE control. Using Visual C++ 2.0 and the OLE Control Developers Kit (CDK), you will follow the steps required to create a functioning OLE control. You will also examine the code in detail as you complete each step.

On completion, the Test Container supplied with the CDK will be used to test the functionality of the control.

This chapter covers the following topics:

- Designing the control

- Using the ControlWizard

- Using the Test Container to test your control

Designing the Control

The control that you are about to develop is an OLE control which displays a random quote whenever the user double-clicks on the control with the mouse. Although the control is simple, it does contain a number of features that are common to most controls:

- *Ambient Properties*. The control will read and use the foreground color, background color, and current font ambient properties.

- *Stock Properties*. The control supports the foreground color, background color, and font stock properties.

- *Custom Properties.* The control will support one custom property.

- *Property Pages.* The control will support property pages for its custom and stock properties.

- *Methods.* The control will expose one method—its About Box—to the user.

- *Licensing.* The control will also make use of a license file to prevent the control from being used in design mode by an unauthorized user.

You will use the ControlWizard supplied with the CDK to generate the initial source files. Then the ClassWizard will be used to add methods and properties to your source files and the control's ODL file.

The ControlWizard

You begin by using the ControlWizard supplied with the CDK to generate the initial source file. Figure 4.1 shows the ControlWizard on startup. This project is called Quote.

Fig. 4.1
Use the ControlWizard to create the initial source files.

Next, select the Control Options command button. The Control Options dialog box appears (see fig 4.2).

Fig. 4.2
The Control Options dialog box is used to select options for your control.

The options available to you in this dialog box are as follows:

Option	Description
Activate When Visible	This option indicates that the control is to be activated when it becomes visible in its container. Containers are not required to act on this request.
Show In Insert Object Dialog	This option should be selected if the control should be listed in the standard OLE Insert Object dialog box. Not all controls will have this option.
Invisible At Runtime	Some types of controls, such as timers, should not be visible to the user at runtime. They are normally only visible when the user is in design-time mode. Like the Activate When Visible option, a container may choose to ignore this request.
Simple Frame	This option enables the simple frame characteristic for an OLE control. This is used to group OLE controls together on a dialog box or a form. The frame operates as an OLE container.
About Box	This option tells the ControlWizard to generate the necessary code to add an About Box to the control.
Subclass Windows Control	This option tells the ControlWizard to generate the code for subclassing common controls such as listboxes and buttons. Subclassing controls will be covered in greater detail in Chapter 11.
Use VBX Control As Template	If you are converting an existing Visual Basic Control VBX to the OCX format, this option will assist you in the process. Chapter 8 is dedicated to this process.
Select VBX Control	This option allows you to select the VBX to port.

For this control, select the Activate When Visible, Show In Insert Object Dialog, and the About Box options.

Finally, you will select the options for the source files generated for this control by selecting the Controls command button. Figure 4.3 shows the options that were selected.

Now that you have selected the options that you want for this control, you ask the ControlWizard to generate the necessary source files by selecting the OK command button.

Fig. 4.3

The Source Files
Options dialog
box shows the
names of the
source files and
classes.

Examining the Code

Next, you'll begin to examine the source code generated by the
ControlWizard. Then, you'll add your methods and properties to the control.
Finally, you will build the control and test it in the Test Container supplied
with the CDK.

The Main Module (Quote.cpp)

The first module of interest is the control's main module, Quote.cpp. The
module contains two methods, InitInstance and ExitInstance, which can be
used for one-time initialization of the control. However, the functions of
most interest to you are the DllRegisterServer and DllUnregisterServer,
which are used to automatically register or unregister your control in the
system registry.

You will remember from Chapter 3 that these functions comprise the new
self-registering mechanism for OLE controls. The container will look in the
resource of an OCX for the string OLESelfRegister. If it finds this string, it
will call LoadLibrary to load the control into memory, use GetProcAddress to
retrieve the address of DllRegisterServer, and then call this function.

As you can see from listing 4.1, your control contains the OLESelfRegister
string:

Listing 4.1   Version Control Information

```
VS_VERSION_INFO   VERSIONINFO
   FILEVERSION       1,0,0,1
   PRODUCTVERSION    1,0,0,1
   FILEFLAGSMASK     VS_FFI_FILEFLAGSMASK
#ifdef _DEBUG
   FILEFLAGS         VS_FF_DEBUG|VS_FF_PRIVATEBUILD|VS_FF_PRERELEASE
#else
   FILEFLAGS         0 // final version
```

```
#endif
#ifdef _WIN32
  FILEOS              VOS__WINDOWS32
#else
  FILEOS              VOS__WINDOWS16
#endif
  FILETYPE            VFT_DLL
  FILESUBTYPE         0   // not used
BEGIN
     BLOCK "StringFileInfo"
     BEGIN
#ifdef _WIN32
         BLOCK "040904B0" // Lang=US English,
                          // CharSet=Unicode
#else
         BLOCK "040904E4" // Lang=US English,
                          // CharSet=Windows Multilingual
#endif
         BEGIN
             VALUE "CompanyName",      "\0"
             VALUE "FileDescription", "QUOTE OLE Control DLL\0"
             VALUE "FileVersion",      "1.0.001\0"
             VALUE "InternalName",     "QUOTE\0"
             VALUE "LegalCopyright",   "Copyright
                     \251 1994, Tangent Software\0"
             VALUE "LegalTrademarks", "\0"
             VALUE "OriginalFilename","QUOTE.DLL\0"
             VALUE "ProductName",      "QUOTE\0"
             VALUE "ProductVersion",   "1.0.001\0"
             VALUE "OLESelfRegister", "\0"
         END
     END
     BLOCK "VarFileInfo"
     BEGIN
#ifdef _WIN32
         VALUE "Translation", 0x409, 1200
             // English language (0x409)
             // and the Unicode codepage (1200)

#else
         VALUE "Translation", 0x409, 1252
             // English language (0x409)
             // and the Windows ANSI codepage (1252)

#endif
     END
END
```

The first function called by your `DllRegisterServer` function is a call to `AfxOleRegisterTypeLib` to register your controls type library. Your type library contains a full description of all your methods and properties. (Type libraries are covered in detail in Chapter 5.) Type libraries are often stored as separate files usually with the TLB or OLB extension. In your case, the type library is stored internally in the control as a resource.

The first parameter is the instance handle of the control and the second parameter is the GUID associated with your control.

Once the type library is registered, you then register the class factory for your control. *Class factories* are the mechanism used by COM to create instances of objects. Once the class factory has been registered with the OLE libraries, containers can then create instances of our control. The COleObjectFactoryEx method UpdateRegistryAll calls UpdateRegistry for each control to perform the actual registration.

Your UpdateRegistry method is defined as follows (this code is generated by the ControlWizard):

```
/////////////////////////////////////////////////////////////////
// CQuoteCtrl::CQuoteCtrlFactory::UpdateRegistry -
// Adds or removes system registry entries for CQuoteCtrl
//
BOOL CQuoteCtrl::CQuoteCtrlFactory::UpdateRegistry(BOOL bRegister)
{
    if (bRegister)
        return AfxOleRegisterControlClass(
            AfxGetInstanceHandle(),
            m_clsid,
            m_lpszProgID,
            IDS_QUOTE,
            IDB_QUOTE,
            TRUE,                        //  Insertable
            _dwQuoteOleMisc,
            _tlid,
            _wVerMajor,
            _wVerMinor);
    else
        return AfxOleUnregisterClass(m_clsid, m_lpszProgID);
}
```

Depending on whether the bRegister parameter is TRUE or FALSE, the control is registered or unregistered. The API function AfxOleRegisterControlClass takes 10 parameters (see table 4.1).

Table 4.1   The Parameters for *AfxOleRegister* Control Class

Parameter	Description
hInstance	The instance handle of the module associated with the control class.
clsid	The unique class ID of the control.
pszProgID	The unique program ID of the control.
idTypeName	The resource ID of the string that contains a user-readable type name for the control.
idBitmap	The resource ID of the bitmap used to represent the OLE control in a toolbar or palette.
bInsertable	Allows the control to be inserted from a container's Insert Object dialog box if set to True; False prevents the control from being inserted.
dwMiscStatus	Contains one or more status flags. For more information on the following flags (or bits), see table 4.2 for the new status flags defined for OLE controls.
tlid	The unique ID of the control class.
wVerMajor	The major version number of the control class.
wVerMinor	The minor version number of the control class.

Table 4.2   The Status Flags for *IOleObject::GetMiscStatus*

Status Flag	Description
OLEMISC_RECOMPOSEONRESIZE	If the object's container resizes the space allocated to the object, the object will resize itself.
OLEMISC_ONLYICONIC	The object can be displayed only as an icon.
OLEMISC_INSERTNOTREPLACE	The object is not to replace the current selection during insertion, particularly if the object is being created as a link to the current selection.
OLEMISC_STATIC	The object is static.
OLEMISC_CANTLINKINSIDE	The object cannot be a link source for a link. For example, a static object cannot be a link source.
OLEMISC_CANLINKBYOLE1	The object can be linked by an OLE 1.0 server.

(continues)

Table 4.2 Continued	
Status Flag	**Description**
OLEMISC_ISLINK	The object is linked and is being used in OLE 1.0 compatibility code.
OLEMISC_INSIDEOUT	The object can be activated in-place without being UI-active (that is, without activating its menus, toolbars, and so on).
OLEMISC_ACTIVATEWHENVISIBLE	The object should be active whenever it is visible.
OLEMISC_INVISIBLEATRUNTIME	Used by a container that has a distinction between designtime and runtime—as most control containers do—to only show the object when in design mode. A Timer control that fires a Click event at preset intervals might use this bit; it would be visible at designtime (so the user can set properties on the timer), but not at runtime.
OLEMISC_ALWAYSRUN	Used by a container to always put objects with this bit set into the running state, even when not visible. That is, the container should request that it not be given the standard handler for this object, but that the server be activated instead. This allows the object to fire events and take other proactive action; again, this is useful for timer-like objects. This bit is not normally required for in-process servers.
OLEMISC_ACTSLIKEBUTTON	Used by a container that provides Default/ Cancel buttons. Controls that provide this flag are capable of acting like buttons. In particular, the control's primary event can be triggered in its IOleControl::OnMnemonic method, and the control is prepared to render itself as the default button based on the ambient DisplayAsDefaultButton.
OLEMISC_ACTSLIKELABEL	Used by a container that potentially allows OLE controls to replace the container's native label. The container is responsible for determining what to do with this flag (or whether to ignore it). A container that uses this flag will typically intercept mnemonics and/or mouse clicks targeted for the label-like control at runtime and reinterpret these messages as attempts to move to the field associated with the label.
OLEMISC_NOUIACTIVATE	Used by a container to determine if a control doesn't support UI activation. Under OLE 2, such an object was not very useful, since activating it was generally the only way to edit it. With OLE controls, the user can program the

Status Flag	Description
	control using OLE automation or set its properties using property pages; therefore, it can use a non UI-activated control. Note that controls can already indicate that they don't support a separate In-Place Active state by not including the OLEMISC_INSIDEOUT bit.
OLEMISC_ALIGNABLE	Used by a container that supports aligned controls. This bit is used by a control that is most useful when aligned on some side of its container. Containers that support such aligned controls can use this bit to decide whether the user should be allowed to align a particular control.
OLEMISC_IMEMODE	Marks a control that understands IME Mode. This only makes sense for DBCS versions of Windows. Containers will typically add an IME Mode property to the extended control for controls that mark themselves with this bit.
OLEMISC_SIMPLEFRAME	Used by containers to determine if a control supports the ISimpleFrameSite protocol. Containers that also support this interface will use simple frame controls as parents for other controls in the container. In effect, the simple frame control operates as an OLE compound document container, but the frame control's container does almost all the work.
OLEMISC_SETCLIENTSITEFIRST	Used by new OLE containers to identify controls that support having SetClientSite called first—immediately after being created—and before the control has been completely constructed. Normal OLE compound document containers are written to call SetClientSite on embedded objects after calling IPersistStorage::Load or IPersistStorage::InitNew on the object. Since OLE controls get state through their client site and that state is useful during the load process, they need to have the client site available during Load or InitNew.

The DllUnregisterServer, which is written by the programmer, is called to remove the control from the list of registered object servers. The type library is also de-registered.

You'll notice from the module definition file in listing 4.2 that each of these functions are exported and that the keyword RESIDENTNAME is used to ensure that these functions are always locked in memory.

The two other exported functions, DllCanUnloadNow and DllGetClassObject are worth mentioning. The MFC class library hides the implementation details of how a user retrieves a pointer to a class factory to use in creating instances of your object or control.

When the API function CoGetClassObject is called, the OLE libraries will locate the object server associated with the CLSID assigned to a particular object or control. Once the DLL server is located, it will then call GetProcAddress to retrieve the address of DllGetClassObject. A call to this function will return a pointer to the class factory interface. Note that this mechanism of retrieving a class factory interface pointer applies only to in-proc server DLLs. Local servers (EXE server) will call CoRegisterClassObject to register the class factory pointer with the OLE libraries.

From time to time, the OLE libraries will call DllCanUnloadNow to give an in-proc server the opportunity to unload itself. Normally a DLL will not decide itself when it should be unloaded. When DllCanUnloadNow is called, the DLL will check if any clients are currently using the DLL by checking its internal reference count. If the DLL is not being used, then this function will return TRUE to its caller and the OLE libraries will unload the DLL.

If you write an OLE control or an in-proc object server without using a class library, you will have to implement both these functions yourself. In the case of MFC, these functions are implemented by the framework and you will not normally have to worry about them (see listing 4.2).

Listing 4.2   The Control Module Definition File

```
; quote32.def : Declares the module parameters.

LIBRARY     QUOTE.OCX

EXPORTS
    DllCanUnloadNow     @1 RESIDENTNAME
    DllGetClassObject   @2 RESIDENTNAME
    DllRegisterServer   @3 RESIDENTNAME
    DllUnregisterServer @4 RESIDENTNAME
```

That completes your look at the implementation of your control's main module. Listing 4.3 shows the complete source for the quote.cpp module.

Listing 4.3   The Quote.h and Quote.cpp Source Files

```
#if !defined( __AFXCTL_H__ )
    #error include 'afxctl.h' before including this file
#endif

#include "resource.h"        // main symbols


/////////////////////////////////////////////////////////////////
// CQuoteApp : See quote.cpp for implementation.

class CQuoteApp : public COleControlModule
{
public:
    BOOL InitInstance();
    int ExitInstance();
};

extern const GUID CDECL _tlid;
extern const WORD _wVerMajor;
extern const WORD _wVerMinor;

#include "stdafx.h"
#include "quote.h"

#ifdef _DEBUG
#undef THIS_FILE
static char BASED_CODE THIS_FILE[] = __FILE__;
#endif


CQuoteApp NEAR theApp;

const GUID CDECL BASED_CODE _tlid =
        { 0x7c647083, 0xf1cb, 0x101b,
        { 0x81, 0xec, 0xb2, 0x31, 0x69, 0x42, 0x46, 0x30 } };
const WORD _wVerMajor = 1;
const WORD _wVerMinor = 0;

/////////////////////////////////////////////////////////////////
// CQuoteApp::InitInstance - DLL initialization
//
BOOL CQuoteApp::InitInstance()
{
    BOOL bInit = COleControlModule::InitInstance();

    if (bInit)
    {
        // TODO: Add your own module initialization code here.
    }

    return bInit;
}
```

(continues)

Listing 4.3 Continued

```
/////////////////////////////////////////////////////////////////
// CQuoteApp::ExitInstance - DLL termination

int CQuoteApp::ExitInstance()
{
    // TODO: Add your own module termination code here.

    return COleControlModule::ExitInstance();
}


/////////////////////////////////////////////////////////////////
// DllRegisterServer - Adds entries to the system registry
//
STDAPI DllRegisterServer(void)
{
    AFX_MANAGE_STATE(_afxModuleAddrThis);

    if (!AfxOleRegisterTypeLib(AfxGetInstanceHandle(), _tlid))
        return ResultFromScode(SELFREG_E_TYPELIB);

    if (!COleObjectFactoryEx::UpdateRegistryAll(TRUE))
        return ResultFromScode(SELFREG_E_CLASS);

    return NOERROR;
}
//----------------------------------------------------------------
STDAPI DllUnregisterServer(void)
{
    AFX_MANAGE_STATE(_afxModuleAddrThis);

    if (!AfxOleUnregisterTypeLib(_tlid))
        return ResultFromScode(SELFREG_E_TYPELIB);

    if (!COleObjectFactoryEx::UpdateRegistryAll(FALSE))
        return ResultFromScode(SELFREG_E_CLASS);

    return NOERROR;
}
//----------------------------------------------------------------
//----------------------------------------------------------------
```

Implementing the Actual Control

You will now begin to implement the code for the control. You start by adding a number of stock properties to the control using the ClassWizard, continue with a custom property, and finally add code to respond to events such as a mouse click. You will also add Property Pages to your control to enable the user to manipulate the control at designtime.

Finally, you will build the control and test it using the Test Container supplied with the CDK.

Initializing the Control

`COleControl::InitializeIIDs` is called to inform the framework of your two primary interface IIDs. The first parameter is the `IID` of your `IDispatch` interface, which is used to drive the control. The second parameter is the `IID` of the `IDispatch` that will be used to fire events.

Next, you initialize the quote table by filling it with quotes and their authors.

One important feature for all controls to support is *ambient properties*. Ambient properties are properties that are exposed by a container and usually describe properties that affect the look of the container, such as current font and background color. Not all containers will support ambient properties; in particular, standard OLE containers will not.

Supporting ambient properties using MFC is pretty straightforward. You use the `AmbientForeGround` and `AmbientBackGround` methods to retrieve the currently defined foreground and background colors. If the container does not support ambient properties, then these methods will return the currently defined colors for Windows.

You then set the initial size of your control by calling `COleControl::SetInitialSize`. This method takes two parameters which are the length and height of the control. The units used are in device units, or pixels.

Adding Stock Properties

As you saw in Chapter 3, stock properties are those properties that are common to most controls. Microsoft has defined a set of `DIPIDs` to represent each of the properties.

Your control is going to support three stock properties—the foreground and background color of the control and the font that is used to draw the text in the control.

You begin by pressing Ctrl+W to access the ClassWizard. The Automation tab is then selected. `CQuoteCtrl` is the name of the class that you will be adding the properties to.

Selecting the Add Property command button will lead you to figure 4.4, which is the Add Property dialog box. You select the External name for the property; in this case, you select `BackColor`. Because this property is a stock property—that is, it is one of the predefined properties—the ClassWizard will automatically select the `Get()` and `Set()` functions for you. The type of the property is also pre-selected as `OLE_COLOR`.

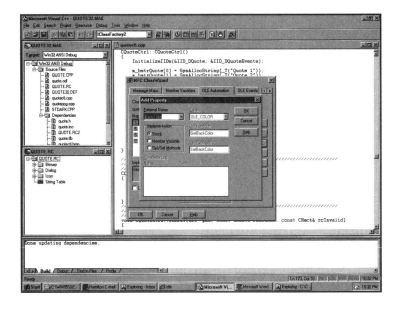

Fig. 4.4

The Add Property dialog box is used to add properties to your control.

When you press OK, the ClassWizard will generate the dispatch map for processing calls to the methods used to get and set the property value. In the following listing, you will notice that the ClassWizard has inserted the `DISP_STOCKPROP_BACKCOLOR` into your dispatch map. (Dispatch maps are covered in greater detail in Chapter 5.)

```
//////////////////////////////////////////////////////////////////
// Dispatch map
//
BEGIN_DISPATCH_MAP(CQuoteCtrl, COleControl)
    //{{AFX_DISPATCH_MAP(CQuoteCtrl)
    DISP_STOCKPROP_BACKCOLOR()
    //}}AFX_DISPATCH_MAP
END_DISPATCH_MAP()
```

This macro expands as follows:

```
#define DISP_STOCKPROP_BACKCOLOR() \
    DISP_PROPERTY_PARAM_ID(COleControl, "BackColor",
    ➥DISPID_BACKCOLOR, \
    COleControl::GetBackColor, COleControl::SetBackColor, \
                VT_COLOR, VTS_STOCK)
```

The parameters used in the `DISP_PROPERTY_PARAM_ID` macro are used to fill in the array of `AFX_DISPMAP_ENTRY` data structures in the dispatch map. This data structure is declared as follows:

```
struct AFX_DISPMAP_ENTRY
{
    LPCTSTR lpszName;       // member/property name
    long lDispID;           // DISPID (may be DISPID_UNKNOWN)
    LPCSTR lpszParams;      // member parameter description
    WORD vt;                // return value type
                            // or type of property
    AFX_PMSG pfn;           // normal member
                            // On<membercall> or, OnGet<property>
    AFX_PMSG pfnSet;        // special member for OnSet<property>
    size_t nPropOffset;     // property offset
};
```

The framework uses a list of `AFX_DISPMAP_ENTRY` structures to locate methods to handle calls made through an `IDispatch::Invoke` call. Chapter 5, "The OLE Controls SDK," examines the internal workings of the framework.

Adding a Custom Property

Now that you have added stock properties to your control, it's now time to add a custom property. Custom properties are properties that have not been predefined by Microsoft. Once again, you start the ClassWizard and select the Add Property command button from the Automation tab. You type the name, `ShowAuthor`, in the External name control (see fig. 4.5). The ClassWizard will automatically create a member variable, `m_ShowAuthor`, and a notification callback, `OnShowAuthorChanged`. The callback is called by the framework whenever the property is updated.

Fig. 4.5
Add a custom property with the ControlWizard.

The callback, `OnShowAuthorChanged`, begins by setting the modified flag for the control. This flag is used to indicate that the properties should be saved when the control is shut down.

You then call `InvalidateControl` to force an update to the control. This function is similar to the `InvalidateRect` function which is used in standard Windows programming to force a repaint of a window.

```
/////////////////////////////////////////////////////////////////////
// CQuoteCtrl message handlers
//
void CQuoteCtrl::OnShowAuthorChanged()
{
    //---
    // The ShowAuthor property is persistent.
    SetModifiedFlag();
    InvalidateControl();
}
```

Adding Property Pages

Property pages are a new UI widget that allows the user of a control to change properties in design mode. Figure 4.6 shows the Property pages that are supported by your control. You invoke the property dialog box from the View menu in the Test Container.

Fig. 4.6
The Fonts property page is used to select the font used by the control.

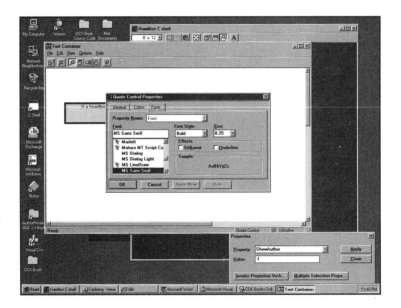

Property pages are very similar to the property sheets or tabbed dialog boxes that are ubiquitous in Windows 95. Property pages share a common interface. The following table shows the actions assigned to the default command buttons.

Button Title	Task
OK	Applies all changes on the current property page and closes the Property dialog box.
Cancel	Ignores changes on the current property page and closes the Property dialog box.
Apply	Applies all changes on the current property page but does not close the Property dialog box.
Help	Displays help for the current property page.

As you saw earlier, your control supports a number of stock properties and one custom property. In order to allow the user easy access to these controls at designtime, you need to add three property pages to your control.

MFC adds a new class, CPropertyPageDialog, to support development of property pages. When you use the ControlWizard to generate the initial code for your control, a default property page is created for you.

You are now going to add a property page for your custom property, ShowAuthor. The first step is to double-click on the quote.rc file in your project window. You then select the dialog resource, IDD_PROPPAGE_QUOTE. This default property page was created for you by the ControlWizard.

Because your property is a simple boolean value, you select a checkbox control to allow the user to toggle the value of the property. Once you have added the control, your next task is to connect the value of the control with the actual property.

As usual, you can use the ClassWizard to help you out. Invoke the ClassWizard by pressing Ctrl+W and select the Member Variables tab. You will notice from figure 4.7 that your checkbox control's ID is visible in the listbox.

Selecting the Add Variable command button will invoke the Add Variable dialog box (see fig. 4.8). Here you type in the name of the variable that you will use, m_ShowAuthor; its category, VALUE; its type, BOOLEAN; and finally, the property name to associate with this variable.

As you probably know from regular MFC programming, all data transfer between your code and a dialog box is handled by the DoDataExchange method. For exchanging data to and from dialog box controls, the DDX_ macros are used.

Fig. 4.7
The Member
Variables tab is
used to connect
the member
variable to a
property.

Fig. 4.8
The Add Variable
dialog box is used
to add new
variables to your
application. These
variables are then
connected to
the control's
properties.

A new set of macros has been introduced to handle OLE properties. These
macros begin with the DDP_ prefix. They take the same parameters with the
exception of the property name which is the last parameter. The following
code demonstrates this:

```
void CQuotePropPage::DoDataExchange(CDataExchange* pDX)
{
    //{{AFX_DATA_MAP(CQuotePropPage)
    DDP_Check(pDX, IDC_SHOWAUTHOR, m_bShowAuthor,
    ➡T("ShowAuthor") );
    DDX_Check(pDX, IDC_SHOWAUTHOR, m_bShowAuthor);
    //}}AFX_DATA_MAP
    DDP_PostProcessing(pDX);
}
```

Table 4.3 lists the currently available DDP_ macros that can be used to associate a control's properties with Property Page variables.

Table 4.3 The DDP Macros	
Function Name	**Purpose**
DDP_CBIndex	Use this function to link the selected string's index in a combo box with a control's property.

Function Name	Purpose
DDP_CBString	Use this function to link the selected string in a combo box with a control's property. The selected string can begin with the same letters as the property's value but need not match it fully.
DDP_CBStringExact	Use this function to link the selected string in a combo box with a control's property. The selected string and the property's string value must match exactly.
DDP_Check	Use this function to link a checkbox with a control property.
DDP_LBIndex	Use this function to link the selected string's index in a listbox with a control's property.
DDP_LBString	Use this function to link the selected string in a listbox with a control's property. The selected string can begin with the same letters as the property's value but need not match it fully.
DDP_LBStringExact	Use this function to link the selected string in a listbox with a control's property. The selected string and the property's string value must match exactly.
DDP_Radio	Use this function to link a radio button with a control property.
DDP_Text	Use this function to link text with a control property.

Now that you have added a property page for your custom property, it is time to add a number of stock property pages.

MFC currently supports three stock property pages—a font property page, a color property, and a picture property page. The actual pages are implemented in the runtime DLL that you must ship with your application.

Adding the new property pages is simply a matter of manually editing the array of property page IDs. The following code from quotectl.cpp demonstrates this:

```
/////////////////////////////////////////////////////////////////////
// Property pages
//   Remember to increase the count!
BEGIN_PROPPAGEIDS(CQuoteCtrl, 3)
    PROPPAGEID(CQuotePropPage::guid)
    PROPPAGEID(CLSID_CColorPropPage)
    PROPPAGEID(CLSID_CFontPropPage)
END_PROPPAGEIDS(CQuoteCtrl)
```

Here you can see that two new entries have been added to the array. Each entry is identified by its CLSID. Once you add these new entries, it is important that you update the count in the BEGIN_PROPPAGEIDS macros.

That's it. Your control now supports three property pages that can be accessed by invoking the OLEIVERB_PROPERTIES verb on your control. Listings 4.4 and 4.5 shows the complete code for quoteppg.cpp.

Listing 4.4   The *CQuotePropPage* Implementation

```
/////////////////////////////////////////////////////////////////////
/////////////////////////////////////////////////////////////////////
// CQuotePropPage : See quoteppg.cpp for implementation.

class CQuotePropPage : public COlePropertyPage
{
    DECLARE_DYNCREATE(CQuotePropPage)
    DECLARE_OLECREATE_EX(CQuotePropPage)

// Constructor
public:
    CQuotePropPage();

// Dialog Data
    //{{AFX_DATA(CQuotePropPage)
    enum { IDD = IDD_PROPPAGE_QUOTE };
    BOOL    m_showAuthor;
    //}}AFX_DATA

// Implementation
protected:
    virtual void DoDataExchange(CDataExchange* pDX);
                    // DDX/DDV support

// Message maps
protected:
    //{{AFX_MSG(CQuotePropPage)
        // NOTE - ClassWizard will add and
        // remove member functions here.
        // DO NOT EDIT what you see in
        // these blocks of generated code!
    //}}AFX_MSG
    DECLARE_MESSAGE_MAP()

};
```

Listing 4.5   Quoteppg.cpp

```cpp
#include "stdafx.h"
#include "quote.h"
#include "quoteppg.h"

#ifdef _DEBUG
#undef THIS_FILE
static char BASED_CODE THIS_FILE[] = __FILE__;
#endif


IMPLEMENT_DYNCREATE(CQuotePropPage, COlePropertyPage)


/////////////////////////////////////////////////////////////////
// Message map

BEGIN_MESSAGE_MAP(CQuotePropPage, COlePropertyPage)
    //{{AFX_MSG_MAP(CQuotePropPage)
    //}}AFX_MSG_MAP
END_MESSAGE_MAP()


/////////////////////////////////////////////////////////////////
// Initialize class factory and guid

IMPLEMENT_OLECREATE_EX(CQuotePropPage, "QUOTE.QuotePropPage.1",
    0x7c647084, 0xf1cb, 0x101b, 0x81,
    0xec, 0xb2, 0x31, 0x69, 0x42, 0x46, 0x30)


/////////////////////////////////////////////////////////////////
// CQuotePropPage::CQuotePropPageFactory::UpdateRegistry -
// Adds or removes system registry entries for CQuotePropPage

BOOL CQuotePropPage::CQuotePropPageFactory::
                UpdateRegistry(BOOL bRegister)
{
    if (bRegister)
        return  AfxOleRegisterPropertyPageClass(
                AfxGetInstanceHandle(),
            m_clsid, IDS_QUOTE_PPG);
    else
        return AfxOleUnregisterClass(m_clsid, NULL);
}


/////////////////////////////////////////////////////////////////
// CQuotePropPage::CQuotePropPage - Constructor

CQuotePropPage::CQuotePropPage() :
    COlePropertyPage(IDD, IDS_QUOTE_PPG_CAPTION)
{
```

(continues)

```
Listing 4.5   Continued

        //{{AFX_DATA_INIT(CQuotePropPage)
        m_showAuthor = FALSE;
        //}}AFX_DATA_INIT
    }


    /////////////////////////////////////////////////////////////////
    // CQuotePropPage::DoDataExchange - Moves data
    // between page and properties

    void CQuotePropPage::DoDataExchange(CDataExchange* pDX)
    {
        //{{AFX_DATA_MAP(CQuotePropPage)
        DDP_Check(pDX, IDC_SHOWAUTHOR, m_showAuthor,
                _T("ShowAuthor"));
        DDX_Check(pDX, IDC_SHOWAUTHOR, m_showAuthor);
        //}}AFX_DATA_MAP
        DDP_PostProcessing(pDX);
    }
    /////////////////////////////////////////////////////////////////
```

Generating Events

As discussed in Chapter 3, one of the main differences between a standard OLE container and a control container is the ability of the control container to respond to events generated by its controls.

You are now going to add one stock event to your control. Stock events, like stock properties, are predefined events with assigned DISPIDs. You will add the DblClk event to your control.

You begin by calling the ClassWizard and selecting the OLE Events tab. You then select the Add Event command button. From the Add Event dialog box, you select DblClick as the external name for the event. This is a stock event, so the ClassWizard disables the internal name, FireDblClick.

ClassWizard will then add the following line to your event table in quotectl.cpp:

```
/////////////////////////////////////////////////////////////////
// Event map
//
BEGIN_EVENT_MAP(CQuoteCtrl, COleControl)
    //{{AFX_EVENT_MAP(CQuoteCtrl)
    EVENT_STOCK_DBLCLICK()
    //}}AFX_EVENT_MAP
END_EVENT_MAP()
```

This line will be added to your ODL file:

```
//{{AFX_ODL_EVENT(CQuoteCtrl)
[id(DISPID_DBLCLICK)] void DblClick();
//}}AFX_ODL_EVENT
```

The event table is the mechanism provided by the framework for supporting events. Events maps are similar in nature to the message maps that are used to route messages to various windows.

The COleControl class provides a number of default implementations for stock events such as DblClick. The current release of the CDK provides default implementations for eight stock events. These events are described in table 4.4.

Table 4.4 **The Stock Events**		
Event	**Firing Function**	**Comments**
Click	void FireClick( )	EVENT_STOCK_CLICK(). Fired when the control has captured the mouse, any BUTTONUP (left, middle, or right) message is received, and the button is released over the control. The stock MouseDown and MouseUp events occur before this event.
DblClick	void FireDblClick( )	EVENT_STOCK_DBLCLICK(). Similar to Click but fired when any BUTTONDBLCLK message is received.
Error	void FireError(SCODE scode, LPCSTR lpszDescription, UINT nHelpID = 0)	EVENT_STOCK_ERROR(). Fired when an error has occurred within your OLE control.
KeyDown	void FireKeyDown(short nChar, short nShiftState)	EVENT_STOCK_KEYDOWN(). Fired when a WM_SYSKEYDOWN or WM_KEYDOWN message is received.
KeyPress	void FireKeyPress(short* pnChar)	EVENT_STOCK_KEYPRESS(). Fired when a WM_CHAR message is received.
KeyUp	void FireKeyUp(short nChar, short nShiftState)	EVENT_STOCK_KEYUP(). Fired when a WM_SYSKEYUP or WM_KEYUP message is received.

(continues)

Table 4.4 Continued		
Event	**Firing Function**	**Comments**
MouseDown	void FireMouseDown(short nButton, short nShiftState, float x, float y)	EVENT_STOCK_MOUSEDOWN(). Fired if any BUTTONDOWN (left, middle, or right) is received. The mouse is captured immediately before this event is fired.
MouseMove	void FireMouseMove(short nButton, short nShiftState, float x, float y)	EVENT_STOCK_MOUSEMOVE(). Fired when a WM_MOUSEMOVE message is received.
MouseUp	void FireMouseUp(short nButton, short nShiftState, float x, float y)	EVENT_STOCK_MOUSEUP(). Fired if any BUTTONUP (left, middle, or right) is received. The mouse capture is released before this event is fired.

Licensing Issues

One important issue facing you as a developer of OLE controls is how to en-sure that users are not copying your controls. After all, one of the reasons you spent so much time developing your control was to make some money.

In general, there are two situations that you must consider. The first one is how another developer or user will use your control to build an application, and secondly how the user of that application will use your control. Nor-mally, you will not expect to get paid by users of applications developed using your controls.

The person who purchases the control from you will be allowed to use it in design mode. That is, he or she will be able to access the control from pro-gramming purposes alone. The user of the application developed with your control should not be able to use the control for any other purpose.

The License File

Microsoft's solution to this problem is the inclusion of a license file that you ship with your control. When the developer of a container uses your control, he or she will make a call to IClassFactory2::GetLicInfo. This call will verify that the license file is available. If it isn't, the developer will not be able to use the control.

Extending the *ClassFactory* to Support Licensing

In order to add support for licensing to OLE, Microsoft needs to extend the current implementation of IClassFactory, the COM interface responsible for creating instances of COM objects. A new class factory interface, IClassFactory2, was defined to ensure backward compatibility with older software. This new interface contains the methods used by the original IClassFactory with the addition of three new methods for the licensing implementation.

These three methods are as follows:

■ GetLicInfo. This method verifies the existence of the license file associated with the control.

■ RequestLicKey. This method is used by a control container to retrieve the unique license information from a control. This information is usually embedded within the container and used when the container uses the controls as part of an application.

■ CreateInstanceLic. This method is used by a control container to create an instance of a particular control. This method will verify that the unique string embedded within the container matches that provided by the control. If the strings do not match, the control will not be instanced.

These methods are all encapsulated by the COleObjectFactoryEx MFC class supplied with the CDK. Listing 4.6 shows the definition of the IClassFactory2 interface.

Listing 4.6   The *IClassFactory2* Interface Definition

```
DECLARE_INTERFACE_(IClassFactory2, IClassFactory)
{
    // IUnknown methods
    STDMETHOD(QueryInterface)
            (THIS_ REFIID riid, LPVOID FAR* ppvObj) PURE;
    STDMETHOD_(ULONG,AddRef)(THIS) PURE;
    STDMETHOD_(ULONG,Release)(THIS) PURE;

    // IClassFactory methods
    STDMETHOD(CreateInstance)
            (THIS_ LPUNKNOWN pUnkOuter, REFIID riid,
        LPVOID FAR* ppvObject) PURE;
    STDMETHOD(LockServer)(THIS_ BOOL fLock) PURE;
```

(continues)

Listing 4.6 Continued

```
    // IClassFactory2 methods
    STDMETHOD(GetLicInfo)(THIS_ LPLICINFO pLicInfo) PURE;
    STDMETHOD(RequestLicKey)
        (THIS_ DWORD dwResrved, BSTR FAR* pbstrKey) PURE;
    STDMETHOD(CreateInstanceLic)(THIS_ LPUNKNOWN pUnkOuter,
        LPUNKNOWN pUnkReserved, REFIID riid, BSTR bstrKey,
        LPVOID FAR* ppvObject) PURE;
};
```

If you ask the ControlWizard to add licensing support to your controls, then a number of additions will be made to the generated source code.

The first pieces of code added are the macros for generating the control's class factory definition. Because you are using licensing, this definition will be from `IClassFactory2`. Note the addition of `VerifyUserLicense` and `GetLicenseKey` in listing 4.7. These two methods of the class `COleObjectFactoryEx` are used to encapsulate the licensing methods of `IClassFactory2`.

Listing 4.7 The Control's Class Factory Definition

```
    BEGIN_OLEFACTORY(CQuoteCtrl)        // Class factory and guid
        virtual BOOL VerifyUserLicense();
        virtual BOOL GetLicenseKey(DWORD, BSTR FAR*);
    END_OLEFACTORY(CQuoteCtrl)
```

The following two declarations are added to Quotectl.cpp.

```
    // Licensing strings

    static const TCHAR BASED_CODE _szLicFileName[] = _T("QUOTE.LIC");

    static const TCHAR BASED_CODE _szLicString[] =
        _T("Copyright (c) 1994 Tangent Software");
```

These strings contain the name of your control's license file and the name of the license string embedded in it. Finally, listing 4.8 shows the implementations of the licensing methods.

Listing 4.8   The Licensing Methods

```
/////////////////////////////////////////////////////////////////////
// CQuoteCtrl::CQuoteCtrlFactory::VerifyUserLicense -
// Checks for existence of a user license

BOOL CQuoteCtrl::CQuoteCtrlFactory::VerifyUserLicense()
{
    return AfxVerifyLicFile(AfxGetInstanceHandle(),
          _szLicFileName,
        _szLicString);

    BOOL bfound = AfxVerifyLicFile(
          AfxGetInstanceHandle(), _szLicFileName,
                              _szLicString);

    if (bfound)
        AfxMessageBox(_T("Found license file"));
    else
        AfxMessageBox(_T("License file NOT found"));

    return (bfound);
}


/////////////////////////////////////////////////////////////////////
// CQuoteCtrl::CQuoteCtrlFactory::GetLicenseKey -
// Returns a runtime licensing key

BOOL CQuoteCtrl::CQuoteCtrlFactory::GetLicenseKey(DWORD dwReserved,
    BSTR FAR* pbstrKey)
{
    if (pbstrKey == NULL)
        return FALSE;

    *pbstrKey = SysAllocString(_szLicString);
    return (*pbstrKey != NULL);
}
```

VerifyUserLicense is called to verify that the license file for the controls exists. The method returns non-zero if the license file is found; otherwise, it returns zero.

GetLicenseKey is called by the control container to retrieve the license key associated with the control.

A third method, VerifyLicenseKey, is used to verify that a container is licensed to create an instance of the control. Licensed containers will contain embedded license string of the controls that they are licensed to use. When the container tries to create a control through `IClassFactory2::CreateInstanceLic`, the framework will call this method to compare the license strings. The default implementations do a simple string comparison of the two strings. It is possible to override this method to perform a more sophisticated check on the licensing information.

Listing 4.9 shows the implementation of the `CQuoteCtrl` class.

Listing 4.9   Quotectl.cpp

```
#define MAXQUOTES       6
/////////////////////////////////////////////////////////////////
// CQuoteCtrl : See quotectl.cpp for implementation.
//
class CQuoteCtrl : public COleControl
{
    DECLARE_DYNCREATE(CQuoteCtrl)

// Constructor
public:
    CQuoteCtrl();

    // Drawing function
    virtual void OnDraw(CDC* pdc,
        const CRect& rcBounds, const CRect& rcInvalid);

    // Persistence
    virtual void DoPropExchange(CPropExchange* pPX);

    // Reset control state
    virtual void OnResetState();

    BSTR m_bstrQuote[MAXQUOTES];
    BSTR m_bstrAuthor[MAXQUOTES];
    int m_nQID;
// Implementation
protected:
    ~CQuoteCtrl();

    BEGIN_OLEFACTORY(CQuoteCtrl)          // Class factory and guid
        virtual BOOL VerifyUserLicense();
        virtual BOOL GetLicenseKey(DWORD, BSTR FAR*);
    END_OLEFACTORY(CQuoteCtrl)

    DECLARE_OLETYPELIB(CQuoteCtrl)        // GetTypeInfo
    DECLARE_PROPPAGEIDS(CQuoteCtrl)       // Property page IDs
    DECLARE_OLECTLTYPE(CQuoteCtrl)        // Type name
                                          // and misc status
```

```
        // Message maps
        //{{AFX_MSG(CQuoteCtrl)
        afx_msg void OnLButtonDblClk(UINT nFlags, CPoint point);
        //}}AFX_MSG
        DECLARE_MESSAGE_MAP()

        // Dispatch maps
        //{{AFX_DISPATCH(CQuoteCtrl)
        BOOL m_showAuthor;
        afx_msg void OnShowAuthorChanged();
        //}}AFX_DISPATCH
        DECLARE_DISPATCH_MAP()

        afx_msg void AboutBox();

        // Event maps
        //{{AFX_EVENT(CQuoteCtrl)
        //}}AFX_EVENT
        DECLARE_EVENT_MAP()

// Dispatch and event IDs
public:
        enum {
        //{{AFX_DISP_ID(CQuoteCtrl)
        dispidShowAuthor = 1L,
        //}}AFX_DISP_ID
        };
};


#include "stdafx.h"
#include "quote.h"
#include "quotectl.h"
#include "quoteppg.h"


#ifdef _DEBUG
#undef THIS_FILE
static char BASED_CODE THIS_FILE[] = __FILE__;
#endif


IMPLEMENT_DYNCREATE(CQuoteCtrl, COleControl)


/////////////////////////////////////////////////////////////////
// Message map

BEGIN_MESSAGE_MAP(CQuoteCtrl, COleControl)
        //{{AFX_MSG_MAP(CQuoteCtrl)
        ON_WM_LBUTTONDBLCLK()
        //}}AFX_MSG_MAP
        ON_OLEVERB(AFX_IDS_VERB_EDIT, OnEdit)
        ON_OLEVERB(AFX_IDS_VERB_PROPERTIES, OnProperties)
END_MESSAGE_MAP()
```

(continues)

Listing 4.9   Continued

```
//////////////////////////////////////////////////////////////////
// Dispatch map
//
BEGIN_DISPATCH_MAP(CQuoteCtrl, COleControl)
    //{{AFX_DISPATCH_MAP(CQuoteCtrl)
    DISP_PROPERTY_NOTIFY(CQuoteCtrl, "ShowAuthor",
        m_showAuthor, OnShowAuthorChanged, VT_BOOL)
    DISP_STOCKPROP_BACKCOLOR()
    DISP_STOCKPROP_FORECOLOR()
    DISP_STOCKPROP_FONT()
    //}}AFX_DISPATCH_MAP
    DISP_FUNCTION_ID(CQuoteCtrl, "AboutBox",
        DISPID_ABOUTBOX, AboutBox, VT_EMPTY, VTS_NONE)
END_DISPATCH_MAP()


//////////////////////////////////////////////////////////////////
// Event map
//
BEGIN_EVENT_MAP(CQuoteCtrl, COleControl)
    //{{AFX_EVENT_MAP(CQuoteCtrl)
    EVENT_STOCK_DBLCLICK()
    //}}AFX_EVENT_MAP
END_EVENT_MAP()


//////////////////////////////////////////////////////////////////
// Property pages
//   Remember to increase the count!
BEGIN_PROPPAGEIDS(CQuoteCtrl, 3)
    PROPPAGEID(CQuotePropPage::guid)
    PROPPAGEID(CLSID_CColorPropPage)
    PROPPAGEID(CLSID_CFontPropPage)
END_PROPPAGEIDS(CQuoteCtrl)

//////////////////////////////////////////////////////////////////
// Initialize class factory and guid
//
IMPLEMENT_OLECREATE_EX(CQuoteCtrl, "QUOTE.QuoteCtrl.1",
    0x7c647080, 0xf1cb, 0x101b,
    0x81, 0xec, 0xb2, 0x31, 0x69, 0x42, 0x46, 0x30)


//////////////////////////////////////////////////////////////////
// Type library ID and version
//
IMPLEMENT_OLETYPELIB(CQuoteCtrl, _tlid, _wVerMajor, _wVerMinor)


//////////////////////////////////////////////////////////////////
// Interface IDs
//
const IID BASED_CODE IID_DQuote =
```

```
            { 0x7c647081, 0xf1cb, 0x101b,
            { 0x81, 0xec, 0xb2, 0x31, 0x69, 0x42, 0x46, 0x30 } };
const IID BASED_CODE IID_DQuoteEvents =
            { 0x7c647082, 0xf1cb, 0x101b,
            { 0x81, 0xec, 0xb2, 0x31, 0x69, 0x42, 0x46, 0x30 } };


/////////////////////////////////////////////////////////////////
// Control type information
//
static const DWORD BASED_CODE _dwQuoteOleMisc =
    OLEMISC_ACTIVATEWHENVISIBLE |
    OLEMISC_SETCLIENTSITEFIRST |
    OLEMISC_INSIDEOUT |
    OLEMISC_CANTLINKINSIDE |
    OLEMISC_RECOMPOSEONRESIZE;

IMPLEMENT_OLECTLTYPE(CQuoteCtrl, IDS_QUOTE, _dwQuoteOleMisc)


/////////////////////////////////////////////////////////////////
// CQuoteCtrl::CQuoteCtrlFactory::UpdateRegistry -
// Adds or removes system registry entries for CQuoteCtrl
//
BOOL CQuoteCtrl::CQuoteCtrlFactory::UpdateRegistry(BOOL bRegister)
{
    if (bRegister)
        return AfxOleRegisterControlClass(
            AfxGetInstanceHandle(),
            m_clsid,
            m_lpszProgID,
            IDS_QUOTE,
            IDB_QUOTE,
            TRUE,                    //  Insertable
            _dwQuoteOleMisc,
            _tlid,
            _wVerMajor,
            _wVerMinor);
    else
        return AfxOleUnregisterClass(m_clsid, m_lpszProgID);
}


/////////////////////////////////////////////////////////////////
// Licensing strings

static const TCHAR BASED_CODE _szLicFileName[] = _T("QUOTE.LIC");

static const TCHAR BASED_CODE _szLicString[] =
    _T("Copyright (c) 1994 Tangent Software");


/////////////////////////////////////////////////////////////////
// CQuoteCtrl::CQuoteCtrlFactory::VerifyUserLicense -
// Checks for existence of a user license
```

(continues)

Listing 4.9 Continued

```
BOOL CQuoteCtrl::CQuoteCtrlFactory::VerifyUserLicense()
{
    return AfxVerifyLicFile(AfxGetInstanceHandle(),
            szLicFileName,
        _szLicString);

    BOOL bfound = AfxVerifyLicFile(
            AfxGetInstanceHandle(), _szLicFileName,
                            _szLicString);

    if (bfound)
        AfxMessageBox(_T("Found license file"));
    else
        AfxMessageBox(_T("License file NOT found"));

    return (bfound);
}


/////////////////////////////////////////////////////////////////
// CQuoteCtrl::CQuoteCtrlFactory::GetLicenseKey -
// Returns a runtime licensing key

BOOL CQuoteCtrl::CQuoteCtrlFactory::GetLicenseKey(DWORD dwReserved,
    BSTR FAR* pbstrKey)
{
    if (pbstrKey == NULL)
        return FALSE;

    *pbstrKey = SysAllocString(_szLicString);
    return (*pbstrKey != NULL);
}


/////////////////////////////////////////////////////////////////
// CQuoteCtrl::CQuoteCtrl - Constructor
//
CQuoteCtrl::CQuoteCtrl()
{
    InitializeIIDs(&IID_DQuote, &IID_DQuoteEvents);

    m_bstrQuote[0] = SysAllocString(
      _T("If a headline ends in a question mark, the answer is no"));
    m_bstrQuote[1] = SysAllocString(
      _T("Nothing is ever so bad that it can't get worse"));
    m_bstrQuote[2] = SysAllocString(
      _T("A crisis is when you can't say,
                            Let's forget the whole thing."));
    m_bstrQuote[3] = SysAllocString(
      _T("If you mess with a thing long enough, it will break."));
    m_bstrQuote[4] = SysAllocString(
      _T("It is easier to get forgiveness than permission."));
    m_bstrQuote[5] = SysAllocString(
```

```
    _T("If you can't fix it, feature it"));

    m_bstrAuthor[0] = SysAllocString(_T("Davis' Law"));
    m_bstrAuthor[1] = SysAllocString(_T("Murphy"));
    m_bstrAuthor[2] = SysAllocString(_T("Ferguson"));
    m_bstrAuthor[3] = SysAllocString(_T("Schmidt's Law"));
    m_bstrAuthor[4] = SysAllocString(
      _T("Stewart's Law of Retroaction"));
    m_bstrAuthor[5] = SysAllocString(
      _T("Last Law of Product Design"));

    m_nQID = 0;

    SetInitialSize(400,50);

    //---
    // Set the default values to the
    // current ambient properties.
    SetForeColor(AmbientForeColor());
    SetBackColor(AmbientBackColor());
}

/////////////////////////////////////////////////////////////////
// CQuoteCtrl::~CQuoteCtrl - Destructor
//
CQuoteCtrl::~CQuoteCtrl()
{
    for(int i = 0; i < MAXQUOTES;i++)
    {
        SysFreeString(m_bstrQuote[i]);
    }
}
/////////////////////////////////////////////////////////////////
// CQuoteCtrl::OnDraw - Drawing function
//
void CQuoteCtrl::OnDraw(CDC* pdc,
➥const CRect& rcBounds, const CRect& rcInvalid)
{

    CFont* pOldFont;

    //---
    // Get stock properties - foreground &
    // background color & Font.

    CBrush bkBrush(TranslateColor(GetBackColor()));
    pdc->SetTextColor(TranslateColor(GetForeColor()));
    pdc->SetBkColor(TranslateColor(GetBackColor()));
    pOldFont = SelectStockFont(pdc);
    pdc->SetBkMode(TRANSPARENT);


    pdc->FillRect(rcBounds, &bkBrush);
    if(m_showAuthor)
    {
        CString s = m_bstrQuote[m_nQID];
```

(continues)

Listing 4.9 Continued

```
            s += "\n ";
            s += m_bstrAuthor[m_nQID];
            pdc->DrawText(s,-1,rcBounds,DT_CENTER);
        }
        else
            pdc->DrawText(m_bstrQuote[m_nQID]
            ➡,-1,rcBounds,DT_CENTER¦DT_VCENTER);

    //---
    // Clean up.
    pdc->SelectObject(pOldFont);
}
/////////////////////////////////////////////////////////////////////
// CQuoteCtrl::DoPropExchange - Persistence support
//
void CQuoteCtrl::DoPropExchange(CPropExchange* pPX)
{
    ExchangeVersion(pPX, MAKELONG(_wVerMinor, _wVerMajor));

    //---
    // Set the default values for our custom properties.
    PX_Bool(pPX, _T("ShowAuthor"), m_showAuthor,TRUE);

    COleControl::DoPropExchange(pPX);
}
/////////////////////////////////////////////////////////////////////
// CQuoteCtrl::OnResetState - Reset control to default state
//
void CQuoteCtrl::OnResetState()
{
    COleControl::OnResetState();
    // Resets defaults found in DoPropExchange

    // TODO: Reset any other control state here.
}
/////////////////////////////////////////////////////////////////////
// CQuoteCtrl::AboutBox - Display an "About" box to the user
//
void CQuoteCtrl::AboutBox()
{
    CDialog dlgAbout(IDD_ABOUTBOX_QUOTE);
    dlgAbout.DoModal();
}
/////////////////////////////////////////////////////////////////////
// CQuoteCtrl message handlers
//
void CQuoteCtrl::OnShowAuthorChanged()
{
    //---
    // The ShowAuthor property is persistent.
    SetModifiedFlag();
    InvalidateControl();
}
//----------------------------------------------------------------
```

```
void CQuoteCtrl::OnLButtonDblClk(UINT nFlags, CPoint point)
{
    m_nQID = rand() % MAXQUOTES;
    InvalidateControl();

}
// ------------------------------------------------------------
// ------------------------------------------------------------
```

The Type Library and ODL

Type libraries and ODL (Object Description Language) have always been
available and used when implementing OLE automation. However, creating
type libraries using the ODL language is a tedious business. With the introduction of Visual C++ 2.0, the ClassWizard directly supports the creation of
ODL files, and the Project Manager will compile the ODL files into type libraries as part of the build process.

Every time you add a new method or property to your control, the
ClassWizard will add the necessary code to the ODL file.

ODL is a language that is used to describe objects and their methods and
properties. Chapter 6 discusses type libraries and the ODL language in greater
detail. Listing 4.10 shows the source code for the ODL file.

Listing 4.10   The ODL File

```
// quote.odl : type library source for OLE Custom Control project.

// This file will be processed by the Make Type
// Library (mktyplib) tool to produce the type library (quote.tlb)
// that will become a resource in
// quote.ocx.

#include <olectl.h>

[ uuid(7C647083-F1CB-101B-81EC-B23169424630), version(1.0),
  helpstring("Quote OLE Custom Control module") ]
library QuoteLib
{
    importlib(STDOLE_TLB);
    importlib(STDTYPE_TLB);

    //  Primary dispatch interface for CQuoteCtrl

    [ uuid(7C647081-F1CB-101B-81EC-B23169424630),
      helpstring("Dispatch interface for Quote Control") ]
```

(continues)

Listing 4.10   Continued

```
dispinterface _DQuote
{
    properties:
        //    Use extreme caution when editing this section.
        //{{AFX_ODL_PROP(CQuoteCtrl)
        [id(DISPID_BACKCOLOR), bindable,
        ➥requestedit] OLE_COLOR BackColor;
        [id(DISPID_FORECOLOR), bindable,
        ➥requestedit] OLE_COLOR ForeColor;
        [id(DISPID_FONT), bindable] IFontDisp* Font;
        [id(1)] boolean ShowAuthor;
        //}}AFX_ODL_PROP

    methods:
        //    Use extreme caution when editing this section.
        //{{AFX_ODL_METHOD(CQuoteCtrl)
        [id(DISPID_DOCLICK)] void DoClick();
        //}}AFX_ODL_METHOD

        [id(DISPID_ABOUTBOX)] void AboutBox();
};

// Event dispatch interface for CQuoteCtrl

[ uuid(7C647082-F1CB-101B-81EC-B23169424630),
  helpstring("Event interface for Quote Control") ]
dispinterface _DQuoteEvents
{
    properties:
        // Event interface has no properties

    methods:
        //    Use extreme caution when editing this section.
        //{{AFX_ODL_EVENT(CQuoteCtrl)
        [id(DISPID_DBLCLICK)] void DblClick();
        //}}AFX_ODL_EVENT
};

// Class information for CQuoteCtrl

[ uuid(7C647080-F1CB-101B-81EC-B23169424630), licensed,
  helpstring("Quote Control") ]
CoClass Quote
{
    [default] dispinterface _DQuote;
    [default, source] dispinterface _DQuoteEvents;
};


//{{AFX_APPEND_ODL}}
};
```

Testing the Control

Your coding of the control is now complete. It is now time to test its functionality. In order to properly test your control, you need to use an OLE control container. At the time of this writing, the only commercially available container is Microsoft Access 2.0. The next version of Visual Basic is rumored to be a fully functional container. Microsoft supplies a Test Container with the CDK that is a very useful debugging tool.

When you install the CDK on your system, a number of programs are added to the Tools menu in the VC++ 2.0 IDE. One of these tools is used to register your control in the system registry. Once you have built the control, you will then use this option to register it.

The next step is to test the code using Test Container. You begin by executing the Test Container from the Tools menu:

1. From the Edit menu, choose Insert OLE Control. The Insert OLE Control dialog box appears. Your control quote will appear in the list box.

2. From the Control Class list box, you select the Quote Control and choose the OK command button to insert the control in your container.

The control will appear in the container. Notice that the background color of the control is white and the text is displayed in black.

From the Edit menu, select Set Ambient Properties. This will invoke the Ambient Properties dialog box (see fig. 4.9). From the Standard properties combo-box, select BackColor. Next, you change the BackColor property to yellow and, using the ForeColor property, set the foreground property to Red.

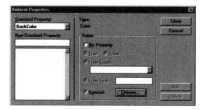

Fig. 4.9
Set the Ambient Properties in the Test Container.

Once again, you select Insert Object from the Edit menu and create a new object. This time the background color of the object will be yellow and the text will be written in red letters. Any time the ambient properties of the container are changed, these changes will be reflected in your control.

Now, you will change some of the properties of the control. You'll remove the display of the author from the control by changing the ShowAuthor property, and change the font used to draw the text. Follow these steps:

1. From the Edit menu, select the Embedded Object Function and select Properties from the resulting sub-menu. The Properties dialog box appears.

2. You will now see the property page that you designed in the dialog edit (see fig. 4.10).

Fig. 4.10
Invoke the
Property dialog
box to change
the control's
properties.

Do not deselect the Show Author checkbox.

3. Choose the Apply button. Your control is redrawn showing the quote and not the author. It is immediately redrawn because changing the ShowAuthor property caused the notification function to be called. The OnShowAuthorChanged function invalidated the control, causing the control to be redrawn.

You'll notice the standard property pages for changing the font and colors used in the control. Selecting the font tab will allow you to select a new font. Again, choosing the Apply command button will cause the control to be repainted using the new font.

Figure 4.11 shows your controls displaying multiple fonts and colors within the test container.

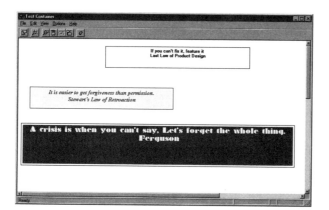

Fig. 4.11
Your control in
action.

From Here...

That concludes your look at creating a simple OLE control using the MFC class library and the OLE Control Developers Kit. As you can see, the class framework takes care of many of the details for you, leaving you to concentrate on the actual implementation of your control. In fact, creating an OLE control using the Visual C++ 2.0 system and the OLE Control Developers Kit is many times easier that creating VBXs or standard custom controls.

In the next chapter, you examine the support offered by the MFC framework in greater detail and also examine the internal implementation of the OLE Control classes. An understanding of what goes on behind the scenes is essential to fully understanding OLE controls. Refer to the following chapters for more information:

- Chapter 2, "The Component Object Model," provides a detailed look at the Component Object Model and how they relate to OLE controls.

- Chapter 5, "The OLE Controls SDK," examines the MFC support for OLE controls in detail.

- Chapters 9, "Building the Comm Custom Control," and 10, "Building the Timer Custom Control," provide information about the actual development of OLE controls.

Chapter 5

The OLE Controls SDK

by Edward B. Toupin

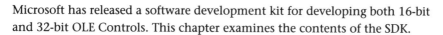

Microsoft has released a software development kit for developing both 16-bit and 32-bit OLE Controls. This chapter examines the contents of the SDK.

The following topics will be discussed in detail:

- Using the ControlWizard

- Working with the Test Container

- Learning the new MFC classes that have been added to support OLE Controls

The SDK which ships with Visual C++ 2.0 integrates seamlessly into the VC++ IDE and provides a number of extensions to MFC and the standard Wizards.

If you choose to install the 16-bit version of the SDK, the installation program will create a subdirectory under the MSVC directory called CDK16. If you install the 32-bit version, the subdirectory will be called CDK32.

The installation procedure will install a new Wizard for creating controls, a control container application for testing OLE controls, new MFC classes for creating controls, header files, samples code, and complete on-line documentation.

The ControlWizard, Test Container, and two utilities to register and unregister controls will be added to the Tools menu in the Visual C++ IDE.

In addition to the utilities and MFC classes, the installation will also install the following runtime DLLs in your Windows system directory:

Library	Description
OC25.DLL	Release version: 16-bit OLE control
OC25D.DLL	Debug version: 16-bit OLE control
OC30.DLL	Release version: 32-bit OLE controls with ANSI/DBCS support
OC30D.DLL	Debug version: 32-bit OLE controls with ANSI/DBCS support
OC30U.DLL	Release version: 32-bit OLE controls with Unicode support
OC30UD.DLL	Debug version: 32-bit OLE controls with Unicode support

The ControlWizard

If you are creating an OLE control, then you can look to the ControlWizard as a replacement for the AppWizard. Its primary function is to create a set of templates that are used to create the control. The ControlWizard will generate starter files for all the CPP files, headers files, the ODL file, and a makefile. Figure 5.1 shows the ControlWizard in action.

Fig. 5.1
The Control-Wizard dialog box allows you to select a name for your control's makefile and select the directory in which to place the generated files.

The following options in table 5.1 are available in the Project Options dialog box:

Table 5.1	The Project Options Dialog Box Options
Option	**Description**
Context-Sensitive Help	ControlWizard generates a set of help files that are used to provide context-sensitive help. These files can be compiled with the Windows help compiler.

Option	Description
External Makefile	By default, ControlWizard creates a project file that is compatible with the environment (and NMAKE). Select this option if you want ControlWizard to create an NMAKE makefile that can only be directly edited. This means that the project cannot be edited while inside the development environment.
Source Comments	ControlWizard inserts comments in the source and header files that guide you in writing your control. The comments indicate where you need to add your own code. This option is enabled by default.
License Validation	ControlWizard inserts several function calls and generates a separate LIC file that supports licensing for your control. Licensing is covered in detail in the next chapter.

For most controls, you will choose all the options except the external makefile. Most programmers prefer to work within the IDE. This allows easy access to the ControlWizard, the class browsers, and context sensitive help. However, for those of you who still prefer to use the command line compiler, you will select the external makefile option. The makefile is compatible with the NMAKE utility.

The Control Options dialog box allows you to select various attributes for each of your controls. Table 2.2 describes each of these options in detail:

Table 5.2   The Control Options Dialog Box Options

Option	Description
Activate When Visible	Check this box to have your control indicate to the container that the control "prefers" to be activated automatically when it is visible. The container is not required to support this request.
Show in Insert Object Dialog	Check this box to have your control listed in the Insert Object dialog box.
Invisible at Runtime	Check this box to have your control indicate a "preference" to its container that the control should be invisible in the container's "runtime" mode and visible in the container's "designtime" mode. A container may ignore the control's "preference." In such a container, your control will be visible at all times.

(continues)

Table 5.2 **Continued**	
Option	**Description**
Simple Frame	Check this box to have your control support the `ISimpleFrameSite` protocol. When the container and the control both support this protocol, the container uses simple frame controls as parents for other controls in the container. In effect, the simple frame control operates as an OLE compound document container, but the frame control's container does nearly all the work.
About box	Check this box to create a standard About dialog box for your control.
Subclass Windows Control	Check this box to subclass common Windows controls, such as buttons, toolbars, and edit boxes. Then choose a Windows control from the Windows control class list box.
Use VBX Control as Template	Check this box to enable the Select VBX Template Control button, then choose that button to select the Use VBX Control as Template dialog box.
Select VBX Control	Choose this button to select the Use VBX Control as Template dialog box.

Finally, the Controls command button allows you to specify the names of the implementation files for the generated control. You also set the exposed names for your control in this dialog box. Table 5.3 describes each of these options in detail.

Table 5.3 **The Control Options**	
Option	**Description**
Short Name	This is the base name of the class. The default is the name of the project. If you change the default, ControlWizard changes the other names that appear on this dialog box.
Class	Use the Class box to select either the control class or the property page class. You can then modify various names pertaining to that class, such as the Short name, the User Type name, and the Programmatic ID.
C++ Class Name	This is the name of the main class of the control or of its property page. The selection in the Class list box determines whether this box displays the name of the control class or the property page class. The default name for the control class is `CPrjnameCtrl`. The default name for the property page class is `CPrjnamePropPage`.

Option	Description
Header File	This is the name of the header file that contains the class definition.
User Type Name	This is the name exposed to the control's user.
Implementation File	This is the name of the source file that contains the class implementation.
Programmatic ID	This is the ID of the OLE control class.
Add Control	Click this button to add new control and property page classes to your project. You must name the header and implementation files for each class. You can also change the default class names that are created.
Delete Control	Click this button to delete the selected control and property page from your project.

The Test Container

One of the most important utilities supplied with the SDK is the Test Container. This control container will allow you to completely test your controls under all conditions. While you must test each of your controls with commercial containers such as Microsoft Access and Visual Basic, the Test Container will allow you to test every aspect of your control.

The Test Container will allow you to test changes to a control's properties, invoke its methods, and fire its events. It provides a complete log of all notifications and even allows you to test the persistence support of a control. You can save and reload the control's properties to a compound file. The Test Container allows you to display a log of data-binding notifications. In addition, you can control the Test Container's response to OnRequestEdit notifications.

The Test Container also provides full support for Ambient Properties.

Figure 5.2 shows the Test Container with an embedded control.

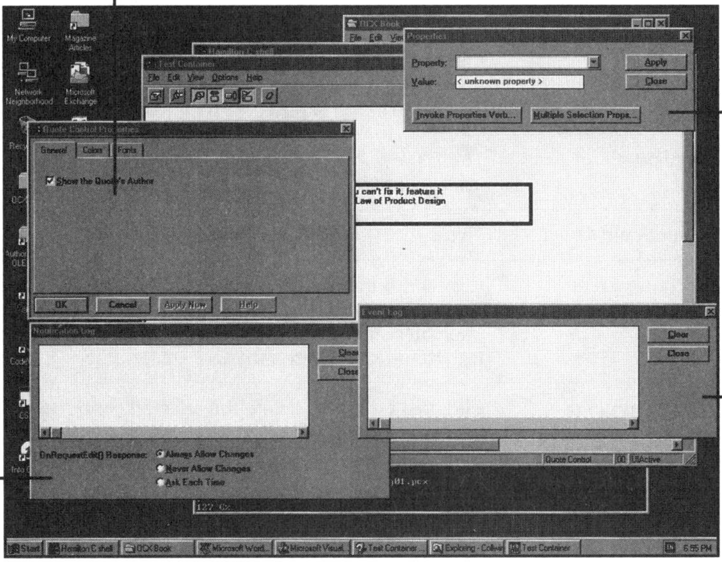

The properties selection dialog box

Fig. 5.2
The Test Container showing the embedded control and the various debug windows available from the test container—the events log, the notification log, the properties selection dialog box, and finally your property selection dialog box.

Your property selection dialog box

The events log

The notification log

MFC Classes

Microsoft has added a number of new classes to the MFC to provide support for OLE controls. This section will examine each of these new classes in detail. While it is quite possible to implement an OLE control without using these classes, it would require a significant amount of programming time and it is doubtful if you could generate the same quality code as the AFX development team within Microsoft. These classes represent an enormous amount of tested source code that is designed to get you up and running with your controls in the shortest amount of time.

COleControl

By far the largest of the new classes is COleControl. This class encapsulated much of the functionality required of any OLE control. COleControl will be the base class for all your OLE controls. All communication between your control and its container is handled by the COleControl class. This class inherits from CWnd so all the code needed to draw and paint your control is also available here.

Figure 5.3 shows the relationship between the OLE control container, the COleControl base class, and your class which inherits from COleControl.

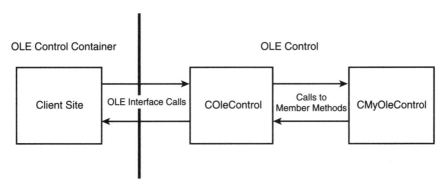

Fig. 5.3
This diagram describes the relationship between control containers and your control when using the MFC control classes.

The COleControl class provides implementation of a number of standard COM interfaces. These interfaces are as follows:

- IPersistStorage
- IPerstistStreamInit
- IOleObject
- IViewObject2
- IDataObject
- IOleInPlaceObject
- IOleInPlaceActiveObject
- IDispatch

- IOleCache
- IOleControl
- IProvideClassInfo
- ISpecifyPropertyPages
- IPerPropertyBrowsing
- IConnectPointContainer
- IPropertyNotifySink

The functionality of the COleControl class can be divided into a number of sections. Each of these sections describe each stage of the control's lifetime from construction, through its use and finally its destruction.

Construction

The following group of methods is involved with the initial creation of the control:

Method dialog box	Description
COleControl	Creates a COleControl object. Usually called from the control's class factory.
RecreateControlWindow	Destroys and re-creates the control's window. Normally would only be used if you needed to change the window's style bits.

Initialization

During the construction of your control, these methods are used to initialize the control:

Method	Description
InitializeIIDs	This method is called in the control's constructor to inform the base class of the IIDs that the control will use.
IsConvertingVBX	This method will tell you if the control that is being loaded is a VBX. This allows you to have special loading code for a VBX control.
SetInitialSize	This method sets the size in device units of an OLE control when first displayed in a container. Usually called from the control's constructor.

Modification Methods

These methods are used to check the current state of the "dirty" flag or to set the flag:

Method	Description
IsModified	Determines if the control state has changed by modifying a control property.
SetModifiedFlag	Sets the flag that the IsModified method checks.

Persistence

The persistence group is used when you need to store or retrieve state information about the control. This information is usually stored in a compound file:

Method	Description
ExchangeExtent	Serializes the control's width and height in HIMETRIC units. Normally called by the default implementation of DoPropertyExchange.
ExchangeStockProps	Serializes the control's stock properties. Normally called by the default implementation of DoPropertyExchange.
ExchangeVersion	Serializes the control's version number. For more information on versioning, refer to Chapter 6.

Method	Description
WillAmbientsBeValidDuringLoad	Determines whether ambient properties will be available the next time the control is loaded. If they are not, then the control should not use them as default values.

Painting Methods

The following group is involved with the display of the control:

Method	Description
DoSuperclassPaint	Redraws an OLE control that has been subclassed from a Windows control. Called from the control's OnDraw method.
InvalidateControl	Invalidates an area of the displayed control, causing it to be redrawn. This method is similar to the InvalidateRect API function.
SelectFontObject	Selects a custom Font property into a device context.
SelectStockFont	Selects the stock Font property into a device context.
TranslateColor	Converts an OLE_COLOR value to a COLORREF value. Used to translate the stock ForeColor and BackColor value to values that can be used by CDC members.

Dispatch Exceptions

Dispatch exceptions are used to convey error information to a control's container:

Method	Description
GetNotSupported	Prevents access to a control's property value by the user.
SetNotPermitted	Indicates that an edit request has failed. This method is called when BoundPropertyRequestEdit fails.
SetNotSupported	Prevents modification to a control's property value by the user.
ThrowError	Signals that an error has occurred in an OLE control. Called from within a Get or Set function for a property.

Ambient Properties

A control container may support ambient properties. These are default properties such as the currently selected font, the current background, or the current foreground color. This group of methods in table 5.4 is used to retrieve these values:

Table 5.4 Methods Dealing with Ambient Properties

Method	Description
AmbientBackColor	Returns the value of the ambient BackColor property.
AmbientDisplayName	Returns the name of the control as specified by the container.
AmbientForeColor	Returns the value of the ambient ForeColor property.
AmbientFont	Returns the value of the ambient Font property.
AmbientLocaleID	Returns the container's locale ID.
AmbientScaleUnits	Returns the type of units used by the container.
AmbientShowGrabHandles	Determines if grab handles should be displayed.
AmbientShowHatching	Determines if hatching should be displayed.
AmbientTextAlign	Returns the type of text alignment specified by the container.
AmbientUIDead	Determines if the control should respond to user-interface actions.
AmbientUserMode	Determines the mode of the container.
GetAmbientProperty	Returns the value of the specified ambient property.

Event Firing

Controls communicate with their containers through events. The following group of methods in table 5.5 is used to fire various types of events:

Table 5.5 Methods Dealing with Events	
Method	**Description**
FireClick	Fires the stock Click event.
FireDblClick	Fires the stock DblClick event.
FireError	Fires the stock Error event.
FireEvent	Fires a custom event.
FireKeyDown	Fires the stock KeyDown event.
FireKeyPress	Fires the stock KeyPress event.
FireKeyUp	Fires the stock KeyUp event.
FireMouseDown	Fires the stock MouseDown event.
FireMouseMove	Fires the stock MouseMove event.
FireMouseUp	Fires the stock MouseUp event.

Stock Methods and Properties

Stock methods and properties are methods and properties that have pre-defined characteristics. Their DISPIDs are defined by Microsoft. This set of methods in table 5.6 is used to manipulate these stock properties and methods:

Table 5.6 Methods Dealing with Stock Methods and Properties	
Method	**Description**
DoClick	Implements the stock DoClick method.
Refresh	Forces a repaint of a control's appearance.
GetBackColor	Returns the value of the stock BackColor property.
SetBackColor	Sets the value of the stock BackColor property.
GetBorderStyle	Returns the value of the stock BorderStyle property.
SetBorderStyle	Sets the value of the stock BorderStyle property.
GetEnabled	Returns the value of the stock Enabled property.

(continues)

Table 5.6   Continued

Method	Description
SetEnabled	Sets the value of the stock Enabled property.
GetForeColor	Returns the value of the stock ForeColor property.
SetForeColor	Sets the value of the stock ForeColor property.
GetFont	Returns the value of the stock Font property.
InternalGetFont	Returns a CFontHolder object for the stock Font property.
SetFont	Sets the value of the stock Font property.
SelectStockFont	Selects the control's stock Font property into a device context.
GetHwnd	Returns the value of the stock hWnd property.
GetText	Returns the value of the stock Text or Caption property.
InternalGetText	Retrieves the stock Text or Caption property.
SetText	Sets the value of the stock Text or Caption property.

Sizing Methods

This group is used to set and retrieve information about the current size and position of the control within a container:

Method	Description
GetControlSize	Returns the position and size of the OLE control.
SetControlSize	Sets the position and size of the OLE control.
GetRectInContainer	Returns the control's rectangle relative to its container.
SetRectInContainer	Sets the control's rectangle relative to its container.

Data Binding Methods
Data binding is the term used to refer to controls that are bound to data sources such as an SQL database. Its methods are as follows:

Method	Description
BoundPropertyChanged	Notifies the container that a bound property has been changed.
BoundPropertyRequestEdit	Requests permission to edit the property value.

Simple Frame Methods
A simple frame allows visual containment of a group of OLE controls. A group box in a data entry form is an example of a simple frame. The simple frame methods are as follows:

Method	Description
EnableSimpleFrame	Enables simple frame support for a control.

Control Site Methods
These methods deal with the control's interaction with its container:

Method	Description
ControlInfoChanged	Calls this function after the set of mnemonics handled by the control has changed.
GetExtendedControl	Retrieves a pointer to an extended control object belonging to the container.
LockInPlaceActive	Determines if your control can be deactivated by the container.
TransformCoords	Transforms coordinate values between a container and the control.

Modal Dialog Box Methods

These methods are used by the control to inform the container that it is using a modal dialog box. These could be used when the property dialog box is displayed:

Method	Description
PreModalDialog	Notifies the container that a modal dialog box is about to be displayed.
PostModalDialog	Notifies the container that a modal dialog box has been closed.

Overridables

These are the methods (shown in table 5.7) that you would normally provide implementations for. MFC provides defaults implementations for most of them:

Table 5.7   Methods Which Can Be Overridden

Method	Description
DisplayError	Displays stock Error events to the control's user.
DoPropExchange	Serializes the properties of a COleControl object.
GetClassID	Retrieves the OLE class ID of the control.
GetMessageString	Provides status bar text for a menu item.
OnClick	Called to fire the stock Click event.
OnDoVerb	Called after a control verb has been executed.
OnDraw	Called when a control is requested to redraw itself.
OnDrawMetafile	Called by the container when a control is requested to redraw itself using a metafile device context.
OnEnumVerbs	Called by the container to enumerate a control's verbs.
OnEventAdvise	Called when event handlers are connected or disconnected from a control.
OnGetColorSet	Notifies the control that IOleObject::GetColorSet has been called.
OnKeyDownEvent	Called after the stock KeyDown event has been fired.

Method	Description
OnKeyPressEvent	Called after the stock KeyPress event has been fired.
OnKeyUpEvent	Called after the stock KeyUp event has been fired.
OnProperties	Called when the control's "Properties" verb has been invoked.
OnResetState	Resets a control's properties to the default values.

Changes Notification Methods

The following group of callbacks is called when any of the stock properties change:

Method	Description
OnBackColorChanged	Called when the stock BackColor property is changed.
OnBorderStyleChanged	Called when the stock BorderStyle property is changed.
OnEnabledChanged	Called when the stock Enabled property is changed.
OnFontChanged	Called when the stock Font property is changed.
OnForeColorChanged	Called when the stock ForeColor property is changed.
OnTextChanged	Called when the stock Text or Caption property is changed.

OLE Interface Notification Methods

This group of callbacks, shown in table 5.8, is associated with the various COM interfaces that each control supports. They are called when the container wants to retrieve data or other information from the control:

Table 5.8 Notification Methods	
Method	**Description**
OnAmbientPropertyChange	Called when an ambient property is changed.
OnFreezeEvents	Called when a control's events are frozen or unfrozen.
OnGetControlInfo	Provides mnemonic information to the container.

(continues)

Table 5.8 Continued	
Method	**Description**
OnMnemonic	Called when a mnemonic key of the control has been pressed.
OnRenderData	Called by the framework to retrieve data in the specified format.
OnRenderFileData	Called by the framework to retrieve data from a file in the specified format.
OnRenderGlobalData	Called by the framework to retrieve data from global memory in the specified format.
OnSetClientSite	Notifies the control that IOleControl::SetClientSite has been called.
OnSetData	Replaces the control's data with another value.
OnSetExtent	Called after the control's extent has changed.
OnSetObjectRects	Called after the control's dimensions have been changed.

Visual Editing Methods

These callbacks are called by the container during visual editing:

Method	**Description**
OnGetInPlaceMenu	Requests the handle of the control's menu that will be merged with the container menu.
OnHideToolBars	Called by the container when the control is UI-deactivated.
OnShowToolBars	Called when the control has been UI-activated.

Property Browsing Methods

This group of callbacks is called to retrieve property values:

Method	**Description**
OnGetDisplayString	Called to obtain a string to represent a property value.
OnGetPredefinedStrings	Returns strings representing possible values for a property.

Method	Description
`OnGetPredefinedValue`	Returns the value corresponding to a predefined string.
`OnMapPropertyToPage`	Indicates which property page to use for editing a property.

Listing 5.1 shows the class definition for `COleControl`. It is easy to see from looking at this code that using MFC in your OLE development saves enormous amounts of development time. Apart from the utility functions supplied with the class, `COleControl` from the MFC classes implements a total of 15 COM interfaces for you.

Listing 5.1 *COleControl*

```
class COleControl : public CWnd
{
    DECLARE_DYNAMIC(COleControl)

// Constructors
public:
    COleControl();

// Operations

    // Initialization
    void SetInitialSize(int cx, int cy);
    void InitializeIIDs(const IID* piidPrimary,
        const IID* piidEvents);

    // Invalidating
    void InvalidateControl(LPCRECT lpRect = NULL);

    // Modified flag
    BOOL IsModified();
    void SetModifiedFlag(BOOL bModified = TRUE);

    // Drawing operations
    void DoSuperclassPaint(CDC* pDC, const CRect& rcBounds);

    // Property exchange
    BOOL ExchangeExtent(CPropExchange* pPX);
    void ExchangeStockProps(CPropExchange* pPX);
    BOOL ExchangeVersion(CPropExchange* pPX, DWORD
    ➥dwVersionDefault,
        BOOL bConvert = TRUE);
    BOOL IsConvertingVBX();
```

(continues)

Listing 5.1 Continued

```
// Stock methods
void Refresh();
void DoClick();

// Stock properties
OLE_COLOR GetBackColor();
void SetBackColor(OLE_COLOR);
short GetBorderStyle();
void SetBorderStyle(short);
BOOL GetEnabled();
void SetEnabled(BOOL);
CFontHolder& InternalGetFont();
LPFONTDISP GetFont();
void SetFont(LPFONTDISP);
OLE_COLOR GetForeColor();
void SetForeColor(OLE_COLOR);
OLE_HANDLE GetHwnd();
const CString& InternalGetText();
BSTR GetText();
void SetText(LPCTSTR);

// Using colors
COLORREF TranslateColor(OLE_COLOR clrColor, HPALETTE hpal =
➥NULL);

// Using fonts
CFont* SelectStockFont(CDC* pDC);
CFont* SelectFontObject(CDC* pDC, CFontHolder& fontHolder);
void GetStockTextMetrics(LPTEXTMETRIC lptm);
void GetFontTextMetrics(LPTEXTMETRIC lptm,
                CFontHolder& fontHolder);

// Client site access
LPOLECLIENTSITE GetClientSite();

// Generic ambient property access
BOOL GetAmbientProperty(DISPID dispid,
        VARTYPE vtProp, void* pvProp);
BOOL WillAmbientsBeValidDuringLoad();

// Specific ambient properties
OLE_COLOR AmbientBackColor();
CString AmbientDisplayName();
LPFONTDISP AmbientFont();
OLE_COLOR AmbientForeColor();
LCID AmbientLocaleID();
CString AmbientScaleUnits();
short AmbientTextAlign();
BOOL AmbientUserMode();
BOOL AmbientUIDead();
BOOL AmbientShowGrabHandles();
BOOL AmbientShowHatching();
```

```
// Firing events
void FireEvent(DISPID dispid, BYTE FAR* pbParams, ...);

// Firing functions for stock events
void FireKeyDown(USHORT* pnChar, short nShiftState);
void FireKeyUp(USHORT* pnChar, short nShiftState);
void FireKeyPress(USHORT* pnChar);
void FireMouseDown(short nButton, short nShiftState,
    OLE_XPOS_PIXELS x, OLE_YPOS_PIXELS y);
void FireMouseUp(short nButton, short nShiftState,
    OLE_XPOS_PIXELS x, OLE_YPOS_PIXELS y);
void FireMouseMove(short nButton, short nShiftState,
    OLE_XPOS_PIXELS x, OLE_YPOS_PIXELS y);
void FireClick();
void FireDblClick();
void FireError(SCODE scode,
    LPCTSTR lpszDescription, UINT nHelpID = 0);

// Changing size and/or rectangle
BOOL GetRectInContainer(LPRECT lpRect);
BOOL SetRectInContainer(LPCRECT lpRect);
void GetControlSize(int* pcx, int* pcy);
BOOL SetControlSize(int cx, int cy);

// Window management
void RecreateControlWindow();

// Modal dialog operations
void PreModalDialog(HWND hWndParent = NULL);
void PostModalDialog(HWND hWndParent = NULL);

// Data binding operations
void BoundPropertyChanged(DISPID dispid);
BOOL BoundPropertyRequestEdit(DISPID dispid);

// Dispatch exceptions
void ThrowError(SCODE sc,
    UINT nDescriptionID, UINT nHelpID = -1);
void ThrowError(SCODE sc,
    LPCTSTR pszDescription = NULL, UINT nHelpID = 0);
void GetNotSupported();
void SetNotSupported();
void SetNotPermitted();

// Communication with the control site
void ControlInfoChanged();
BOOL LockInPlaceActive(BOOL bLock);
LPDISPATCH GetExtendedControl();
void TransformCoords(POINTL FAR* lpptlHimetric,
    POINTF FAR* lpptfContainer, DWORD flags);

// Simple frame
void EnableSimpleFrame();
```

(continues)

Listing 5.1 Continued

```
// Overridables
    virtual void DoPropExchange(CPropExchange* pPX);
    virtual void OnResetState();
    virtual void OnDraw(CDC* pDC,
        const CRect& rcBounds, const CRect& rcInvalid);
    virtual void OnDrawMetafile(CDC* pDC, const CRect& rcBounds);

    // Class ID (implemented by IMPLEMENT_OLECREATE_EX macro)
    virtual HRESULT GetClassID(LPCLSID pclsid) = 0;

    // For customizing the default messages on the status bar
    virtual void GetMessageString(UINT nID, CString& rMessage)
        const;

    // Display of error events to user
    virtual void DisplayError(SCODE scode,
        LPCTSTR lpszDescription,
        LPCTSTR lpszSource, LPCTSTR lpszHelpFile, UINT nHelpID);

    // IOleObject notifications
    virtual void OnSetClientSite();
    virtual BOOL OnSetExtent(LPSIZEL lpSizeL);

    // IOleInPlaceObject notifications
    virtual BOOL OnSetObjectRects(LPCRECT lpRectPos,
        LPCRECT lpRectClip);

    // Event connection point notifications
    virtual void OnEventAdvise(BOOL bAdvise);

    // Override to hook firing of Click event
    virtual void OnClick(USHORT iButton);

    // Override to get character after key events
    // have been processed.
    virtual void OnKeyDownEvent(USHORT nChar, USHORT nShiftState);
    virtual void OnKeyUpEvent(USHORT nChar, USHORT nShiftState);
    virtual void OnKeyPressEvent(USHORT nChar);

    // Change notifications
    virtual void OnBackColorChanged();
    virtual void OnBorderStyleChanged();
    virtual void OnEnabledChanged();
    virtual void OnTextChanged();
    virtual void OnFontChanged();
    virtual void OnForeColorChanged();

    // IOleControl notifications
    virtual void OnGetControlInfo(LPCONTROLINFO pControlInfo);
    virtual void OnMnemonic(LPMSG pMsg);
    virtual void OnAmbientPropertyChange(DISPID dispid);
    virtual void OnFreezeEvents(BOOL bFreeze);
```

```
        // In-place activation
        virtual HMENU OnGetInPlaceMenu();
        virtual void OnShowToolBars();
        virtual void OnHideToolBars();

        // IViewObject
        virtual BOOL OnGetColorSet(DVTARGETDEVICE FAR* ptd,
                           HDC hicTargetDev,
                    LPLOGPALETTE FAR* ppColorSet);

        // IDataObject - see COleDataSource for a description of these
        // overridables
        virtual BOOL OnRenderGlobalData(LPFORMATETC lpFormatEtc,
             HGLOBAL* phGlobal);
        virtual BOOL OnRenderFileData(LPFORMATETC lpFormatEtc,
             CFile* pFile);
        virtual BOOL OnRenderData(LPFORMATETC lpFormatEtc,
             LPSTGMEDIUM lpStgMedium);
        virtual BOOL OnSetData(LPFORMATETC lpFormatEtc,
             LPSTGMEDIUM lpStgMedium,
           BOOL bRelease);

        // Verbs
        virtual BOOL OnEnumVerbs(LPENUMOLEVERB FAR* ppenumOleVerb);
        virtual BOOL OnDoVerb(LONG iVerb, LPMSG lpMsg,
             HWND hWndParent, LPCRECT lpRect);
        virtual BOOL OnEdit(LPMSG lpMsg,
             HWND hWndParent, LPCRECT lpRect);
        virtual BOOL OnProperties(LPMSG lpMsg,
             HWND hWndParent, LPCRECT lpRect);

        // IPerPropertyBrowsing overrides
        virtual BOOL OnGetDisplayString(DISPID dispid, CString&
             strValue);
        virtual BOOL OnMapPropertyToPage(DISPID dispid, LPCLSID
             lpclsid,
           BOOL* pbPageOptional);
        virtual BOOL OnGetPredefinedStrings(DISPID dispid,
           CStringArray* pStringArray, CDWordArray* pCookieArray);
        virtual BOOL OnGetPredefinedValue(DISPID dispid, DWORD
             dwCookie,
           VARIANT FAR* lpvarOut);

        // Window procedure
        virtual LRESULT WindowProc(UINT message,
             WPARAM wParam, LPARAM lParam);

// Implementation
        ~COleControl();

#ifdef _DEBUG
        void AssertValid() const;
        void Dump(CDumpContext& dc) const;
#endif // _DEBUG
```

(continues)

Listing 5.1 Continued

```
protected:
    // Friend classes
    friend class CReflectorWnd;
    friend class CControlFrameWnd;

    // Interface hook for primary automation interface
    LPUNKNOWN GetInterfaceHook(const void* piid);

    // Shutdown
    virtual void OnFinalRelease();

    // Window management
    BOOL CreateControlWindow(HWND hWndParent, const CRect& rcPos);
    void CreateWindowForSubclassedControl();
    BOOL IgnoreWindowMessage(UINT msg, WPARAM wParam, LPARAM
            lParam,
        LRESULT* plResult);

    // Serialization
    HRESULT SaveState(IStream* pStm);
    HRESULT LoadState(IStream* pStm);
    virtual void Serialize(CArchive& ar);

    // Drawing
    void DrawContent(CDC* pDC, CRect& rc);
    void DrawMetafile(CDC* pDC, CRect& rc);
    BOOL GetMetafileData(LPFORMATETC lpFormatEtc,
            LPSTGMEDIUM lpStgMedium);

    // IDataObject formats
    void SetInitialDataFormats();
    BOOL GetPropsetData(LPFORMATETC lpFormatEtc,
            LPSTGMEDIUM lpStgMedium,
        REFCLSID fmtid);
    BOOL SetPropsetData(LPFORMATETC lpFormatEtc,
            LPSTGMEDIUM lpStgMedium, CCC
        REFCLSID fmtid);

    // Type library
    virtual HRESULT GetTypeLib(LCID, LPTYPELIB FAR*);
    virtual CTypeLibCache* GetTypeLibCache();
    HRESULT GetTypeInfoOfGuid(LCID, REFGUID, LPTYPEINFO FAR*);

    // Connection point container
    LPCONNECTIONPOINTCONTAINER GetConnectionPointContainer();
    virtual LPCONNECTIONPOINT GetConnectionHook(REFIID iid);

    // Events
    static AFX_DATA AFX_EVENTMAP_ENTRY BASED_CODE _eventEntries[];
    virtual AFX_EVENTMAP FAR* GetEventMap() const;
    static AFX_DATA AFX_EVENTMAP BASED_CODE eventMap;
    AFX_EVENTMAP_ENTRY FAR* GetEventMapEntry(LPCTSTR pszName,
```

```
        DISPID* pDispid) const;
void FireEventV(DISPID dispid, BYTE FAR* pbParams,
        va_list argList);

// Stock events
void KeyDown(USHORT* pnChar);
void KeyUp(USHORT* pnChar);
void ButtonDown(USHORT iButton, UINT nFlags, CPoint point);
void ButtonUp(USHORT iButton, UINT nFlags, CPoint point);
void ButtonDblClk(USHORT iButton, UINT nFlags, CPoint point);

// Masks to identify which stock events
// and properties are used
void InitStockEventMask();
void InitStockPropMask();

// Support for subclassing a Windows control
BOOL ContainerReflectsMessages();
CWnd* GetOuterWindow() const;
void OnReflectorDestroyed();

// Aggregation of default handler
BOOL OnCreateAggregates();

// State change notifications
void SendAdvise(UINT uCode);

// Non-in-place activation
HRESULT OnOpen(BOOL bTryInPlace, LPMSG pMsg);
void ResizeOpenControl(int cx, int cy);
virtual CControlFrameWnd* CreateFrameWindow();
void ResizeFrameWindow(int cx, int cy);
void OnFrameClose();
HRESULT OnHide();

// In-place activation
HRESULT OnActivateInPlace(BOOL bUIActivate, LPMSG pMsg);
void ForwardActivationMsg(LPMSG pMsg);
void AddFrameLevelUI();
void RemoveFrameLevelUI();
BOOL BuildSharedMenu();
void DestroySharedMenu();

// Property sheet
virtual LPCLSID GetPropPageIDs(ULONG& cPropPages);

// IOleObject implementation
CString& GetUserType();
virtual UINT GetUserTypeNameID() = 0;
virtual DWORD GetMiscStatus() = 0;

// Data members
AFX_MODULE_STATE* m_pModuleState;
    // Pointer to your module's state
```

(continues)

Listing 5.1   Continued

```
const IID* m_piidPrimary;        // IID for control automation
const IID* m_piidEvents;         // IID for control events
CTypeLibCache* m_pTypeLibCache;  // Type library cache
DWORD m_dwVersionLoaded;         // Version number of loaded state
COleDispatchDriver m_ambientDispDriver;
DWORD m_dwStockEventMask;  // Which stock events are used?
DWORD m_dwStockPropMask;   // Which stock properties are used?
ULONG m_cEventsFrozen; // Event freeze count (>0 means frozen)
CControlFrameWnd* m_pWndOpenFrame;  // Open frame window.
CString m_strFrameTitle;  // Title string for open frame
                          // window.
CRect m_rcPos;            // Control's position rectangle
CRect m_rcBounds;         // Bounding rectangle for drawing
long m_cxExtent;          // Control's width in HIMETRIC units
long m_cyExtent;          // Control's height in HIMETRIC units
class CReflectorWnd* m_pReflect;    // Reflector window
UINT m_nIDTracking;       // Tracking command ID or string IDS
UINT m_nIDLastMessage;    // Last displayed message string IDS
BYTE m_bAutoMenuEnable;   // Disable menu items without
                          // handlers?
BYTE m_bFinalReleaseCalled; // Are we handling the final
                            // Release?
BYTE m_bModified;           // "Dirty" bit.
BYTE m_bCountOnAmbients;   // Can we count on Ambients
                          // during load?
BYTE m_iButtonState;         // Which buttons are down?
BYTE m_iDblClkState;    // Which buttons involved in dbl click?
BYTE m_bInPlaceActive;             // Are we in-place active?
BYTE m_bUIActive;                  // Are we UI active?
BYTE m_bPendingUIActivation;  // Are we about to become
                              // UI active?
BYTE m_bOpen;             // Are we open (non-in-place)?
BYTE m_bChangingExtent;   // Extent is currently being changed
BYTE m_bConvertVBX;            // VBX conversion in progress
BYTE m_bSimpleFrame;           // Simple frame support
BYTE m_bTranslatingAccelerator;
        // Currently inside TranslateAcclerator?
BYTE m_bUIDead;                // UIDead ambient property value

// Stock properties
OLE_COLOR m_clrBackColor;  // BackColor
OLE_COLOR m_clrForeColor;  // ForeColor
CString m_strText;         // Text/Caption
CFontHolder m_font;        // Font
HFONT m_hFontPrev;         // Previously selected font object
short m_sBorderStyle;      // BorderStyle
BOOL m_bEnabled;           // Enabled

// Shared OLE menu data
OLEMENUGROUPWIDTHS m_menuWidths;
HMENU m_hSharedMenu;
HOLEMENU m_hOleMenu;
```

```
        // Default Handler aggregation
        LPUNKNOWN m_pDefIUnknown;
        LPOLEOBJECT m_pDefIOleObject;
        LPPERSISTSTORAGE m_pDefIPersistStorage;
        LPVIEWOBJECT m_pDefIViewObject;
        LPOLECACHE m_pDefIOleCache;
#ifdef OLE2ANSI
        LPUNKNOWN m_pUnkWrapper;
#endif

        // OLE client site interfaces
        LPOLECLIENTSITE m_pClientSite;          // Client site
        LPOLEINPLACESITE m_pInPlaceSite;        // In-place site
        LPOLECONTROLSITE m_pControlSite;        // Control site
        LPOLEADVISEHOLDER m_pOleAdviseHolder;   // Advise holder
        LPDATAADVISEHOLDER m_pDataAdviseHolder; // Data advise holder
        LPSIMPLEFRAMESITE m_pSimpleFrameSite;   // Simple frame site

        // OLE in-place activation info
        LPOLEINPLACEFRAME m_pInPlaceFrame;
        OLEINPLACEFRAMEINFO m_frameInfo;
        LPOLEINPLACEUIWINDOW m_pInPlaceDoc;
        CString m_strUserTypeName;

        // Implementation of IDataObject
        // CControlDataSource implements
        //OnRender reflections to COleControl
        class CControlDataSource : public COleDataSource
        {
        protected:
            virtual BOOL OnRenderGlobalData(LPFORMATETC
                    lpFormatEtc, HGLOBAL* phGlobal);
            virtual BOOL OnRenderFileData(LPFORMATETC
                    lpFormatEtc, CFile* pFile);
            virtual BOOL OnRenderData(LPFORMATETC
                    lpFormatEtc, LPSTGMEDIUM lpStgMedium);

            virtual BOOL OnSetData(LPFORMATETC lpFormatEtc,
                    LPSTGMEDIUM lpStgMedium,
                BOOL bRelease);
        };
        CControlDataSource m_dataSource;
        friend class CControlDataSource;

// Message Maps
protected:
        //{{AFX_MSG(COleControl)
        afx_msg void OnKeyDown(UINT nChar, UINT nRepCnt, UINT nFlags);
        afx_msg void OnKeyUp(UINT nChar, UINT nRepCnt, UINT nFlags);
        afx_msg void OnChar(UINT nChar, UINT nRepCnt, UINT nFlags);
        afx_msg void OnMouseMove(UINT nFlags, CPoint point);
        afx_msg void OnLButtonDown(UINT nFlags, CPoint point);
        afx_msg void OnLButtonUp(UINT nFlags, CPoint point);
        afx_msg void OnLButtonDblClk(UINT nFlags, CPoint point);
```

(continues)

Listing 5.1 Continued

```
    afx_msg void OnMButtonDown(UINT nFlags, CPoint point);
    afx_msg void OnMButtonUp(UINT nFlags, CPoint point);
    afx_msg void OnMButtonDblClk(UINT nFlags, CPoint point);
    afx_msg void OnRButtonDown(UINT nFlags, CPoint point);
    afx_msg void OnRButtonUp(UINT nFlags, CPoint point);
    afx_msg void OnRButtonDblClk(UINT nFlags, CPoint point);
    afx_msg void OnInitMenuPopup(CMenu*, UINT, BOOL);
    afx_msg void OnMenuSelect(UINT nItemID,
                    UINT nFlags, HMENU hSysMenu);
    afx_msg LRESULT OnSetMessageString(WPARAM wParam,
                    LPARAM lParam);
    afx_msg void OnEnterIdle(UINT nWhy, CWnd* pWho);
    afx_msg void OnCancelMode();
    afx_msg void OnPaint(CDC* pDC);
    afx_msg void OnSysKeyDown(UINT nChar, UINT nRepCnt,
                    UINT nFlags);
    afx_msg void OnSysKeyUp(UINT nChar, UINT nRepCnt,
                    UINT nFlags);
    afx_msg int  OnMouseActivate(CWnd *pDesktopWnd,
                    UINT nHitTest, UINT message);
    afx_msg LRESULT OnSetText(WPARAM wParam, LPARAM lParam);
    afx_msg BOOL OnNcCreate(LPCREATESTRUCT lpCreateStruct);
    afx_msg void OnDestroy();
    afx_msg  void OnKillFocus(CWnd* pNewWnd);
    afx_msg void OnSetFocus(CWnd* pOldWnd);
    //}}AFX_MSG

#ifdef _WIN32
    afx_msg LRESULT OnOcmCtlColorBtn(WPARAM wParam,
                    LPARAM lParam);
    afx_msg LRESULT OnOcmCtlColorDlg(WPARAM wParam,
                    LPARAM lParam);
    afx_msg LRESULT OnOcmCtlColorEdit(WPARAM wParam,
                    LPARAM lParam);
    afx_msg LRESULT OnOcmCtlColorListBox(WPARAM wParam,
                    LPARAM lParam);
    afx_msg LRESULT OnOcmCtlColorMsgBox(WPARAM wParam,
                    LPARAM lParam);
    afx_msg LRESULT OnOcmCtlColorScrollBar(WPARAM wParam,
                    LPARAM lParam);
    afx_msg LRESULT OnOcmCtlColorStatic(WPARAM wParam,
                    LPARAM lParam);
#else
    afx_msg LRESULT OnOcmCtlColor(WPARAM wParam, LPARAM lParam);
#endif
    DECLARE_MESSAGE_MAP()
```

```
// Interface Maps
protected:
    // IPersistStorage
    BEGIN_INTERFACE_PART(PersistStorage, IPersistStorage)
        INIT_INTERFACE_PART(COleControl, PersistStorage)
        STDMETHOD(GetClassID)(LPCLSID);
        STDMETHOD(IsDirty)();
        STDMETHOD(InitNew)(LPSTORAGE);
        STDMETHOD(Load)(LPSTORAGE);
        STDMETHOD(Save)(LPSTORAGE, BOOL);
        STDMETHOD(SaveCompleted)(LPSTORAGE);
        STDMETHOD(HandsOffStorage)();
    END_INTERFACE_PART(PersistStorage)

    // IPersistStreamInit
    BEGIN_INTERFACE_PART(PersistStreamInit, IPersistStreamInit)
        INIT_INTERFACE_PART(COleControl, PersistStreamInit)
        STDMETHOD(GetClassID)(LPCLSID);
        STDMETHOD(IsDirty)();
        STDMETHOD(Load)(LPSTREAM);
        STDMETHOD(Save)(LPSTREAM, BOOL);
        STDMETHOD(GetSizeMax)(ULARGE_INTEGER FAR *);
        STDMETHOD(InitNew)();
    END_INTERFACE_PART(PersistStreamInit)

    // IOleObject
    BEGIN_INTERFACE_PART(OleObject, IOleObject)
        INIT_INTERFACE_PART(COleControl, OleObject)
        STDMETHOD(SetClientSite)(LPOLECLIENTSITE);
        STDMETHOD(GetClientSite)(LPOLECLIENTSITE FAR*);
        STDMETHOD(SetHostNames)(LPCTSTR, LPCTSTR);
        STDMETHOD(Close)(DWORD);
        STDMETHOD(SetMoniker)(DWORD, LPMONIKER);
        STDMETHOD(GetMoniker)(DWORD, DWORD, LPMONIKER FAR*);
        STDMETHOD(InitFromData)(LPDATAOBJECT, BOOL, DWORD);
        STDMETHOD(GetClipboardData)(DWORD, LPDATAOBJECT FAR*);
        STDMETHOD(DoVerb)(LONG, LPMSG, LPOLECLIENTSITE,
                    LONG, HWND, LPCRECT);
        STDMETHOD(EnumVerbs)(IEnumOLEVERB FAR* FAR*);
        STDMETHOD(Update)();
        STDMETHOD(IsUpToDate)();
        STDMETHOD(GetUserClassID)(CLSID FAR*);
        STDMETHOD(GetUserType)(DWORD, LPTSTR FAR*);
        STDMETHOD(SetExtent)(DWORD, LPSIZEL);
        STDMETHOD(GetExtent)(DWORD, LPSIZEL);
        STDMETHOD(Advise)(LPADVISESINK, LPDWORD);
        STDMETHOD(Unadvise)(DWORD);
        STDMETHOD(EnumAdvise)(LPENUMSTATDATA FAR*);
        STDMETHOD(GetMiscStatus)(DWORD, LPDWORD);
        STDMETHOD(SetColorScheme)(LPLOGPALETTE);
    END_INTERFACE_PART(OleObject)
```

(continues)

Listing 5.1 Continued

```
// IViewObject2
BEGIN_INTERFACE_PART(ViewObject, IViewObject2)
    INIT_INTERFACE_PART(COleControl, ViewObject)
    STDMETHOD(Draw)(DWORD, LONG,
                void FAR*, DVTARGETDEVICE FAR*, HDC, HDC,
            LPCRECTL, LPCRECTL, BOOL (CALLBACK*)(DWORD), DWORD);
    STDMETHOD(GetColorSet)(DWORD, LONG,
                void FAR*, DVTARGETDEVICE FAR*,
            HDC, LPLOGPALETTE FAR*);
    STDMETHOD(Freeze)(DWORD, LONG, void FAR*, DWORD FAR*);
    STDMETHOD(Unfreeze)(DWORD);
    STDMETHOD(SetAdvise)(DWORD, DWORD, LPADVISESINK);
    STDMETHOD(GetAdvise)(DWORD FAR*,
                DWORD FAR*, LPADVISESINK FAR*);
    STDMETHOD(GetExtent) (DWORD,
                LONG, DVTARGETDEVICE FAR*, LPSIZEL);
END_INTERFACE_PART(ViewObject)

// IDataObject
BEGIN_INTERFACE_PART(DataObject, IDataObject)
    INIT_INTERFACE_PART(COleControl, DataObject)
    STDMETHOD(GetData)(LPFORMATETC, LPSTGMEDIUM);
    STDMETHOD(GetDataHere)(LPFORMATETC, LPSTGMEDIUM);
    STDMETHOD(QueryGetData)(LPFORMATETC);
    STDMETHOD(GetCanonicalFormatEtc)(LPFORMATETC,
                LPFORMATETC);
    STDMETHOD(SetData)(LPFORMATETC, LPSTGMEDIUM, BOOL);
    STDMETHOD(EnumFormatEtc)(DWORD, LPENUMFORMATETC FAR*);
    STDMETHOD(DAdvise)(LPFORMATETC, DWORD,
                LPADVISESINK, LPDWORD);
    STDMETHOD(DUnadvise)(DWORD);
    STDMETHOD(EnumDAdvise)(LPENUMSTATDATA FAR*);
END_INTERFACE_PART(DataObject)

// IOleInPlaceObject
BEGIN_INTERFACE_PART(OleInPlaceObject, IOleInPlaceObject)
    INIT_INTERFACE_PART(COleControl, OleInPlaceObject)
    STDMETHOD(GetWindow)(HWND FAR*);
    STDMETHOD(ContextSensitiveHelp)(BOOL);
    STDMETHOD(InPlaceDeactivate)();
    STDMETHOD(UIDeactivate)();
    STDMETHOD(SetObjectRects)(LPCRECT, LPCRECT);
    STDMETHOD(ReactivateAndUndo)();
END_INTERFACE_PART(OleInPlaceObject)

// IOleInPlaceActiveObject
BEGIN_INTERFACE_PART(OleInPlaceActiveObject,
        // IOleInPlaceActiveObject)
    INIT_INTERFACE_PART(COleControl, OleInPlaceActiveObject)
    STDMETHOD(GetWindow)(HWND FAR*);
    STDMETHOD(ContextSensitiveHelp)(BOOL);
    STDMETHOD(TranslateAccelerator)(LPMSG);
    STDMETHOD(OnFrameWindowActivate)(BOOL);
```

```
            STDMETHOD(OnDocWindowActivate)(BOOL);
            STDMETHOD(ResizeBorder)(LPCRECT,
                    LPOLEINPLACEUIWINDOW, BOOL);
            STDMETHOD(EnableModeless)(BOOL);
        END_INTERFACE_PART(OleInPlaceActiveObject)

        // IDispatch
        BEGIN_INTERFACE_PART(Dispatch, IDispatch)
            INIT_INTERFACE_PART(COleControl, Dispatch)
            STDMETHOD(GetTypeInfoCount)(unsigned int FAR* pctinfo);
            STDMETHOD(GetTypeInfo)(unsigned int itinfo, LCID lcid,
                ITypeInfo FAR* FAR* pptinfo);
            STDMETHOD(GetIDsOfNames)(REFIID riid,
                    LPTSTR FAR* rgszNames,
                unsigned int cNames, LCID lcid,
                    DISPID FAR* rgdispid);
            STDMETHOD(Invoke)(DISPID dispidMember,
                    REFIID riid, LCID lcid,
                unsigned short wFlags, DISPPARAMS FAR* pdispparams,
                VARIANT FAR* pvarResult, EXCEPINFO FAR* pexcepinfo,
                unsigned int FAR* puArgErr);
        END_INTERFACE_PART(Dispatch)

        // IOleCache
        BEGIN_INTERFACE_PART(OleCache, IOleCache)
            INIT_INTERFACE_PART(COleControl, OleCache)
            STDMETHOD(Cache)(LPFORMATETC, DWORD, LPDWORD);
            STDMETHOD(Uncache)(DWORD);
            STDMETHOD(EnumCache)(LPENUMSTATDATA FAR*);
            STDMETHOD(InitCache)(LPDATAOBJECT);
            STDMETHOD(SetData)(LPFORMATETC, STGMEDIUM FAR*, BOOL);
        END_INTERFACE_PART(OleCache)

        // IOleControl
        BEGIN_INTERFACE_PART(OleControl, IOleControl)
            INIT_INTERFACE_PART(COleControl, OleControl)
            STDMETHOD(GetControlInfo)(LPCONTROLINFO pCI);
            STDMETHOD(OnMnemonic)(LPMSG pMsg);
            STDMETHOD(OnAmbientPropertyChange)(DISPID dispid);
            STDMETHOD(FreezeEvents)(BOOL bFreeze);
        END_INTERFACE_PART(OleControl)

        // IProvideClassInfo
        BEGIN_INTERFACE_PART(ProvideClassInfo, IProvideClassInfo)
            INIT_INTERFACE_PART(COleControl, ProvideClassInfo)
            STDMETHOD(GetClassInfo)(LPTYPEINFO FAR* ppTypeInfo);
        END_INTERFACE_PART(ProvideClassInfo)

        // ISpecifyPropertyPages
        BEGIN_INTERFACE_PART(SpecifyPropertyPages,
                    ISpecifyPropertyPages)
            INIT_INTERFACE_PART(COleControl, SpecifyPropertyPages)
            STDMETHOD(GetPages)(CAUUID FAR*);
        END_INTERFACE_PART(SpecifyPropertyPages)
```

(continues)

Listing 5.1 Continued

```
    // IPerPropertyBrowsing
    BEGIN_INTERFACE_PART(PerPropertyBrowsing,
                IPerPropertyBrowsing)
        INIT_INTERFACE_PART(COleControl, PerPropertyBrowsing)
        STDMETHOD(GetDisplayString)(DISPID dispid,
                BSTR FAR* lpbstr);
        STDMETHOD(MapPropertyToPage)(DISPID dispid,
                LPCLSID lpclsid);
        STDMETHOD(GetPredefinedStrings)(DISPID dispid,
            CALPOLESTR FAR* lpcaStringsOut,
                CADWORD FAR* lpcaCookiesOut);
        STDMETHOD(GetPredefinedValue)(DISPID dispid,
                DWORD dwCookie,
            VARIANT FAR* lpvarOut);
    END_INTERFACE_PART(PerPropertyBrowsing)

    // IConnectionPointContainer
    BEGIN_INTERFACE_PART(ConnPtContainer,
                IConnectionPointContainer)
        INIT_INTERFACE_PART(COleControl, ConnPtContainer)
        STDMETHOD(EnumConnectionPoints)(
                LPENUMCONNECTIONPOINTS FAR* ppEnum);
        STDMETHOD(FindConnectionPoint)(
            REFIID iid, LPCONNECTIONPOINT FAR* ppCP);
    END_INTERFACE_PART(ConnPtContainer)

    // IPropertyNotifySink for font updates (not exposed via
    // QueryInterface)
    BEGIN_INTERFACE_PART(FontNotification, IPropertyNotifySink)
        INIT_INTERFACE_PART(COleControl, FontNotification)
        STDMETHOD(OnChanged)(DISPID dispid);
        STDMETHOD(OnRequestEdit)(DISPID dispid);
    END_INTERFACE_PART(FontNotification)

    DECLARE_INTERFACE_MAP()

// Connection maps
protected:
    // Connection point for events
    BEGIN_CONNECTION_PART(COleControl, EventConnPt)
        virtual void OnAdvise(BOOL bAdvise);
        virtual REFIID GetIID();
    END_CONNECTION_PART(EventConnPt)

    // Connection point for property notifications
    BEGIN_CONNECTION_PART(COleControl, PropConnPt)
        CONNECTION_IID(IID_IPropertyNotifySink)
    END_CONNECTION_PART(PropConnPt)

    DECLARE_CONNECTION_MAP()
};
```

COleControlModule

In a normal MFC application—one that does not use OLE Controls—you would normally create a class that derives from CWinApp. In the case of applications that use OLE Controls, your application object must derive from COleControlModule. As you can see, in listing 5.2, this class in turn derives from CWinApp.

Listing 5.2 *COleControlModule* **from the MFC Classes**

```
class COleControlModule : public CWinApp
{
     DECLARE_DYNAMIC(COleControlModule)
public:
     virtual BOOL InitInstance();
     virtual int ExitInstance();
};
```

CConnectionPoint

A connection point implements outgoing dispatch interfaces. Outgoing interfaces allow a control access to code implemented in control containers or other controls. With an outgoing interface, the actual code that is called is not implemented by the control. The connection points are used to fire events and notify control containers of changes in properties. Most controls will only support two connection points—one for events and the other for properties.

These two connection points are implemented by the COleControl class. If you need to use additional connection pointers, you must implement them yourself. The CConnectionPoint class in listing 5.3 would be used to implement these additional connection points:

Method	Description
GetConnections	Retrieves all connection points in a connection map.
GetContainer	Retrieves the container of the control that owns the connection map.
GetIID	Retrieves the interface ID of a connection point.
GetMaxConnections	Retrieves the maximum number of connection points supported by a control.
OnAdvise	Called by the framework when establishing or breaking connections.

Listing 5.3 *CConnectionPoint* **from the MFC Classes**

```
class CConnectionPoint : public CCmdTarget
{
// Constructors
public:
    CConnectionPoint();

// Operations
    const CPtrArray* GetConnections();

// Overridables
    virtual LPCONNECTIONPOINTCONTAINER GetContainer() = 0;
    virtual REFIID GetIID() = 0;
    virtual void OnAdvise(BOOL bAdvise);
    virtual int GetMaxConnections();

// Implementation
    ~CConnectionPoint();

protected:
    size_t m_nOffset;
    AFX_MODULE_STATE* m_pModuleState;
    CPtrArray m_Connections;

// Interface Maps
public:
    BEGIN_INTERFACE_PART(ConnPt, IConnectionPoint)
        INIT_INTERFACE_PART(CConnectionPoint, ConnPt)
        STDMETHOD(GetConnectionInterface)(IID FAR* pIID);
        STDMETHOD(GetConnectionPointContainer)(
            IConnectionPointContainer FAR* FAR* ppCPC);
        STDMETHOD(Advise)(LPUNKNOWN pUnkSink, DWORD FAR*
                pdwCookie);
        STDMETHOD(Unadvise)(DWORD dwCookie);
        STDMETHOD(EnumConnections)(LPENUMCONNECTIONS FAR*
                ppEnum);
    END_INTERFACE_PART(ConnPt)
};
```

CFontHolder

This class is used to implement the functionality of the CFont class. It also implements the IFont interface. This class is used to implement the stock fonts for a control. Table 5.8 shows a description of each of the methods. Listing 5.4 shows the class definition for this class.

Table 5.8 *CFontHolder*

Method	Description
m_pFont	A pointer to the CFontHolder object's IFont interface.

Method	Description
CFontHolder	Constructs a CFontHolder object.
GetFontDispatch	Returns the font's IDispatch interface.
GetDisplayString	Retrieves the string displayed in a Visual Basic property sheet.
GetFontHandle	Returns a handle to a Windows font.
InitializeFont	Initializes a CFontHolder object.
ReleaseFont	Disconnects the CFontHolder object from the IFont and IFontNotification interfaces.
Select	Selects a font resource into a device context.
SetFont	Connects the CFontHolder object to an IFont interface.

Listing 5.4 *CFontHolder* from the MFC Classes

```
class CFontHolder
{
// Constructors
public:
    CFontHolder(LPPROPERTYNOTIFYSINK pNotify);

// Attributes
    LPFONT m_pFont;

// Operations
    void InitializeFont(
            const FONTDESC FAR* pFontDesc = NULL,
            LPDISPATCH pFontDispAmbient = NULL);
    void SetFont(LPFONT pNewFont);
    void ReleaseFont();
    HFONT GetFontHandle();
    HFONT GetFontHandle(long cyLogical, long cyHimetric);
    CFont* Select(CDC* pDC, long cyLogical, long cyHimetric);
    BOOL GetDisplayString(CString& strValue);
    LPFONTDISP GetFontDispatch();
    void QueryTextMetrics(LPTEXTMETRIC lptm);

// Implementation
public:
    ~CFontHolder();

protected:
    DWORD m_dwConnectCookie;
    LPPROPERTYNOTIFYSINK m_pNotify;
}
```

CPictureHolder

The CPictureHolder class is used to implement the Picture property. The class can be used to display bitmaps, icons, or metafiles.

A property page to allow the user to select the picture is provided by this class. The class also supports properties of type LPPICTUREDISP. These properties can be manipulated by using the appropriate Get/Set methods. Table 5.9 describes each of these methods. Listing 5.9 shows the class defination for the CPictureHolder class.

Table 5.9   CPictureHolder

Method	Description
m_pPict	Points to a font object.
GetDisplayString	Retrieves the string displayed in a Visual Basic property sheet.
CreateEmpty	Creates an empty CPictureHolder object.
CreateFromBitmap	Creates a CPictureHolder object from a bitmap.
CreateFromMetafile	Creates a CPictureHolder object from a metafile.
CreateFromIcon	Creates a CPictureHolder object from an icon.
GetPictureDispatch	Returns the CPictureHolder object's IDispatch interface.
SetPictureDispatch	Sets the CPictureHolder object's IDispatch interface.
GetType	Tells whether the CPictureHolder object is a bitmap, a metafile, or an icon.
Render	Renders the picture.

Listing 5.5   CPictureHolder from the MFC Classes

```
class CPictureHolder
{
// Constructors
public:
    CPictureHolder();
    ~CPictureHolder();

// Attributes
    LPPICTURE m_pPict;

// Operations
```

```
    BOOL CreateEmpty();

    BOOL CreateFromBitmap(UINT idResource);
    BOOL CreateFromBitmap(CBitmap* pBitmap, CPalette* pPal = NULL,
        BOOL bTransferOwnership = TRUE);
    BOOL CreateFromBitmap(HBITMAP hbm, HPALETTE hpal = NULL,
        BOOL bTransferOwnership = FALSE);

    BOOL CreateFromMetafile(HMETAFILE hmf, int xExt, int yExt,
        BOOL bTransferOwnership = FALSE);

    BOOL CreateFromIcon(UINT idResource);
    BOOL CreateFromIcon(HICON hIcon,
            BOOL bTransferOwnership = FALSE);

    short GetType();
    BOOL GetDisplayString(CString& strValue);
    LPPICTUREDISP GetPictureDispatch();
    void SetPictureDispatch(LPPICTUREDISP pDisp);
    void Render(CDC* pDC, const CRect& rcRender,
            const CRect& rcWBounds);
};
```

COlePropertyPage

This class, which inherits from CDialog, provides the user interface to allow the user to manipulate a control's properties. The interface is in the form of a tabbed dialog box.

Each property that your control supports can have its own property tab in the tabbed dialog. Table 5.10 describes each of the methods in this class.

Table 5.10 *COlePropertyPage*	
Method	**Description**
GetObjectArray	Returns the array of objects being edited by the property page.
SetModifiedFlag	Sets a flag indicating whether the user has modified the property page.
IsModified	Indicates whether the user has modified the property page.
GetPageSite	Returns a pointer to the property page's IPropertyPageSite interface.
SetDialogResource	Sets the property page's dialog resource.

(continues)

Method	Description
SetPageName	Sets the property page's name (caption).
SetHelpInfo	Sets the property page's brief help text, the name of its help file, and its help context.
GetControlStatus	Indicates whether the user has modified the value in the control.
SetControlStatus	Sets a flag indicating whether the user has modified the value in the control.
IgnoreApply	Determines which controls do not enable the Apply button.
OnHelp	Called by the framework when the user invokes help.
OnInitDialog	Called by the framework when the property page is initialized.
OnEditProperty	Called by the framework when the user edits a property.
OnSetPageSite	Called by the framework when the property frame provides the page's site.

Listing 5.6 *COlePropertyPage* from the MFC Classes

```
class COlePropertyPage : public CDialog
{
    DECLARE_DYNAMIC(COlePropertyPage)

// Constructors
public:
    COlePropertyPage(UINT idDlg, UINT idCaption);

// Operations
    LPDISPATCH FAR* GetObjectArray(ULONG FAR* pnObjects);
    void SetModifiedFlag(BOOL bModified = TRUE);
    BOOL IsModified();
    LPPROPERTYPAGESITE GetPageSite();
    void SetDialogResource(HGLOBAL hDialog);
    void SetPageName(LPCTSTR lpszPageName);
    void SetHelpInfo(LPCTSTR lpszDocString,
                LPCTSTR lpszHelpFile = NULL,
        DWORD dwHelpContext = 0);

    BOOL GetControlStatus(UINT nID);
    BOOL SetControlStatus(UINT nID, BOOL bDirty);
    void IgnoreApply(UINT nID);

    int MessageBox(LPCTSTR lpszText, LPCTSTR lpszCaption = NULL,
            UINT nType = MB_OK);
    // note this is a non-virtual override of CWnd::MessageBox()
```

```
// Overridables
    virtual void OnSetPageSite();
    virtual void OnObjectsChanged();
    virtual BOOL OnHelp(LPCTSTR lpszHelpDir);
    virtual BOOL OnInitDialog();
    virtual BOOL OnEditProperty(DISPID dispid);

// Implementation

    // DDP_ property get/set helper routines
    BOOL SetPropText(LPCTSTR pszPropName, BYTE &Value);
    BOOL GetPropText(LPCTSTR pszPropName, BYTE* pValue);
    BOOL SetPropText(LPCTSTR pszPropName, int &Value);
    BOOL GetPropText(LPCTSTR pszPropName, int* pValue);
    BOOL SetPropText(LPCTSTR pszPropName, UINT &Value);
    BOOL GetPropText(LPCTSTR pszPropName, UINT* pValue);
    BOOL SetPropText(LPCTSTR pszPropName, long &Value);
    BOOL GetPropText(LPCTSTR pszPropName, long* pValue);
    BOOL SetPropText(LPCTSTR pszPropName, DWORD &Value);
    BOOL GetPropText(LPCTSTR pszPropName, DWORD* pValue);
    BOOL SetPropText(LPCTSTR pszPropName, CString &Value);
    BOOL GetPropText(LPCTSTR pszPropName, CString* pValue);
    BOOL SetPropText(LPCTSTR pszPropName, float &Value);
    BOOL GetPropText(LPCTSTR pszPropName, float* pValue);
    BOOL SetPropText(LPCTSTR pszPropName, double &Value);
    BOOL GetPropText(LPCTSTR pszPropName, double* pValue);
    BOOL SetPropCheck(LPCTSTR pszPropName, int Value);
    BOOL GetPropCheck(LPCTSTR pszPropName, int* pValue);
    BOOL SetPropRadio(LPCTSTR pszPropName, int Value);
    BOOL GetPropRadio(LPCTSTR pszPropName, int* pValue);
    BOOL SetPropIndex(LPCTSTR pszPropName, int Value);
    BOOL GetPropIndex(LPCTSTR pszPropName, int* pValue);
    CMapWordToOb m_DDPmap;   // Map of member
                             // vars to pending DDP data

    // Destructors
    ~COlePropertyPage();

protected:
    LRESULT WindowProc(UINT msg, WPARAM wParam, LPARAM lParam);
    BOOL OnCommand(WPARAM wParam, LPARAM lParam);
    BOOL PreTranslateMessage(LPMSG lpMsg);
    virtual void OnFinalRelease();
    void CleanupObjectArray();
    static BOOL CALLBACK EXPORT EnumChildProc(HWND hWnd,
                LPARAM lParam);
    static BOOL CALLBACK EXPORT EnumControls(HWND hWnd,
                LPARAM lParam);

    // Member data
protected:
    AFX_MODULE_STATE* m_pModuleState;

private:
    BOOL m_bDirty;
```

(continues)

Listing 5.6 Continued

```
                    UINT m_idDlg;
                    UINT m_idCaption;
                    CString m_strPageName;
                    SIZE m_sizePage;
                    CString m_strDocString;
                    CString m_strHelpFile;
                    DWORD m_dwHelpContext;
                    LPPROPERTYPAGESITE m_pPageSite;

                    LPDISPATCH FAR* m_ppDisp; // Array of IDispatch
                                              // pointers, used to
                                              // access the properties of each
                                              // control
                    LPDWORD m_pAdvisors;      // Array of connection tokens used by
                                       // IConnectionPoint::Advise/UnAdvise.
                    BOOL m_bPropsChanged;
                                       // IPropertyNotifySink::OnChanged has been
                                       // called, but not acted upon yet.
                    ULONG m_nObjects; // Objects in m_ppDisp,
                                      //m_ppDataObj, m_pAdvisors
                    BOOL m_bInitializing;  // TRUE if the
                                           // contents of the fields of
                                           // the dialog box are being initialized
                    int m_nControls;
                    AFX_PPFIELDSTATUS* m_pStatus;   // Array containing
                                                    // information on
                                                    // which fields are dirty
                    CWordArray m_IDArray;
                                // controls to ignore when deciding if
                                // the apply button is to be enabled
                    HGLOBAL m_hDialog;          // Handle of the dialog resource
            // Interface Maps
            protected:
                BEGIN_INTERFACE_PART(PropertyPage, IPropertyPage2)
                    INIT_INTERFACE_PART(COlePropertyPage, PropertyPage)
                    STDMETHOD(SetPageSite)(LPPROPERTYPAGESITE);
                    STDMETHOD(Activate)(HWND, LPCRECT, BOOL);
                    STDMETHOD(Deactivate)();
                    STDMETHOD(GetPageInfo)(LPPROPPAGEINFO);
                    STDMETHOD(SetObjects)(ULONG, LPUNKNOWN FAR*);
                    STDMETHOD(Show)(UINT);
                    STDMETHOD(Move)(LPCRECT);
                    STDMETHOD(IsPageDirty)();
                    STDMETHOD(Apply)();
                    STDMETHOD(Help)(LPCTSTR);
                    STDMETHOD(TranslateAccelerator)(LPMSG);
                    STDMETHOD(EditProperty)(DISPID);
                END_INTERFACE_PART(PropertyPage)

                BEGIN_INTERFACE_PART(PropNotifySink, IPropertyNotifySink)
                    INIT_INTERFACE_PART(COlePropertyPage, PropNotifySink)
                    STDMETHOD(OnRequestEdit)(DISPID);
```

```
        STDMETHOD(OnChanged)(DISPID);
    END_INTERFACE_PART(PropNotifySink)

    DECLARE_INTERFACE_MAP()
};
```

CPropExchange

CPropExchange provides support for OLE Controls. It allows controls to save state information about its properties to a storage medium. In fact, it is the base class for two additional classes, CArchivePropExchange and CResetPropExchange. The CArchivePropExchange class is used to store properties to a storage medium. CResetPropExchange is used to initialize properties.

The COleControl::DoPropExchange takes a pointer to one of the following classes as a parameter. Listing 5.7 shows the class defination.

Method	Description
ExchangeFontProp	Exchanges a font property.
ExchangeProp	Exchanges properties of any built-in type.
ExchangeBlobProp	Exchanges a binary large object (BLOB) property.
ExchangePersistentProp	Exchanges a property between a control and a file.
ExchangeVersion	Exchanges the version number of an OLE control.
IsLoading	Indicates whether properties are being loaded into the control or saved from it.
GetVersion	Retrieves the version number of an OLE control.

Listing 5.7   *CPropExchange*

```
class CPropExchange
{
// Operations
public:
    BOOL IsLoading();
    DWORD GetVersion();
    BOOL ExchangeVersion(DWORD& dwVersionLoaded,
            DWORD dwVersionDefault,
        BOOL bConvert);

    virtual BOOL ExchangeProp(LPCTSTR pszPropName, VARTYPE vtProp,
```

(continues)

Listing 5.7 Continued

```
                    void* pvProp, const void*
                        pvDefault = NULL) = 0;
        virtual BOOL ExchangeBlobProp(LPCTSTR pszPropName,
                    HGLOBAL* phBlob,
                    HGLOBAL hBlobDefault = NULL) = 0;
        virtual BOOL ExchangeFontProp(LPCTSTR pszPropName,
                    CFontHolder& font,
                    const FONTDESC FAR* pFontDesc,
                    LPFONTDISP pFontDispAmbient) = 0;
        virtual BOOL ExchangePersistentProp(LPCTSTR pszPropName,
                    LPUNKNOWN FAR* ppUnk,
                        REFIID iid, LPUNKNOWN pUnkDefault) = 0;

// Implementation
protected:
    CPropExchange();
    BOOL m_bLoading;
    DWORD m_dwVersion;
};
```

COleObjectFactoryEx

This class extends the functionality of the standard `COleObjectFactory` which is used to create COM objects. `COleObjectFactory` was extended to add licensing support for OLE Controls.

If you ask the ControlWizard to add licensing support to your control, a pair of macros—`BEGIN_OLEFACTORY` and `END_OLEFACTORY`—are inserted in the class declaration for the control. These macros expand to create an `COleObjectFactoryEx` object as an embedded member of the control class. The following table lists each of the methods and a description. Listing 5.8 shows the definition of the class.

Method	Description
`GetNextFactory`	Gets the next object factory in the DLL.
`UpdateRegistryAll`	Registers all the DLL's object factories with the OLE system registry.
`IsLicenseValid`	Indicates whether the control is licensed for design-time use.
`UpdateRegistry`	Registers this object factory with the OLE system registry.
`VerifyUserLicense`	Verifies that the control is licensed for design-time use.
`GetLicenseKey`	Requests a unique key from the control's DLL.

Method	Description
VerifyLicenseKey	Verifies that the key embedded in the control matches the key embedded in the container.

Listing 5.8 *COleObjectFactoryEx* **from the MFC Classes**

```
class COleObjectFactoryEx : public COleObjectFactory
{
    DECLARE_DYNAMIC(COleObjectFactoryEx)

// Constructors
public:
    COleObjectFactoryEx(REFCLSID clsid,
            CRuntimeClass* pRuntimeClass,
        BOOL bMultiInstance, LPCTSTR lpszProgID);

// Operations
    static BOOL PASCAL UpdateRegistryAll(BOOL bRegister);
    COleObjectFactory* GetNextFactory();
    BOOL IsLicenseValid();

// Overridables
    virtual BOOL UpdateRegistry(BOOL bRegister) = 0;
    virtual BOOL VerifyUserLicense();
    virtual BOOL GetLicenseKey(DWORD dwReserved,
            BSTR FAR* pbstrKey);
    virtual BOOL VerifyLicenseKey(BSTR bstrKey);

// Implementation
protected:
    AFX_MODULE_STATE* m_pModuleState;
    BYTE m_bLicenseChecked;
    BYTE m_bLicenseValid;

// Interface Maps
    BEGIN_INTERFACE_PART(ClassFactory2, IClassFactory2)
        INIT_INTERFACE_PART(COleObjectFactoryEx, ClassFactory2)
        STDMETHOD(CreateInstance)(LPUNKNOWN, REFIID,
                LPVOID FAR*);
        STDMETHOD(LockServer)(BOOL);
        STDMETHOD(GetLicInfo)(LPLICINFO);
        STDMETHOD(RequestLicKey)(DWORD, BSTR FAR*);
        STDMETHOD(CreateInstanceLic)(LPUNKNOWN,
                LPUNKNOWN, REFIID, BSTR,
            LPVOID FAR*);
    END_INTERFACE_PART(ClassFactory2)

    DECLARE_INTERFACE_MAP()
};
```

Event Maps

As you saw in Chapter 3, the ability of OLE controls to generate events is an important part of their functionality. In this section, you will see how events are handled in MFC.

Adding an event to your control application begins with invoking the ClassWizard. Once the ClassWizard appears, select the Events tab (see fig. 5.4). Here, you select the external and internal name for the event that you are creating.

Fig. 5.4
The ClassWizard shows the OLE Events tab for configuring OLE events.

The ClassWizard will then set up the Event Maps for this event in the source code. The following lines will be added to your modules header file:

```
// Event maps
//{{AFX_EVENT(CQuoteCtrl)
void FireMyEvent()
    {FireEvent(eventidMyEvent,EVENT_PARAM(VTS_NONE));}
//}}AFX_EVENT
DECLARE_EVENT_MAP()
```

As you can see, the event map declares and implements the FireMyEvent function. The FireEvent function is the standard function, implemented by the framework, for firing events. It takes a DISPID as its first parameter and a variable list of other parameters. In this case, your event does not take any parameters so the parameter list is VTS_NONE.

The DISPID is defined in the AFX_DISP_ID enum:

```
public:
    enum {
    //{{AFX_DISP_ID(CQuoteCtrl)
    dispidShowAuthor = 1L,
    eventidMyEvent = 1L,
    //}}AFX_DISP_ID
    };
```

The DECLARE_EVENT_MAP is very similar to the DECLARE_MESSAGE_MAP that most of you are familiar with. In fact, the macro expands to the same code as you can see here:

```
private:
    static AFX_DATA AFX_EVENTMAP_ENTRY BASED_CODE _eventEntries[];
protected:
    static AFX_DATA AFX_EVENTMAP BASED_CODE eventMap;
    virtual AFX_EVENTMAP FAR* GetEventMap() const;
```

_eventEntries is an array that is used to hold the event map entries. eventMap will hold a pointer to the event map and GetEventMap will return a pointer to an event map.

In the CPP source file, the event map is declared as follows:

```
///////////////////////////////////////////////////////////////
// Event map
//
BEGIN_EVENT_MAP(CQuoteCtrl, COleControl)
    //{{AFX_EVENT_MAP(CQuoteCtrl)
    EVENT_CUSTOM("MyEvent", FireMyEvent, VTS_NONE)
    //}}AFX_EVENT_MAP
END_EVENT_MAP()
```

These macros expand as follows:

```
AFX_EVENTMAP FAR* CQuoteCtl::GetEventMap() const
{
    return &eventMap;
}

AFX_DATADEF AFX_EVENTMAP BASED_CODE CQuoteCtl::eventMap =
{
    &(COleControl::eventMap),
    CQuoteCtl::_eventEntries
};

AFX_DATADEF AFX_EVENTMAP_ENTRY BASED_CODE
CQuoteCtl::_eventEntries[] =
{
    { afxEventCustom, DISPID_UNKNOWN, _T("MyEvent"), VTS_NONE},
    { afxEventCustom, DISPID_UNKNOWN, NULL, NULL },
};
```

As you can see, the event array is now initialized to include the name and parameter list for your custom event. The GetEventMap method returns a pointer to your event map. Your event map itself contains a pointer to your base class' (`COleControl`) event map and a pointer to your array of event entries.

MFC now has all the information that it needs to locate your event handlers. When an event needs to be fired, the framework will walk the chain of event maps until it locates the actual handler.

In this case, your handler is called `FireMyEvent` and is implemented inline in the event map declaration:

```
// Event maps
//{{AFX_EVENT(CQuoteCtrl)
void FireMyEvent()
    {FireEvent(eventidMyEvent,EVENT_PARAM(VTS_NONE));}
//}}AFX_EVENT
DECLARE_EVENT_MAP()
```

`FireMyEvent` calls the MFC `FireEvent` method. `FireEvent` takes a `DISPID` as its first parameter. The `DISPID`, which is a 32-bit value, uniquely identifies the method or property within a particular dispatch interface. `FireEvent` takes a variable number of parameters. Once the parameter list has been parsed, it will then retrieve a dispatch interface pointer. Once the pointer has been retrieved, `IDispatch::Invoke` will be called using the `DISPID` and the parameter list. The following code shows the implementation of `COleControl::FireEvent`:

```
void COleControl::FireEventV(DISPID dispid,
        BYTE FAR* pbParams, va_list argList)
{
    COleDispatchDriver driver;

    const CPtrArray* pConnections =
        m_xEventConnPt.GetConnections();
    ASSERT(pConnections != NULL);

    int i;
    int cConnections = pConnections->GetSize();
    LPDISPATCH pDispatch;

    for (i = 0; i < cConnections; i++)
    {
        pDispatch = (LPDISPATCH)(pConnections->GetAt(i));
        ASSERT(pDispatch != NULL);
        driver.AttachDispatch(pDispatch, FALSE);
        TRY
            driver.InvokeHelperV(dispid,
                    DISPATCH_METHOD, VT_EMPTY, NULL,
                        pbParams, argList);
        END_TRY
        driver.DetachDispatch();
```

```
        }
    }

    void COleControl::FireEvent(DISPID dispid, BYTE FAR* pbParams, ...)
    {
        va_list argList;
        va_start(argList, pbParams);
        FireEventV(dispid, pbParams, argList);
        va_end(argList);
    }
```

Connection Maps

You have already examined connection points in the OLE control architecture. To assist you in creating connections between OLE controls and their containers, MFC has added connection maps. These maps work in a very similar fashion to the event maps that you examined in the previous section.

Normally, a control will only support two connections—one for events and the other for notifications, such as advise sinks. The COleControl class provides a default implementation of each of these connections for you. However, if you need to provide other connections, you will need to implement them yourself. The ControlWizard will not be of any help. The macros defined in the following table show a brief description of each.

Macro	Description
BEGIN_CONNECTION_PART	Declares an embedded class that implements an additional connection point (must be used in the class declaration).
END_CONNECTION_PART	Ends the declaration of a connection point (must be used in the class declaration).
CONNECTION_IID	Specifies the interface ID of the control's connection point.
DECLARE_CONNECTION_MAP	Declares that a connection map will be used in a class (must be used in the class declaration).
BEGIN_CONNECTION_MAP	Begins the definition of a connection map (must be used in the class implementation).
END_CONNECTION_MAP	Ends the definition of a connection map (must be used in the class implementation).
CONNECTION_PART	Specifies a connection point in the control's connection map.

Global MFC Functions

In addition to the new MFC classes that have been previewed here, a number of global functions have been added to MFC to assist you when developing OLE controls. Because each of these functions is not part of any specific class with the MFC freamwork, you can access them from anywhere within your program. They are as follows:

Table 5.11 Global MFC Functions	
Function	**Description**
AfxConnectionAdvise	This function is used to establish a connection between a source and a sink.
AfxConnectionUnadvise	This function breaks an already established connection between a source and a sink.
AfxOleRegisterControlClass	This function registers the control's class with the system registry. Once a control is registered, it can be used by OLE control containers.
AfxOleRegisterPropertyPageClass	This function registers the control's property page class with the system registry.
AfxOleRegisterTypeLib	This function registers the control's type library with the system registry.
AfxOleUnregisterTypeLib	This function is used to remove a registered type library from the system registry.
AfxOleUnregisterClass	This function removes the property page class or the control class from the system registry.
AfxVerifyLicFile	This function verifies that the container is licensed to use the control.

From Here...

This chapter completes your look at the OLE controls SDK and the additions to MFC that Microsoft added to support OLE controls. As you can see, everything that you need to quickly create OLE controls is included in this chapter. For more information on topics in this chapter, refer to the following:

- Chapter 6, "Type Libraries, Licensing, and Versioning," examines type libraries and discusses how they are used with OLE controls. It also looks at versioning and licensing issues.

- Chapter 9, "Building the Comm Custom Control," provides information about the actual development of OLE controls.

Chapter 6

Type Libraries, Licensing, and Versioning

In this chapter, you examine type libraries in detail. Type libraries are used extensively by OLE automation controllers and controls. They are used to describe and expose methods and properties. You will see how they are created and used by OLE controls.

You then examine the licensing mechanisms employed by OLE controls. The issue of licensing is very important to developers of component software because it is the only means of ensuring that they get paid for their work.

Finally, you look at how OLE supports versioning of objects. As more and more OLE controls become available and developers begin shipping new versions, this is an issue that everybody will have to contend with.

In this chapter, the following topics are covered:

- OLE type libraries
- Licensing issues
- Version control for OLE objects

Introduction to Type Libraries

Type libraries were first introduced with OLE automation. They provide a means for developers to expose and describe their object's functionality. Type libraries can be accessed by Object Browsers and Scripting tools such as Visual

Basic's `ITypeLib` and `ITypeInfo` COM interfaces. Type libraries are necessary for the run-time binding of objects.

Type libraries are made available in three ways:

- *Type libraries can be a resource in an application's DLL.* This resource's type should be declared as `typelib`, and its integer ID should be 1. The following line shows how it should be declared:

    ```
    1 typelib mylib.tlb
    ```

    There can be only one resource of this type. Application developers use the resource compiler to add the TLB file to their own DLL. A DLL with a type-library resource typically has the extension OLB (object library).

- *Type libraries can be stored within compound files.* The sub-storage used for type libraries must be called:

    ```
    "\006typelib"
    ```

    The name is a quoted string that begins with a control character (ASCII 6) plus the identifier `typelib` (`\006` represents 6 within the string, using octal notation).

- *Type libraries may also be distributed as stand-alone files.* The output from the `Mktyplib` utility is a type library. Libraries usually have a TLB or OLB extension.

Developers of OLE automation servers describe all their exposed methods and properties through a type library. With the introduction of OLE controls, new extensions to type libraries were needed. In some cases, OLE controls use the `MiscStatus` bits in the system registry, but in cases where these simple bits are not enough, a type library is used. OLE controls use type libraries to expose properties and methods to OLE control containers.

Object Description Language

The Object Description Language (ODL) is the language used by developers to describe an object's methods and properties.

You now examine the structure of a type library as it is described using ODL. The basic syntax for a type library is

```
[attributes] library libraryname { librarycontents };
```

The `attributes` for a type library include the library's `UUID`, a default help string that describes the function of the library, and the library's local ID. The local ID describes what national language the type library is written in.

Next comes the keyword—Library—followed by the actual name of the library. This is the name used to load the library to access its exposed interfaces.

`librarycontents` contains information about various interfaces supported by the library, enumerations, structures, and other data types. Information about COM classes are also described here. Table 6.1 shows most of the common keywords found in a type library.

Table 6.1   Elements of a Type Library

Category	Library Element	Description
Directive for referencing other type libraries. Must precede all other library contents entries.	`importlib (lib1)`	Specifies an external type library (in this case `lib1`) whose definitions may be referenced in this type library.
Data type declarations used by the objects in this type library. Must appear before any references to the types.	`typedef[attributes]`	An alias declared using C syntax. Must have at least one attribute to be included in the type library.
`typedef`	`[attributes] enum`	An enumeration declared using C `typedef` and `enum` keywords.
`typedef`	`[attributes] struct`	A structure declared using C `typedef` and `struct` keywords.
`typedef`	`[attributes] union`	A union declared using C `typedef` and `union` keywords.
DLL description functions (make querying the DLL possible)	`[attributes] module`	Constants and a group of general data functions whose actions are not restricted to any specified class of objects (functions exposed by a DLL and not accessed through `vtable` entries).
Interface descriptions	`[attributes] dispinterface`	An IDispatch interface describing the methods and properties for an object that can be accessed through `IDispatch::Invoke`. The property accessor functions and methods are not in the vtable of the interface.

(continues)

Table 6.1 Continued		
Category	**Library Element**	**Description**
		Therefore, `DispInvoke` and `CreateStdDispatch` can't be used to provide an implementa tion of `IDispatch::Invoke`.
`[attributes]`	`interface`	Interface describing functions, including property accessor functions and methods of an object. These functions are in the `vtable` of the interface, so `DispInvoke` and `CreateStdDispatch` can be used to provide an implementation of `IDispatch::Invoke`.
OLE class descriptions	`[attributes]` `CoClass`	Specifies a top-level object, with all its interfaces and dispinterfaces, which can be created by OLE's `CoCreateInstance` or DispTest's `CreateObject` function.

Example ODL Files

You now examine some sample ODL files that are used to build type libraries. The first file is used to create a type library for an OLE automation server. The second ODL file is generated by the ControlWizard supplied with the OLE control SDK. The ODL file is used by an OLE control.

In the first section of the ODL file in listing 6.1, you see the `attributes` for the library listed. As you can see, you begin with the UUID for the library. This UUID is required and ensures that the library has a unique name. Next, you have the help string that can be used to identify the library. The help string is often followed by a help context that gives the value of a context jump within a help file.

The `LCID` file is the local ID for the help file. Because type libraries are used to describe methods and properties to the end-user via scripting languages such as Visual Basic, localizing the names of the methods and properties in differ-ent national languages is very important. The local ID is used to identify the national language.

Finally, you use a version number to further identify the type library in the future. That completes the `attributes` section of this type library.

You then name the library; in this case, it is `AutoSrv`. This is the name that is registered in the system registry and used by applications that want to access information from this type library.

Now you come to the contents of the library. This library describes one Component Object Class, `AutoSrv`; one dispatch interface, `_DAutoSrv`; and one COM interface, `_IAutoSrv`. Notice that the syntax for each of these sections follows the same format as the structure of the library itself. In other words, you begin with the `attributes`, then the name, and finally the contents.

Before you examine the interfaces described in this ODL file, one line is worth mentioning. The `importlib` command is used to import another type library into this one. In this case, you are importing `stdole.tlb`. This type library, which is supplied with the OLE SDK, contains the definitions for the `IDispatch` interface. Anytime you create a type library for an OLE automation controller, you must include this type library.

You begin by using the keyword `CoClass` to define a component object class. In this case, the class name is `AutoSrv`. The `AutoSrv` class has the attributes of a `CLSID`, which is used to uniquely identify the class and a help string that give a human readable name to the class.

The `CoClass` defines two interfaces. The first one is the `IDispatch` interface that is the primary OLE automation interface. You look at the implementation of `_DAutoSrv` in a moment. The other interface is your own interface `_IAutoSrv`.

The `IDispatch` interface is prefixed with the keyword `dispinterface`. As usual, you have a set of attributes associated with each section. The `UUID` is the Interface ID (IID) associated with your interface. You also have a help string that can be used to identify the interface. The dispatch interface is implemented by the `_IAutoSrv` interface.

As before, the interface definition is prefixed by its attributes. Your interface, like all COM interfaces, inherits from `IUnknown`. You can now list the methods exposed by this interface. In this case, there is only one—`GetQuote`—which does not take any parameters and returns a BSTR data type as a return value. If you had any properties, they are also listed here.

Listing 6.1   The ODL File

```
[
    uuid(82D56580-591B-101B-BB57-00608CC0BA93),
    helpstring("Creating OLE Controls"),
    lcid(0x0409),
    version(1.0)
]
library AutoSrv
{
    importlib("stdole.tlb");

    [
        // The uuid for the interface IID_IObject.
        odl,
        uuid(8B0D9560-591B-101B-BB57-00608CC0BA93),
        helpstring("Automation Quote Server")
    ]

    interface _IAutoSrv : IUnknown
    {
        BSTR GetQuote(void);
    }


    [
        uuid(910B1780-591B-101B-BB57-00608CC0BA93),
        helpstring("Automation Quote Server DispInterface")
    ]

    dispinterface _DAutoSrv
    {
        interface _IAutoSrv;
    }


    [
        // This is the UUID for our object class
        uuid(72B15100-591B-101B-BB57-00608CC0BA93),
        helpstring("Automation Quote Server")
    ]
    CoClass AutoSrv
    {
        dispinterface _DAutoSrv;
        interface _IAutoSrv;
    }
};
```

You now continue and examine an ODL file generated by the ControlWizard in listing 6.2. As before you begin with the attributes for the library, then the name for the library, and finally the contents.

Notice that in addition to the `stdole.tlb` that you import for `IDispatch` support, you now include an additional library for supporting OLE controls.

You begin with the COM class Quote. A new attribute, licensed, indicates that this control supports licensing. Your interface supports two dispatch interfaces, _Dquote and _DQuoteEvents. Each of these definitions is also preceded by attributes. The first interface has the attribute default. This means that this interface is the default one for this sink. The other attribute, source, means that this interface is called by your control, rather than implemented by your control.

As you can see, the ControlWizard takes care of defining the methods and properties for each interface. Notice that each method and property is prefixed by the ID keyword. This keyword is used to define the DISPID for each method or property. The DISPID is a unique 32-bit value that is used to identify the property or method.

Listing 6.2   The ODL File as Generated by the ControlWizard

```
#include <olectl.h> // Standard MFC include file
                    // for Control support

[ uuid(7C647083-F1CB-101B-81EC-B23169424630), version(1.0),
  helpstring("Quote OLE Custom Control module") ]
library QuoteLib
{
    importlib(STDOLE_TLB);
    importlib(STDTYPE_TLB);

    //  Primary dispatch interface for CQuoteCtrl

    [ uuid(7C647081-F1CB-101B-81EC-B23169424630),
      helpstring("Dispatch interface for Quote Control") ]
    dispinterface _DQuote
    {
        properties:
            // {{AFX_ODL_PROP(CQuoteCtrl)
            [id(DISPID_BACKCOLOR), bindable,
            ➡requestedit] OLE_COLOR BackColor;
            [id(DISPID_FORECOLOR), bindable,
            ➡requestedit] OLE_COLOR ForeColor;
            [id(DISPID_FONT), bindable] IFontDisp* Font;
            [id(1)] boolean ShowAuthor;
            //}}AFX_ODL_PROP

        methods:
            //{{AFX_ODL_METHOD(CQuoteCtrl)
            [id(DISPID_DOCLICK)] void DoClick();
            //}}AFX_ODL_METHOD

            [id(DISPID_ABOUTBOX)] void AboutBox();
    };

    //  Event dispatch interface for CQuoteCtrl
```

(continues)

```
Listing 6.2   Continued

    [ uuid(7C647082-F1CB-101B-81EC-B23169424630),
      helpstring("Event interface for Quote Control") ]
    dispinterface _DQuoteEvents
    {
        properties:
            //  Event interface has no properties

        methods:
            //{{AFX_ODL_EVENT(CQuoteCtrl)
            [id(DISPID_DBLCLICK)] void DblClick();
            //}}AFX_ODL_EVENT
    };

    //  Class information for CQuoteCtrl

    [ uuid(7C647080-F1CB-101B-81EC-B23169424630), licensed,
      helpstring("Quote Control") ]
    CoClass Quote
    {
        [default] dispinterface _DQuote;
        [default, source] dispinterface _DQuoteEvents;
    };


    //{{AFX_APPEND_ODL}}
};
```

Type Library Attributes

As you saw in the previous sections, various keywords in a type library can have a number of different attributes. Table 6.2 shows the available attributes.

Table 6.2   Type Library Attributes

Attribute	Used On	Effect	Comments
appobject	CoClass	Identifies the Application object.	Indicates that the members of the class may be accessed without qualification when accessing this type of library.
bindable	Property	Indicates that the property supports data binding.	Refers to the property as a whole, so it must be specified wherever the property is defined. This may mean specifying the attribute on both

Attribute	Used On	Effect	Comments
			the property Get description and on the property Set description. Representations: FUNCFLAG_FBINDABLE, VARFLAG_FBINDABLE
default	Member of a CoClass	Indicates that the interface or dispinterface represents the default for the source or sink.	Representation: IMPLTYPEFLAG_ FDEFAULT
defaultbind	Property	Indicates the single bindable property that best represents the object. Used by containers having a user model that involves binding to an object rather than binding to a property of an object.	An object can support data binding but not have this attribute. Properties having the defaultbind attribute must also have the bindable attribute. Can't specify defaultbind on more than one property in a dispinterface. Representation: FUNCFLAG_ FDEFAULTBIND, VARFLAG_ FDEFAULTBIND
displaybind	Property	Set on those properties recommended by the object to be displayed to the user as bindable.	An object can support data binding but not have this attribute. The property that has the displaybind attribute must also have the bindable attribute. Representations: FUNCFLAG_ FDISPLAYBIND, VARFLAG_ FDISPLAYBIND
dllname(str)	Module		Defines the name of the DLL that contains the module entry points.
entry(entryid)	Function in a Module	Identifies the entry point in the DLL. If entryid is a string, this	Provides a way to obtain the address of a function in a module.

(continues)

Table 6.2 Continued

Attribute	Used On	Effect	Comments
		is a named entry point. If `entryid` is a number, the entry point is defined by an ordinal.	
`helpcontext` `(numctxt)`	Interface, library, dispinterface, struct, enum, union, module, typedef, method, struct member, enum value, property, CoClass, const	Retrieved via the GetDocumentation functions in the `ITypeLib` and `ITypeInfo` interfaces.	The `numctxt` is a 32-bit Help context within the Help file.
`helpfile` `(filenam)`	Library	Retrieved via the GetDocumentation functions in the `ITypeLib` and `ITypeInfo` interfaces.	All types in a library share the same Help file.
`helpstring` `(string)`	Library, interface, dispinterface, struct, enum, union, module, typedef, method, struct member, enum value, property, CoClass, const	Retrieved via the GetDocumentation functions in the `ITypeLib` and `ITypeInfo` interfaces.	

Attribute	Used On	Effect	Comments
id(num)	Method or property in interface or disp-interface	Identifies the DISPID of the member.	The num is a 32-bit integral value.
in	Parameter	Parameter receives a value.	Specifies an input parameter. The parameter may be a pointer (as with char *) but the value it refers to is not returned.
lcid(numid)	Library	Identifies the locale for the library.	The numid is a 32-bit local ID as used in Win32 National Language Support. This is typically entered in hexadecimal.
licensed	CoClass	Indicates that the class is licensed.	Representation: TYPEFLAG_FLICENSED
odl	Interface (required)	Identifies an interface as an ODL interface. This attribute must appear on all interfaces.	
optional	Parameter	Parameter may be omitted.	Specifies an optional. Valid only if the parameter is of type VARIANT. All subsequent parameters of the function must be optional.
parameter	Parameter supplies a value	Specifies an output parameter. The parameter must be a pointer to memory that receives a result.	
propget	Functions; methods in interfaces and disp-interfaces	Causes the INVOKEKIND in the funcdesc to be INVOKE_PROPERTY-GET.	Specifies a property-accessor function for the property with the same name as the function. At most, one of propget, propput, and propputref can be specified for a function.

(continues)

Table 6.2	Continued		
Attribute	**Used On**	**Effect**	**Comments**
propput	Functions; methods in interfaces and disp-interfaces	Causes the INVOKEKIND in the funcdesc to INVOKE_PROPERTY-PUT.	Specifies a property-setting function for the property with the same name as the function. At most, one of propget, propput, and propputref can be specified.
propputref	Functions; methods in interfaces and disp-interfaces	Causes the INVOKEKIND in the funcdesc to be INVOKE_PROPERTYPUTREF.	Specifies a property-setting function that sets the reference for the property with the name of the function. At most, one of propget, propput, and propputref can be specified.
public	Aliases declared with typedef	Causes an alias to be included in the type library.	Specifies that an alias created with typedef (and having no other attributes) should be included in the type library. Otherwise, an alias created with typedef (and having no other attributes) is treated as a #define.
readonly		Causes the variable's VARDESC structure to have its wVarFlags element set with VAR-FLAG_FREADONLY.	If the flag is set, assignment to the variable should not be allowed.
requestedit	Property	The property supports the OnRequestEdit notification, raised by a property before it is edited.	An object can support data binding but not have this attribute. Representations: FUNCFLAG_FREQUESTEDIT, VARFLAG_FREQUESTEDIT
restricted	Member of a CoClass	Prevents the interface or dispinterface from being used by a macro programmer.	Allowed on a member of a CoClass, independent of whether the member is a dispinterface or interface, and

Attribute	Used On	Effect	Comments
			independent of whether the member is a sink or source. A member of a CoClass cannot have both the restricted and default attributes. Representation: `IMPLTYPEFLAG_FRESTRICTED`
`restricted`	`Type libraries and members in modules and interfaces`	If specified, the FUNCDESC will have its wFuncFlags element set with `FUNCFLAG_FRESTRICTED`	Indicates that the function should not be called from macro languages. Corresponds to `FUNCFLAG_FRESTRICTED`
`source`	`Member of a CoClass`	Specified on a member of a CoClass that is called rather than implemented.	Representation: `IMPLTYPEFLAG_FSOURCE`.
`string`	`Struct, member, parameter, property`		Included only for compatibility with IDL; use LPSTR for a zero-terminated string.
`uuid(uuidval)`	`Library, dispinter-face, struct, enum, union, module, typedef, interface, CoClass`	This value is returned in the TypeAttr structure retrieved via `TypeInfo::Get-TypeAttr`	Optional for all but library, CoClass, and dispinterface. The `uuidval` is a 16-byte value formatted as hexadecimal digits in the following format: 12345678-1234-1234-1234-123456789ABC.
`vararg`	`All functions`		Indicates that the last parameter must be a safe array of VARIANT type.
`version (versionval)`	`Library, struct, module, dispinter-face, interface, CoClass, enum, union`		The argument `versionval` is a real number of the format $n.m$, where n is a major version number and m is a minor version number.

Type Library Extensions

A number of extensions have been added to type libraries with the release of OLE controls (see table 6.3). These extensions are new attributes; and these attributes are used to further describe control properties, methods, and controls themselves.

Table 6.3	Type Library Extensions		
Attribute	**Allowed On**	**Effect**	**Comments**
Bindable	Property	The property supports property binding.	Refers to the property as a whole, so it must be specified wherever the property is defined. This may mean specifying the attribute on both the property Get description and on the property Set description. Representations: FUNCFLAG_FBINDABLE, VARFLAG_FBINDABLE
Default	CoClass	Indicates that the interface or dispatch interface represents the default for the source or sink.	Representation: IMPLTYPEFLAG_FDEFAULT
DefaultBind	Property	Indicates the single bindable property that best represents the object. Used by containers having a user model that involves binding to an object rather than binding to a property of an object.	An object can support property binding but not have this attribute. Property having DefaultBind attribute must also have the Bindable attribute. Cannot specify DefaultBind on more than one property in a dispinterface. Representation: FUNCFLAG_FDEFAULTBIND, VARFLAG_FDEFAULTBIND
DisplayBind	Property	Set on those properties recommended by the object to be displayed to the user as bindable.	An object can support property binding but not have this attribute. The property that has the DisplayBind attribute must also have the Bindable attribute. Representations: FUNCFLAG_FDISPLAYBIND, VARFLAG_FDISPLAYBIND

Attribute	Allowed On	Effect	Comments
Licensed	CoClass	Indicates that the class is licensed.	Representation: TYPEFLAG_FLICENSED
RequestEdit	Property	The property supports the OnRequestEdit notification, raised by a property before it is edited.	An object can support property binding but not have this attribute. Representations: FUNCFLAG_ FREQUESTEDITBIND, VARFLAG_FREQUESTEDITBIND
Restricted	CoClass	Prevents the interface or dispatch interface from being used by a macro programmer.	Allowed on a member of a CoClass, independent of whether the member is a dispatch or other type interface, and independent of whether the member is a sink or source. A member of a CoClass cannot have both the Restricted and Default attributes.
Source	CoClass	Specified on a member of a CoClass that is called rather than implemented.	Representation: IMPTYPEFLAG_FSOURCE

Creating a Type Library

A type library compiler is supplied with the OLE SDK. This tool, which is called Mktyplib, is used to generate type libraries from ODL files. The tool can be invoked from the command line or from the Tools menu in the Visual C++ IDE. If you are using Visual C++ 2.0, then the type library compiler is automatically called when you build your control.

The compiler can also generate an optional header file that can be used by C or C++ programs that want to access the functionality exposed by the type library. The compiler is invoked as follows. Table 6.4 describes each of the parameters available.

```
MkTypLib [options] ODLfile
```

Table 6.4 Command Line Options Available for *Mytyplib*

Option	Description
/? or /help	Displays command-line Help. The ODLfile does not need to be specified in this case.
/align:alignment	Sets the default alignment for types in the library. An alignment value of 1 indicates natural alignment; n indicates alignment on byte n.
/D define[=value]	Defines the name define for the C preprocessor. The value is its optional value. No space is allowed between the equal sign and the value.
/I includedirectory	Specifies includedirectory as the directory where include files are located for the C preprocessor.
/tlb filename	Specifies filename as the name of the output TLB file. If not specified, this is the same as the name of the ODL file with the extension TLB.
/h filename	Specifies filename as the name for a stripped version of the input file. This file can be used as a C or C++ header file. The output is defined in the section H file output.
/Win16, /Win32, /mac, /mips, /alpha, /ppc, or /ppc32	Specifies type of output that the type library is to produce. The default is /Win16.
/nologo	Disables display of the copyright banner.
/nocpp	Suppresses invocation of the C preprocessor.
/cpp_cmd cpppath	Specifies cpppath as the command to run the C preprocessor. By default, MkTypLib invokes CL.
/cpp_opt "options"	Specifies options for the C preprocessor. The default is "/C /E /D__MKTYPLIB__".
/o outputfile	Redirects output (for example, error messages) to specified outputfile.
/w0	Disables warnings.

With the release of the OLE control SDK for Visual C++ 2.0, it is now possible to invoke the Mktyplib compiler directly from a project file. If you are using the 16-bit CDK with Visual C++ 1.5, you need to invoke the type-library compiler separately from the Tools menu.

Motivation for Licensing

For developers of component objects such as OLE controls, the question of controlling and licensing the component is an important one. The main problem is that the controls must be distributed with each application, and there is nothing to stop users from reusing the controls in another application. After all, this is supposed to be one of the benefits of component software.

In order to distinguish between the buyer of a control using the control in building an application and the user of that application using the control, two modes of use are required—design-time mode and run-time mode.

The control is in design-time mode when it is being used to build an application. The control is in run-time mode when it is being used as part of an application.

Licensing Implementation

The licensing scheme is designed such that the control can verify access to its functionality through a key. When an application developer buys a control, the developer receives a DLL containing the control and a license file.

When the developer loads the control into his or her container and attempts to initialize it, the control looks for the license file. (The license file, which usually has the extension LIC, is located in the same directory as the control.) If it finds the file, then an instance of the control is created (see fig. 6.1).

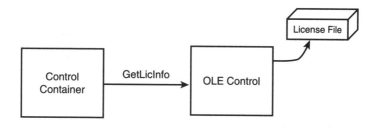

Fig. 6.1
Verifying the existence of the license file.

Once the control has been successfully created, the control container may request the key from the control. The container then stores the key in its own compound file (see fig. 6.2).

Fig. 6.2
Requesting the
license key from
the control.

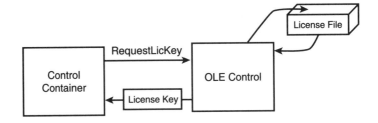

If the control is then distributed with the completed application, the license file is not included. When the container attempts to create an instance of the control, the license file cannot be found, and you cannot use the control. In this case, the control asks the container for the cached (stored) key. If the key matches the key stored within the control, the control allows itself to be instantiated (see fig. 6.3).

Fig. 6.3
Verifying the
license.

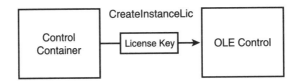

If a user attempts to use a control in a container that does not contain the correct cached key and the license file is not available, the control cannot be used. The license file is known as the design-time key, and the cached key is the run-time key.

The licensing scheme described here is extremely flexible. Instead of using the license–key-file mechanism, the control developer can use Licensing APIs (LSAPI) to control usage of a control on a network. A developer can also implement various tiers of functionality that unlock with different license keys. This enables the developer to ship a "lite" version of a control for say $40, with an upgrade to a "professional" version for an additional $100.

COM Extensions To Support Licensing

Licensing support was not originally built into OLE and a number of extensions to COM were necessary in order to support it. The fact that these extensions can be transparently added demonstrates the extendibility of the COM architecture.

The obvious place to add licensing support is in the `IClassFactory` interface. However, because of the COM requirement that interfaces not be versioned, a new interface needs to be created. This interface is called `IClassFactory2`. It provides exactly the same functionality as the standard `IClassFactory` interface with the addition of three methods that are added for licensing support.

Listing 6.3   The *IClassFactory2* Interface

```
interface IClassFactory2 : public IClassFactory
{
    GetLicInfo(LICINFO FAR *plicinfo);
    RequestLicKey(DWORD dwReserved, BSTR FAR *pbstrKey);
    CreateInstanceLic(

        LPUNKNOWN pUnkOuter,
        LPUNKNOWN pUnkReserved,
        REFIID riid,
        BSTR bstrKey,
        LPVOID FAR *ppvObject);
};
```

A new datastructure, `LICINFO`, is defined to hold information about the licensing information. This structure is returned when `IClassFactory2::GetLicInfo` is called.

```
typedef struct licinfo
{
    long    cbLicInfo;    // Size of licinfo structure
    bool    fRuntimeKeyAvail;    // True if class offers a runtime
                                 // key for building into solution
    bool    fLicVerified;    // True if component has already
                             // verified machine/user lic
} LICINFO;
```

`IClassFactory2::RequestLicKey` is used to retrieve the actual license key. The `BSTR` type is used to allow developers to use more than just a simple string as a key. The `BSTR` data type has its length embedded as the first character, and it may also contain embedded '`\0`'s.

`IClassFactory2::CreateInstanceLic` is similar to the standard `IClassFactory::CreateInstance`. The only difference is that the license key is passed as a parameter. This method is used to perform verification on the license key. How the verification is performed is totally up to the developer; it can be as simple as comparing two strings, or a more sophisticated method can be employed.

Motivation for Versioning

Versioning of component objects can become quite a problem as more and more applications ship with third-party components. This issue affects not only control developers but also users of controls.

Two issues need to be addressed. The first one concerns how the new control works with older control containers. The second issue is how new containers function with older versions of the control.

To address these issues, Microsoft has defined two kinds of compatibility: *binary compatibility* and *source compatibility*.

Before you examine these issues in detail, it should be noted that OLE currently supports versioning of compound document objects. If you select an embedded object in a compound document, you see the Convert option. This option allows you to convert the object to a newer format or to a compatible format. Because this implementation relies on using IStorage and generic compound document interfaces, it is not suitable for use with OLE controls.

Binary Compatibility

Microsoft refers to binary compatibility between controls if the new control can fulfill the obligations of the original control through its CLSID and its interface IDs (IIDs).

Microsoft, in the OLE CDK documentation, states that for a control to support binary compatibility between revisions, it must fulfill the following rules:

- The new implementation must at least support the original CLSID. This means that the implementation is registered under the original CLSID in the registry, and that the class factory registered is available via DllGetClassObject on the server (or via CoRegisterClassObject for local servers).

- The new implementation of a component must support all the interfaces, including connection points, exactly as they were described in the original implementation's type library. This means that the new component's implementation of QueryInterface is able to return all the interfaces named in the old type library. The component's FindConnectionPointFromIID method, which is supplied to the container, should be able to return a connection point to the container for each outgoing interface named in the old type library. In addition, the component's `EnumConnectionPoints` enumerator should enumerate a connection point for each as well.

Following the normal OLE conventions, it's acceptable for the component to return an interface pointer to a new version of `IID` for the incoming interface, assuming that the new interface is a strict superset of the old interface. This can greatly simplify the task of continuing to support old interfaces. In `Dispatch` case, doing `GetTypeInfo` / `GetTypeInfoCount` may return a description of the new interface, rather than the old interface.

Similarly, it's acceptable for the component to map connection requests for an old `IID` connection point onto the connection point for the new version of the outgoing interface. When firing an event via `Invoke` (for a `Dispatch`-based connection point), the component may invoke methods that the event sink (receiving event handler) isn't expecting, corresponding to events that are part of the new version of the outgoing interface. The sink should simply ignore these and return `S_OK`.

With interface-based connection points, supporting multiple versions of the same interface on a single connection point is slightly more complicated. When attempting to `Advise` to a new event sink, the connection point first calls `QueryInterface` (QI) for the most derived interface— that is, the most recent version. If this QI fails, then the connection point calls QIs for the next most derived interface, and so on. The connection then keeps track of which version of the interface was supported by each event sink and only calls methods on the event sink that it supports.

■ It is acceptable for the new implementation to support additional interfaces and connection points. Furthermore, if the component supports `IProvideClassInfo`, the description returned from a running instance of the component may describe the interfaces for the new version of the component.

■ The new implementation must be capable of reading, without loss of information, a persistent image of the component saved by the original implementation. By definition, because an instance of the component was created via its original `CLSID`, any persistent load is an emulation.

■ The new implementation must be capable of writing out a persistent image of the component that can be read by the original implementation, where the only loss of information relates to functionality that was not part of the original implementation.

`IStream` objects can't use the `Read/WriteFmtUserTypeStg` or `Read/WriteClassStg` mechanisms to determine the originating version of a persistent image. It is recommended that some kind of version stamp be included in the stream format for such a class.

Source Compatibility

When a new version of a control is released, it can be assumed that the developer has added additional functionality. The new functionality can only be accessed by a newer version of the control container. If the changes are such that only minor changes to the source in the container are required in order to access this new functionality, then the control is said to be source compatible.

Microsoft, in the OLE CDK documentation, states that for a control to support source compatibility between revisions, the following rules must be fulfilled:

- If an interface is left intact syntactically and semantically, its corresponding `TypeInfo` in the type library can remain unchanged, and the interface should retain its original name and `IID`.

- If an interface is extended through the addition of new members and all original members are intact, then the interface should retain its original name but be given a new `IID`.

- If an interface is modified in other ways, for example, by adding a parameter to an existing method, the original interface must be described and supported via its original name, and the new interface must be given a new name and `IID`.

- The `CoClass` description for the component must contain all interfaces and connection points, according to their names, that the original `CoClass` description for the component contained. It may contain additional interfaces and connection points. The `CoClass` should retain its original name but be given a new `CLSID`.

- The new type library should be registered under the same `GUID/LCID` as the original type library. It should be given a higher version number.

- The new implementation of the component (created from its new `CLSID`) must be capable of reading a persistent image created by the original implementation of the component. It is not strictly required that it be able to write a persistent image that the original component implementation can read.

If the component supports IStream persistence, it should assume that loading a previously saved instance corresponds to a Conversion request. If the component supports IStorage persistence, it can distinguish between emulation and conversion requests via the normal OLE 2 IStorage-based conventions.

■ If the component uses another class, K, such that instances of K are exposed via one of the component's interfaces, and K also has source-compatible changes, then the source-compatible upgrade of the component must include or require a source-compatible upgrade of K so that the application can be correctly rebuilt.

Of course, it is possible for a control to provide both binary- and source-level compatibility. This is achieved through a new CLSID that provides access to the additional functionality and a new type library. It is vital that any changes made to an interface are provided by a new interface. If this interface is a superset of the original interface, then the control can map all QueryInterface calls on the old IID to the new IID. The user of the IID is not aware of the additional methods and properties provided by this new interface. The control should, however, be aware of what version of the CLSID that the control was created with. This helps the control provides any CLSID specific behavior that may be required.

From Here...

That concludes your look at type libraries, licensing issues, and versioning with OLE controls. In the next chapter, you examine the architecture of OLE control containers and see what changes need to be made to standard OLE containers in order to support the embedding of OLE controls.

For more information, see the following chapters:

■ Chapter 5, "The OLE Controls SDK," examines the MFC support for OLE controls in detail.

■ Chapters 9, "Building the Comm Custom Control," and 10, "Building the Timer Custom Control," will provide information about the actual development of OLE controls.

Chapter 7

Control Containers

by Edward B. Toupin

In this chapter, you learn about containers and how they utilize the functionality of OLE custom controls. You first take a look at standard OLE containers and how these containers incorporate OLE controls. You then delve into the object model interfaces that are used between custom controls and containers. Finally, you develop a container in Visual C++ in order to explore how containers operate with the controls discussed in Chapters 9, 10, and 11.

This chapter covers the following topics:

- Standard OLE containers

- Component Object Model interfaces

- The Component Object Model (COM)

- Creating a control container

What Is a Control Container?

A container provides a means of interfacing the functionality of a custom control with the environment. The capabilities of a container are very similar to those of a control and, in some cases, a container may be useful as a control itself.

Most of the necessary attributes for a control container are provided by the *Component Object Model* interfaces, which are required for in-place capable embedding containers. A control container, in addition, must supply two other sets of information and functionality to each control:

■ *Ambient properties* are named characteristics or values of the container itself that generally apply to all controls in the container. Some examples of ambient properties are color, font, and whether the container is in *design-time* or *run-time mode.*

Fig. 7.1
A control container allows you to build applications based on the Component Object Model with custom controls.

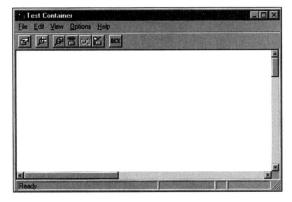

■ *Events* are translated by a control by converting external events from the user or another program into events useful to the container. The container must provide entry points to the control for each event the control might trigger.

NOTE

A *compound document* is a document within a container application that integrates data of different formats, such as sound clips, spreadsheets, text, and bitmaps. Each piece of integrated data, also known as a *compound document object,* is created and maintained by its object application. Rather than being concerned with managing multiple object applications, users can focus on the compound document and the task being performed.

Combining the capabilities previously described with the behavior of a compound document container and the requirements of a control, you have four necessary mechanisms for a control container:

■ Create, place, size, and save the runtime program that manages and interacts with controls.

■ Expose ambient properties to all controls.

■ Provide and expose event entry points to each specific control.

■ Inform controls of keyboard events.

Design-time Interaction

Assume that you are going to place two controls in a control container. When you select the type of control to place from the Insert Object dialog box, the control is automatically placed and sized in the document. To create the document with two controls, as shown in figure 7.2, you perform this process twice.

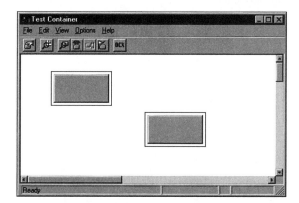

Fig. 7.2

A container application can contain multiple custom controls to create a fully operational component application. This container contains two button custom controls that operate independently of one another.

If you are reloading the object instead of creating a new one, the same process occurs, except the container calls OleLoad() instead of OleCreate().

When the rectangle for the control is set in the container, the container calls the OleCreate() function with the CLSID of the selected button control. As with other compound document objects, OLE looks up CLSID for the button in the system registry to find the BUTTON.OCX (BUTTON.DLL for 16-bit) listed as the server for that CLSID (see fig. 7.3). OLE then loads that OCX (DLL for 16-bit) and obtains the control's IClassFactory pointer to create a new instance of the object. In return, the container gets an IOleObject interface pointer back, which is used for communications between the control and the container.

The container now has its first interface pointer to the control through which the container tells the control of its height and width—IOleObject::SetExtents(). The container also checks if the object wants to be activated in-place through IOleObject::GetMiscStatus().

If the control wants to be activated, the container activates the control by calling IOleObject::DoVerb() with the standard verb OLEIVERB_INPLACEACTIVATE. This allows the control to become in-place *active* but not *UI-active*. Active means that the object has its own window in the container's window; while UI-active means that the object is utilizing its own user interface within the container. Essentially, UI-active applies to those applications that provide in-place activation and does not apply to custom controls.

Fig. 7.3

The system registry contains the CLSID for each control as well as the name of the control's server. OLE uses the system registry to provide a simple means of locating and loading custom control servers for container applications.

If the control uses a window when activated in-place, the control draws its bitmap in the window by using the default of the control. The buttons from figure 7.2 always use the font defined in the container's ambient property with the dispatch ID DISPID_AMBIENT_FONT. The control retrieves a pointer to the container's ambient properties from a call to IOleObject::SetClientSite() during the creation phase.

In order to access the container's font property, the control calls IOleClientSite::QueryInterface() to retrieve the container's ambient properties. The control then calls IDispatch::Invoke() with DISPID_AMBIENT_FONT to retrieve the required font information. The control can now draw itself with the correct font. If the control wants other information, such as colors, it calls IDispatch::Invoke() again with different IDs for those other ambient properties.

If the control is not using a window for in-place activation, it may still ask for the same properties from the container—the control needs those properties in order to draw itself in the container. In this case, in absence of a control window, the container calls OleDraw(), which calls the control's Draw()

member function. The control receives the container window's device context, and the control draws itself in a rectangle in the device context of the container.

Run-time Interaction

From the container in figure 7.2, you have a document with two buttons where clicking either button displays a message for the button click event. At this point, the container is connected to the control except for the IOleControl interface. The properties, methods, and the events of the control are in place, and the control is activated.

For the last part of this example, you need to review the *mnemonics* for the controls. When the container first enters run-time mode, it queries all controls in the container for their IOleControl interfaces and calls IOleControl::GetControlInfo() to obtain each control's keyboard flags. Whenever a key is pressed, the container first calls OleTranslateAccelerator(), which allows the control with the focus to access any keyboard messages before other controls. In this case, pressing the spacebar activates the button that has focus at the time of the event, which changes the control's visuals and fires a ButtonClicked event.

If you press the Alt+2 combination, for example, OleTranslateAccelerator() bypasses the active control and allows the container to capture the keystroke. The control container then checks each control's accelerator table, obtained from IOleControl::GetControlInfo(). If it finds a match to the Alt+2 keystroke, the container calls that control's IOleControl::OnMnemonic() function that lets the control change state, repaint, and fire events as appropriate.

Component Object Model Interfaces

Being the key to OLE's extensible architecture, the Component Object Model (COM) defines how objects interact with one another both within an application and between separate applications. The foundation of the model on which the rest of OLE is built provides mechanisms that support multiple interfaces between an object application and controlling applications (see fig. 7.4). The architecture is divided into services supported by the component object model (interface negotiation, memory management, error and status reporting, and interprocess communications) and other basic services built on the model.

A component object conforms to this model, implementing and using the interfaces that support object interaction. Component objects can be implemented using C++ classes or C structures. Component objects can be independent, stand-alone entities or a combination of other objects. Using a composition technique known as *aggregation*, a new object can be built using one or more existing objects that support some or all of the new object's required interfaces. This technique enables the new object to appear as a seamless whole rather than as a collection of independent parts.

Fig. 7.4
The Component Object Model is a layered architecture defining how objects interact with one another.

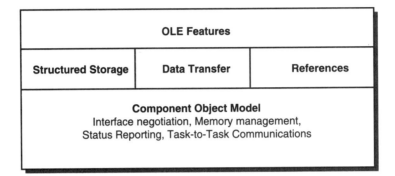

The model defines an interface by which a controlling application can communicate with a control or object application that provides a service for the requesting controlling application. Through the model, each object application can support multiple interfaces in order to service multiple controlling applications that may query about support for a specific interface or service.

The model provides a mechanism for interprocess communications that provides a means of allowing objects to communicate with controlling applications. This mechanism allows communications to exist across application boundaries so that controlling applications can pass information to the objects of object applications and vice versa.

The model also provides a means of dynamically loading and destroying objects. When an object is requested, the object application in which the requested object exists is loaded or, if the application is already running, the existing object application is accessed. Each access made by a controlling application increments a *reference counter* so that the model knows how many interfaces are currently active for an object application. Likewise, as controlling applications release control of an object application, the reference counter is decremented. When all references, and subsequent interfaces, are released, the object application is removed from memory and that memory is freed by the model.

The Component Object Model defines the following:

- An interface by which a client communicates with a service provider. The service provider, whether it is implemented in a DLL, OCX, VBX, or EXE is referred to as the object.

- An architecture where objects can support multiple interfaces such that potential clients can query an object about support for a specific interface.

- A reference counting model for object management that allows simultaneous use of objects by multiple clients as well as a way to determine when an object is no longer in use and can safely be destroyed.

- A mechanism where memory passed between clients and objects can be allocated and freed.

- A model for error and status reporting.

- A mechanism for allowing objects communication across process boundaries.

- A mechanism where an object implementation can be identified and loaded into a running system. The implementation may be local or remote and the difference is handled transparently.

Interfaces

Interfaces are the binary standard for component object interaction. Each interface contains a set of functions that defines how an object and its clients communicate. The interface communications includes the name of the interface, the function names, and the parameter names and types.

Clients use pointers to reference interfaces, obtaining them either by instantiating or querying the object. An interface pointer points to an array of function pointers known as a virtual table (VTBL). The functions that are pointed to by the members of the VTBL are called the *methods* or *member functions* of the interface. Figure 7.5 represents a run-time interface instance. A variable of a client points to the object's VTBL pointer, which in turn, points to the VTBL instance.

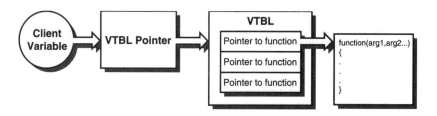

Fig. 7.5
The OLE interface model defines how client applications access the methods and members of an object.

Interfaces are abstract base classes that specify behavior in a general manner with no implementation. Interfaces are defined by OLE to be *pure virtual*—no implementation in the base class. OLE provides implementations for the interfaces that support the Component Object Model and parts of the model as well as for interfaces that support application features. Applications typically implement some of the interfaces, such as those that support data transfer, and some of the feature-specific interfaces. If an OLE implementation of a particular interface is somehow unsuitable, an application can provide its own unique implementation, either adding onto what OLE has provided or completely replacing it.

Figure 7.6 shows all interfaces available to OLE applications by functional area. The Component Object Model interfaces are placed in the center of the diagram because they provide the foundation on which all other interfaces are built. All interface names are prefixed with either `IOle` or `I`. Interfaces that begin with `IOle` provide services relating to compound document management. Those that begin with `I` provide services that are more general in nature. For example, `IOleObject` contains methods used by a client of an embedded or linked compound document object. `IOleObject` is implemented and used only by applications that participate in compound document management. `IDataObject` contains methods that are used by all applications and provide the means by which data of any type is transferred.

Fig. 7.6
The functional area view of OLE depicts many methods separated by functionality.

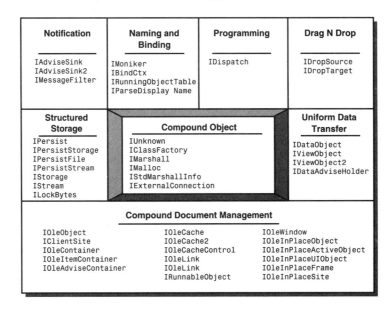

Interface Negotiation

Objects use interfaces through a mechanism known as *interface negotiation*. An interface has a unique *interface identifier* (IID) by which it is known at runtime. The IID allows clients to dynamically determine, with a call to IUnknown::QueryInterface(), the capabilities and supported interfaces of other objects.

IUnknown::QueryInterface() is the method that allows clients to query for and obtain pointers to needed interfaces. IUnknown is implemented by all component objects because it is the base interface from which all other interfaces are derived. Given an interface pointer, a caller can invoke QueryInterface() to get pointers to other interface implementations that are supported by the object supporting the interface referenced by the pointer. The caller passes the IID of the desired interface to IUnknown::QueryInterface(). The function returns either a NULL pointer, signifying that the interface is not supported, or a valid pointer to the interface.

There are two strategies for obtaining interface pointers in OLE applications. Some applications acquire all the interface pointers they will use over the lifetime of the application at initialization time. These applications typically store copies of the pointers with the objects that make calls to the interface's methods. Other applications postpone the acquisition of interface pointers until an interface is needed. These applications do not store pointer copies, instead the interface pointer is used and then released.

Reference Counting

Reference counting is a method that allows the model to keep a count of each instance of a pointer to an interface that is derived from IUnknown. Reference counting ensures that an object is not destroyed before all references to it are released and that these objects are kept alive if there are one or more references to one or more of their interfaces. An object is not deleted when its reference count is not zero. The reference counting mechanism of the model allows independent components to obtain and release pointers to a single object without any type of coordination.

Memory Management

OLE uses two kinds of memory: *local task memory* and *shared memory*. All non-shared task memory allocated by the OLE libraries and by object handlers is allocated using either an application-supplied allocation method or a default allocation method provided by OLE if an application does not provide its own. An application controls how memory is actually allocated and benefits from the improved efficiency that results from not being required to allocate copies of data to pass as parameters to OLE functions. This allocation method is robust during failures because the task memory is owned by an application and freed by Windows when the application terminates.

Shared memory is used less frequently in OLE than is task memory. The primary use of shared memory is to optimize data copying between tasks. If an application knows that the data it is allocating is passed as a parameter to another task, allocating it in shared memory is more efficient.

The management of memory allocated for pointers to interfaces is handled by the previously discussed reference counting mechanism. Memory management for parameters to functions or methods that are passed between processes is handled by a method where the communicating applications agree on the allocation and deallocation of memory for function parameters. OLE function parameters are defined as either *in-parameters*, *out-parameters*, or *in-out-parameters*. For each parameter type, the responsibility for allocating and freeing of resources is as shown in table 7.1.

 A *caller* (the calling task) is one that calls a function and passes parameters to that function. A *callee* (the receiver of a call) is a task that accepts the function call from a caller and executes the function accordingly.

Table 7.1 Parameter Types and Allocation

Parameter Type	How It Is Allocated and Freed
In-Parameter	In-parameters are allocated and freed by a caller. Either the task or the shared allocation method can be used to allocate the parameter.
Out-Parameter	Out-parameters are allocated by the callee, using only the task allocator of the callee. The parameter is then freed by the caller.
In-Out-Parameter	In-out-parameters are initially allocated by a caller, using only the task allocator, and are freed and reallocated by the callee as required. The caller is responsible for freeing the final returned value.

 These memory management conventions apply only to interfaces and APIs. Memory allocation performed internal to tasks does not have to follow the specifications in table 7.1.

Pointers passed as in-parameters are temporarily owned and can be inspected and modified depending on the semantics of the function for the parameter. To hold data longer than a call's duration, such as a global collection, the data must be copied.

If a function containing an out-parameter returns an error result, the out-parameter must be set to a value that can be cleaned up without any effort by the caller—such as NULL. In-out-parameters should be left untouched when the function returns an error, thus remaining in the state set by the caller.

Error and Status Reporting

OLE interface methods and API functions return result handles, HRESULT, that consist of a severity code, context information, a facility code, and a status code. The returned HRESULT can be interpreted at two levels. At the simplest level, zero indicates success and non-zero indicates failure. At a more complex level, the non-zero value can be examined with GetScode() to determine the severity code—thus Scode—and retrieve a more detailed reason for the failure.

Interprocess Communications

Similar to *dynamic data exchange* (DDE), OLE uses a *lightweight remote procedure call* (LRPC) communication mechanism based on posting messages or events to window handles to transfer data between processes. The communication mechanism is referred to as *lightweight* because it only handles communications between processes on one machine. LRPC is not a protocol because there is no need for a conversation between the communicating processes—data is simply sent to a predefined space in memory.

Remote procedure calls (RPC) provide the mechanism by which communications can occur across a network between tasks.

Sending and receiving interface parameters across process boundaries, referred to as *marshaling* and *unmarshaling*, is the job of proxy- and stub-component objects. Interfaces have proxy objects that can package method parameters for that interface. On the receiving side, there is an interface stub object that unpackages the parameters and makes the required method call. A proxy manager establishes connections to the LRPC channel and loads and unloads proxy objects as needed. In most cases, callers of interface methods are not affected when calls cross process boundaries.

Fig. 7.7
LRPC provides a
means where
clients can
perform remote
procedure calls
with servers
located on the
same machine as
the client.

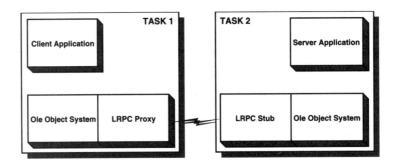

Dynamic Object Loading

One of the key features of the Component Object Model is that a client of a
component object can locate the code that is responsible for the object and
dynamically load it into a running system. By associating each component
object with a class identifier (CLSID), OLE can match the CLSID with the
implementation of the associated object. Once loaded, OLE makes a call to
the object implementation to retrieve an instance of the specific interface
requested by the client.

Firing Object Events

OLE controls introduce a standard way for OLE component object model
(COM) objects to fire events. The OLE controls architecture allows objects to
have outgoing interfaces, and defines a new connection architecture where
outgoing interfaces complement the normal interfaces that an object provides. An object provides normal (or incoming) interfaces by implementing
them; however, an object supports outgoing interfaces by calling other objects' implementations of those interfaces.

The set of events fired by a control is modeled as a single outgoing dispatch
(IDispatch) interface and is the complement for the primary interface exposed by objects. An OLE control collects its set of properties and methods
into its primary interface; however, it collects its set of events into the primary event set.

Creating a Container

Creating a control container in Visual C++ is simple with the AppWizard,
a part of the Application Workbench. Let's step through the creation of a
simple control container that you can use with the controls you will develop
in Chapters 9, 10, and 11.

To begin the development of a container, run Visual C++ from the Program Manager. Once Visual C++ is started, close any project that may have been saved during your last Visual C++ session. Now select File, New, Project (or press Ctrl+N) from the main menu in order to begin the creation of the control container application.

The New Project dialog box appears and prompts you for information regarding your new project. Select the directory and application type for the project (see fig. 7.8). Options for the New Project dialog box include the following:

- Project Type is the type of program that the project builds. You view the list of types by clicking the arrow. For this project, you want to create an executable that uses the Microsoft Foundation Classes—MFC AppWizard (exe). You can also select to create an MFC DLL, a non-MFC application, a non-MFC DLL, a 32-bit DOS shell application, and a simple static library.

- Platforms specifies the type of application your project creates. This application is being developed to run under the Windows 32-bit operating system.

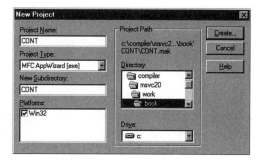

Fig. 7.8
The New Project dialog box allows you to configure a project to create a skeleton for your application.

Once you have established the name and directory for the application, you can select the Create button to access the MFC AppWizard Step 1 dialog box (see fig. 7.9). From this dialog box, you can select the type of window interface you want to have. Options for this dialog box include:

- Single Document (SDI) specifies that AppWizard creates an application that allows access to just one document at a time. An example of an SDI application is the Windows Notepad. For this application, you utilize an SDI.

- Multiple Documents (MDI) specifies that the application that AppWizard creates provides multiple documents, each with its own window. An example of an MDI application is the Windows File Manager.

- Dialog-Based specifies that the application that AppWizard creates uses simple dialog boxes and is based on a dialog-template resource.

- Language specifies the language you want to use for your resources from the DLLs that are available on your system.

Selecting the Next button of the MFC AppWizard Step 1 dialog box displays the MFC AppWizard Step 2 of 6 dialog box in which you select the type of database support to have in the application (see fig. 7.10). For your application, you do not need database support, so select the None radio button control. Options available for this dialog include:

- None specifies that AppWizard does not include database support.

- Only Include Header Files specifies that the application that AppWizard creates provides basic database support. The application can create recordsets and use them to examine and update records.

Fig. 7.9

The MFC AppWizard Step 1 dialog box allows you to select the type of application window desired.

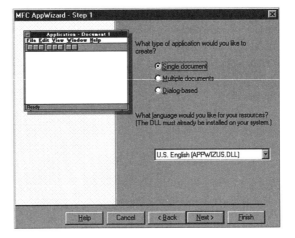

- A Database View, Without File Support specifies that the application that AppWizard creates has a CRecordView-derived class as its view class. This class is associated with a CRecordset-derived class, which AppWizard creates. This gives you a form-based application in which the record view is used to view and update records using its recordset. This type of application does not support serialization, which allows you to save documents to files other than databases.

- Both a Database View and File Support is similar to the previous selection, except that this type of application does support file serialization in addition to the database support.

- Data Source opens the SQL Data Sources dialog box, which is used to specify the database files for the application. This option is available only if you choose to include a database view in the application.

Applications that contain file support can support document serialization, which you can use, for example, to update a user profile file for an operating system's security system.

Most database applications operate on a per-record basis rather than on a per-file basis. Therefore, applications that support database views do not support serialization. If you choose to include a database view, you must specify the source of the data with the Data Source button control.

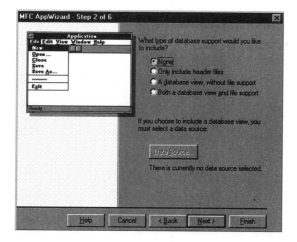

Fig. 7.10
The MFC AppWizard Step 2 dialog box allows you to select the type of database support you want for your application.

Selecting the Next button displays the MFC AppWizard Step 3 of 6 dialog box in which you select the type of OLE support you want in your application (see fig. 7.11). For this application, you want to support OLE container capabilities.

Options available for OLE application support include the following:

- None option specifies that no OLE support is included in the application.

- Container specifies that the application contain linked and embedded objects.

- Mini-Server specifies that the application have the ability to create and manage compound document objects. Mini-servers cannot run as stand-alone applications and only support embedded objects.

- Full-Server specifies that the application have the ability to create and manage compound document objects. Full-servers are able to run as stand-alone applications and support both linked and embedded objects.

- Both Container and Server specifies that the application is both a container and a server.

- Yes, Please specifies that the application's members are exposed to OLE automation clients. This allows your application to be accessed by OLE automation clients such as Microsoft Excel.

- No Automation specifies that the application is not exposed to allow OLE automation clients access to its members.

Fig. 7.11

The MFC AppWizard Step 3 dialog box allows you to select the type of OLE support you desire for your application.

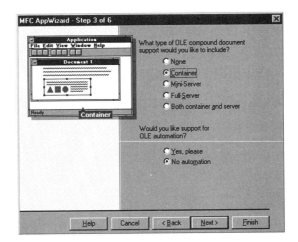

Selecting the Next button displays the MFC AppWizard Step 4 of 6 dialog box in which you select the features available in the user interface of the application (see fig. 7.12). The defaults for the dialog box are shown in the figure; use these defaults in your container application. Options for this dialog include:

- Dockable Toolbar specifies whether the toolbar that AppWizard generates can be placed along the border of your application window. The default toolbar is dockable and contains buttons for creating a new document, opening and saving document files, cutting, copying, pasting, printing, displaying the About dialog box, and invoking Help.

- Initial Status Bar specifies whether your application has a status bar. The status bar contains automatic indicators for the keyboard's Caps Lock,

Num Lock, and Scroll Lock keys and a message line that displays help strings for menu commands and toolbar buttons.

■ Printing and Print Preview signals the AppWizard to generate the code to handle print, print setup, and print preview commands by calling member functions in the CView class from the Microsoft Foundation Class library (MFC).

■ Context Sensitive Help allows the AppWizard to generate a set of help files that are used to provide context-sensitive help. Help support requires the help compiler.

■ Use 3D Controls specifies whether the visual interface of the application provides a 3D view of the application's controls.

■ MRU files list specifies the number of files to be listed on the "most recently used" list—defaulted to 4.

■ Advanced opens the Advanced Options dialog box, which allows you to specify options for document template strings and user interface frame characteristics.

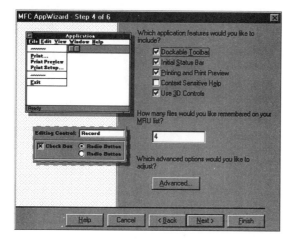

Fig. 7.12
The MFC AppWizard Step 4 dialog box allows you to select additional features for your application including help, printing capabilities, and toolbars.

Selecting the Next button displays the MFC AppWizard Step 5 of 6 dialog box in which you select how the AppWizard creates the source code for the application (see fig. 7.13). Options for this dialog box include:

■ Yes, Please specifies that AppWizard generate and insert comments in the source files that guide you in writing your program.

■ No Comments specifies that AppWizard does not insert comments in the source files it generates.

- ■ Visual C++ Makefile specifies that AppWizard generate a project file compatible with Visual C++ and NMAKE.

- ■ External Makefile specifies that AppWizard generate an NMAKE makefile that you can edit directly but must use as an external project from within Visual C++.

- ■ Use MFC in a Static Library specifies that MFC be linked to your application as a static library.

- ■ Use MFC in a Shared DLL specifies that MFC be linked to your application as a shared DLL.

Fig. 7.13
The MFC AppWizard Step 5 dialog box allows you to specify the contents and creation options of your source code.

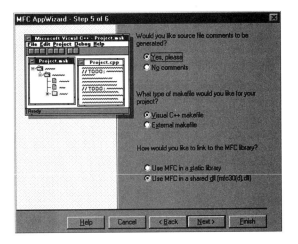

Selecting the Next button displays MFC AppWizard Step 6 of 6 dialog box in which you select how the AppWizard creates the source code for the application (see fig. 7.14). Options for this dialog include:

- ■ New Classes contains a list of the new classes that AppWizard generates for the application.

- ■ Class Name specifies the name of the class that you have selected in the New Classes list box. You can change the name of the class by typing the new name in the edit control.

- ■ Base Class, accessible by pressing Alt+A when the derived class is selected, specifies the class from which the selected class is derived.

- ■ Header File, also accessible by pressing Alt+H, specifies the name of the header file associated with the selected class.

■ Implementation File, also accessible by pressing Alt+I, specifies the name of the source code file associated with the selected class.

Once all of the options are selected you can select the Finish button. This button causes AppWizard to display the New Project Information dialog box, which contains a summary of the options you selected (see fig. 7.15). If you are satisfied with the application's options, select OK to create the application in the directory shown in the Install Directory label. Selecting Cancel will abort the project creation and clear all options for the project that was being created.

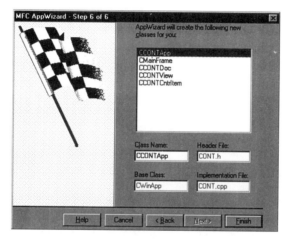

Fig. 7.14
The MFC AppWizard Step 6 dialog box describes the classes and associated header and implementation files for your application.

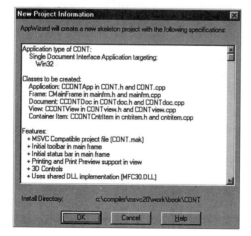

Fig. 7.15
The New Project Information dialog box displays the options selected for the control.

Testing the Container Application

Once the code has been created by AppWizard, you can compile, link, and test the container application. Selecting Project, Build CONT.EXE (or pressing Shift+F8) from the main menu notifies the Application Workbench to compile and link the code for the container to create an executable.

To test the application, you run it from the Application Workbench by selecting Project, Execute CONT.EXE (or pressing Ctrl+F5) from the main menu. The container starts and provides a single document interface (see fig. 7.16).

Fig. 7.16
The CONT application, as created by the AppWizard, allows you to insert controls as well as embed objects.

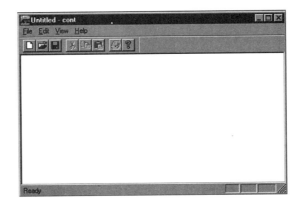

The AppWizard includes basic code to support OLE within the container so you can execute OLE operations immediately. For this test, include a button control on the container and test the control in the container. To do so, select Edit, Insert New Object (or press Alt+E+N) from the container's menu to access the Insert Object dialog box (see fig. 7.17).

Fig. 7.17
The Insert Object dialog box allows you to select an object from the system registry to insert into the container.

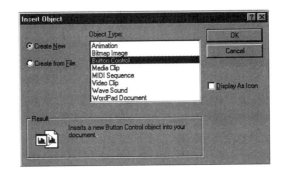

If you select the Create <u>N</u>ew radio button of the dialog box, you embed an object or control into your container application. You can select a class from the Object <u>T</u>ype list by double-clicking the class or clicking the OK button. If the class supports automation or in-place-activation, the container acquires a menu from the class's server and an image of the selected class appears in the container. If the class does not support in-place-activation, the server for the selected class executes and appears for editing. For example, selecting Microsoft Excel Worksheet places an image of a spreadsheet in the control; however, selecting Microsoft Graph executes the Graph application. To test this container with custom controls, select Button Control to insert a button into your container.

If you select the Create from <u>F</u>ile radio button, you select a particular file from your hard disk to load as the object (see fig. 7.18). If you select the <u>L</u>ink check box, a reference to the object is placed into your container so that it is updated whenever it is changed by the server application of the object. If you do not select the <u>L</u>ink check box, the image from the file is loaded into the container; however, changes are not reflected if the object's file should be changed by the server. The latter is similar to embedding an object in that the object from the file is wholly contained in the container. As with object embedding, you may edit the object by double-clicking that object to access the object's server.

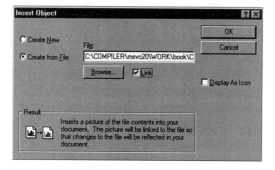

Fig. 7.18
The Insert Object dialog box also allows you to select a file that can be linked to the control.

Double-clicking the Button Control selection from the Insert Object dialog box places a button control into the container (see fig. 7.19). To test the control, simply select the button with the mouse to fire custom events for the custom control.

Fig. 7.19
Once inserted in the container, the Button control— or any custom control for that matter—can be activated and used as part of the container application.

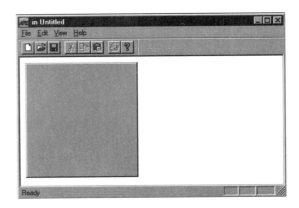

From Here...

In this chapter, you learned how to create a container application using the AppWizard of Visual C++. You have also seen how to use OLE controls to create an application that is indistinguishable from an application written at a lower level using raw Windows function calls. For more information on the topics discussed in this chapter, see the following:

■ Chapter 2, "The Component Object Model," provides information on the OLE object model, marshaling, and interfaces.

■ Chapter 11, "Subclassing Standard Controls," delves into information on subclassing controls and on the use of stock controls.

Chapter 8

Converting VBXs to OLE Custom Controls

by Edward B. Toupin

Visual Basic 3.0 introduced the VBX control which allowed you to incorporate the functionality of custom controls into Visual Basic applications. With the newer 32-bit environment, 32-bit containers, and Visual C++ 2.0, you were introduced to the OLE custom control (OCX) that combined the functionality of VBXs with OLE 2.0. The one problem with this movement to OCXs was that a large base of existing VBXs would be left totally useless which, of course, produced some opposition to the OCX specifications. To remedy this, Microsoft provided a simple method for migrating VBXs to OCXs using Visual C++.

This chapter will overview the migration of VBXs to OCXs using Visual C++. You will take a look at some of the things to watch for during migration, how the migration is implemented, and how the control will operate after the migration is complete.

This chapter will examine the following topics:

- Overview of control migration

- Preparing VBX code for migration

- Using the ControlWizard VBX template tool

- What is affected in migration

- Building and testing the migrated OLE control

VBX Control Migration

As part of the development of a test Visual Basic 3.0 application for real-time process control in Windows, I was introduced to the development of VBXs. These VBXs were developed to maintain the functionality of a particular field device including valves, pumps, tanks, and sensors. There were already many applications out there that could easily have been utilized for real-time control; however, the use of Visual Basic with *plug-n-play* controls was intriguing. The idea behind development environments such as Visual Basic is to implement an interface without a lot of actual coding. Implementing individual representations of field devices in Visual Basic was definitely out of the question; however, encapsulating the functionality of these field devices into plug-in modules made the development of the mentioned system quite easy. So now that Visual C++ 2.0, OCXs, and 32-bit containers are arriving on the scene, what do we do with the VBXs?

In essence, a VBX is a special form of DLL consisting of properties with a message processing function (WndProc()) to handle the GETPROPERTY and SETPROPERTY messages from Visual Basic in addition to standard Windows messages. Visual Basic itself provides memory management for storage of properties and a system for managing their settings between design-time mode and run-time mode. At designtime, properties can be set in Properties window, and at runtime, they can be programmed using the BASIC language. If a developer has already developed a DLL containing the functionality required, the VBX is merely a wrapper for mapping a set of properties to the DLL's traditional function call API.

With OLE 2.0, the emphasis shifted from the concept of the compound document to an object-oriented approach, which is intended to affect the way in which Windows is used and programmed. OLE 2.0 also introduced *in-place activation*, or Visual Editing, that allows a server application to activate within the visual context of a container. Automation, also a part of OLE 2.0, makes OLE a more viable solution now than does the standard VBX. OLE Automation means that any *automation-aware* client application can control OLE server objects.

To make you aware of where the OCX fits into the grand scheme of things, it is useful for you to know that there are several types of OLE servers available for OLE client applications—automation, full, mini, in-process, and in-process handlers. A full server is like Microsoft Excel, which is a standalone application and can support both embedded and linked objects. Excel can also provide OLE automation server support for controlling client applications. A mini server can only support embedded objects and can only run in the context of a container application—Microsoft Graph is such a server. Both full and mini servers that are implemented as EXEs are known as *local servers*. These applications operate in their own environments and communicate with container applications through OLE's lightweight remote procedure call (LRPC) mechanism.

An in-process server is like a mini server, but is implemented as a DLL rather than an EXE. It is more tightly bound to its container application than a mini server is. This is because it operates in the same environment as its container and provides communications through direct function calls instead of LRPC. Finally, an in-process handler exists simply to display an object without the overhead of having to load a local server. It is almost identical to an in-process server but with minimum functionality, excluding in-place activation and automation.

As an in-process server, an OCX supports object embedding, in-place activation, and OLE Automation. Unlike the OLE server just mentioned, an OCX also supports events and is therefore functionally equivalent to a VBX. For the capabilities of an OCX to be of any use, a container application must also be enhanced to provide the framework to handle event notification. An OCX will work in most containers where a standard OLE 2.0 server can be used (such as in the VB 3.0 OLE 2.0 control); however, the additional functionality of the OCX will be ignored.

For developers with existing VBX controls, the Microsoft CDK provides a way to convert VBX controls to the OLE 2 custom control (OCX) format using the VBX template tool found in the ControlWizard. The VBX template tool helps you turn your VBX custom control into an OLE control. The template tool uses model information in the VBX file and creates a Visual C++ project file, as well as source code files for creating the OLE control. These files can be compiled and linked to produce a working skeleton for the OLE control. Once the skeleton is built and tested, the next step is to take code from your VBX source files and place it in the appropriate areas of the generated OCX source files.

Preparing the VBX Custom Control for Migration

In order for the VBX template tool of the ControlWizard to properly translate the VBX control, you must expose the VBX control's model information to the template builder. If your VBX source code does not already define the function VBGetModelInfo(), you must define the function and rebuild your VBX before you can use the template tool. This function should be defined as an exported function. You must also define a MODELINFO structure containing a specific Visual Basic version number, and a NULL-terminated array of MODEL structures that will be utilized within the VBGetModelInfo(). The following example illustrates this:

```
LPMODEL modellistcontrol[] =
    {
    &modelcontrol,
    NULL
    };

MODELINFO modelinfocontrol =
    {
    VB_VERSION,        // VB version being used
    modellistcontrol   // MODEL list
    };

LPMODELINFO FAR PASCAL _export VBGetModelInfo(USHORT usVersion)
{
    if (usVersion <= VB100_VERSION)
        return &modelinfocontrol_Vb1;

    if (usVersion <= VB200_VERSION)
        return &modelinfocontrol_Vb2;
    else
        return &modelinfocontrol;
}
```

NOTE If your VBX file supports multiple versions, you will need to create similar MODELINFO structures to point to those models. You could define ModelinfoControl_VB1 and ModelinfoControl_VB2 structures to contain the required information for each version.

Performing Migration with the VBX Template Tool

After your VBX control has been built with the VBGetModelInfo() function as previously described, you can build a control skeleton by running the ControlWizard VBX template tool on the VBX control. To start the process, load Visual C++ and close any projects that may have been saved during the last session in the Workbench. Once loaded and cleared, select Tools, ControlWizard from the Workbench menu to access the ControlWizard (see fig. 8.1).

The ControlWizard will be discussed in the next few chapters during the development of several OCXs.

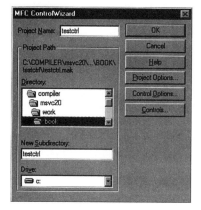

Fig. 8.1
The main dialog box of the ControlWizard allows you to select options for the creation of a custom control.

Select the drive from the Drive list box where you would like the control project to reside; then select the name of the project's parent directory from the Directory list. In the Project Name edit control, enter the name that you want to call the project. For this example, call the project TESTCTRL.

From the main ControlWizard dialog box, select the Project button control. In the Project Options dialog box, you want to clear all checkboxes except for the Source Comments checkbox so that you will have comments inserted into the generated source code (see fig. 8.2). Click OK to accept the selections.

Fig. 8.2
The Project Options dialog box allows you to select options that determine the specialized skeleton code inserted into your controls implementation and header files.

Now select the Control Options button control from the ControlWizard dialog box, and check the Select when Visible and the Show in Insert Object Dialog checkboxes (see fig. 8.3). In addition, select the Use VBX Control as Template checkbox so that you may select a VBX to utilize as part of the control construction. Once the latter checkbox is selected, the Select VBX Control button control will become active so that you may select the VBX to incorporate into the project.

Fig. 8.3
The Control
Options dialog
box allows you to
select options that
determine the
behavior of your
control within
a container
application.

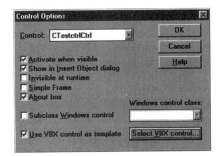

Choose the Select VBX Control button from the Control Options dialog box to access the VBX selection dialog box shown in figure 8.4. From this dialog box, you should select the Browse button control to locate the VBX that you want to use as a template for the current project. Once you locate the appropriate VBX, you will be able to select which control from the VBX you want to use as the template from the Control Name listbox. After selecting the VBX for the control, click the OK button control to accept the changes and return you to the main ControlWizard dialog box.

Fig. 8.4
Select the file of
a prior custom
control style
(VBXs) to use as a
template for your
new custom
control (OCX).

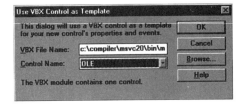

If you select a VBX file that does not properly export the model information previously described, Visual C++ may crash at this point.

From the main dialog box of the ControlWizard, select the Controls button control to access the Controls dialog box shown in figure 8.5. From this dialog box, you can change the names that will be used for the classes, header, and implementation files of the controls for the project. For this project, however, you will use the defaults shown in the edit controls of the dialog box. Select the OK button to accept the information and return to the main ControlWizard dialog box.

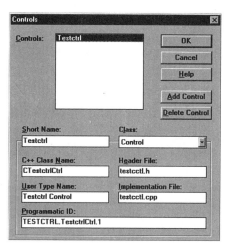

Fig. 8.5
The Controls
dialog box presents
the class names
used in your
custom control
and the file names
in which your
skeleton code is
stored.

You are now ready to generate the control skeleton, which is accomplished
by selecting the OK button control. The New Control Information dialog box
shows the configuration information for the new control (see fig. 8.6). This
information contains the class name for the control, the filename information, and also indicates that you are converting an existing VBX to an OCX.

To generate the files for the project in the directory listed at the bottom of
the dialog box, select the Create button control. The ControlWizard will
generate all of the header, implementation, and resource files required for the
new control.

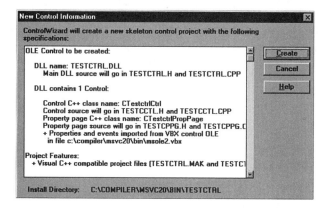

Fig. 8.6
The New Control
Information dialog
box displays
information about
your new control
that you have
selected in the
ControlWizard's
dialog boxes.

In addition to creating the source files, a subdirectory for the Type library file is created. The 16-bit version of the CDK is placed into TLB16, and the 32-bit version of the CDK is stored into OBJD32. The README.TXT file generated by the ControlWizard contains a description of the files created by the VBX template tool and is required to build a complete working skeleton of the new OLE control.

Building and Testing the Skeleton

After ControlWizard generates a template for your VBX control, you should build and test the control to familiarize yourself with the behavior of the migrated OLE control. The following sections describe this process and demonstrate how to test your new OLE control using the Test Container.

Compiling, Linking, and Registering the OLE Control Skeleton

To compile and link the new control, simply select Project, Build TESTCTRL.EXE from the Workbench main menu. The Workbench will compile the control and then perform a link on the generated object files. When the project is successfully built, you must register the new control before you can test it. Choose Tools, Register Control from the main menu. A message box will appear indicating that the control was successfully registered in the system registry and is ready for use.

Testing the OLE Control Skeleton

Once the control is built and registered in system registry, you can immediately test the functionality of the new control skeleton using the Test Container.

To test your new OLE control skeleton, follow these steps:

1. If the control was not registered in the system registry after you compiled and linked, you should select Tools, Register Control from the Workbench menu to register the control in the system registry.

2. Select Tools, Test Container from the Workbench menu to load the Test Container application.

3. From the menu of the Test Container, select Edit, Insert OLE Control. This will load the Insert OLE Control dialog box so that you may select the control to insert into the container.

4. In the Insert OLE Control dialog box, select the desired control and choose OK. The control will then appear in the control container.

If your control is not listed in the Insert OLE Control dialog box, go back to step 1 and start over.

At this point, you can test your control's properties or events. To test properties, follow these steps:

1. From the Test Container's menu select Edit, Control Object, Properties.

2. Modify the value of a property on the property page for the control.

3. Click the Apply Now button control to apply the new value to the control. The property for the control now contains the new value you just entered (see fig. 8.7).

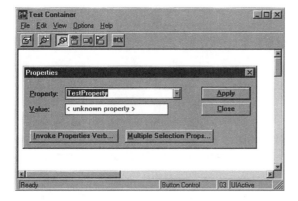

Fig. 8.7
The Property page information dialog box allows you to view and set values for properties of your control.

To test the events for the control, follow these steps:

1. From the menu of the Test Container select View, Event Log.

2. Perform an action that causes the control to fire an event. The fired event will appear in the Event Log window (see fig. 8.8).

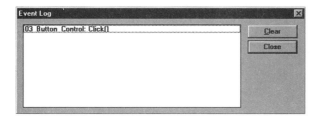

Fig. 8.8
Performing an action that causes a control in the Test Container to fire an event will place an entry describing the event in the Test Container Event Log.

Once you have completed testing your control, close the Test Container by selecting File, Exit in the menu, or double-click the system menu button located in the upper left corner of the window.

Final Steps of the Migration

When you are satisfied that the built skeleton for the control is working properly, the next step is to port the implementation of your OLE control's custom properties and events from your VBX source code to the new control's source code files. For safety's sake, remember to back up your files frequently and test each new block of code as you go, using the Test Container.

Properties and Events

The Type Library contains a description of the object, and can be queried to determine the object's capabilities. A Type Library is created as a text file with the ODL (for Object Description Language) extension, and is then compiled to a TLB using MKTYPLIB in the Workbench before compiling the C++ code for the object.

The Type Library is the OCX's equivalent to the VBX's model structure and property/event lists. It lists the properties and their types, and gives each one an ID. It lists events, their IDs, and their parameters, as well as the methods for the control. Unlike the VBX, an OCX can have its own custom methods, which can be genuine methods with parameters or property getting and setting methods.

The names listed in the Type Library are the names by which the outside world knows them—they are equivalent to the names in quotation marks in the VBX's property/event lists (see listing 8.1). A VBX's properties are either standard or custom, while an OCX has four types—stock, ambient, extender, and custom. Stock properties are equivalent to the VBX's standard properties, but some standard properties are no longer accessible and have been renamed extender properties in an OCX, as discussed earlier in this chapter. Ambient properties provide information about the container in which your object is embedded. Finally, custom properties are your properties—the same as in a VBX.

Just like a VBX, an OCX has two types of event—stock (standard) and custom. The same set of stock events is supported by COleControl as for a VBX.

Listing 8.1 · Type Library File

```
// testctrl.odl : type library source for OLE Custom Control
// project.

// This file will be processed by the Make Type Library (mktyplib)
// tool to produce the type library (testctrl.tlb) that will become
// a resource in testctrl.ocx.

#include <olectl.h>

[ uuid(F32F9E93-3444-11CE-960F-524153480005), version(1.0),
  helpstring("Testctrl OLE Custom Control module") ]
library TestctrlLib
{
    importlib(STDOLE_TLB);
    importlib(STDTYPE_TLB);

    //  Primary dispatch interface for CTestctrlCtrl

    [ uuid(F32F9E91-3444-11CE-960F-524153480005),
      helpstring("Dispatch interface for Testctrl Control") ]
    dispinterface _DTestctrl
    {
        properties:
            // NOTE - ClassWizard will maintain property
            // information here.
            //    Use extreme caution when editing this section.
            //{{AFX_ODL_PROP(CTestctrlCtrl)
            [id(1)] short InnerTop;
            [id(2)] short InnerLeft;
            [id(3)] short InnerRight;
            [id(4)] short InnerBottom;
            [id(5)] short Min;
            [id(6)] short Max;
            [id(7)] short Value;
            [id(8)] short Style;
            [id(9)] boolean Autosize;
            [id(10)] IPictureDisp* Picture;
            [id(11)] short NeedleWidth;
            [id(DISPID_ENABLED),bindable,requestedit]
               boolean Enabled;
            [id(DISPID_BACKCOLOR),bindable,requestedit]
               OLE_COLOR BackColor;
            [id(DISPID_FORECOLOR),bindable,requestedit]
               OLE_COLOR ForeColor;
            [id(DISPID_HWND)] short hWnd;

            //}}AFX_ODL_PROP

        methods:
            // NOTE - ClassWizard will maintain method
            // information here.
```

(continues)

Listing 8.1 Continued

```
                    //    Use extreme caution when editing this section.
                    //{{AFX_ODL_METHOD(CTestctrlCtrl)
                    //}}AFX_ODL_METHOD

                    [id(DISPID_ABOUTBOX)] void AboutBox();
          };

          //  Event dispatch interface for CTestctrlCtrl

          [ uuid(F32F9E92-3444-11CE-960F-524153480005),
            helpstring("Event interface for Testctrl Control") ]
          dispinterface _DTestctrlEvents
          {
              properties:
                      //  Event interface has no properties

              methods:
                      // NOTE - ClassWizard will maintain event
                      // information here.
                      //    Use extreme caution when editing this section.
                      //{{AFX_ODL_EVENT(CTestctrlCtrl)
                      [id(1)] void Change();
                      [id(DISPID_CLICK)] void Click();
                      [id(DISPID_DBLCLICK)] void DblClick();
                      [id(DISPID_KEYDOWN)] void KeyDown(short* KeyCode,
                          short Shift);
                      [id(DISPID_KEYPRESS)] void KeyPress(short*
                          KeyAscii);
                      [id(DISPID_KEYUP)] void KeyUp(short* KeyCode, short
                          Shift);
                      [id(DISPID_MOUSEDOWN)] void MouseDown(short Button,
                          short Shift, OLE_XPOS_PIXELS X, OLE_YPOS_PIXELS Y);
                      [id(DISPID_MOUSEMOVE)] void MouseMove(short Button,
                          short Shift, OLE_XPOS_PIXELS X, OLE_YPOS_PIXELS Y);
                      [id(DISPID_MOUSEUP)] void MouseUp(short Button,
                          short Shift, OLE_XPOS_PIXELS X, OLE_YPOS_PIXELS Y);

                      //}}AFX_ODL_EVENT
          };

          //  Class information for CTestctrlCtrl

          [ uuid(F32F9E90-3444-11CE-960F-524153480005),
            helpstring("Testctrl Control") ]
          CoClass Testctrl
          {
              [default] dispinterface _DTestctrl;
              [default, source] dispinterface _DTestctrlEvents;
          };


          //{{AFX_APPEND_ODL}}
      };
```

Getting and Setting Properties

Using OLE Automation, a container application has two ways of interactively setting an OCX's properties at designtime. The first approach is for the container to use the Type Library to establish the set of properties supported by the OCX and allow the user to get and set them by using a Property window in much the same way VB does for a VBX.

The second approach is for the container to get the OCX to do this on its own behalf using a feature called the *property page*, which is a dialog box that can be designed with AppStudio. An OCX can have as many property pages as is required, with each page managing any number of properties. The property page system is the OCX's personal user interface, but with an imposed style so that multiple OCXs within an application have property pages of consistent appearance and behavior. While it's an open-ended enhancement of the rather crude Property window approach of Visual Basic, the property page avoids complete free-for-all that would occur if every OCX had its own proprietary user interface.

Each property page is an individual OLE object, making it a separate entity from the OCX object, even though each property page implementation is a C++ class (CPropertyPage) created by the SDK's Control Wizard. In order to make this system work, there is a DoDataExchange(), which transfers the property values into the property page upon its creation and the updated values back out again upon termination. These values are then updated in the OCX object by OLE Automation. COleControl does all this for you, leaving you to merely design the dialog boxes for the property pages.

Internally, an OCX uses the same mechanism for getting and setting its properties at runtime as it does at designtime, just like a VBX. Again, like a VBX, an OCX can find out whether it's being used in design-time mode or run-time mode. As mentioned earlier, the user's view of an OCX's run-time interface depends on the container implementation. Ultimately, OLE Automation is the mechanism through which an OCX's properties are manipulated both at designtime and runtime.

Let's compare the dispatch map of an OCX (see listing 8.2) and the VBX's GETPROPERTY and SETPROPERTY messages. The dispatch map is the OCX's equivalent to the VBX's GETPROPERTY and SETPROPERTY structures in its WndProc() function, and it contains additional information from the VBX's property descriptions. The entries in the dispatch map are different according to the get and set requirements of the properties. For a VBX property, there are three possibilities:

- A property is a member variable, such that no special action is required for the variable.

- A property is a member variable, and notification is required when the variable is changed (set).

- A property requires special action, and notification is required when the value of the variable is retrieved (get) and changed (set).

Property validation is important, so some type of notification will probably be required for your control when a property variable changes. VBXs provided a mechanism to check property values before allowing them to be set. In an OCX, there is no special assistance, so you must code up your validation logic in the member functions listed in your dispatch map and throw an OLE exception if your validation fails.

Listing 8.2 Dispatch Map for TESTCTRL in TESTCCTL.CPP

```
/////////////////////////////////////////////////////////////////
// Dispatch map

BEGIN_DISPATCH_MAP(CTestctrlCtrl, COleControl)
    //{{AFX_DISPATCH_MAP(CTestctrlCtrl)
    // NOTE - ClassWizard will add and remove dispatch map entries
    //     DO NOT EDIT what you see in these blocks of generated code!
    DISP_PROPERTY_EX(CTestctrlCtrl, "InnerTop", GetInnerTop,
     SetInnerTop, VT_I2)
    DISP_PROPERTY_EX(CTestctrlCtrl, "InnerLeft", GetInnerLeft,
     SetInnerLeft, VT_I2)
    DISP_PROPERTY_EX(CTestctrlCtrl, "InnerRight", GetInnerRight,
     SetInnerRight, VT_I2)
    DISP_PROPERTY_EX(CTestctrlCtrl, "InnerBottom", GetInnerBottom,
     SetInnerBottom, VT_I2)
    DISP_PROPERTY_EX(CTestctrlCtrl, "Min", GetMin, SetMin, VT_I2)
    DISP_PROPERTY_EX(CTestctrlCtrl, "Max", GetMax, SetMax, VT_I2)
    DISP_PROPERTY_EX(CTestctrlCtrl, "Value", GetValue, SetValue,
     VT_I2)
    DISP_PROPERTY_EX(CTestctrlCtrl, "Style", GetStyle,
     SetStyle, VT_I2)
    DISP_PROPERTY_EX(CTestctrlCtrl, "Autosize", GetAutosize,
     SetAutosize, VT_BOOL)
    DISP_PROPERTY_EX(CTestctrlCtrl, "Picture", GetPicture,
     SetPicture, VT_PICTURE)
    DISP_PROPERTY_EX(CTestctrlCtrl, "NeedleWidth", GetNeedleWidth,
     SetNeedleWidth, VT_I2)
    DISP_STOCKPROP_ENABLED()
    DISP_STOCKPROP_BACKCOLOR()
    DISP_STOCKPROP_FORECOLOR()
```

```
        DISP_STOCKPROP_HWND()
        DISP_DEFVALUE(CTestctrlCtrl, "Value")

        //}}AFX_DISPATCH_MAP
        DISP_FUNCTION_ID(CTestctrlCtrl, "AboutBox", DISPID_ABOUTBOX,
          AboutBox, VT_EMPTY, VTS_NONE)
    END_DISPATCH_MAP()
```

COleControl does the majority of the event handling for you (see fig. 8.9). In a VBX, you use the API function VBFireEvent(); whereas in an OCX, you simply define a list of custom events you support and fire them when appropriate. When an event that you establish in the ClassWizard is fired, COleControl notifies the container through an OLE interface.

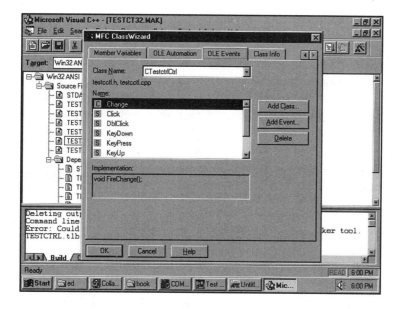

Fig. 8.9
The ClassWizard allows you to add events to the control that are fired whenever you perform an action on the control.

Drawing the Control

VBXs maintain their own windows, and you simply respond to the Windows WM_PAINT message in order to draw your control. Managing your own window also makes it straightforward to implement event-driven functionality triggered by mouse and keyboard activity—you simply fire events based on incoming messages. Graphical controls don't have their own windows, but instead rely on VB passing an equivalent set of messages to the controls and are drawn directly on the underlying form.

OLE is more complicated than this. An embedded OLE object can be in one of three states—*passive*, *loaded*, or *running*. Passive means that the container is closed. Loaded means that the container is open and the object may be visible, but it will be a rendition of the object only—the object will maintain its own window. Running means that the object has been activated, and its own window is present in the container and is ready for manipulation. In fact, there are two active states—*active* and *UI-active*. There can only be one UI-active object at a time in a container, and that is the one that is being edited.

To further complicate matters, OLE objects can be either *outside-in* or *inside-out*. Most OLE objects are outside-in, which means that the user must double-click them to activate them for editing. An inside-out object doesn't really have a loaded state because it's activated the moment the container document is opened, as long as the container understands inside-out objects and activates them.

OCXs are inside-out objects because, in run-time mode, they need to be in a position to generate events as soon as they become visible. To assist you, `COleControl` provides an `OnDraw()` member function that provides the opportunity to draw the control into the device context of the container that is passed as a parameter to the function.

Listing 8.3 *OnDraw()* **Member Function of TESTCTRL**

```
///////////////////////////////////////////////////////////////
//
// CTestctrlCtrl::OnDraw - Drawing function

void CTestctrlCtrl::OnDraw(
            CDC* pdc, const CRect& rcBounds,
            const CRect& rcInvalid)
{
    // TODO: Replace the following code with your
    // own drawing code.
    pdc->FillRect(rcBounds, CBrush::FromHandle(
      (HBRUSH)GetStockObject(WHITE_BRUSH)));
    pdc->Ellipse(rcBounds);
}
```

The Effects of Migration

The template, or skeleton, generated by the template tool of the ControlWizard is similar to the templates generated when you use

ControlWizard to create a new control with the following exceptions. (The development of new controls is discussed in more detail in Chapters 9 and 10.)

Custom Properties and Events

Custom properties and events in your VBX are provided in the template as *stub functions*. In order to make these properties and events functional, you need to port the implementation code from your VBX source files into the appropriate files in the new control template. As shown in the following example, the ControlWizard places comments in your source file to note where you are to place the VBX implementation code:

```
// TODO: Initialize your control's instance data here.
```

Stock Properties and Events

Many of the standard properties and events in your VBX will be converted to fully implemented stock properties and events in the new control's template. Stock properties supported during the migration include BorderStyle, Enabled, Font, Caption, Text, ForeColor, BackColor, and hWnd. Stock events supported during the migration include Click, DblClick, KeyDown, KeyPress, KeyUp, MouseDown, MouseMove, and MouseUp. These standard properties are now stock properties of MFC and are fully implemented.

> Properties that were standard in the VBX control model (for example, Left, Top, Height, Width) are automatically supported by OLE as standard *extender properties*. Extender properties are not needed in the new OLE control model and are not converted by the ControlWizard template tool.

Unimplemented Properties and Events

During the migration process, some stock properties of the VBX model will not be migrated to the OCX. These include DragIcon, DragMode, MouseCursor, and MousePointer. Stock events not supported include DragDrop, DragOver, LinkOpen, LinkClose, LinkError, and LinkNotify. These properties and events are no longer stock members of COleControl for the new OCX architecture since the control container has responsibility for managing these aspects of the control. Drag-and-drop is specifically handled by COleDropSource and COleDropTarget, while DDE is handled by CWinApp.

From Here...

In this chapter, you learned about the migration of VBX control to the OCX standard. Also discussed was how the migration occurs, the development of an OCX control skeleton, porting your VBX implementation, and building and testing the new control in the Test Container.

In the next few chapters, you explore the development of a new control from the ground up and how to use the control in development environments. For further information, see the following:

■ Chapter 9, "Building the Comm Custom Control," helps you go one step further and create a new control with the ControlWizard.

■ *Using Visual C++ 2.0, Special Edition*, published by Que, provides additional reading on Visual C++ 2.0, OCXs, and OLE.

■ The Microsoft Control Development Kit discusses the specifics of custom control development.

Chapter 9

Building the Comm Custom Control

by Edward B. Toupin

This is the first of two chapters that delves into the intricacies of developing an OLE custom control in Visual C++. In this chapter, you will develop a portion of a small communications custom control which, when used within a container, will allow you to specify a phone number for dialing. The control will dial that number, wait 5 seconds, then hang up the modem. This application is used primarily as the basis for a full communications wrapper control for use in container applications and container application development environments.

During the development of a custom control, there is not actually a lot of coding involved. Much of the framework is developed for you by ControlWizard, whereas many of the enhancements required for the control are added through the ClassWizard. As you will see, you add the basic coding for the control to the properties and methods of the control provided within the framework of the application.

This chapter explores the following topics:

- ■ Creating the Comm Control with ControlWizard
- ■ Customizing the Comm Control
- ■ Registering the Comm Control
- ■ Testing the Comm Control

The ControlWizard

As with the other tools available in Visual C++, you have access to a wizard specifically designed for the development of custom controls. The ControlWizard allows you to specify the basic characteristics of a control and then generates the framework for the control.

The first step involved in creating a custom control is, of course, to start Visual C++ and to clear the workspace. You can clear the workspace by merely closing all of the active code and project windows, if any, that are visible. You can then activate ControlWizard by selecting Tools, ControlWizard from the Visual C++ menu (see fig. 9.1).

Fig. 9.1
The
ControlWizard.

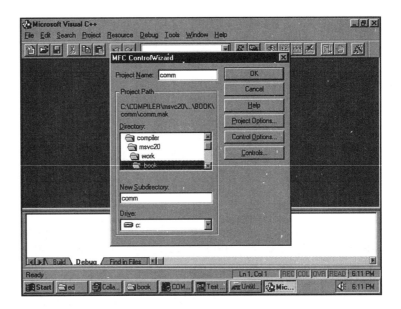

As is shown in figure 9.1, you can select a directory in the Directory list box that will be the parent directory for your control project. When you enter the name of the control project into the Project Name edit control, you will see that the name of the project is also used to create a new directory of the same name in the New Subdirectory edit field. You have the option of changing the name of the new directory or leaving that name to be used by Visual C++.

The Project Options button control allows you to access the Project Options dialog box, shown in figure 9.2.

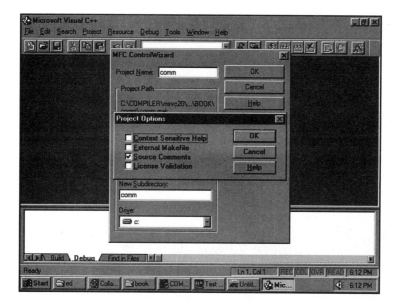

Fig. 9.2
The Project
Options dialog
box.

In this dialog box, you can select several options for the control:

- *Context Sensitive Help.* Selecting this checkbox informs ControlWizard that it is to generate code for building context-sensitive help. These files are generated so that you can modify them to provide help about the control for the user or developer. For this control we are not interested in providing context-sensitive help, so we will leave the checkbox unchecked.

- *External Makefile.* The ControlWizard can generate makefiles for 16- and 32-bit development environments as well as for the NMAKE utility available with Visual C++. Selecting this checkbox tells ControlWizard to generate a makefile for NMAKE that is compatible with the Visual Workbench. Under normal circumstances, the Workbench modifies your makefiles for you; however, with this option selected, you must make all changes to the makefile manually. For this control, leave the External Makefile checkbox unchecked so that all modifications to the project makefile will be completed by the Visual Workbench.

- *Source Comments.* When selected, this checkbox informs ControlWizard to insert comments into the source files it generates. The box is checked by default, and I suggest you leave it checked. These comments, as well as any other comments that you may add, are useful to read when modifying the source code and to follow the flow of the code.

■ *License Validation.* Selecting this checkbox notifies ControlWizard to generate files, data, and functions to perform license validation for the control. Licensing a control prevents unauthorized use of the control by developers. You authorize, or license, a developer to use your control for development by shipping an LIC file with the control. This file resides in the same directory as the control or in the Windows system directory so that the control can find it when used. When a developer ships your control, they do not ship the LIC file; so your control can be used only in a runtime mode. The LIC file, when present, enables the control to be used for development; otherwise, the control is usable at runtime.

Selecting the Control Options button in ControlWizard's main window accesses the Control Options dialog box (see fig. 9.3).

NOTE The OLE custom control file, OCX, can contain multiple controls. Each control within the OCX can have different characteristics, but it is best to keep controls with similar functionality within one OCX.

Fig. 9.3
The Control
Options dialog
box.

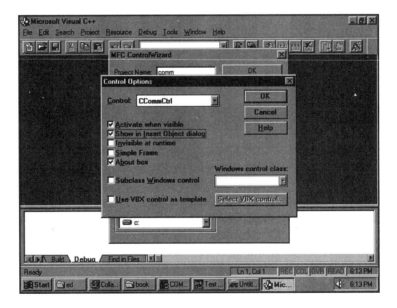

This dialog box contains the properties that directly affect the operation of the control within a container application. The Control Options dialog box contains the following options:

■ The Control drop-down list contains the names of all of the OLE controls in ControlWizard's project makefile. You can have multiple controls within one OLE custom control (OCX). For this OLE custom control, the default—and only—control is `CCommCtrl`.

■ The Activate When Visible checkbox allows your control to become active when it is visible within a container application. Active controls are aware of the Windows environment and can respond to messages and events in a manner similar to that of standard Windows applications. Inactive controls may only respond to notification events sent by the control's container, but will not receive normal Windows messages and events. Essentially, an inactive control is responsive to container messages only while an active control is responsive to container and Windows messages.

■ The Show in Insert Object Dialog checkbox allows your control to appear in the Insert Object dialog box. This dialog box appears when you dynamically insert an object into a container application using the Edit, Insert Object or Insert, Object menu selections from most Windows-based applications.

■ The Invisible at Runtime checkbox makes your control invisible while the container of the control is running. Currently, most VBX custom controls support this feature in that they are hidden within a container if they do not need to be visible to perform their specific function. Such controls include the Timer control, database management controls, and communications controls. All functionality of the hidden control is available through the methods and properties of the control.

■ The Simple Frame checkbox controls the inclusion or exclusion of a border around the control within the container application.

■ The About Box checkbox informs ControlWizard to create an About dialog box for your control. The ControlWizard adds a dialog resource to your resource file (RC) and a member function to your control class. When a container application invokes the `AboutBox()` function, an About dialog box appears.

■ The Subclass Windows Control checkbox tells ControlWizard to generate code appropriate for a particular type of subclassing. You should select this checkbox if you plan on subclassing an existing Windows class. Control subclassing is discussed in more detail in Chapter 11.

■ The Windows Control Class drop-down list box contains available Windows classes from which you can select to subclass. All of the standard Windows controls are available for subclassing, including `BUTTON`, `COMBOBOX`, `EDIT`, `LISTBOX`, `STATIC`, and `SCROLLBAR`.

■ The Use VBX Control as Template checkbox allows you to select an existing VBX control as a template for your custom control. For more information on the use of VBXs with OCXs, refer back to Chapter 8 on "Converting VBXs to OLE Custom Controls."

■ The Select VBX Control button is enabled for you to select only if the Use VBX Control as Template checkbox is selected. This button displays a dialog box from which you can select an existing VBX control (see fig. 9.4).

Fig. 9.4
The Use VBX
Control as
Template dialog
box.

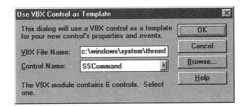

The Controls dialog box is accessible by clicking the Controls button in the ControlWizard window (see fig. 9.5). This dialog box allows you to manage the names of existing components for your control as well as add new controls to the OCX.

Fig. 9.5
The Controls
dialog box.

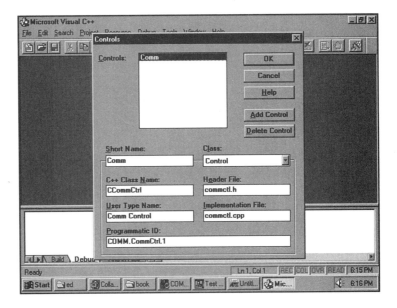

The options in this dialog box include the following:

- The Controls list box lists the names of all of the OLE controls in your project. When you select a control from the list box, the information about the selected control populates the rest of the dialog box's edit controls with information about the selected OLE control.

- The Short Name edit control displays the return value used by your control's OLE interface. Since MFC hides the implementation details of the OLE interface, the name is used to provide a means of allowing access to the implementation interface. The default name is fine unless you specifically require another name for the control to be seen by the application that uses the interface.

- The C++ Class Name is the name of the control's class as it will appear in the code generated by ControlWizard.

- The User Type Name displays a description for your control's interface. For this control, the descriptive return value is Comm Control.

- The Class drop-down list box enables you to define further the names that you are changing. Initially, this list box is set to Control, which indicates that you are working with the information used to generate code for the Comm control. If you select Property Page from the list, you can change the various names, files, and classes for your control's property page information.

- The Header File edit control displays the file name that ControlWizard will use for your control's header file.

- The Implementation File edit control displays the name of your source file for the current class.

- The Programmatic ID edit box displays the text that is used when you register your control in the system registry. This text consists of your control's name, class, and version number. Once the control is registered, this information is used by the container application to load your OCX and be able to access the controls available within the OCX.

- The Add Control button allows you to add controls to your project if you need to add more than one type. When you click this button, a new control appears with the name of the default control followed by a numeric value. You can then edit this new control's information.

■ The Delete Control button deletes the control currently highlighted in the Controls list box.

After you have completed the configuration of your control in ControlWizard, you can click the OK button on the main ControlWizard window. The ControlWizard verifies the information and displays the New Control Information dialog box, which contains a summary of the framework that you specified for your control (see fig. 9.6). If you are satisfied with your selections, you can click the Create button to have ControlWizard create your source files in the directory you specified.

Fig. 9.6
The New Control Information dialog box.

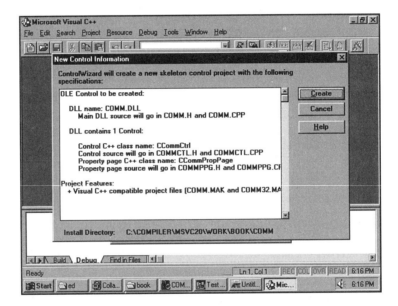

The ControlWizard and MFC provide complete cross-platform compatibility, so you can compile your generated code in both 16- and 32-bit development environments without modifying the code. To prepare for this compilation, ControlWizard creates two makefiles—one for 16-bit (COMM.MAK) and one for 32-bit (COMM32.MAK). The ControlWizard also creates two directories for the storage of 32-bit information (\OBJD32) and 16-bit type libraries (\TLB16).

After ControlWizard has completed its generation of the source files based on the specifications you have provided in the ControlWizard window, you will have everything you need for a working control. Table 9.1 is a list of the files, along with the descriptions for each, that are generated by ControlWizard for the Comm custom control.

Table 9.1 Files Generated by ControlWizard

Filename	File Size	Description
comm32.mak	18,074	The project makefile for building a 32-bit OLE custom control. This project file is compatible with the Visual C++ 2.0 Workbench and is also compatible with NMAKE.
comm.mak	2,540	The project makefile for building your 16-bit OLE custom control. This project file is compatible with the Visual C++ 1.5 Workbench and is also compatible with NMAKE.
makefile	1,431	A makefile that is used by the NMAKE utility from the command prompt. Use the following parameters with NMAKE:
comm.cpp	1,876	This is the main source file that contains the OLE DLL initialization, termination, and other housekeeping.
comm.h	516	This is the main include file for the OLE custom control DLL. It includes project-specific includes such as RESOURCE.H.
comm.def	502	This file contains information about the OLE custom control DLL that must be provided to run with Microsoft Windows. It defines parameters such as the name and description of the DLL, and the size of the initial local heap. The numbers generated in this file are typical for OLE custom control DLLs.
comm32.def	236	This is a version of COMM.DEF for building a 32-bit version of the OLE custom control DLL.
comm.ico	768	This file contains an icon that will appear in the About box. This icon is included in the main resource file COMM.RC.
comm.odl	1,781	This file contains the Object Description Language source code for the type library of your OLE control.

Within the `makefile` row:

```
DEBUG=0      Builds retail version
DEBUG=1      Builds debug version (default)
WIN32=0      Builds 16-bit version (default)
WIN32=1      Builds 32-bit version
UNICODE=0    Builds ANSI/DBCS version
             (default for WIN32=0)
UNICODE=1    Build Unicode version
             (default for WIN32=1)
```

(continues)

Table 9.1 Continued

File name	File Size	Description
comm.rc	3,001	This is a listing of the Microsoft Windows resources that the project uses. This file can be directly edited with the Visual C++ resource editor.
comm.rc2	2,075	This file contains resources that are not edited by the resource editor. Initially this contains a VERSIONINFO resource that you can customize for your OLE custom control DLL, and a TYPELIB resource for your DLL's type library. You should place other manually maintained resources for your control in this file.
commctl.cpp	7,599	This file contains the implementation of the CCommCtrl C++ class.
commctl.h	1,447	This file contains the declaration of the CCommCtrl C++ class.
commppg.cpp	2,091	This file contains the implementation of the CCommPropPage C++ class.
commppg.h	711	This file contains the declaration of the CCommPropPage C++ class.
resource.h	844	This is the standard header file, which defines new resource IDs that are read and updated by AppStudio.
comm.clw	1,020	This file contains information used by ClassWizard to edit existing classes or add new classes. ClassWizard also uses this file to store information needed to generate and edit message maps and dialog data maps and to generate prototype member functions.
commctl.bmp	240	This file contains a bitmap that a container will use to represent the CCommCtrl control when it appears on a tool palette. This bitmap is included by the main resource file COMM.RC.
stdafx.cpp stdafx.h	204 240	These files are used to build a precompiled header (PCH) file named DAFX.PCH and a precompiled types (PCT) file named STDAFX.OBJ.

Details of the Control

The code to develop the communications custom control, included on the CD accompanying this book, is very simple—especially since most of it is generated by ControlWizard. You will step through the code in the following sections to give you a feel for the code that makes up the control, and provide you some insight into how you can put together a full control of your own.

The comm.h File

Listing 9.1 contains the source code for the Comm control's application class header file. In this file, you will find the definition for the control's application class as well as the global variables used by the rest of the OCX.

Listing 9.1   comm.h—The Comm Control's Header File

```
// comm.h : main header file for COMM.DLL
#if !defined( __AFXCTL_H__ )
    #error include 'afxctl.h' before including this file
#endif

#include "resource.h"        // main symbols

/////////////////////////////////////////////////////////////////////
// CCommApp : See comm.cpp for implementation.

class CCommApp : public COleControlModule
{
public:
    BOOL InitInstance();
    int ExitInstance();
};

extern const GUID CDECL _tlid;
extern const WORD _wVerMajor;
extern const WORD _wVerMinor;
```

The comm.cpp File

The source code in listing 9.2 contains the implementation of the application class CCommApp, as well as the application instance theApp. All MFC applications can maintain only one application instance; however, you can have multiple instances of the control. One OLE-specific data member important here is the _tlid global variable. This variable is utilized by the DLLRegisterServer() and DLLUnregisterServer() functions to register and unregister the Comm control from the system registry.

The InitInstance() function is called to initialize a new instance of a control, while ExitInstance() is called when the instance is destroyed. You can add instance-specific code to these two functions to customize the creation and destruction functionality of your control.

Listing 9.2 comm.cpp—The Comm Control's Implementation File

```cpp
// comm.cpp : Implementation of CCommApp and DLL registration.

#include "stdafx.h"
#include "comm.h"

#ifdef _DEBUG
#undef THIS_FILE
static char BASED_CODE THIS_FILE[] = __FILE__;
#endif

CCommApp NEAR theApp;

const GUID CDECL BASED_CODE _tlid =
        { 0x5b83b083, 0x14f0, 0x11ce,
        { 0x96, 0xf, 0x52, 0x41, 0x53, 0x48, 0x0, 0x5 } };
const WORD _wVerMajor = 1;
const WORD _wVerMinor = 0;

/////////////////////////////////////////////////////////////////
// CCommApp::InitInstance - DLL initialization

BOOL CCommApp::InitInstance()
{
    BOOL bInit = COleControlModule::InitInstance();

    if (bInit)
    {
        // TODO: Add your own module initialization code here.
    }

    return bInit;
}

/////////////////////////////////////////////////////////////////
// CCommApp::ExitInstance - DLL termination

int CCommApp::ExitInstance()
{
    // TODO: Add your own module termination code here.

    return COleControlModule::ExitInstance();
}

/////////////////////////////////////////////////////////////////
// DllRegisterServer - Adds entries to the system registry
```

```
STDAPI DllRegisterServer(void)
{
    AFX_MANAGE_STATE(_afxModuleAddrThis);

    if (!AfxOleRegisterTypeLib(AfxGetInstanceHandle(), _tlid))
        return ResultFromScode(SELFREG_E_TYPELIB);

    if (!COleObjectFactoryEx::UpdateRegistryAll(TRUE))
        return ResultFromScode(SELFREG_E_CLASS);

    return NOERROR;
}

/////////////////////////////////////////////////////////////////////
// DllUnregisterServer - Removes entries from the system registry

STDAPI DllUnregisterServer(void)
{
    AFX_MANAGE_STATE(_afxModuleAddrThis);

    if (!AfxOleUnregisterTypeLib(_tlid))
        return ResultFromScode(SELFREG_E_TYPELIB);

    if (!COleObjectFactoryEx::UpdateRegistryAll(FALSE))
        return ResultFromScode(SELFREG_E_CLASS);

    return NOERROR;
}
```

The comm.rc File

The comm.rc file, in listing 9.3, contains the resource script for resources that
are maintained with the AppStudio resource editor. This file defines your
About dialog box and the string table used by the Comm control. The resource script also includes the icon displayed in your container's toolbar and
the bitmap used to render your control in a container's visible workspace.

Listing 9.3   comm.rc—The Comm Control's Resource File

```
//Microsoft Visual C++ generated resource script.
//
#include "resource.h"

#define APSTUDIO_READONLY_SYMBOLS
/////////////////////////////////////////////////////////////////////
//
// Generated from the TEXTINCLUDE 2 resource.
//
#include "afxres.h"
```

(continues)

Listing 9.3 Continued

```
//////////////////////////////////////////////////////////////////
#undef APSTUDIO_READONLY_SYMBOLS


#ifdef APSTUDIO_INVOKED
//////////////////////////////////////////////////////////////////
//
// TEXTINCLUDE
//

1 TEXTINCLUDE DISCARDABLE
BEGIN
    "resource.h\0"
END

2 TEXTINCLUDE DISCARDABLE
BEGIN
    "#include ""afxres.h""\r\n"
    "\0"
END

3 TEXTINCLUDE DISCARDABLE
BEGIN
    "#include ""afxres.rc""\r\n"
    "#include ""comm.rc2""  // non-App Studio edited resources\r\n"
    "#if 0\r\n"
    "#include "".\\tlb16\\comm.tlb""  // 16-bit: force dependency
                                      // on .TLB file\r\n"
    "#endif\r\n"
    "\0"
END

//////////////////////////////////////////////////////////////////
#endif    // APSTUDIO_INVOKED


//////////////////////////////////////////////////////////////////
//
// Icon
//

IDI_ABOUTDLL            ICON    DISCARDABLE     "comm.ico"


//////////////////////////////////////////////////////////////////
//
// Bitmap
//

IDB_COMM                BITMAP  DISCARDABLE     "commctl.bmp"
IDB_BITMAP1             BITMAP  DISCARDABLE     "bitmap1.bmp"
```

```
/////////////////////////////////////////////////////////////////////
//
// Dialog
//

IDD_ABOUTBOX_COMM DIALOG DISCARDABLE  34, 22, 260, 55
STYLE DS_MODALFRAME ¦ WS_POPUP ¦ WS_CAPTION ¦ WS_SYSMENU
CAPTION "About Comm Control"
FONT 8, "MS Sans Serif"
BEGIN
    ICON            IDI_ABOUTDLL,IDC_STATIC,10,10,18,20
    LTEXT           "Communications Test OCX",
                    IDC_STATIC,40,10,170,8
    LTEXT           "Copyright \251 1994, Edward B. Toupin",
                    IDC_STATIC,40,25,170,8
    DEFPUSHBUTTON   "OK",IDOK,220,10,32,14,WS_GROUP
END


IDD_PROPPAGE_COMM DIALOG DISCARDABLE  0, 0, 250, 62
STYLE WS_CHILD
FONT 8, "MS Sans Serif"
BEGIN
END


/////////////////////////////////////////////////////////////////////
//
// String Table
//

STRINGTABLE DISCARDABLE
BEGIN
    IDS_COMM                "Comm Control"
    IDS_COMM_PPG            "Comm Property Page"
END

STRINGTABLE DISCARDABLE
BEGIN
    IDS_COMM_PPG_CAPTION    "General"
END

#ifndef APSTUDIO_INVOKED
/////////////////////////////////////////////////////////////////////
//
// Generated from the TEXTINCLUDE 3 resource.
//
#include "afxres.rc"
#include "comm.rc2"           // non-App Studio edited resources
#if 0
#include ".\tlb16\comm.tlb"  // 16-bit: force dependency
                             // on .TLB file
#endif


/////////////////////////////////////////////////////////////////////
#endif    // not APSTUDIO_INVOKED
```

The comm.rc2 File

The comm.rc2 file, in listing 9.4, contains the resource script for resources that cannot be edited by AppStudio. The resource information contains the VERSIONINFO and the control's type library information. This file is included into your comm.rc file as a separate file so that you can manually edit the information without disturbing the contents of comm.rc. Obviously, you will want to manually change the version number, trademarks, and copyright information of your OCX for your specific implementation.

Listing 9.4 comm.rc2—The Comm Control's Resource File

```
//
// COMM.RC2 - resources App Studio does not edit directly
//

#ifdef APSTUDIO_INVOKED
    #error this file is not editable by App Studio
#endif //APSTUDIO_INVOKED

/////////////////////////////////////////////////////////////////////
// Version stamp for this DLL

#ifdef _WIN32
#include "winver.h"
#else
#include "ver.h"
#endif

VS_VERSION_INFO     VERSIONINFO
   FILEVERSION      1,0,0,1
   PRODUCTVERSION   1,0,0,1
   FILEFLAGSMASK    VS_FFI_FILEFLAGSMASK
#ifdef _DEBUG
   FILEFLAGS        VS_FF_DEBUG¦VS_FF_PRIVATEBUILD¦VS_FF_PRERELEASE
#else
   FILEFLAGS        0 // final version
#endif
#ifdef _WIN32
   FILEOS           VOS__WINDOWS32
#else
   FILEOS           VOS__WINDOWS16
#endif
   FILETYPE         VFT_DLL
   FILESUBTYPE      0   // not used
BEGIN
    BLOCK "StringFileInfo"
    BEGIN
#ifdef _WIN32
        BLOCK "040904B0" // Lang=US English, CharSet=Unicode
```

```
        #else
                BLOCK "040904E4" // Lang=US English, CharSet=Windows
                                 // Multilingual
        #endif
                BEGIN
                    VALUE "CompanyName",       "\0"
                    VALUE "FileDescription",   "COMM OLE Control DLL\0"
                    VALUE "FileVersion",       "1.0.001\0"
                    VALUE "InternalName",      "COMM\0"
                    VALUE "LegalCopyright",
                        "Copyright \251 1994, Edward B. Toupin\0"
                    VALUE "LegalTrademarks",  "\0"
                    VALUE "OriginalFilename", "COMM.DLL\0"
                    VALUE "ProductName",       "COMM\0"
                    VALUE "ProductVersion",   "1.0.001\0"
                    VALUE "OLESelfRegister",  "\0"
                END
            END
            BLOCK "VarFileInfo"
            BEGIN
        #ifdef _WIN32
                VALUE "Translation", 0x409, 1200
                        // English language (0x409) and the Unicode
                        // codepage (1200)
        #else
                VALUE "Translation", 0x409, 1252
                        // English language (0x409) and the Windows ANSI
                        // codepage (1252)
        #endif
            END
        END

        /////////////////////////////////////////////////////////////////
        // Type library for controls in this DLL

        1 TYPELIB comm.tlb

        /////////////////////////////////////////////////////////////////
        // Add additional manually edited resources here...

        /////////////////////////////////////////////////////////////////
```

The comm.def File

The comm.def file, in listing 9.5, contains the definition for the 16-bit Comm control. The library NAME and DESCRIPTION clauses contain the Comm project name as well as the exports contained in COMM.DLL. These exports are the functions made visible to Windows so that Windows can call them as required.

Listing 9.5 comm.def—The Comm Control's 16-bit Definition File

```
; comm.def : Declares the module parameters.

LIBRARY        'COMM'
DESCRIPTION    'COMM OLE Custom Control module'
EXETYPE        WINDOWS

CODE           PRELOAD MOVEABLE DISCARDABLE
DATA           PRELOAD MOVEABLE SINGLE

HEAPSIZE       1024    ; initial heap size

EXPORTS
    WEP                    @1   RESIDENTNAME
    DLLCANUNLOADNOW        @2   RESIDENTNAME
    DLLGETCLASSOBJECT      @3   RESIDENTNAME
    DLLREGISTERSERVER      @4   RESIDENTNAME
    DLLUNREGISTERSERVER    @5   RESIDENTNAME

SEGMENTS
    WEP_TEXT FIXED
```

The comm32.def File

The comm32.def file, in listing 9.6, contains the definitions for the 32-bit Comm control. The most important difference between this definition and the 16-bit definition is that the EXETYPE and the SEGMENTS clause are not included in this definition. The primary reason for the missing parameters is that you do not need to be concerned about defining segments and executable types under 32-bit Windows.

Listing 9.6 comm32.def—The Comm Control's 32-bit Definition File

```
; comm32.def : Declares the module parameters.

LIBRARY        COMM.OCX

EXPORTS
    DllCanUnloadNow        @1 RESIDENTNAME
    DllGetClassObject      @2 RESIDENTNAME
    DllRegisterServer      @3 RESIDENTNAME
    DllUnregisterServer    @4 RESIDENTNAME
```

The commctl.h File

Listing 9.7 shows the contents of the commctl.h header file, which contains the class definition for the CCommCtl class. As you can see, CCommCtrl is derived from the C0leObject base class, providing much of the functionality required by the Comm control. The derived class contains a public constructor, a protected destructor, the message-handling function OnDraw(), and the control reset function OnResetState().

Note the macros in the following list, which further define the functionality of the OLE control:

- DECLARE_OLECREATE_EX declares your control's class factory and provides the GetClassId() member function.

- DECLARE_OLETYPELIB declares the member function GetTypeLib(), which returns your control's type library. MFC utilizes the type library for the control internally for your control's OLE interface.

- DECLARE_PROPPAGEIDS prepares your control for the binding of your property pages to the control's properties. Property pages provide a tabbed visual interface to your control's properties.

Listing 9.7 commctl.h—The Header File for the *CCommCtrl* Class

```
// commctl.h : Declaration of the CCommCtrl OLE control class.

/////////////////////////////////////////////////////////////////////
// CCommCtrl : See commctl.cpp for implementation.

class CCommCtrl : public COleControl
{
    DECLARE_DYNCREATE(CCommCtrl)

// Constructor
public:
    CCommCtrl();

// Overrides

    // Drawing function
    virtual void OnDraw(
        CDC* pdc, const CRect& rcBounds, const CRect& rcInvalid);

    // Persistence
    virtual void DoPropExchange(CPropExchange* pPX);

    // Reset control state
    virtual void OnResetState();

// Implementation
protected:
    ~CCommCtrl();
```

(continues)

```
Listing 9.7   Continued

        DECLARE_OLECREATE_EX(CCommCtrl)    // Class factory and guid
        DECLARE_OLETYPELIB(CCommCtrl)      // GetTypeInfo
        DECLARE_PROPPAGEIDS(CCommCtrl)     // Property page IDs
        DECLARE_OLECTLTYPE(CCommCtrl)      // Type name and misc status

    // Message maps
        //{{AFX_MSG(CCommCtrl)
        //}}AFX_MSG
        DECLARE_MESSAGE_MAP()

    // Dispatch maps
        //{{AFX_DISPATCH(CCommCtrl)
        //}}AFX_DISPATCH
        DECLARE_DISPATCH_MAP()

        afx_msg void AboutBox();

    // Event maps
        //{{AFX_EVENT(CCommCtrl)
        //}}AFX_EVENT
        DECLARE_EVENT_MAP()

    // Dispatch and event IDs
    public:
        enum {
        //{{AFX_DISP_ID(CCommCtrl)
        //}}AFX_DISP_ID
        };
};
```

The commctl.cpp File

Listing 9.8 contains the code for the implementation file, commctl.cpp, of
the Comm control. This file contains the primary code for the functionality
of the control itself. This is also where the code that provides customized
features for the control will reside.

The sections of the implementation file for the control are as follows:

- The *message map* contains a correspondence list of messages to functions. Each message listed in the message map corresponds to a member
  function for the class. Each time that the control receives a particular
  message, such as ON_WM_LBUTTONDOWN() or ON_WM_RBUTTONDOWN(), the associated member function is fired, thus executing your code.

- The *dispatch map* exposes functions and properties so that containers
  and other Windows applications can access the methods and properties
  of your control. The default entry created by ControlWizard, About

box, activates the control's About dialog box when an external application makes a request for the `AboutBox()` member function.

■ The *event map* allows you to add events to communicate with the control's container. These events are Windows messages that are passed to the control when certain events occur on the control.

■ The *property page IDs* identify the property pages that change the values of the control's properties. All controls generated by the ClassWizard start with one property page, General, which is the only entry in the current set of property pages. You add controls to the General property page as well as add user-defined property pages as required.

■ The *OLE macros* `IMPLEMENT_OLECREATE_EX` and `IMPLEMENT_OLETYPELIB` create the class factory and type library code needed to implement the control as an OLE object.

■ The *interface IDs* `IID_DComm` and `IID_DCommEvents` are the unique IDs for the Comm control and its events.

■ The `CCommCtrlFactory::UpdateRegistry()` function adds or removes entries in the system registry. The code and the control's default parameters are generated for you automatically and are usually adequate for the implementation.

■ The *constructor* initializes the `IID`s for the control.

■ The *destructor* is currently an empty shell, but you can add your own code to be executed when the control is destroyed as required.

■ The `OnDraw()` function contains minimal code to at least draw something when the function is called—in this case an ellipse in a square. You can replace this code with your own rendering code as required to appropriately represent the control in the container's visible workspace.

■ The `DoPropExchange()` function provides a method of serialization for your control. Simply, the property information for your control is loaded and saved through a stream in this function. This is useful in saving the OLE workspace for the control and later loading it back into a container.

■ The `OnResetState()` is called to reset the control's contents. Any properties included in the `DoPropExchange()` function should, through coding of your own, be reset to default values. You also can use this function to reinitialize internal class and data members.

- The AboutBox() function is called to display your control's About dialog
  box and is currently the only member of the dispatch map. A CDialog
  object is instantiated to display the About dialog box, which is then
  executed by the DoModal() member function.

**Listing 9.8   commctl.cpp—The Implementation File for the
CCommCtrl Class**

```
// commctl.cpp : Implementation of the CCommCtrl OLE control class.

#include "stdafx.h"
#include "comm.h"
#include "commctl.h"
#include "commppg.h"


#ifdef _DEBUG
#undef THIS_FILE
static char BASED_CODE THIS_FILE[] = __FILE__;
#endif

IMPLEMENT_DYNCREATE(CCommCtrl, COleControl)


/////////////////////////////////////////////////////////////////
// Message map

BEGIN_MESSAGE_MAP(CCommCtrl, COleControl)
    //{{AFX_MSG_MAP(CCommCtrl)
    //}}AFX_MSG_MAP
    ON_OLEVERB(AFX_IDS_VERB_EDIT, OnEdit)
    ON_OLEVERB(AFX_IDS_VERB_PROPERTIES, OnProperties)
END_MESSAGE_MAP()


/////////////////////////////////////////////////////////////////
// Dispatch map

BEGIN_DISPATCH_MAP(CCommCtrl, COleControl)
    //{{AFX_DISPATCH_MAP(CCommCtrl)
    //}}AFX_DISPATCH_MAP
    DISP_FUNCTION_ID(CCommCtrl, "AboutBox", DISPID_ABOUTBOX,
      AboutBox, VT_EMPTY, VTS_NONE)
END_DISPATCH_MAP()


/////////////////////////////////////////////////////////////////
// Event map

BEGIN_EVENT_MAP(CCommCtrl, COleControl)
    //{{AFX_EVENT_MAP(CCommCtrl)
    //}}AFX_EVENT_MAP
END_EVENT_MAP()
```

```
//////////////////////////////////////////////////////////////////
// Property pages

// TODO: Add more property pages as needed.
// Remember to increase the count!
BEGIN_PROPPAGEIDS(CCommCtrl, 1)
    PROPPAGEID(CCommPropPage::guid)
END_PROPPAGEIDS(CCommCtrl)


//////////////////////////////////////////////////////////////////
// Initialize class factory and guid

IMPLEMENT_OLECREATE_EX(CCommCtrl, "COMM.CommCtrl.1",
    0x5b83b080, 0x14f0, 0x11ce, 0x96, 0xf, 0x52, 0x41, 0x53,
    0x48, 0x0, 0x5)


//////////////////////////////////////////////////////////////////
// Type library ID and version

IMPLEMENT_OLETYPELIB(CCommCtrl, _tlid, _wVerMajor, _wVerMinor)


//////////////////////////////////////////////////////////////////
// Interface IDs

const IID BASED_CODE IID_DComm =
        { 0x5b83b081, 0x14f0, 0x11ce,
        { 0x96, 0xf, 0x52, 0x41, 0x53, 0x48, 0x0, 0x5 } };
const IID BASED_CODE IID_DCommEvents =
        { 0x5b83b082, 0x14f0, 0x11ce,
        { 0x96, 0xf, 0x52, 0x41, 0x53, 0x48, 0x0, 0x5 } };


//////////////////////////////////////////////////////////////////
// Control type information

static const DWORD BASED_CODE _dwCommOleMisc =
    OLEMISC_ACTIVATEWHENVISIBLE |
    OLEMISC_SETCLIENTSITEFIRST |
    OLEMISC_INSIDEOUT |
    OLEMISC_CANTLINKINSIDE |
    OLEMISC_RECOMPOSEONRESIZE;

IMPLEMENT_OLECTLTYPE(CCommCtrl, IDS_COMM, _dwCommOleMisc)


//////////////////////////////////////////////////////////////////
// CCommCtrl::CCommCtrlFactory::UpdateRegistry -
// Adds or removes system registry entries for CCommCtrl

BOOL CCommCtrl::CCommCtrlFactory::UpdateRegistry(BOOL bRegister)
{
    if (bRegister)
```

(continues)

Listing 9.8 Continued

```
            return AfxOleRegisterControlClass(
                AfxGetInstanceHandle(),
                m_clsid,
                m_lpszProgID,
                IDS_COMM,
                IDB_COMM,
                TRUE,                           //  Insertable
                _dwCommOleMisc,
                _tlid,
                _wVerMajor,
                _wVerMinor);
    else
            return AfxOleUnregisterClass(m_clsid, m_lpszProgID);
}


/////////////////////////////////////////////////////////////////
// CCommCtrl::CCommCtrl - Constructor

CCommCtrl::CCommCtrl()
{
    InitializeIIDs(&IID_DComm, &IID_DCommEvents);

    // TODO: Initialize your control's instance data here.
}


/////////////////////////////////////////////////////////////////
// CCommCtrl::~CCommCtrl - Destructor

CCommCtrl::~CCommCtrl()
{
    // TODO: Clean up your control's instance data here.
}


/////////////////////////////////////////////////////////////////
// CCommCtrl::OnDraw - Drawing function

void CCommCtrl::OnDraw(
                CDC* pdc, const CRect& rcBounds,
                    const CRect& rcInvalid)
{
    // TODO: Replace the following code with your
    // own drawing code.
    pdc->FillRect(rcBounds,
        CBrush::FromHandle((HBRUSH)GetStockObject(WHITE_BRUSH)));
    pdc->Ellipse(rcBounds);
}


/////////////////////////////////////////////////////////////////
// CCommCtrl::DoPropExchange - Persistence support
```

```
void CCommCtrl::DoPropExchange(CPropExchange* pPX)
{
    ExchangeVersion(pPX, MAKELONG(_wVerMinor, _wVerMajor));
    COleControl::DoPropExchange(pPX);
    // TODO: Call PX_ functions for each persistent custom
    // property.
}


//////////////////////////////////////////////////////////////////
// CCommCtrl::OnResetState - Reset control to default state

void CCommCtrl::OnResetState()
{
    COleControl::OnResetState();  // Resets defaults found in
                                  // DoPropExchange

    // TODO: Reset any other control state here.
}


//////////////////////////////////////////////////////////////////
// CCommCtrl::AboutBox - Display an "About" box to the user

void CCommCtrl::AboutBox()
{
    CDialog dlgAbout(IDD_ABOUTBOX_COMM);
    dlgAbout.DoModal();
}


//////////////////////////////////////////////////////////////////
// CCommCtrl message handlers
```

The commppg.h File

Listing 9.9 shows the contents of the commppg.h header file. This file contains the class definition for CCommPropPage. This class provides the definition of the class required for the General property page and is derived from the CDialog MFC class.

Listing 9.9   commppg.h—The Header File for the *CCommPropPage* Class

```
// commppg.h : Declaration of the CCommPropPage
// property page class.

//////////////////////////////////////////////////////////////////
// CCommPropPage : See commppg.cpp for implementation.

class CCommPropPage : public COlePropertyPage
```

(continues)

Listing 9.9   Continued

```
{
     DECLARE_DYNCREATE(CCommPropPage)
     DECLARE_OLECREATE_EX(CCommPropPage)

// Constructor
public:
     CCommPropPage();

// Dialog Data
     //{{AFX_DATA(CCommPropPage)
     enum { IDD = IDD_PROPPAGE_COMM };
     //}}AFX_DATA

// Implementation
protected:
     virtual void DoDataExchange(CDataExchange* pDX);    // DDX/DDV
                                                         // support

// Message maps
protected:
     //{{AFX_MSG(CCommPropPage)
     //}}AFX_MSG
     DECLARE_MESSAGE_MAP()

};
```

The commppg.cpp File

Listing 9.10 shows the contents of the commppg.h header file. This file contains the class definition for CCommPropPage. This class provides the functionality for the General property page based on the class defined in the respective header file.

The sections of the property page implementation file for the control are as follows:

■ The *message map* is a shell for modifications to be made later. This message map, as with CCommCtrl, contains a correspondence list of messages to member functions.

■ The IMPLEMENT_OLECREATE_EX macro declares the class factory for the control and the GetClassID() function. Since CCommPropPage is an OLE class, it is registered in the system registry using the class factory.

■ The CCommPropPageFactory::UpdateRegistry() function registers and deregisters the CCommPropPage class.

■ The *constructor* is included so that you can add your own initialization code for the instantiation of the control's property pages as required.

- The `DoDataExchange()` function overrides the standard `CHWnd::DoDataExchange()` function to provide data transfer between the control and the property pages.

Listing 9.10   commppg.cpp—The Implementation File for the *CCommPropPage* Class

```
// commppg.cpp : Implementation of the CCommPropPage
// property page class.

#include "stdafx.h"
#include "comm.h"
#include "commppg.h"

#ifdef _DEBUG
#undef THIS_FILE
static char BASED_CODE THIS_FILE[] = __FILE__;
#endif


IMPLEMENT_DYNCREATE(CCommPropPage, COlePropertyPage)


/////////////////////////////////////////////////////////////////
// Message map

BEGIN_MESSAGE_MAP(CCommPropPage, COlePropertyPage)
    //{{AFX_MSG_MAP(CCommPropPage)
    //}}AFX_MSG_MAP
END_MESSAGE_MAP()


/////////////////////////////////////////////////////////////////
// Initialize class factory and guid

IMPLEMENT_OLECREATE_EX(CCommPropPage, "COMM.CommPropPage.1",
    0x5b83b084, 0x14f0, 0x11ce, 0x96, 0xf, 0x52, 0x41, 0x53,
    0x48, 0x0, 0x5)


/////////////////////////////////////////////////////////////////
// CCommPropPage::CCommPropPageFactory::UpdateRegistry -
// Adds or removes system registry entries for CCommPropPage

BOOL CCommPropPage::CCommPropPageFactory::UpdateRegistry
    (BOOL bRegister)
{
    if (bRegister)
        return
AfxOleRegisterPropertyPageClass(AfxGetInstanceHandle(),
            m_clsid, IDS_COMM_PPG);
    else
```

(continues)

Listing 9.10 Continued

```
            return AfxOleUnregisterClass(m_clsid, NULL);
}


/////////////////////////////////////////////////////////////////////
// CCommPropPage::CCommPropPage - Constructor

CCommPropPage::CCommPropPage() :
    COlePropertyPage(IDD, IDS_COMM_PPG_CAPTION)
{
    //{{AFX_DATA_INIT(CCommPropPage)
    //}}AFX_DATA_INIT
}


/////////////////////////////////////////////////////////////////////
// CCommPropPage::DoDataExchange - Moves data between
// page and properties

void CCommPropPage::DoDataExchange(CDataExchange* pDX)
{
    //{{AFX_DATA_MAP(CCommPropPage)
    //}}AFX_DATA_MAP
    DDP_PostProcessing(pDX);
}


/////////////////////////////////////////////////////////////////////
// CCommPropPage message handlers
```

The stdafx.h File

Listing 9.11 shows the stdafx.h file, which contains a single #include statement. This #include statement provides MFC support for OLE controls.

Listing 9.11 stdafx.h—The Standard System Include File

```
// stdafx.h : include file for standard system include files,
// or project-specific include files that are used frequently
// but are changed infrequently

#include <afxctl.h>          // MFC support for OLE Custom Controls
```

The stdafx.cpp File

Listing 9.12 shows the stdafx.cpp file, which is the implementation file for MFC OLE control support.

Listing 9.12   stdafx.cpp—The Standard System Implementation File

```
// stdafx.cpp : source file that includes just the standard
// includes
// stdafx.pch will be the pre-compiled header
// stdafx.obj will contain the pre-compiled type information

#include "stdafx.h"
```

The resource.h File

Listing 9.13 shows the resource.h file. This file contains several #define statements that are used by the comm.rc resource script file. The #define statements correspond to the following:

IDS_?????	Strings in a string table
IDS_?????	Dialog box identifiers
IDB_?????	Bitmap identifiers
IDI_?????	Icon identifiers

When you load the comm.rc file in the AppStudio, these names will also be loaded and used when you view the properties for the resources edited in the resource file. You should recognize these names as identifiers for the various resources you can edit.

Listing 9.13   resource.h—The Resource Header File

```
//{{NO_DEPENDENCIES}}
// Microsoft Visual C++ generated include file.
// Used by comm.rc
//
#define IDS_COMM                   1
#define IDB_COMM                   1
#define IDS_COMM_PPG               2
#define IDI_ABOUTDLL              10
#define IDD_ABOUTBOX_COMM        100
#define IDS_COMM_PPG_CAPTION     101
#define IDD_PROPPAGE_COMM        101
#define IDB_BITMAP1              201

// Next default values for new objects
//
#ifdef APSTUDIO_INVOKED
#ifndef APSTUDIO_READONLY_SYMBOLS
```

(continues)

Listing 9.13 Continued

```
#define _APS_NEXT_RESOURCE_VALUE          202
#define _APS_NEXT_COMMAND_VALUE           32768
#define _APS_NEXT_CONTROL_VALUE           206
#define _APS_NEXT_SYMED_VALUE             101
#endif
#endif
```

The comm.odl File

The Comm control's type library information is stored in the comm.odl file, which is shown in listing 9.14. The ClassWizard maintains the information stored in this file; however, you should be aware of the information in this file to understand how the control is registered and accessed by container applications.

The sections of the type library file for the control are as follows:

- The *dispatch interface* corresponds directly to the dispatch map in commctl.cpp. This information is added to the resources of your control so that applications requesting access to the control's members and properties can find out about the interfaces that your control supports. This section consists of properties and methods subsections containing the properties and methods that you are making accessible.

- The *event dispatch* section stores information about the events that your OLE control generates. The container can then respond to events generated by your control. The event dispatch also consists of properties and methods subsections; however, there are no properties associated with events, usually only methods.

- The *class information* section exports the interface for both the primary dispatch interface and the event dispatch interface. Containers refer to this section to learn about all of the various interfaces that your OLE control supports.

Listing 9.14 comm.odl—Type Library File

```
// comm.odl : type library source for OLE Custom Control project.

// This file will be processed by the Make Type Library (mktyplib)
// tool to produce the type library (comm.tlb) that will become a
// resource in comm.ocx.

#include <olectl.h>
```

```
[ uuid(5B83B083-14F0-11CE-960F-524153480005), version(1.0),
  helpstring("Comm OLE Custom Control module") ]
library CommLib
{
    importlib(STDOLE_TLB);
    importlib(STDTYPE_TLB);

    //  Primary dispatch interface for CCommCtrl

    [ uuid(5B83B081-14F0-11CE-960F-524153480005),
      helpstring("Dispatch interface for Comm Control") ]
    dispinterface _DComm
    {
        properties:
            // NOTE - ClassWizard will maintain property
            // information here.
            //    Use extreme caution when editing this section.
            //{{AFX_ODL_PROP(CCommCtrl)
            //}}AFX_ODL_PROP

        methods:
            // NOTE - ClassWizard will maintain method
            // information here.
            //    Use extreme caution when editing this section.
            //{{AFX_ODL_METHOD(CCommCtrl)
            //}}AFX_ODL_METHOD

            [id(DISPID_ABOUTBOX)] void AboutBox();
    };

    //  Event dispatch interface for CCommCtrl

    [ uuid(5B83B082-14F0-11CE-960F-524153480005),
      helpstring("Event interface for Comm Control") ]
    dispinterface _DCommEvents
    {
        properties:
            //  Event interface has no properties

        methods:
            // NOTE - ClassWizard will maintain event
            // information here.
            //    Use extreme caution when editing this section.
            //{{AFX_ODL_EVENT(CCommCtrl)
            //}}AFX_ODL_EVENT
    };

    //  Class information for CCommCtrl

    [ uuid(5B83B080-14F0-11CE-960F-524153480005),
      helpstring("Comm Control") ]
    CoClass Comm
    {
        [default] dispinterface _DComm;
```

(continues)

Listing 9.14 Continued

```
        [default, source] dispinterface _DCommEvents;
    };


    //{{AFX_APPEND_ODL}}
};
```

Customizing the Control

Now that the framework is available, as generated by ControlWizard, you need to enhance the control's code to meet the needs of the design. The purpose of this control is to dial a number, which you enter into the property page, when you click with the left mouse button. The control also will respond to the right mouse button click by accessing the About dialog box.

Changing the Control Rendering

The first code change that you should implement is that of altering the way the control is rendered in a container's visible workspace when the container loads the control. As you saw in the OnDraw() member function generated by ControlWizard, the control displays an ellipse in a square within a container control (see fig. 9.7). You need to change the representation of the control to be something more suitable. Because this control performs a dial operation, you could change the rendering to a telephone.

Listing 9.15 Modifying the *OnDraw()* Member Function

```
void CCommCtrl::OnDraw(
            CDC* pdc, const CRect& rcBounds,
                const CRect& rcInvalid)
{
    // TODO: Replace the following code with your own drawing
    // code.
    CBitmap bitmap;
    BITMAP  bmp;
    CPictureHolder picHolder;
    CRect rcSrcBounds;

    // Load clock bitmap
    bitmap.LoadBitmap(IDB_BITMAP1);
    bitmap.GetObject(sizeof(BITMAP), &bmp);
    rcSrcBounds.right = bmp.bmWidth;
    rcSrcBounds.bottom = bmp.bmHeight;

    // Create picture and render
    picHolder.CreateFromBitmap((HBITMAP)bitmap.m_hObject,
```

```
      NULL, FALSE);
    picHolder.Render(pdc, rcBounds, rcSrcBounds);
}
```

The preceding code replaces the CCommCtrl::OnDraw() function in the commctl.cpp implementation file. This code loads a bitmap resource called IDB_BITMAP1 into the rectangle used to display the control. This bitmap is that of a telephone and was created using the resource editor of the Visual Workbench in the comm.rc file. When the control is loaded into a container, the control looks like figure 9.8.

Fig. 9.7
The original rendering.

Fig. 9.8
The modified rendering.

Modifying the Property Page

The property page for this control will provide a means of entering a phone number so that the other functions of the control can have a number to dial. In modifying the property page, you need to first access the resource editor for the project and load the dialog box named IDD_PROPPAGE_COMM, as shown in figure 9.9. This dialog box is the default property page, General, for the control.

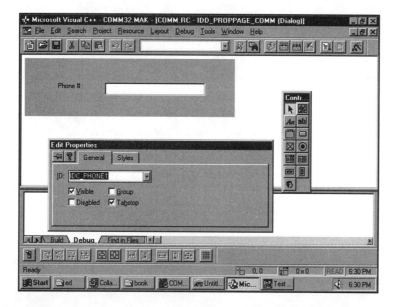

Fig. 9.9
Modifying the property page.

When ControlWizard creates the property page for your control, the page is originally empty. To make this page suit the needs of the control, add an edit control called IDC_PHONE1. This edit control will allow you to enter the phone number to be dialed by the control.

Once the edit control is added, you need to add a variable using the ClassWizard. Select the Member Variables tab in the ClassWizard dialog box in order to add a variable attached to the edit control. Click the Add Variable button and enter the information associated with that variable (see fig. 9.10). For this control, the variable will be of the CString class so that it can store a text representation of the phone number. You also need to add the OLE Property Name PhoneNumber, or a tagname of sorts, to the new variable. This tagname will be used to access the value of the property from those member functions or applications that require access to the property.

Fig. 9.10
Adding a variable.

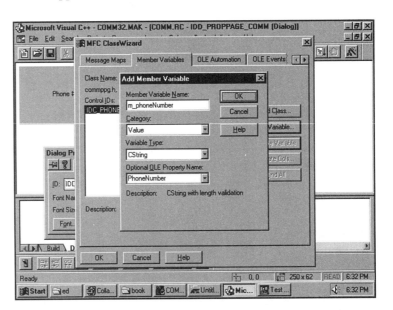

Listing 9.16 The Modified *DoDataExchange()* Function

```
void CCommPropPage::DoDataExchange(CDataExchange* pDX)
{
    //{{AFX_DATA_MAP(CCommPropPage)
    DDP_Text(pDX, IDC_PHONE1, m_phoneNumber, _T("PhoneNumber") );
    DDX_Text(pDX, IDC_PHONE1, m_phoneNumber);
    DDV_MaxChars(pDX, m_phoneNumber, 14);
    //}}AFX_DATA_MAP
    DDP_PostProcessing(pDX);
}
```

As shown in listing 9.16, when you add the m_phoneNumber member variable to the CCommPropPage class, the DDX_Text() and DDV_Text() functions are added as part of the operation of the ClassWizard. DDX_Text() implements data exchange with a dialog box—being the property page in this context. DDV_MaxChars() validates the edit control IDC_PHONE1 to make sure that the number of characters entered does not exceed 14.

The DDP_Text() function is used to synchronize the value of the property with the associated property page control and should always be called before the corresponding DDX_Text() function. You are essentially assigning a tagname by which data exchange operations can access the property by name.

When the value for the edit control you just added changes, you want to receive some kind of notification so that you can perform an operation with the data. To accomplish this, select the CCommCtrl Class Name under the OLE Automation tab of the ClassWizard. Click the Add Property button to access the Add Property dialog box (see fig. 9.11). In this box, you add a property and property notification procedure that is to be executed when the phone number changes.

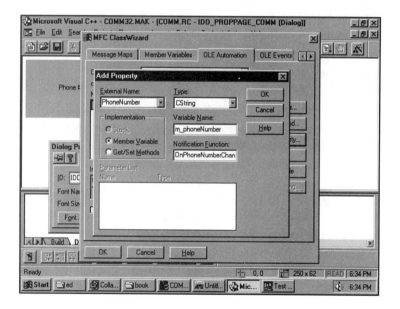

Fig. 9.11
Adding a property.

This property is notified through OnPhoneNumberChanged() when the phone number changes in the property page. The new value of the phone number is also stored in the m_phoneNumber variable for use within the CCommCtrl class.

As you can see in listing 9.17, the dispatch map is modified to provide a method of firing a procedure whenever the phone number changes in the property page. The macro DISP_PROPERTY_NOTIFY takes arguments of the class name, property name, member variable, the notification function, and the variable type.

Listing 9.17   The Dispatch Map

```
BEGIN_DISPATCH_MAP(CCommCtrl, COleControl)
    //{{AFX_DISPATCH_MAP(CCommCtrl)
    DISP_PROPERTY_NOTIFY(CCommCtrl, "PhoneNumber", m_phoneNumber,
        OnPhoneNumberChanged, VT_BSTR)
    //}}AFX_DISPATCH_MAP
    DISP_FUNCTION_ID(CCommCtrl, "AboutBox", DISPID_ABOUTBOX,
        AboutBox, VT_EMPTY, VTS_NONE)
END_DISPATCH_MAP()
```

In addition to adding the dispatch map to the control's code, the notification functions associated with the dispatch map are also added to the ccommctl.cpp file. As you can see in listing 9.18, the function OnPhoneNumberChanged() is added to the code and is fired each time the phone number in the property page changes.

Listing 9.18   The Notification Function

```
void CCommCtrl::OnPhoneNumberChanged()
{
    // TODO: Add notification handler code
    SetModifiedFlag(TRUE);
}
```

The SetModifiedFlag() function sets a new value for the control's modified flag. True, the default, indicates that the control's state has been modified; whereas False indicates that the control's state has been saved since the last time it changed. This function is called whenever a change occurs that would affect your control's persistent state. For example, if the value of a persistent property changes, this function should be called, passing a value of True as an argument to the function.

On the other side, you can use the IsModified() function to determine whether a control's state has been changed. A return value of 0 means the control has not been changed; however, a non-zero value means that the control has been changed since the last time it was saved.

Setting Default Values

When the control is placed into a container and activated, a default phone number is placed into the m_phoneNumber property. This defaulting operation is merely to provide an initial starting point for the dialing operation. To provide a default for the m_phoneNumber variable, modify the DoPropExchange() function as shown in listing 9.19.

Listing 9.19   Setting a Default

```
void CCommCtrl::DoPropExchange(CPropExchange* pPX)
{
    ExchangeVersion(pPX, MAKELONG(_wVerMinor, _wVerMajor));
    COleControl::DoPropExchange(pPX);
    // TODO: Call PX_ functions for each persistent custom
    // property.
    PX_String(pPX,_T("PhoneNumber"),m_phoneNumber,DEF_PHONE);
}
```

The modification includes the addition of the PX_String() function, which allows you to either extract or set the value of the property with the OLE Property Name of PhoneNumber. In this case, you are sending a string to the property page that is stored in the DEF_PHONE constant. The value stored in DEF_PHONE is defined as #define DEF_PHONE "13031234567" at the top of the commctl.cpp file.

Responding to Mouse Click Events

Since you want to dial a number when you click on the control with the mouse, the program needs a way of responding to these mouse clicks. To be able to react to mouse clicks, you need to add two event procedures that are executed when you click on the control with either the left or the right mouse button.

To add these procedures, you need to access the ClassWizard from the Project option of the Visual Workbench menu, and select the tab for the Message Map page. The ClassWizard dialog box appears so that you can select the class you want to modify. For this control, select the CCommCtrl class from the Class Name list. In the Object IDs list box, select the CCommCtrl object to access a list of messages for the object in the Messages list (see fig. 9.12).

For this control, you will want to first choose the WM_LBUTTONDOWN messages and click the Add Function button. Doing so adds the function CCommCtrl::OnLButtonDown() and brings that code forward in the code window to allow you to edit. In this function, you will want to modify the function to add the code as it appears in listing 9.20.

Fig. 9.12

Adding the mouse
button messages.

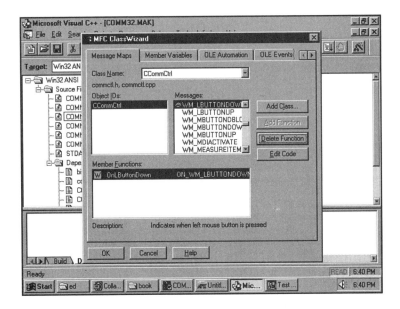

Listing 9.20   The Left Mouse Button Event Function

```
void CCommCtrl::OnLButtonDown(UINT nFlags, CPoint point)
{
    // TODO: Add your message handler code here
    // and/or call default
    LPDCB       lpDevConBlk;
    DWORD       dwLstErr;
    HANDLE      hCommDev;
    int iloop;
    CString     cCommStr;

    //Build a device control block
    if(!BuildCommDCB("COM2: baud=1200 parity=n data=8 stop=1",
lpDevConBlk))
        dwLstErr = GetLastError();

    //Open a handle for the communications port
    hCommDev = CreateFile("COM2:",GENERIC_WRITE,0,NULL,
        OPEN_ALWAYS,FILE_ATTRIBUTE_NORMAL,NULL);

    //Set up the communications port; bypass if an error occurs
    if(!SetCommState(hCommDev,lpDevConBlk))
        MessageBox("Cannot Setup Comm Device");

    //Build a comm string to submit to modem
    cCommStr = "atdt" + m_phoneNumber;

    //Send each character from the property page phone number
    for(iloop=0;iloop<cCommStr.GetLength();iloop++)
```

```
    {
        TransmitCommChar(hCommDev,cCommStr[iloop]);
        Sleep(10);
    }

    //Send a carriage return line-feed to notify the modem that
    //the # is complete
    TransmitCommChar(hCommDev,0x0D);
    Sleep(10);
    TransmitCommChar(hCommDev,0x0A);

    //Wait for 5 seconds
    Sleep(5000);

    //Create a hangup command to the modem
    cCommStr = "ath";

    //Send each character from the hangup command string
    for(iloop=0;iloop<cCommStr.GetLength();iloop++)
    {
        TransmitCommChar(hCommDev,cCommStr[iloop]);
        Sleep(10);
    }

    //Send a carriage return line-feed to notify the modem that
    //the command is complete
    TransmitCommChar(hCommDev,0x0D);
    Sleep(10);
    TransmitCommChar(hCommDev,0x0A);

    //Close the device attached to this handle
    CloseHandle(hCommDev);

    COleControl::OnLButtonDown(nFlags, point);
}
```

The first thing that you do in the function is create a device control block (DCB), open the communications port, and set the communications port to the parameters you supplied for the BuildDCB() function. This code is hard-coded to access COM2 at 1200 baud; however, you can add a couple of radio buttons to the property page to provide a means of dynamically setting the proper communications port and speed.

Once the port is set up, you need to send the phone number entered in the property page out the port to dial the modem. Recall that you have a notification function, OnPhoneNumberChanged, and a variable, m_phoneNumber, that are affected by any changes in the property page. When the phone number changes, it is stored into the CString m_phoneNumber. You are using that variable and appending it to the atdt modem dial command string in order to have the modem dial the number.

The code sends each character of the cCommStr to the modem, followed by a carriage return line-feed combination, to dial the modem on COM2. You have to issue a 10-millisecond pause between each character send in order to provide enough time for the modem to process the character. Once dialed, wait for 5 seconds and then issue the ath hangup command string to the modem.

Now you should add code that will display the About dialog box when the user clicks the right mouse button on the control. This is easily accomplished in a manner similar to what you just did for the left mouse button.

Adding the WM_RBUTTONDOWN message and select is performed in the same fashion by locating the message in the message list and selecting the Add Function button to go to the code. When you select the button, the CCommCtrl::OnRButtonDown() is created and brought forward so that you may edit. To access the About box, you should make the function as is shown in listing 9.21.

Listing 9.21   The Right Mouse Button Event Function

```
void CCommCtrl::OnRButtonDown(UINT nFlags, CPoint point)
{
    // TODO: Add your message handler code here
    // and/or call default
    CDialog dlgAbout(IDD_ABOUTBOX_COMM);
    dlgAbout.DoModal();

    COleControl::OnRButtonDown(nFlags, point);
}
```

This code creates a dialog box of the CDialog class and loads the About dialog box as shown in figure 9.13.

Fig. 9.13
The About
dialog box.

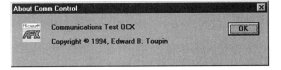

One thing to take note of is the last line of code in listings 9.20 and 9.21. The functions COleControl::OnLButtonDown(nFlags, point) and COleControl::OnRButtonDown(nFlags, point) return the keys and the x,y position of the cursor over the control when the mouse button was selected. The nFlags variable returns a notification as to whether any of the virtual keys (for example, CTRL, SHFT, or a mouse button) is pressed. The point variable specifies the x and y coordinates of the mouse cursor relative to the upper-left corner of the control window.

Building and Registering the Control

Now that the control is completely coded, you need to build the Timer control file from that code. This is accomplished by selecting Project, Build (Shift+F8) from the Visual Workbench menu. The control will first be compiled, then linked, and then it is ready for registration.

Before the control can actually be used by any container application, you must register the control in the system registry. Registering your control involves adding an entry to the system registry that contains a unique ID for each control in your Windows installation. In this control, you have only one control, which looks like figure 9.14 in the system registry.

Fig. 9.14
The Comm OCX in the system registry.

To register your compiled and linked OCX, you should select the Tools, Register Control selection from the Visual Workbench menu. This menu selection invokes the REGSVR32.EXE utility to register the control in the system registry. REGSVR32.EXE loads the OCX as a DLL and calls the DLLRegisterServer() function. Once the control is successfully registered, REGSVR32.EXE will display the dialog box shown in figure 9.15.

Fig. 9.15
REGSVR32.EXE's
successful registra-
tion of the OCX.

Testing the Control

In the days of VBXs, the only way to build and test them was to purchase the professional version of Visual Basic. The new OCX CDK, which comes with Visual C++, includes a utility called the Test Container which enables you to test all aspects and features of your new controls without third-party applications.

A container, as you know, is an application in which you can place any number of OLE objects. The Test Container, however, not only allows you to insert OLE controls, but also any object located in the system registry.

The Test Container is an executable file, called TSTCOM32.EXE, which comes with the Control Development Kit. You can invoke the Test Container manually from the File Manager or Program Manager or through the Tools, Test Container menu selection of the Visual Workbench menu.

To test the Comm control, you must first load it into the Test Container. Choose Edit, Insert OLE Control from the Test Container menu. This selection accesses the Insert OLE Control dialog box, from which you can select the Comm control (see fig. 9.16).

Several things have now happened. First, the Test Container has located the entry for the Comm control in the system registry, loaded it and created a control in the container, and activated the control. When the control is activated, the control's OnDraw() function is called to render the control in the container and display the telephone bitmap (see fig. 9.17).

Fig. 9.16
Selecting the
Comm control
from the Insert
OLE Control
dialog box of the
Test Container.

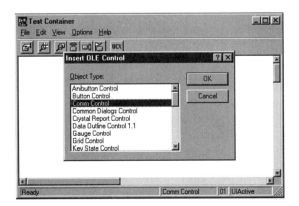

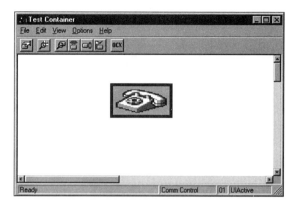

Fig. 9.17
The Comm
control in the
Test Container.

You can move the control by moving the mouse cursor over the thin border lines of the control, pressing the left mouse button, and dragging the control to its new location. Once at the desired location, you can release the left mouse button to drop the control.

Now that the control is loaded, active, and positioned where you want it in the container, you should test it. First, you need to enter a phone number in the property page. Select Edit, Comm Control Object to access the submenu for the Comm Control Object. From the submenu, select Properties to access the property page for the Comm control (see fig. 9.18). You now can see the edit control for the phone number containing the default phone number you added to the code. Enter a new phone number, or leave the default, in the edit control. If you entered a new phone number, click the Apply Now button to apply the new phone number, then click OK; otherwise, just click OK.

Fig. 9.18
The Comm control
property page.

To dial the phone number, move the mouse cursor over the control window and click the left mouse button. The control will execute the `CCommCtrl::OnLButtonDown()` function to dial the phone number entered in the property page.

To access the About box, move the mouse cursor over the control window and click the right mouse button. The control will execute the `CCommCtrl::OnRButtonDown()` function to display the About dialog box.

To view the available properties for the control, select the View, Properties menu selection. A Properties dialog box appears, containing a list control and two buttons. Select the list control to view the PhoneNumber property. Recall that you added this property name to the m_phoneNumber member variable of the commppg.cpp file. Through this name, you can access the property and the property's value. Selecting either of the two buttons on the dialog box, Invoke Properties Verb or Multiple Selection Properties, accesses the property pages of the control.

To perform other operations on the control, some of the options available in the Test Container include the following:

- The File, Save to Stream and File, Save to Substorage commands allow you to test the serialization of your control. You can then invoke the File, Load command to create a new instance of your control in the Test Container.

- The File, Save Property Set and File, Load Property Set commands test serialization as well.

- The File, Register Controls command allows you to register and unregister controls using REGSVGR32.EXE in a manner similar to that of the Tools, Register and Tools, Unregister menu selections of the Visual Workbench.

- The Edit, Set Ambient Properties command allows you to change properties that belong to the container such as font and colors. Many developers use ambient properties over custom properties when it is convenient for the control to share properties with the container. Sharing of ambient properties is one of the primary means of maintaining property consistency across all controls of a container.

- The View, Event Log and View, Event Notification Log allow you to see events that have occurred to the control. The event log shows all events that are fired by the control, whereas the notification log shows changes to the properties of the control.

- The View, Properties command displays a generic dialog box in which you can view the properties of your control. When a control is selected in the Test Container, the bottom of the Edit menu will contain a command for that specific type of control—such as Comm Control Object.

- Selecting the Edit, Comm Control Object command displays a submenu with another Properties command. This second Properties command displays the property pages for the selected control.

From Here...

In this chapter, you learned how to develop a simple OLE control and test it in the Test Container. The next chapter takes control development a little further and develops a licensed Timer control that can be used in development environments. For further information, see the following:

- Chapter 5, "The OLE Controls SDK," should help you understand how MFC operates as part of OLE controls.

- Chapter 10, "Building the Timer Custom Control," helps you understand licensing and the development of an interactive custom control.

Chapter 10

Building the Timer Custom Control

by Edward B. Toupin

In this chapter, you will develop a Timer control that you can incorporate into a container application, such as Visual Basic, to perform interval based operations. The control provides a properties page in which you can enable or disable the control, as well as set the interval at which the control will fire a procedure within a container that you provide. This control actually duplicates, to a very small degree, the timer control within Visual Basic; however, it will give you a feel for how you can develop controls that can be utilized within a programming environment.

As with the Comm control you saw in Chapter 9, there will not be a lot of coding involved to make this Timer control work for you. You will set up the control in the ControlWizard and modify it with the ClassWizard and code windows.

This chapter explores the following topics:

- Creating the Timer Control with the ControlWizard
- Customizing the Timer Control
- Registering the Timer Control
- Licensing the Timer Control
- Using the Timer Control

The ControlWizard

For the Timer control, you need to, of course, start Visual C++ and clear the workspace. You can clear the workspace by merely closing all of the active code and project windows, if any, that are visible. You then activate the ControlWizard by selecting Tools, ControlWizard from the Visual C++ menu.

Fig. 10.1

The ControlWizard project creation dialog allows you to specify options to create the framework for an OLE custom control.

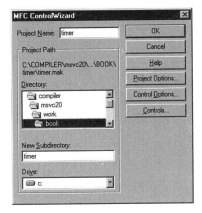

As is shown in figure 10.1, you need to select a directory in the directory list box and enter the name of the control project into the Project Name edit control. This will be the directory in which the control code and executables will reside. Select the Project Options button control to gain access to the dialog box shown in figure 10.2. In this dialog box, you will see the following options:

- *Context Sensitive Help.* For this control, as with the Comm control, you are not providing context-sensitive help, so leave the checkbox unchecked.

- *External Makefile.* For this control, you will leave the External Makefile checkbox unchecked so that all modifications to the project makefile will be completed by the Visual Workbench.

- *Source Comments.* You always want the ControlWizard to generate comments in your source, so leave this checkbox checked.

- *License Validation.* Recall from our discussion in the previous chapter that licensing a control prevents unauthorized use of the control by developers. You authorize, or license, a developer to use your control for development by shipping a LIC file with the control. For this control, you want to have licensing capabilities present in the control, so this box should be checked.

Fig. 10.2
The Project Options dialog box of the ControlWizard allows you to create source comments or insert code for licensing and help into the framework.

From the Control Options dialog box of the ControlWizard, select the Control Options button control and set the options like this (see fig. 10.3):

- The **Control** drop-down list of the dialog box lists all of the OLE controls in the ControlWizard's project makefile. You can have multiple controls within one OLE custom control; however, this control only requires the default CTimerCtrl.

- The **Activate When Visible** checkbox allows your control to become active when it is visible within a container application. Recall from Chapter 9 that active controls are aware of the Windows environment and can respond to messages and events in a manner similar to that of standard Windows applications. For this application, you want the control to be responsive to both Windows messages and to messages issued by the container application.

- The **Show in Insert Object Dialog** checkbox allows your control to appear in the Insert Object dialog box. You want this control to be visible when you select the Edit, Insert Object or Insert, Object menu selections from a container; so you want to check this option.

- The **Invisible at Runtime** checkbox makes your control invisible while the container of the control is running (a.k.a., user-mode or run-time mode). You want to check this checkbox, since you want the Timer control to become invisible when the container is running. This is because all functions of the control do not require any sort of user interface to execute the functions of the control.

- The **Simple Frame** checkbox controls the inclusion or exclusion of a border around the control within the container application. For this control, you want to have a small frame around the control—for display purposes only.

- The **About Box** checkbox informs the ControlWizard to create an About dialog box for your control. Of course, you want a small About dialog box to be available to show ownership and copyright information for the control.

■ The **SubClass <u>W</u>indows Control** checkbox should not be checked since you are not sub-classing any existing Windows controls; so we need not mark this checkbox.

■ The **Windows Control Class** drop-down list box will not be used to select a class to sub-class for this control.

■ The **<u>U</u>se VBX Control as Template** checkbox allows you to select an existing VBX control as a template for your custom control. Since this control is a new control not based on or converted from an existing VBX control, leave this checkbox unchecked.

■ The **Select <u>V</u>BX Control** button displays a file dialog box from which you can select an existing VBX control. Since you did not mark the previous checkbox, this information is not available for editing.

Fig. 10.3
The Control Options dialog box allows you to select options that determine how the control acts within a container application.

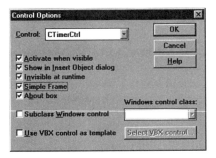

To review the Timer control components, access the Controls dialog box by selecting the Controls button control from the ControlWizard dialog box (see fig. 10.4). From this dialog box, you can manage the names of existing components for your control. Review the information in this dialog box so that you will be aware of the contents of the Timer control as you explore the code for the control.

Options and information available in this dialog box are as follows:

■ The **<u>C</u>ontrols** list box lists the names of all of the OLE controls in your project. The selected control's information is populated in the rest of the dialog box's edit controls. This control's name is Timer.

■ The **<u>S</u>hort Name**, Timer, contains the return value used by your control's OLE interface.

■ The **C++ Class <u>N</u>ame**, CTimerCtrl, is the name of the control's class as it will appear in the code generated by the ControlWizard.

- The **User Type Name**, `Timer Control`, displays a description for your control's interface.

- The **Class** drop-down list box enables you to define further the names that you are changing. For most controls, as with this one, the defaults are Control and Property Page.

- The **Header File**, timerctl.h, and **Implementation File**, timerctl.cpp, are the files to be generated by the ControlWizard that will contain class definition information for the control.

- The **Programmatic ID**, TIMER.TimerCtl.1, is the text used when you register your control in the system registry.

- The **Add Control** button allows you to add additional controls to your project if you find it necessary to add more than one type of control to your project. For this control, you will not be adding additional controls.

- The **Delete Control** button deletes the control currently highlighted in the Controls list box.

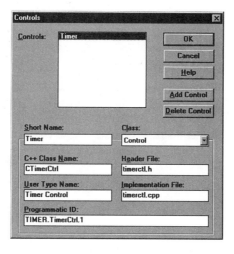

Fig. 10.4
The Controls dialog box contains information about the classes to be used in the framework for the control.

Next, you want to create the control that you have set up in the options of the ControlWizard. Select the OK button on the main ControlWizard dialog box to have the ControlWizard display the New Control Information dialog box (see fig. 10.5). If you are satisfied with your selections for the control, select the Create button to have the ControlWizard create your source files in the directory you specified.

Fig. 10.5

The New Control Information dialog box contains a summary of your choices for the custom control's framework.

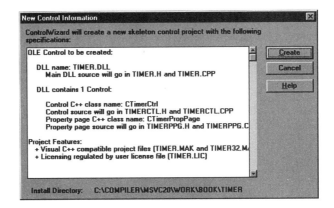

The listing in table 10.1 is a list of the files along with the descriptions for each that are generated by the ControlWizard for the Timer custom control. The ControlWizard will generate the source files based on the specifications you provided in the ControlWizard dialog box. Now that the framework is generated, you have to go into the source and perform some modifications to make the control framework operate in the manner required for the Timer control's operation.

Table 10.1   Files Generated by ControlWizard

Filename	File Size	Description
timer32.mak	18,249	This is the project makefile for building a 32-bit OLE custom control. This project file is compatible with the Visual C++ 2.0 Workbench and is also compatible with NMAKE.
timer.mak	2,571	This is the project makefile for building your 16-bit OLE custom control. This project file is compatible with the Visual C++ 1.5 Workbench and is also compatible with NMAKE.
makefile	1,436	This is a makefile that is used by the NMAKE utility from the timer and prompt. Use the following parameters with NMAKE: DEBUG=0 Builds retail version DEBUG=1 Builds debug version (default) WIN32=0 Builds 16-bit version (default) WIN32=1 Builds 32-bit version UNICODE=0 Builds ANSI/DBCS version (default for WIN32=0) UNICODE=1 Build Unicode version (default for WIN32=1)

Filename	File Size	Description
timer.cpp	1,884	This is the main source file that contains the OLE DLL initialization, termination, and other housekeeping.
timer.h	521	This is the main include file for the OLE custom control DLL. It contains project-specific includes such as RESOURCE.H.
timer.def	505	This file contains information about the OLE custom control DLL that must be provided to run with Microsoft Windows. It defines parameters such as the name and description of the DLL, and the size of the initial local heap. The numbers generated in this file are typical for OLE custom control DLLs.
timer32.def	238	This is a version of TIMER.DEF used for building a 32-bit version of the OLE custom control DLL.
timer.ico	768	This file contains an icon that will appear in the About dialog box. This icon is included in the main resource file TIMER.RC.
timer.odl	1,899	This file contains the Object Description Language (ODL) source code for the type library of your OLE control.
timer.rc	3,140	This is a listing of the Microsoft Windows resources that the project uses. This file can be directly edited with the Visual C++ resource editor.
timer.rc2	2,081	This file contains resources that are not edited by the resource editor. Initially, this contains a VERSIONINFO resource that you can customize for your OLE custom control DLL, and a TYPELIB resource for your DLL's type library. You should place other manually maintained resources for your control in this file.
timerctl.cpp	9,247	This file contains the implementation of the CTimerCtrl C++ class.
timerctl.h	1,926	This file contains the declaration of the CTimerCtrl C++ class.
timerppg.cpp	2,374	This file contains the implementation of the CTimerPropPage C++ class.
timerppg.h	872	This file contains the declaration of the CTimerPropPage C++ class.

(continues)

Table 10.1 Continued		
Filename	**File Size**	**Description**
resource.h	844	This is the standard header file, which defines new resource IDs that are read and updated by AppStudio.
timer.clw	1,091	This file contains information used by ClassWizard to edit existing classes or add new classes. ClassWizard also uses this file to store information needed to generate and edit message maps and dialog data maps, and to generate prototype member functions.
timerctl.bmp	238	This file contains a bitmap that a container will use to represent the CTimerCtrl control when it appears on a tool palette. This bitmap is included by the main resource file TIMER.RC.
timer.lic	396	This is the user license file. This file must be present in the same directory as the control to allow an instance of the control to be created in a design-time environment. Typically, you will distribute this file with your control, but your customers will not distribute it to their users.
stdafx.cpp stdafx.h	204 240	These files are used to build a precompiled header (PCH) file named STDAFX.PCH and a precompiled types (PCT) file named STDAFX.OBJ.

Details of the Control

The code for the Timer custom control, included on the CD accompanying this book, is just as simple as the Comm custom control of the previous chapter. The primary difference is, of course, its function and the fact that the control is licensed. The following sections will step through the code to give you a feel for the contents of a licensed control that can be utilized in container applications such as Visual Basic.

The timer.h File

Listing 10.1 contains the source code for the Timer control's application class header file. This file contains the definition for the control's application class as well as the global variables used by the rest of the custom control.

Listing 10.1   timer.h—The Timer Control's Header File

```
// timer.h : main header file for TIMER.DLL

#if !defined( __AFXCTL_H__ )
    #error include 'afxctl.h' before including this file
#endif

#include "resource.h"        // main symbols

/////////////////////////////////////////////////////////////////////
// CTimerApp : See timer.cpp for implementation.

class CTimerApp : public COleControlModule
{
public:
    BOOL InitInstance();
    int ExitInstance();
};

extern const GUID CDECL _tlid;
extern const WORD _wVerMajor;
extern const WORD _wVerMinor;
```

The timer.cpp File

The source code shown in listing 10.2 contains the implementation of the class CTimerApp as well as the application instance theApp. The _tlid global variable is utilized by the DLLRegisterServer() and DLLUnregisterServer()to register and unregister the Timer control from the system registry.

The InitInstance() function is called to initialize a new instance of a control, while ExitInstance() is called when the instance is destroyed. For this control, you have no need to change the two functions for any additional creation and destruction functionality.

Listing 10.2   timer.cpp—The Timer Control's Implementation File

```
// timer.cpp : Implementation of CTimerApp and DLL registration.

#include "stdafx.h"
#include "timer.h"

#ifdef _DEBUG
#undef THIS_FILE
static char BASED_CODE THIS_FILE[] = __FILE__;
#endif
```

(continues)

Listing 10.2 Continued

```
CTimerApp NEAR theApp;

const GUID CDECL BASED_CODE _tlid =
            { 0x56e0b3b3, 0x1784, 0x11ce,
            { 0x96, 0xf, 0x52, 0x41,0x53, 0x48, 0x0, 0x5 } };
const WORD _wVerMajor = 1;
const WORD _wVerMinor = 0;


/////////////////////////////////////////////////////////////////////
// CTimerApp::InitInstance - DLL initialization

BOOL CTimerApp::InitInstance()
{
    BOOL bInit = COleControlModule::InitInstance();

    if (bInit)
    {
        // TODO: Add your own module initialization code here.
    }

    return bInit;
}


/////////////////////////////////////////////////////////////////////
// CTimerApp::ExitInstance - DLL termination

int CTimerApp::ExitInstance()
{
    // TODO: Add your own module termination code here.

    return COleControlModule::ExitInstance();
}


/////////////////////////////////////////////////////////////////////
// DllRegisterServer - Adds entries to the system registry

STDAPI DllRegisterServer(void)
{
    AFX_MANAGE_STATE(_afxModuleAddrThis);

    if (!AfxOleRegisterTypeLib(AfxGetInstanceHandle(), _tlid))
        return ResultFromScode(SELFREG_E_TYPELIB);

    if (!COleObjectFactoryEx::UpdateRegistryAll(TRUE))
        return ResultFromScode(SELFREG_E_CLASS);

    return NOERROR;
}
```

```
//////////////////////////////////////////////////////////////////
// DllUnregisterServer - Removes entries from the system registry

STDAPI DllUnregisterServer(void)
{
    AFX_MANAGE_STATE(_afxModuleAddrThis);

    if (!AfxOleUnregisterTypeLib(_tlid))
        return ResultFromScode(SELFREG_E_TYPELIB);

    if (!COleObjectFactoryEx::UpdateRegistryAll(FALSE))
        return ResultFromScode(SELFREG_E_CLASS);

    return NOERROR;
}
```

The timer.rc File

The timer.rc file, in listing 10.3, contains the resource script for resources that are maintained with the AppStudio resource editor. This file defines your About Box dialog box and the string table used by the Timer control. The resource script also includes the icon displayed in your container's toolbar, IDB_TIMER, and the bitmap used to render your control in a container's visible workspace, IDB_CLOCK.

Listing 10.3   timer.rc—The Timer Control's Resource File

```
//Microsoft Visual C++ generated resource script.
//
#include "resource.h"

#define APSTUDIO_READONLY_SYMBOLS
//////////////////////////////////////////////////////////////////
//
// Generated from the TEXTINCLUDE 2 resource.
//
#include "afxres.h"


//////////////////////////////////////////////////////////////////
#undef APSTUDIO_READONLY_SYMBOLS


#ifdef APSTUDIO_INVOKED
//////////////////////////////////////////////////////////////////
//
// TEXTINCLUDE
//
1 TEXTINCLUDE DISCARDABLE
```

(continues)

Listing 10.3   Continued

```
BEGIN
    "resource.h\0"
END

2 TEXTINCLUDE DISCARDABLE
BEGIN
    "#include ""afxres.h""\r\n"
    "\0"
END

3 TEXTINCLUDE DISCARDABLE
BEGIN
    "#include ""afxres.rc""\r\n"
    "#include ""timer.rc2""  // non-App Studio edited resources\r\n"
    "#if 0\r\n"
    "#include "".\\tlb16\\timer.tlb""  // 16-bit: force dependency
                                    // on .TLB file\r\n"
    "#endif\r\n"
    "\0"
END


/////////////////////////////////////////////////////////////////////
#endif    // APSTUDIO_INVOKED


/////////////////////////////////////////////////////////////////////
//
// Icon
//

IDI_ABOUTDLL            ICON    DISCARDABLE     "timer.ico"

/////////////////////////////////////////////////////////////////////
//
// Bitmap
//

IDB_TIMER               BITMAP  DISCARDABLE     "timerctl.bmp"
IDB_CLOCK               BITMAP  DISCARDABLE     "bitmap1.bmp"

/////////////////////////////////////////////////////////////////////
//
// Dialog
//

IDD_ABOUTBOX_TIMER DIALOG DISCARDABLE  34, 22, 260, 55
STYLE DS_MODALFRAME ¦ WS_POPUP ¦ WS_CAPTION ¦ WS_SYSMENU
CAPTION "About Timer Control"
FONT 8, "MS Sans Serif"
BEGIN
    ICON            IDI_ABOUTDLL,IDC_STATIC,10,10,20,20
    LTEXT           "Timer Control, Version 1.0",IDC_STATIC,40,10,
                    170,8
```

```
    LTEXT               "Copyright \251 1994, Edward B. Toupin",
                        IDC_STATIC,40,25,170,8
    DEFPUSHBUTTON       "OK",IDOK,220,10,32,14,WS_GROUP
END

IDD_PROPPAGE_TIMER DIALOG DISCARDABLE  0, 0, 250, 62
STYLE WS_CHILD
FONT 8, "MS Sans Serif"
BEGIN
    EDITTEXT            IDC_INTERVALEDIT,110,10,55,15,ES_AUTOHSCROLL
    RTEXT               "Interval",IDC_STATIC,55,10,50,8
    CONTROL             "Enabled",IDC_ENABLEDCHECK,"Button",
                        BS_AUTOCHECKBOX ¦
                        WS_TABSTOP,110,30,55,15
END


/////////////////////////////////////////////////////////////////////
//
// String Table
//

STRINGTABLE DISCARDABLE
BEGIN
    IDS_TIMER               "Timer Control"
    IDS_TIMER_PPG           "Timer Property Page"
END

STRINGTABLE DISCARDABLE
BEGIN
    IDS_TIMER_PPG_CAPTION   "General"
END


#ifndef APSTUDIO_INVOKED
/////////////////////////////////////////////////////////////////////
//
// Generated from the TEXTINCLUDE 3 resource.
//
#include "afxres.rc"
#include "timer.rc2"  // non-App Studio edited resources
#if 0
#include ".\tlb16\timer.tlb"  // 16-bit: force dependency on .TLB file
#endif

/////////////////////////////////////////////////////////////////////
#endif    // not APSTUDIO_INVOKED
```

The timer.rc2 File

The timer.rc2 file, in listing 10.4, contains the resource script for resources that
cannot be edited by AppStudio. You will want to change the version number,
trademarks, and copyright information of your custom control for your specific
implementation.

Listing 10.4   timer.rc2—The Timer Control's Resource File

```
//
// TIMER.RC2 - resources App Studio does not edit directly
//

#ifdef APSTUDIO_INVOKED
    #error this file is not editable by App Studio
#endif //APSTUDIO_INVOKED


/////////////////////////////////////////////////////////////////////
// Version stamp for this DLL

#ifdef _WIN32
#include "winver.h"
#else
#include "ver.h"
#endif

VS_VERSION_INFO       VERSIONINFO
  FILEVERSION         1,0,0,1
  PRODUCTVERSION      1,0,0,1
  FILEFLAGSMASK       VS_FFI_FILEFLAGSMASK
#ifdef _DEBUG
  FILEFLAGS           VS_FF_DEBUG¦VS_FF_PRIVATEBUILD¦VS_FF_PRERELEASE
#else
  FILEFLAGS           0 // final version
#endif
#ifdef _WIN32
  FILEOS              VOS__WINDOWS32
#else
  FILEOS              VOS__WINDOWS16
#endif
  FILETYPE            VFT_DLL
  FILESUBTYPE         0   // not used
BEGIN
    BLOCK "StringFileInfo"
    BEGIN
#ifdef _WIN32
        BLOCK "040904B0" // Lang=US English, CharSet=Unicode
#else
        BLOCK "040904E4" // Lang=US English,
            CharSet=Windows Multilingual
#endif
        BEGIN
            VALUE "CompanyName",     "\0"
            VALUE "FileDescription", "TIMER OLE Control DLL\0"
            VALUE "FileVersion",     "1.0.001\0"
            VALUE "InternalName",    "TIMER\0"
            VALUE "LegalCopyright",
                "Copyright \251 1994, Edward B. Toupin\0"
            VALUE "LegalTrademarks", "\0"
            VALUE "OriginalFilename","TIMER.DLL\0"
```

```
                    VALUE "ProductName",     "TIMER\0"
                    VALUE "ProductVersion",  "1.0.001\0"
                    VALUE "OLESelfRegister", "\0"
            END
        END
        BLOCK "VarFileInfo"
        BEGIN
#ifdef _WIN32
            VALUE "Translation", 0x409, 1200
                    // English language (0x409) and
                    // the Unicode codepage (1200)
#else
            VALUE "Translation", 0x409, 1252
                    // English language (0x409) and
                    // the Windows ANSI codepage (1252)
#endif
        END
END


/////////////////////////////////////////////////////////////////
// Type library for controls in this DLL

1 TYPELIB timer.tlb


/////////////////////////////////////////////////////////////////
// Add additional manually edited resources here...

/////////////////////////////////////////////////////////////////
```

The timer.def File

The timer.def file, in listing 10.5, contains the definition for the 16-bit Timer control. These exports are the functions made visible to Windows so that Windows may call them as required.

Listing 10.5 timer.def—The Timer Control's 16-bit Definition File

```
; timer.def : Declares the module parameters.

LIBRARY     'TIMER'
DESCRIPTION 'TIMER OLE Custom Control module'
EXETYPE     WINDOWS

CODE        PRELOAD MOVEABLE DISCARDABLE
DATA        PRELOAD MOVEABLE SINGLE

HEAPSIZE    1024   ; initial heap size
```

(continues)

```
Listing 10.5   Continued

EXPORTS
    WEP                 @1  RESIDENTNAME
    DLLCANUNLOADNOW     @2  RESIDENTNAME
    DLLGETCLASSOBJECT   @3  RESIDENTNAME
    DLLREGISTERSERVER   @4  RESIDENTNAME
    DLLUNREGISTERSERVER @5  RESIDENTNAME

SEGMENTS
    WEP_TEXT FIXED
```

The timer32.def File

The timer32.def file, in listing 10.6, contains the definitions for the 32-bit Timer control.

```
Listing 10.6   timer32.def—The Timer Control's 32-bit
Definition File

; timer32.def : Declares the module parameters.

LIBRARY     TIMER.OCX

EXPORTS
    DllCanUnloadNow     @1  RESIDENTNAME
    DllGetClassObject   @2  RESIDENTNAME
    DllRegisterServer   @3  RESIDENTNAME
    DllUnregisterServer @4  RESIDENTNAME
```

The timerctl.h File

Listing 10.7 shows the contents of the timerctl.h header file that contains the class definition for the CTimerCtl class. As you can see, CTimerCtrl is derived from the COleObject base class that provides much of the functionality required by the Timer control. The derived class contains a public constructor, a protected destructor, the message handling function OnDraw(), and the control reset function OnResetState().

For this control, you should specifically pay attention to the BEGIN_OLEFACTORY(CTimerCtrl) and END_OLEFACTORY(CTimerCtrl) macros. These macros provide you with a means of defining your own class factory. Recall from the Comm control that you used the macro DECLARE_OLECREATE_EX to declare your control's default class factory and the GetClassID() member function. If your control does not support licensing, you will see DECLARE_OLECREATE_EX. In this control, which uses licensing, the declared macro pair incorporates licensing functionality as part of the OLE control.

Using the DECLARE_OLECREATE_EX macro is the same as using
BEGIN_OLEFACTORY() and END_OLEFACTORY() without function declarations
between the macro instances:

```
BEGIN_OLEFACTORY(CTimerCtrl)
END_OLEFACTORY(CTimerCtrl)
```

**Listing 10.7   timerctl.def—Declaration of the *CTimerCtrl* OLE
Control Class**

```
// timerctl.h : Declaration of the CTimerCtrl OLE control class.

/////////////////////////////////////////////////////////////////////
// CTimerCtrl : See timerctl.cpp for implementation.

const DEFAULT_INTERVAL  = 1000;


class CTimerCtrl : public COleControl
{
    DECLARE_DYNCREATE(CTimerCtrl)

// Constructor
public:
    CTimerCtrl();

// Overrides

    // Drawing function
    virtual void OnDraw(
            CDC*pdc, const CRect& rcBounds,
                const CRect& rcInvalid);

    // Persistence
    virtual void DoPropExchange(CPropExchange* pPX);

    // Reset control state
    virtual void OnResetState();

    virtual void OnAmbientPropertyChange(DISPID dispid);

    virtual void OnEnabledChanged();


// Implementation
protected:
    ~CTimerCtrl();

    BEGIN_OLEFACTORY(CTimerCtrl)            // Class factory and guid
        virtual BOOL VerifyUserLicense();
        virtual BOOL GetLicenseKey(DWORD, BSTR FAR*);
    END_OLEFACTORY(CTimerCtrl)
```

(continues)

Listing 10.7   Continued

```
        DECLARE_OLETYPELIB(CTimerCtrl)        // GetTypeInfo
        DECLARE_PROPPAGEIDS(CTimerCtrl)       // Property page IDs
        DECLARE_OLECTLTYPE(CTimerCtrl)        // Type name and
                                              // misc status

// Message maps
    //{{AFX_MSG(CTimerCtrl)
    afx_msg int OnCreate(LPCREATESTRUCT lpCreateStruct);
    afx_msg void OnDestroy();
    afx_msg BOOL OnEraseBkgnd(CDC* pDC);
    afx_msg void OnTimer(UINT nIDEvent);
    //}}AFX_MSG
    DECLARE_MESSAGE_MAP()

// Dispatch maps
    //{{AFX_DISPATCH(CTimerCtrl)
    short m_interval;
    afx_msg void OnIntervalChanged();
    //}}AFX_DISPATCH
    DECLARE_DISPATCH_MAP()

    afx_msg void AboutBox();

// Event maps
    //{{AFX_EVENT(CTimerCtrl)
    void FireTimer()
        {FireEvent(eventidTimer,EVENT_PARAM(VTS_NONE));}
    //}}AFX_EVENT
    DECLARE_EVENT_MAP()

// Dispatch and event IDs
public:
    enum {
    //{{AFX_DISP_ID(CTimerCtrl)
    dispidInterval = 1L,
    eventidTimer = 1L,
    //}}AFX_DISP_ID
    };

protected:

    void OnSetClientSite();
    void StartTimer();
    void StopTimer();

};
```

In this header code, notice the entries for the message map, dispatch map, and event map. Each of these maps are modified through the ClassWizard as you did for the Comm control.

Figure 10.6 depicts the ClassWizard containing the message map information. Each message added to the control, as shown in the Member Functions list, allows you to process Windows specific messages. In the header file, the respective functions for processing these messages are added to the message map as part of the `DECLARE_MESSAGE_MAP()` macro.

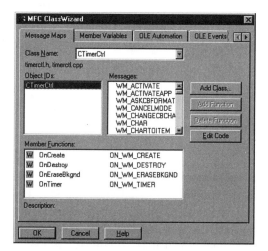

Fig. 10.6

The ClassWizard Message Map page contains mapping declarations to associate class members to Windows messages.

Use the `DECLARE_MESSAGE_MAP()` macro at the end of your class declaration to declare a list of messages that are to be processed by the control. In the implementation CPP file, you need to define the member functions for the class using the `BEGIN_MESSAGE_MAP()` and `END_MESSAGE_MAP()` macros for each of your message-handler functions.

> MFC classes that receive messages have a *message map*. The framework uses message maps to connect messages and commands to their handler functions.

Figure 10.7 depicts the ClassWizard containing the dispatch map information. The entry for `m_interval`, Interval, allows the function `OnIntervalChanged()` to fire whenever the value in `m_interval` changes. This interval ties to the value you enter into the property page for the control.

Fig. 10.7

The ClassWizard OLE Automation page contains method and property information that is accessible by container applications.

The entry for Enabled is known as a stock object and is used by members of the COleControl. The GetEnabled() function (as you will see in listing 10.8) accesses the Enabled property of your control to determine the state of your control. The state of the Enabled property is managed in the property pages of the control to allow you to enable or disable the timer.

A *stock member* is a standard member of a base class from which a class is derived. These members can be used within your applications as though they were defined within your application.

Finally, you have the event map information, as depicted in figure 10.8. This information is specific to events that occur for the control in which a certain action is to occur. For this control, the FireTimer() function fires when the timer expires and calls the FireEvent() stock member function. The FireEvent() function can be called with any number of optional arguments to fire a user-defined event from your control. As is shown in the previous listing (listing 10.7), this function should not be called directly; but should instead be called by the event-firing function, FireTimer(), and generated by ClassWizard in the event map section of the control's class declaration.

Fig. 10.8
The ClassWizard
OLE Events page
contains informa-
tion about stock
and custom events
that are
propogated out to
a container
application.

The timerctl.cpp File

The source in listing 10.8 contains the code for the implementation file,
timerctl.cpp, of the Timer control. This file contains the primary code for the
functionality of the control itself, and is also where your code will reside to
provide customized features for the control.

The sections of the implementation file for the control are as follows:

- The **message map** contains a correspondence list of messages to functions. In this control, you are defining the ON_WM_CREATE(),
  ON_WM_DESTROY(), ON_WM_ERASEBKGND(), and ON_WM_TIMER() messages to be
  processed by the control. The entries here correspond to the message
  map entries in timerctl.h.

- The **dispatch map** exposes methods and properties so that containers
  and other Windows applications can access the methods and properties
  of your control. For the Timer control, you have three methods that are
  accessible to external applications.

- The **event map** allows you to add events to communicate with the
  control's container. In this control, you want to send WM_TIMER messages
  to the control when a timer fires within the control. The container will
  be notified of the event through the reference "Timer" which is associated with the FireTimer() function.

■ The **property page IDs** identify the property pages that manage the values of the control's properties. You only have one property page for the Timer control, and it contains a field for the entry of an interval and a checkbox to enable/disable the timer.

■ The **OLE macros** IMPLEMENT_OLECREATE_EX and IMPLEMENT_OLETYPELIB create the class factory and type library code needed to implement the control as an OLE object.

■ The **interface IDs** IID_DTimer and IID_DTimerEvents are the unique IDs for the Timer control and its events.

■ The CTimerCtrlFactory::UpdateRegistry() function adds or removes entries in the system registry. The code and the control's default parameters are generated for you automatically and are adequate for the Timer control.

■ The CTimerCtrl::CTimerCtrlFactory::VerifyUserLicense() function loads the file named in _szLicFileName and verifies that the license information in the file matches the license information in _szLicString. This function determines if a design-time license exists and is valid for the control to be used in a design-time environment.

■ The CTimerCtrl::CTimerCtrlFactory::GetLicenseKey() function retrieves a unique license key from the control and stores it into pbstrKey. The default implementation of this function returns 0 and stores nothing in pbstrKey. If you use ControlWizard to create your project, as was done with this control, ControlWizard supplies an override that retrieves the control's license key.

■ The **constructor** initializes the IIDs for the control and, for this control, calls the SetInitialSize() function. This function sets the horizontal and vertical size of the control, in pixels, when an instance of it is placed into a container.

■ The **destructor** is currently an empty shell but you can add your own code as required to be executed when the control is destroyed.

■ The OnDraw() function originally contained minimal code to draw an ellipse in a square on the container when the control is instantiated. You replaced this code to draw the bitmap given by the identifier IDB_CLOCK when the timer is instantiated.

- The `DoPropExchange()` function is setting the interval property, for the property page, equal to the `DEFAULT_INTERVAL` of 1000 milliseconds.

- The `OnResetState()` is called to reset the control's contents. Any properties included in the `DoPropExchange()` function should, through coding of your own, be reset to default values.

- The `AboutBox()` function is called to display your control's About dialog box.

The implementation file for the Timer control is shown in listing 10.8.

Listing 10.8   timerctl.cpp—The Implementation File for the *CTime CtrlClass*

```
// timerctl.cpp : Implementation of the CTimerCtrl // OLE control
class.

#include "stdafx.h"
#include "timer.h"
#include "timerctl.h"
#include "timerppg.h"


#ifdef _DEBUG
#undef THIS_FILE
static char BASED_CODE THIS_FILE[] = __FILE__;

#endif

const short ID_TIMER = 1;


IMPLEMENT_DYNCREATE(CTimerCtrl, COleControl)


/////////////////////////////////////////////////////////////////
// Message map

BEGIN_MESSAGE_MAP(CTimerCtrl, COleControl)
    //{{AFX_MSG_MAP(CTimerCtrl)
    ON_WM_CREATE()
    ON_WM_DESTROY()
    ON_WM_ERASEBKGND()
    ON_WM_TIMER()
    //}}AFX_MSG_MAP
    ON_OLEVERB(AFX_IDS_VERB_PROPERTIES, OnProperties)
END_MESSAGE_MAP()
```

(continues)

Listing 10.8 Continued

```
/////////////////////////////////////////////////////////////////
// Dispatch map
BEGIN_DISPATCH_MAP(CTimerCtrl, COleControl)
    //{{AFX_DISPATCH_MAP(CTimerCtrl)
    DISP_PROPERTY_NOTIFY(CTimerCtrl, "Interval",
        m_interval, OnIntervalChanged, VT_I2)
    DISP_STOCKPROP_ENABLED()
    //}}AFX_DISPATCH_MAP
    DISP_FUNCTION_ID(CTimerCtrl, "AboutBox",
        DISPID_ABOUTBOX, AboutBox, VT_EMPTY, VTS_NONE)
END_DISPATCH_MAP()


/////////////////////////////////////////////////////////////////
// Event map

BEGIN_EVENT_MAP(CTimerCtrl, COleControl)
    //{{AFX_EVENT_MAP(CTimerCtrl)
    EVENT_CUSTOM("Timer", FireTimer, VTS_NONE)
    //}}AFX_EVENT_MAP
END_EVENT_MAP()


/////////////////////////////////////////////////////////////////
// Property pages

// TODO: Add more property pages as needed.
// Remember to increase the count!
BEGIN_PROPPAGEIDS(CTimerCtrl, 1)
    PROPPAGEID(CTimerPropPage::guid)
END_PROPPAGEIDS(CTimerCtrl)


/////////////////////////////////////////////////////////////////
// Initialize class factory and guid

IMPLEMENT_OLECREATE_EX(CTimerCtrl, "TIMER.TimerCtrl.1",
    0x56e0b3b0, 0x1784, 0x11ce, 0x96, 0xf, 0x52, 0x41,
    0x53, 0x48, 0x0, 0x5)


/////////////////////////////////////////////////////////////////
// Type library ID and version

IMPLEMENT_OLETYPELIB(CTimerCtrl, _tlid, _wVerMajor, _wVerMinor)


/////////////////////////////////////////////////////////////////
// Interface IDs

const IID BASED_CODE IID_DTimer =
        { 0x56e0b3b1, 0x1784, 0x11ce,
        { 0x96, 0xf, 0x52, 0x41,0x53, 0x48, 0x0, 0x5 } };
const IID BASED_CODE IID_DTimerEvents =
        { 0x56e0b3b2, 0x1784, 0x11ce,
        { 0x96, 0xf, 0x52, 0x41,0x53, 0x48, 0x0, 0x5 } };
```

```
/////////////////////////////////////////////////////////////////////
// Control type information

static const DWORD BASED_CODE _dwTimerOleMisc =
     OLEMISC_INVISIBLEATRUNTIME |
     OLEMISC_ACTIVATEWHENVISIBLE |
     OLEMISC_SETCLIENTSITEFIRST |
     OLEMISC_INSIDEOUT |
     OLEMISC_CANTLINKINSIDE |
     OLEMISC_RECOMPOSEONRESIZE;

IMPLEMENT_OLECTLTYPE(CTimerCtrl, IDS_TIMER, _dwTimerOleMisc)


/////////////////////////////////////////////////////////////////////
// CTimerCtrl::CTimerCtrlFactory::UpdateRegistry -
// Adds or removes system registry entries for CTimerCtrl

BOOL CTimerCtrl::CTimerCtrlFactory::UpdateRegistry(BOOL bRegister)
{
     if (bRegister)
          return AfxOleRegisterControlClass(
               AfxGetInstanceHandle(),
               m_clsid,
               m_lpszProgID,
               IDS_TIMER,
               IDB_TIMER,
               FALSE,                       //  Not insertable
               _dwTimerOleMisc,
               _tlid,
               _wVerMajor,
               _wVerMinor);
     else
          return AfxOleUnregisterClass(m_clsid, m_lpszProgID);
}


/////////////////////////////////////////////////////////////////////
// Licensing strings

static const TCHAR BASED_CODE _szLicFileName[] = _T("TIMER.LIC");

static const TCHAR BASED_CODE _szLicString[] =
     _T("Copyright (c) 1994 Edward B. Toupin");


/////////////////////////////////////////////////////////////////////
// CTimerCtrl::CTimerCtrlFactory::VerifyUserLicense -
// Checks for existence of a user license

BOOL CTimerCtrl::CTimerCtrlFactory::VerifyUserLicense()
{
     return AfxVerifyLicFile(AfxGetInstanceHandle(), _szLicFileName,
          _szLicString);
}
```

(continues)

Listing 10.8 Continued

```
///////////////////////////////////////////////////////////////////
// CTimerCtrl::CTimerCtrlFactory::GetLicenseKey -
// Returns a runtime licensing key

BOOL CTimerCtrl::CTimerCtrlFactory::GetLicenseKey(DWORD dwReserved,
    BSTR FAR* pbstrKey)
{
    if (pbstrKey == NULL)
        return FALSE;

    *pbstrKey = SysAllocString(_szLicString);
    return (*pbstrKey != NULL);
}


///////////////////////////////////////////////////////////////////
// CTimerCtrl::CTimerCtrl - Constructor

CTimerCtrl::CTimerCtrl()
{
    InitializeIIDs(&IID_DTimer, &IID_DTimerEvents);

    // TODO: Initialize your control's instance data here.
    SetInitialSize(24, 22);
}


///////////////////////////////////////////////////////////////////
// CTimerCtrl::~CTimerCtrl - Destructor

CTimerCtrl::~CTimerCtrl()
{
    // TODO: Cleanup your control's instance data here.
}


///////////////////////////////////////////////////////////////////
// CTimerCtrl::OnDraw - Drawing function

void CTimerCtrl::OnDraw(
            CDC*pdc, const CRect& rcBounds,
                const CRect& rcInvalid)
{
    // TODO: Replace the following code with your own drawing code.
    CBitmap bitmap;
    BITMAP  bmp;
    CPictureHolder picHolder;
    CRect rcSrcBounds;

    // Load clock bitmap
    bitmap.LoadBitmap(IDB_CLOCK);
    bitmap.GetObject(sizeof(BITMAP), &bmp);
    rcSrcBounds.right = bmp.bmWidth;
    rcSrcBounds.bottom = bmp.bmHeight;
```

```
        // Create picture and render
        picHolder.CreateFromBitmap
            ((HBITMAP)bitmap.m_hObject, NULL, FALSE);
        picHolder.Render(pdc, rcBounds, rcSrcBounds);
}


/////////////////////////////////////////////////////////////////
// CTimerCtrl::DoPropExchange - Persistence support

void CTimerCtrl::DoPropExchange(CPropExchange* pPX)
{
        ExchangeVersion(pPX, MAKELONG(_wVerMinor, _wVerMajor));
        COleControl::DoPropExchange(pPX);

        // TODO: Call PX_ functions for each persistent custom property.
        PX_Short(pPX, _T("Interval"), m_interval, DEFAULT_INTERVAL);
}


/////////////////////////////////////////////////////////////////
// CTimerCtrl::OnResetState - Reset control to default state

void CTimerCtrl::OnResetState()
{
        COleControl::OnResetState();  // Resets defaults
                                      // found in DoPropExchange

        // TODO: Reset any other control state here.
}


/////////////////////////////////////////////////////////////////
// CTimerCtrl::AboutBox - Display an "About" box to the user

void CTimerCtrl::AboutBox()
{
        CDialog dlgAbout(IDD_ABOUTBOX_TIMER);
        dlgAbout.DoModal();
}


/////////////////////////////////////////////////////////////////
// CTimeCtrl::OnSetClientSite - Force creation of window

void CTimerCtrl::OnSetClientSite()
{
        RecreateControlWindow();
}
```

(continues)

Listing 10.8 Continued

```
/////////////////////////////////////////////////////////////////////////
// CTimerCtrl message handlers

int CTimerCtrl::OnCreate(LPCREATESTRUCT lpCreateStruct)
{
    if (COleControl::OnCreate(lpCreateStruct) == -1)
        return -1;

    // TODO: Add your specialized creation code here

    // Start timer if in user mode and if enabled
    if (AmbientUserMode() && GetEnabled())
        StartTimer();

    return 0;
}

void CTimerCtrl::OnDestroy()
{
    StopTimer();

    COleControl::OnDestroy();

    // TODO: Add your message handler code here

}

BOOL CTimerCtrl::OnEraseBkgnd(CDC* pDC)
{
    // TODO: Add your message handler code here and/or call default

    return COleControl::OnEraseBkgnd(pDC);
}

void CTimerCtrl::OnTimer(UINT nIDEvent)
{
    // TODO: Add your message handler code here and/or call default
    FireTimer();
    COleControl::OnTimer(nIDEvent);
}

void CTimerCtrl::OnIntervalChanged()
{
    // TODO: Add notification handler code
    if (GetEnabled() && AmbientUserMode())
    {
        StopTimer();
        StartTimer();
    }

    MessageBox("OnIntervalChange");

    SetModifiedFlag();
}
```

```
/////////////////////////////////////////////////////////////////////
// CTimeCtrl::OnEnabledChanged - Start/stop the timer
// when the enable state has changed.

void CTimerCtrl::OnEnabledChanged()
{
    if (AmbientUserMode())
    {
        if (GetEnabled())
        {
            if (GetHwnd() != NULL)
                StartTimer();
        }
        else
            StopTimer();
    }

    MessageBox("OnEnabledChange");
}

/////////////////////////////////////////////////////////////////////
// CTimeCtrl::OnAmbientPropertyChange -
// Start the timer if user mode ambient property
// has changed and if timer is enabled.  Stop the
// timer if user  mode ambient property has changed
// and if timer is enabled.

// mode ambient property has changed and if timer is enabled.

void CTimerCtrl::OnAmbientPropertyChange(DISPID dispid)
{
    if (dispid == DISPID_AMBIENT_USERMODE)
    {
        // Start or stop the timer
        if (GetEnabled())
        {
            if (AmbientUserMode())
                StartTimer();
            else
                StopTimer();
        }

        InvalidateControl();
    }
}

/////////////////////////////////////////////////////////////////////
// CTimeCtrl::StartTimer - Start the timer.

void CTimerCtrl::StartTimer()
{
    SetTimer(ID_TIMER, m_interval, NULL);
}
```

(continues)

Listing 10.8   Continued

```
/////////////////////////////////////////////////////////////////
// CTimeCtrl::StopTimer - Stop the timer.

void CTimerCtrl::StopTimer()
{
    KillTimer(ID_TIMER);
};
```

Now let's take a look at the remainder of the code for the control. Each of the additional member functions are not automatically generated by the ControlWizard, but are instead created through the ClassWizard or written by the developer.

The following member functions for the Timer control implementation file are all coded by the developer in order to customize the features of the control:

■ The CTimerCtrl::OnCreate() member function, which executes when a WM_CREATE message is received, is fired when the control is instantiated. The control uses the GetAmbientUserMode() function to determine if the container is in design mode (False) or in run-time mode (True). If in design mode, you do not want to start the timer; if the control is enabled from the property page and in run-time mode, you want to start the timer.

■ The CTimerCtrl::OnDestroy() calls the StopTimer() member function to stop the timer that is set for the control. The COleControl::OnDestroy() function is called after the window for the control is removed from the screen. This function is the default operation for the WM_DESTROY message, which is the message that causes this function to fire.

■ The CTimerCtrl::OnEraseBkgnd() calls the COleControl::OnEraseBkgnd() member function to prepare a window for painting. This function is executed as a result of the control receiving the WM_ERASEBKGND message.

■ The CTimerCtrl::OnTimer() function is called as a result of the reception of the WM_TIMER message by the control. When this function executes, you call the FireTimer() function declared in timerctl.h to perform timer-specific operations in the container. This function provides an event for the container to notify itself that it should perform operations specific to the timer execution.

■ The `CTimerCtrl::OnIntervalChanged()` function is called whenever you change the interval value within the property page for the control. When the function executes, check to see that you are in run-time mode and that the timer is enabled from the property page. If so, stop the timer and then restart the timer with the new interval. For debugging, and purposes of this demonstration control only, a message will appear on the screen to tell you that the interval value has been changed and accepted by the property pages.

■ The `CTimerCtrl::OnEnabledChanged()` function is called whenever you change the enabled state of the control in the property page for the control. When the function executes, check to see that you are in run-time mode and, if so, check the state of the enabled checkbox of the property page. If the OLE control is valid and the control's timer is enabled, start the timer; otherwise, you should stop the timer.

■ The `CTimerCtrl::OnAmbientPropertyChange()` function is called whenever you change any of the ambient properties of the control. However, you are only looking for the state of the container on which you will perform operations—design-time mode or run-time mode (a.k.a., user mode). When the function executes, you start the timer if in run-time mode and if the timer is enabled. You stop the timer if in design mode and if the timer is enabled. The final call of the function, `InvalidateControl()`, invalidates the control and forces it to redraw the bitmap via `OnDraw()`.

■ The control has two developer written functions used to start and stop the timer—`CTimerCtrl::StartTimer()` and `CTimerCtrl::StopTimer()`. In using the `SetTimer()` function, you are setting the timer to the number of milliseconds defined in the property page field for interval. `KillTimer()` halts the timer associated with `ID_TIMER`, the one you started with `SetTimer()`.

The timerppg.h File

Listing 10.9 shows the contents of the timerppg.h header file. This file contains the class definition for `CTimerPropPage`. This class provides the definition of the class required for the General property page and is derived from the `CDialog` MFC class.

Listing 10.9   timerppg.h—The Header File for the *CTimerPropPage* Class

```
// timerppg.h: Declaration of the CTimerPropPage property page class.

/////////////////////////////////////////////////////////////////
// CTimerPropPage : See timerppg.cpp for implementation.

class CTimerPropPage : public COlePropertyPage
{
    DECLARE_DYNCREATE(CTimerPropPage)
    DECLARE_OLECREATE_EX(CTimerPropPage)

// Constructor
public:
    CTimerPropPage();

// Dialog Data
    //{{AFX_DATA(CTimerPropPage)
    enum { IDD = IDD_PROPPAGE_TIMER };
    BOOL    m_Enabled;
    int     m_Interval;
    //}}AFX_DATA

// Implementation
protected:
    virtual void DoDataExchange(CDataExchange* pDX);
        // DDX/DDV support

// Message maps
protected:
    //{{AFX_MSG(CTimerPropPage)
        // NOTE - ClassWizard will add and remove member
        // functions here.
        //    DO NOT EDIT what you see in these blocks
        // of generated code !
    //}}AFX_MSG
    DECLARE_MESSAGE_MAP()

};
```

As you can see in listing 10.9, you have two member variables, m_Enabled and m_Interval. These two variables are used to store information entered into the property page fields for the timer interval and the enabled state. Both of these are entered into the ClassWizard to provide a variable for storage of the information entered into the property pages (see fig. 10.9).

Fig. 10.9
The ClassWizard
Member Variables
page manages the
association of
variables to
controls for the
storage of control
information.

The timerppg.cpp File

Listing 10.10 shows the contents of the timerppg.h header file. This file
contains the class definition for CTimerPropPage. This class provides the
functionality for the General property page based on the class defined in the
respective header file.

The sections of the property page implementation file for the control are as
follows:

- The **message map**, as with CTimerCtrl, contains a correspondence list
  of messages to member functions.

- The IMPLEMENT_OLECREATE_EX macro declares the class factory for the
  control and the GetClassID() function. Since CTimerPropPage is an OLE
  class, it is registered in the system registry using the class factory.

- The CTimerPropPageFactory::UpdateRegistry() function registers and
  deregisters the CTimerPropPage class.

- The **constructor** is included so that you may add your own initialization code for the instantiation of the control's property pages as required.

- The DoDataExchange() function provides data transfer between the control and the property pages. In this function, you are setting the property names with DDP_Check() and DDP_Text(). DDX_Check() and
  DDX_Text() implement data exchange for the checkbox and edit control
  located in the control's property page.

Listing 10.10 timerppg.cpp—The Implementation File for the
***CTimerPropPage* Class**

```
// timerppg.cpp : Implementation of the CTimerPropPage
// property page class.

#include "stdafx.h"
#include "timer.h"
#include "timerppg.h"

#ifdef _DEBUG
#undef THIS_FILE
static char BASED_CODE THIS_FILE[] = __FILE__;
#endif


IMPLEMENT_DYNCREATE(CTimerPropPage, COlePropertyPage)


/////////////////////////////////////////////////////////////////////
// Message map

BEGIN_MESSAGE_MAP(CTimerPropPage, COlePropertyPage)
    //{{AFX_MSG_MAP(CTimerPropPage)
    // NOTE - ClassWizard will add and remove message map entries
    //    DO NOT EDIT what you see in these blocks of generated code!
    //}}AFX_MSG_MAP
END_MESSAGE_MAP()


/////////////////////////////////////////////////////////////////////
// Initialize class factory and guid

IMPLEMENT_OLECREATE_EX(CTimerPropPage, "TIMER.TimerPropPage.1",
    0x56e0b3b4, 0x1784, 0x11ce, 0x96, 0xf, 0x52, 0x41, 0x53,
    0x48, 0x0, 0x5)


/////////////////////////////////////////////////////////////////////
// CTimerPropPage::CTimerPropPageFactory::UpdateRegistry -
// Adds or removes system registry entries for CTimerPropPage

BOOL CTimerPropPage::CTimerPropPageFactory::UpdateRegistry(
   BOOL bRegister)
{
    if (bRegister)
return
   AfxOleRegisterPropertyPageClass(AfxGetInstanceHandle(),
            m_clsid, IDS_TIMER_PPG);
    else
        return AfxOleUnregisterClass(m_clsid, NULL);
}
```

```
//////////////////////////////////////////////////////////////////
// CTimerPropPage::CTimerPropPage - Constructor

CTimerPropPage::CTimerPropPage() :
    COlePropertyPage(IDD, IDS_TIMER_PPG_CAPTION)
{
    //{{AFX_DATA_INIT(CTimerPropPage)
    m_Enabled = FALSE;
    m_Interval = 0;
    //}}AFX_DATA_INIT
}


//////////////////////////////////////////////////////////////////
// CTimerPropPage::DoDataExchange - Moves data between
// page and properties

void CTimerPropPage::DoDataExchange(CDataExchange* pDX)
{
    //{{AFX_DATA_MAP(CTimerPropPage)
    DDP_Check(pDX, IDC_ENABLEDCHECK, m_Enabled, _T("Enabled") );
    DDX_Check(pDX, IDC_ENABLEDCHECK, m_Enabled);
    DDP_Text(pDX, IDC_INTERVALEDIT, m_Interval, _T("Interval") );
    DDX_Text(pDX, IDC_INTERVALEDIT, m_Interval);
    DDV_MaxChars(pDX, m_Interval, 32767);
    //}}AFX_DATA_MAP
    DDP_PostProcessing(pDX);
}


//////////////////////////////////////////////////////////////////
// CTimerPropPage message handlers
```

The stdafx.h File

Listing 10.11 shows the stdafx.h file which contains a single #include statement.
This #include statement provides MFC support for OLE controls.

Listing 10.11   stdafx.h—The Standard System Include File

```
// stdafx.h : include file for standard system include files,
// or project specific include files that are used frequently,
// but are changed infrequently

#include <afxctl.h>           // MFC support for OLE Custom Controls
```

The stdafx.cpp File

Listing 10.12 shows the stdafx.cpp file which is the implementation file for MFC
OLE control support.

Listing 10.12   stdafx.cpp—The Standard System Implementation File

```
// stdafx.cpp : source file that includes just the
//   standard includes
//   stdafx.pch will be the pre-compiled header
//   stdafx.obj will contain the pre-compiled type information

#include "stdafx.h"
```

The resource.h File

Listing 10.13 shows the resource.h file for use with AppStudio. You should recognize these names as identifiers for the various resources you can edit.

Listing 10.13   resource.h—The Resource Header File

```
//{{NO_DEPENDENCIES}}
// Microsoft Visual C++ generated include file.
// Used by timer.rc
//
#define IDS_TIMER                       1
#define IDB_TIMER                       1
#define IDS_TIMER_PPG                   2
#define IDI_ABOUTDLL                    10
#define IDD_ABOUTBOX_TIMER              100
#define IDS_TIMER_PPG_CAPTION           101
#define IDD_PROPPAGE_TIMER              101
#define IDC_INTERVALEDIT                201
#define IDB_CLOCK                       201
#define IDC_ENABLEDCHECK                202

// Next default values for new objects
//
#ifdef APSTUDIO_INVOKED
#ifndef APSTUDIO_READONLY_SYMBOLS
#define _APS_NEXT_RESOURCE_VALUE        202
#define _APS_NEXT_TIMERAND_VALUE        32768
#define _APS_NEXT_CONTROL_VALUE         203
#define _APS_NEXT_SYMED_VALUE           101
#endif
#endif
```

The timer.odl File

The Timer control's type library information is stored in the timer.odl file shown in listing 10.14. The ClassWizard maintains the information stored in this file; however, you should be aware of the information in this file to understand how the control is registered and access by container applications.

Listing 10.14 timer.odl—The Type Library File

```
// timer.odl : type library source for OLE Custom Control project.

// This file will be processed by the Make Type Library
// (mktyplib) tool to
// produce the type library (timer.tlb) that will become a resource
// in timer.ocx.

#include <olectl.h>

[ uuid(56E0B3B3-1784-11CE-960F-524153480005), version(1.0),
  helpstring("Timer OLE Custom Control module") ]
library TimerLib
{
    importlib(STDOLE_TLB);
    importlib(STDTYPE_TLB);

    //  Primary dispatch interface for CTimerCtrl

    [ uuid(56E0B3B1-1784-11CE-960F-524153480005),
      helpstring("Dispatch interface for Timer Control") ]
    dispinterface _DTimer
    {
        properties:
            // NOTE - ClassWizard will maintain property
            // information here.
            //     Use extreme caution when editing this section.
            //{{AFX_ODL_PROP(CTimerCtrl)
            [id(DISPID_ENABLED), bindable,
                requestedit] boolean Enabled;
            [id(1)] short Interval;
            //}}AFX_ODL_PROP

        methods:
            // NOTE - ClassWizard will maintain method
          // information here.
            //     Use extreme caution when editing this section.
            //{{AFX_ODL_METHOD(CTimerCtrl)
            //}}AFX_ODL_METHOD

            [id(DISPID_ABOUTBOX)] void AboutBox();
    };

    //  Event dispatch interface for CTimerCtrl

    [ uuid(56E0B3B2-1784-11CE-960F-524153480005),
      helpstring("Event interface for Timer Control") ]
    dispinterface _DTimerEvents
    {
        properties:
            //  Event interface has no properties
```

(continues)

Listing 10.14 Continued

```
methods:
                    // NOTE - ClassWizard will maintain event
                    // information here.
                    //    Use extreme caution when editing this section.
                    //{{AFX_ODL_EVENT(CTimerCtrl)
                    [id(1)] void Timer();
                    //}}AFX_ODL_EVENT
        };

        //  Class information for CTimerCtrl

        [ uuid(56E0B3B0-1784-11CE-960F-524153480005), licensed,
          helpstring("Timer Control") ]
        CoClass Timer
        {
            [default] dispinterface _DTimer;
            [default, source] dispinterface _DTimerEvents;
        };


        //{{AFX_APPEND_ODL}}
    };
```

Building and Registering the Control

The new control now has to be built and registered with the system registry before it can be used. The build operation is accomplished easily by selecting Project, Build from the Visual Workbench menu. The control will then be compiled and linked and ready for registration.

Registering the Timer control involves adding an entry to the system registry that contains a unique ID for each control in your Timer control. In the case of this control, you only have one control which looks like figure 10.10 in the system registry.

Fig. 10.10
The Timer Control
is registered in the
system registry to
provide access to
the resources of
the control by
container applica-
tions.

To register the control, you should select Tools, Register Control from the
Visual Workbench menu. This menu selection invokes the REGSVR32.EXE
utility to register the control in the system registry. REGSVR32.EXE loads the
OCX as a DLL and calls the DLLRegisterServer() function. Once the control
is successfully registered, REGSVR32.EXE will display the dialog box shown in
figure 10.11.

Fig. 10.11
Once the
REGSVR32.EXE
application
successfully
registers the Timer
control, a dialog
box appears
noting a success-
ful registration.

Using the Control

Let us once again use the Test Container application, as you did in Chapter 9,
to test and use the Timer control. You must first invoke the Test Container
from the File Manager or Program Manager or through the Tools, Test Container menu selection of the Visual Workbench menu.

Fig. 10.12
To use the control
in the Test
Container, you
must first verify
that the control is
registered in the
system registry.

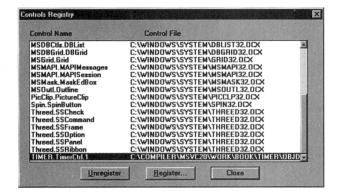

As shown in figure 10.12, you should first check to see if the control was
previously registered in the system registry. From the File menu of the Test
Container, choose Register Controls. A window will appear containing a list
of all registered controls including the Timer control. If the Timer control was
not registered previously, you could do so by selecting the Register button at
the bottom of the window. This button accesses a file dialog box from which
you can select a custom control to load (fig. 10.13).

If you do not register a control in the system registry, it will not appear in the Controls dialog box for you to include into a container.

Caution

Remember that the Timer control is a licensed control. If the TIMER.LIC file is not in
the same directory as the control's library (16-bit DLL or 32-bit OCX), then you will
receive an error message and the control will not be able to be used in the design-
time state of the container. This will not prohibit run-time usage of the control;
however, you will not be able to use it at designtime. Make sure that the LIC file is in
the same directory as the control!

Fig. 10.13
To register a
control in the
system registry,
you can scroll
through available
disk files and
select the control
that you want to
register.

Once your control is registered, you will need to load the Timer Controls into the Test Container. Select Edit, Insert OLE Control from the Test Container menu. This selection accesses the Insert OLE Control dialog box, from which you can select the Timer control (see fig. 10.14).

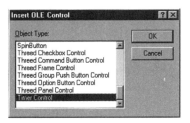

Fig. 10.14
Select the Timer control from the Insert OLE Control dialog box of the Test Container.

Once the Timer control is selected, the Test Container, via OLE, locates the entry for the Timer control in the system registry. The control is then loaded, created, and activated in the container. When the control is activated, the control's OnDraw() function is called to render the control in the container and display the clock bitmap (see fig. 10.15).

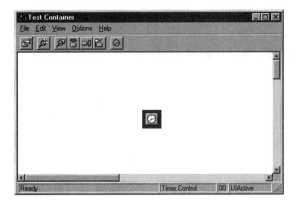

Fig. 10.15
The Timer control is displayed on activation in the Test Container.

Now that the control is loaded, active, and positioned where you want it in the container, you should test it. First, you need to go to the property page for the control and change the interval, as well as make sure the timer is enabled. From the menu, select Edit, Timer Control Object, Properties. As shown in figure 10.16, you can edit the properties for the control once the page is visible. Select OK when the edits are complete.

Fig. 10.16
The property page for the Timer control allows you to change the interval and enabled properties of the control.

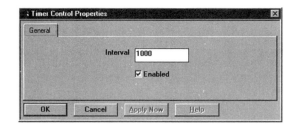

To monitor the firing of the Timer control, you need to watch the `Timer()` procedure. Recall from the code in `timerctl.cpp` that the timer will fire at intervals specified by the interval entered into the property page. Selecting Edit, View Event List allows you to view all event procedures for the control. As in figure 10.17, the only event procedure is the `Timer()` procedure.

The buttons to the right control logging; you select whether you are going to be logging events for one or more events into a log window. For this procedure make sure that the `Log Event?` column is set to `Yes` for the `Timer()` procedure. Once logging is enabled, you can select View, Event Log to access the event log window to view event notifications generated by the control.

Fig. 10.17
Set the log attribute of an event procedure for the Timer control.

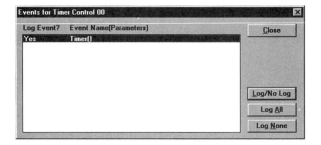

The final test that you need to complete is to make sure that the About dialog box can be displayed. To test the dialog box, you need to invoke the `AboutBox()` method from the container. Selecting Edit, Invoke Methods accesses the Invoke Control Method dialog box (fig. 10.18). In the upper left corner of the dialog box is a method list from which you can select a method to invoke (in this case, you want `AboutBox()` to be invoked). To invoke the method, select the Invoke Method button to invoke the method and display the dialog box.

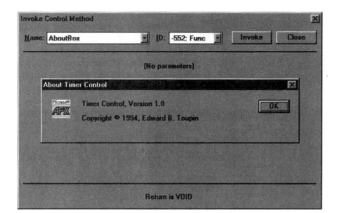

Fig. 10.18
Invoke the
AboutBox method
from the Invoke
Control Method
dialog box.

From Here...

In this chapter, you learned how to develop a simple licensed OLE control, install it into a container, and perform operations on the control. You also learned some of the intricacies of coding with MFC in conjunction with the ControlWizard and ClassWizard.

For further information on topics discussed in this chapter, see the following:

- Chapter 5, "The OLE Controls SDK," shows you how to understand how MFC operates as part of OLE controls.

- Chapter 8, "Converting VBXs to OLE Custom Controls," discusses in detail converting existing VBX custom controls to OLE custom controls.

- Chapter 11, "Subclassing Standard Controls," discusses how to clearly understand control subclassing.

Chapter 11

Subclassing Standard Controls

by Edward B. Toupin

Subclassing allows you to take an existing Windows control, such as a button or edit control, and expand the functionality of the control by adding your own code and capabilities into a control to create a new control. This chapter examines the development and testing of a subclassed control, and details some of the specifics of subclassing with Visual C++.

In this chapter, you build a simple subclassed control—a button control that subclasses the Windows command button control class and provides the Click events for use in container applications. The result is the Button control which operates in a manner similar to the standard Windows command button class that can be used in Visual Basic or any other supporting container application. The difference is that once you understand how to write code duplicating the command button class, you can later enhance it to include the specific features you require for your specific applications.

This chapter explores the following topics:

- What is subclassing?
- Why should you subclass?
- Designing a subclassed control
- Registering the control
- Testing and using the control

Subclassing Windows Controls

The quickest way to write a powerful control is to subclass an existing Windows control. Windows controls are already capable of being displayed and recognizing actions such as mouse clicks. The additional code you write implements properties and events for the control so the control can be used within different 32-bit container applications. Although subclassing a Windows control requires a small amount of code, you do need to understand some important concepts concerning how the code and the superclass interact. Once you understand these concepts, subclassing becomes much faster than writing a control from scratch.

When subclassing, the abilities of the existing control, such as painting and responding to mouse clicks, are handled by the superclass' procedures. Any additional functionality is provided by your subclassing function.

Fig. 11.1
When a Windows control is subclassed, additional processing code is added to the control to intercept operating system messages. These intercepted messages are then processed or passed on to the subclassed control's primary message processing handler.

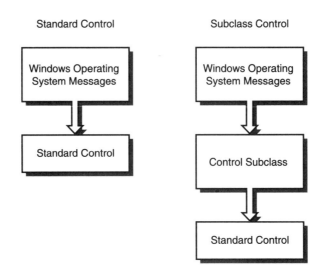

Standard control messages are passed to the superclass, or subclassed control, by calling the default control procedures, as shown in figure 11.1. When you subclass a control, messages are passed to the superclass, as normal, which may process the message itself or pass it along. If there is a superclass, the message gets passed to the window procedure of the superclass; however, if there is no superclass, the message is passed to the default Windows procedure, `DefWindowProc()`. Basically, if neither the control procedure nor the default control procedure does anything with the message, the superclass receives it.

This chapter focuses on the Windows push button class, which provides a good deal of functionality to Windows applications. From the previous controls, you saw that you had to handle the depiction of the control in the container, as well as handle the messages to and from the control. When subclassing, you don't need to write code that handles any of the following because the Windows push button class, the superclass of our control, does it for you:

- Painting the control. The Windows class handles all responses to WM_PAINT, and it can display a push button of any size.

- Setting the window text, which is implemented as the standard Caption property. Windows handles all the following messages: WM_SETTEXT, WM_GETTEXT, and WM_GETTEXTLENGTH.

- Displaying the caption.

For the functionality in the preceding list to work, messages must be passed along to the superclass. Other Windows classes provide similar functionality. So what exactly do you have to do, since some of the functionality is handled by the superclass? When you subclass a Windows control for use in a container application, you have to provide the interface to the container. This means adding properties and events for the subclass, and specifically involves the following:

- Listing properties and events in the property information table.

- Supporting custom events, such as the Click event. If a Windows control sends notification of such an event (most Windows controls do), you can respond to this notification message by firing an event.

- Interpreting mnemonic keys (access keys) by responding to the VBM_MNEMONIC message. This usually involves falling through to the code that handles a mouse click because the response is typically the same.

Subclassing a Windows Control

Subclassing a Windows control is quite straightforward. To do so, perform the following tasks:

- Override two member functions of COleControl, called PreCreateWindow() and GetSuperWndProcAddr().

- Modify your OnDraw() member function.

■ Handle any OCM messages reflected to your control.

 Much of the work of handling OCM messages is done for you by ControlWizard if you select the Subclass Windows Control option in the Control Options dialog box.

Overriding *PreCreateWindow* and *GetSuperWndProcAddr*

Overriding `PreCreateWindow()` and `GetSuperWndProcAddr()` involves the addition of the following lines of code to the protected section of your control's class declaration:

```
BOOL PreCreateWindow( CREATESTRUCT& cs );
WNDPROC* GetSuperWndProcAddr( );
```

In your control's implementation file, the following lines of code exist to implement the two overridden functions:

```
BOOL CSampleCtrl::PreCreateWindow( CREATESTRUCT& cs )
{
    cs.lpszClass = _T("BUTTON");
    return COleControl::PreCreateWindow(cs);
}

WNDPROC* CSampleCtrl::GetSuperWndProcAddr( )
{
    static WNDPROC NEAR pfnSuper;
    return &pfnSuper;
}
```

Notice that the Windows button control is specified in `PreCreateWindow()`; however, you have the capability of subclassing any of the standard Windows controls. When subclassing a Windows control, you may want to specify a particular window style (`WS_`) or extended window style (`WS_EX_`) flag to be used in creating the control's window. You can set values for these parameters in the `PreCreateWindow()` member function by modifying the `cs.style` and `cs.dwExStyle` structure fields. Modifications to these fields should be made using an OR operation in order to preserve the default flags that are set by the `COleControl` base class. For example, if your control is subclassing the button control and you want the control to appear as a checkbox, insert the following line of code into the implementation of `CSampleCtrl::PreCreateWindow()`:

```
cs.style |= BS_CHECKBOX;
```

This operation will add the `BS_CHECKBOX` style flag, while leaving the default style flag (`WS_CHILD`) of the `COleControl` base class intact.

Modifying the *OnDraw* Member Function

The OnDraw() member function for your subclassed control should contain only a call to the DoSuperclassPaint() member function, as in the following example:

```
void CSampleCtrl::OnDraw( CDC* pdc, const CRect& rcBounds,
    const CRect& rcInvalid )
{
    DoSuperclassPaint( pdc, rcBounds );
}
```

The DoSuperclassPaint() member function, implemented by COleControl, uses the window procedure of the Windows control to cause the control to be drawn in the specified device context within the bounding rectangle. This enables the control to be visible even when it is not active.

The DoSuperclassPaint() member function works with only those control types that allow a device context to be passed as the wParam of a WM_PAINT message, such as SCROLLBAR and BUTTON. For controls that do not support this behavior, you will have to write the code to display the control in the inactive state.

Reflected Window Messages

Windows controls typically send certain window messages to their parent window. Some of these messages, such as WM_COMMAND, provide notification of an action by the user. Others, such as WM_CTLCOLOR, are used to obtain information from the parent window. For an OLE control, this kind of communication with the parent window is usually accomplished by other means. Notifications occur through the firing of events, whereas information about the control container is obtained by accessing the container's ambient properties. Because these communication techniques exist, OLE control containers are not expected to process any window messages sent by the control.

To prevent the container from receiving the window messages sent by a Windows control to its parent window, the COleControl base class causes an extra window to be created to serve as the control's parent. Note that this extra window is created only for an OLE control that subclasses a Windows control. This window, called the *reflector window*, intercepts window messages and sends similar messages back to the control itself. The control, in its window procedure, can then process these reflected messages by performing some appropriate action for an OLE control (for example, firing an event). Table 11.1 shows the messages that are intercepted and the corresponding messages that the reflector window sends.

Table 11.1 Reflected Messages

Message Sent by Control	Message Reflected to Control
WM_COMMAND	OCM_COMMAND
WM_CTLCOLOR	OCM_CTLCOLOR
WM_DRAWITEM	OCM_DRAWITEM
WM_MEASUREITEM	OCM_MEASUREITEM
WM_DELETEITEM	OCM_DELETEITEM
WM_VKEYTOITEM	OCM_VKEYTOITEM
WM_CHARTOITEM	OCM_CHARTOITEM
WM_COMPAREITEM	OCM_COMPAREITEM
WM_HSCROLL	OCM_HSCROLL
WM_VSCROLL	OCM_VSCROLL
WM_PARENTNOTIFY	OCM_PARENTNOTIFY

An OLE control container may choose to perform message reflection itself, eliminating the need for COleControl to create the reflector window and reducing the runtime overhead for a subclassed Windows control. COleControl can detect whether the container supports this capability by checking for a MessageReflect ambient property with a value of True.

To handle a reflected window message, you need to add an entry to your control's message map and implement a handler function. Because the reflected messages are not part of the standard set of messages defined by Windows, there is no support provided by ClassWizard for adding such message handlers. However, it is not difficult to add a handler manually.

To add a message handler for a reflected window message, you must perform the following:

1. In the .H file of your control's class, declare a handler function. The function should have a return type of LRESULT and two parameters with types WPARAM and LPARAM, respectively. For example:

```
LRESULT OnOcmCommand( WPARAM wParam, LPARAM lParam );
```

2. In the .CPP file of your control's class, add an ON_MESSAGE entry to the message map. The parameters of this entry should be the message identifier and the name of the handler function. For example:

```
ON_MESSAGE( OCM_COMMAND, OnOcmCommand )
```

3. Also in the .CPP file, implement the OnOcmCommand member function to process the reflected message. The wParam and lParam parameters are the same as those of the original window message.

The ControlWizard

This control will take on a slight variation from what you have been doing thus far—you will be subclassing a standard button control. As with the controls of Chapters 9 and 10, you need to start Visual C++ and clear the workspace. Activate the ControlWizard by selecting Tools, ControlWizard from the Visual C++ menu.

Fig. 11.2
The ControlWizard dialog box allows you to select options for creating a subclassed Windows control.

As shown in figure 11.2, select a directory in the Directory list box and enter the name of the control project in the Project Name edit control—BUTTON. Select the Project Options button to access the dialog box shown in figure 11.3. For this control, you will not be using the licensing feature. However, you will want source comments, so you can leave them defaulted, as shown in the figure.

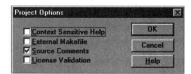

Fig. 11.3
The dialog box allows you to select the type of functionality and code.

Return to the ControlWizard's main window. Click the Control Options button and set the options to match figure 11.4. For your subclassed button control, you want the control to be activated when visible so it can process standard Windows messages. You also want the control to show up in the Insert Object dialog box.

Fig. 11.4

The Control Options dialog box allows you to select the options for the behavior of the control in a container as well as the Windows control that is to be subclassed.

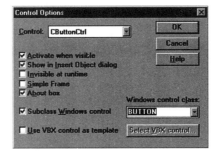

What's new for this control is that you should select the Subclass Windows Control checkbox to tell the ControlWizard that the new control will sub-class an existing Windows control. Once you have selected this option, you will have access to the Windows Control Class drop-down list box so you can select the Windows class you want to subclass. In the case of this control, select the entry for the BUTTON control from the list.

To review the Button control components, access the Controls dialog box by clicking the Controls button in the ControlWizard main window (see fig. 11.5). As with the controls from Chapters 9 and 10, you can manage the names of existing components for your control. Review the information in this dialog box so that you will be aware of the contents of the Button control as you read about the code for the control.

Now you want to create the subclassed Button control that you have set up in the options of the ControlWizard. Click the OK button in the ControlWizard main window to have the ControlWizard display the New Control Information dialog box (see fig. 11.6). Once you have reviewed the information, click the Create button to have the ControlWizard create your source files in the directory you specified.

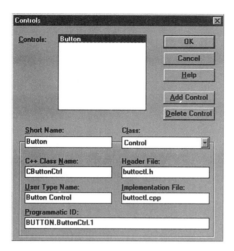

Fig. 11.5
The Controls
dialog box
contains informa-
tion about the
classes and files for
the subclassed
control.

Table 11.2 is a list of the files generated by ControlWizard, along with the
descriptions for each that are generated for the Button custom control. Now
that the framework is generated, you can use the ClassWizard to modify the
Button control to operate the way you want.

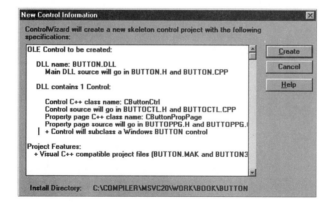

Fig. 11.6
The New Control
Information dialog
box contains a
summary of the
options selected
for the new
custom control.

Table 11.2 Files Generated by ControlWizard		
File Name	**File Size**	**Description**
BUTTON.MAK	2,589	The project makefile for building your 16-bit OLE custom control. This project file is compatible with the Visual C++ 1.5 Workbench. It is compatible also with NMAKE.

(continues)

Table 11.2 Continued		
File Name	**File Size**	**Description**
BUTTON32.MAK	18,384	The project makefile for building your 32-bit OLE custom control. This project file is compatible with the Visual C++ 2.0 Workbench. It is compatible also with NMAKE.
MAKEFILE	1,441	A makefile that makes it easy to run NMAKE from the command prompt. Use the following parameters with NMAKE:

<table>
<tr><td>DEBUG=0</td><td>Builds retail version</td></tr>
<tr><td>DEBUG=1</td><td>Builds debug version (default)</td></tr>
<tr><td>WIN32=0</td><td>Builds 16-bit version (default)</td></tr>
<tr><td>WIN32=1</td><td>Builds 32-bit version</td></tr>
<tr><td>UNICODE=0</td><td>Builds ANSI/DBCS version (default for WIN32=0)</td></tr>
<tr><td>UNICODE=1</td><td>Builds Unicode version (default for WIN32=1)</td></tr>
</table>

File Name	File Size	Description
BUTTON.H	526	This is the main include file for the OLE custom control DLL. It has other project-specific includes such as RESOURCE.H.
BUTTON.CPP	1,892	This is the main source file that contains the OLE DLL initialization, termination, and other bookkeeping.
BUTTON.RC	2,452	This is a listing of the Microsoft Windows resources that the project uses. This file can be directly edited with the Visual C++ resource editor.
BUTTON.RC2	2,087	This file contains resources that are not edited by the resource editor. Initially, this contains a VERSIONINFO resource that you can customize for your OLE custom control DLL, and a TYPELIB resource for your DLL's type library. You should place other manually maintained resources in this file.
BUTTON.DEF	508	This file contains information about the OLE custom control DLL that must be provided to run with Microsoft Windows. It defines parameters such as the name and description of the DLL, and the size of the initial local heap. The numbers in this file are typical for OLE custom control DLLs.
BUTTON32.DEF	240	This is a version of BUTTON.DEF for when you are building a 32-bit version of the OLE custom control DLL.

File Name	File Size	Description
BUTTON.CLW	876	This file contains information used by ClassWizard to edit existing classes or add new classes. ClassWizard also uses this file to store information needed to generate and edit message maps and dialog data maps, and to generate prototype member functions.
BUTTON.ODL	1,789	This file contains the Object Description Language source code for the type library of your OLE control.
BUTTON.ICO	768	This file contains an icon that will appear in the About dialog box. This icon is included by the main resource file BUTTON.RC.
BUTTOCTL.H	1,996	This file contains the declaration of the CButtonCtrl C++ class.
BUTTOCTL.CPP	6,333	This file contains the implementation of the CButtonCtrl C++ class.
BUTTOPPG.H	967	This file contains the declaration of the CButtonPropPage C++ class.
BUTTOPPG.CPP	2,356	This file contains the implementation of the CButtonPropPage C++ class.
BUTTOCTL.BMP	240	This file contains a bitmap that a container will use to represent the CButtonCtrl control when it appears on a tool palette. This bitmap is included by the main resource file BUTTON.RC.
STDAFX.H	240	The header file is used to build a precompiled header (PCH) file named STDAFX.PCH and a precompiled types (PCT) file named STDAFX.OBJ.
STDAFX.CPP	204	The implementation file is used to build a precompiled header (PCH) file named STDAFX.PCH and a precompiled types (PCT) file named STDAFX.OBJ.
RESOURCE.H	532	This is the standard header file, which defines new resource IDs. AppStudio reads and updates this file.

Details of the Control

The code for the Button custom control is very similar to the Comm and Timer controls, except that you are importing some of the functionality from the standard button control. The following listings step through the code to give you a feel for the contents of a subclassed control that will be tested in the Test Container to demonstrate how such a control can be utilized in container applications. The purpose of this subclassed control is to incorporate the functionality of the stock Windows Button control with your own customized code.

The button.h File

Listing 11.1 contains the source code for the Button control's application class header file. As you can see, the basic elements of this file are not much different than the Comm and Timer controls except for the name of the control application's base class. This file is created and maintained by the ControlWizard.

Listing 11.1 button.h—The Button Control's Header File

```
// button.h : main header file for BUTTON.DLL

#if !defined( __AFXCTL_H__ )
    #error include 'afxctl.h' before including this file
#endif

#include "resource.h"        // main symbols

/////////////////////////////////////////////////////////////////////////
// CButtonApp : See button.cpp for implementation.

class CButtonApp : public COleControlModule
{
public:
    BOOL InitInstance();
    int ExitInstance();
};

extern const GUID CDECL _tlid;
extern const WORD _wVerMajor;
extern const WORD _wVerMinor;
```

The button.cpp File

The source code in listing 11.2 contains the implementation of the class CButtonApp, as well as the theApp application instance. Again, the basic code did not change much between the Comm, Timer, and Button controls.

The purpose of the functions DllRegisterServer() and
DllUnregisterServer(), as with all custom controls, is to register and
unregister the control in the system registry. As you have seen with the
Comm and Timer controls, when registering the control with REGSRVR32,
DllRegisterServer() is called to register the control. Likewise, when
unregistering the control, DllUnregisterServer() is called to remove the
control from the system registry.

Listing 11.2   button.cpp—The Button Control's Implementation File

```
// button.cpp : Implementation of CButtonApp and DLL registration.

#include "stdafx.h"
#include "button.h"

#ifdef _DEBUG
#undef THIS_FILE
static char BASED_CODE THIS_FILE[] = __FILE__;
#endif


CButtonApp NEAR theApp;

const GUID CDECL BASED_CODE _tlid =
        { 0x56a2c5a3, 0x240a, 0x11ce, { 0x96, 0xf, 0x52, 0x41,
        0x53, 0x48, 0x0, 0x5 } };
const WORD _wVerMajor = 1;
const WORD _wVerMinor = 0;


/////////////////////////////////////////////////////////////////////
// CButtonApp::InitInstance - DLL initialization

BOOL CButtonApp::InitInstance()
{
    BOOL bInit = COleControlModule::InitInstance();

    if (bInit)
    {
        // TODO: Add your own module initialization code here.
    }

    return bInit;
}


/////////////////////////////////////////////////////////////////////
// CButtonApp::ExitInstance - DLL termination

int CButtonApp::ExitInstance()
```

(continues)

Listing 11.2 Continued

```
{
    // TODO: Add your own module termination code here.

    return COleControlModule::ExitInstance();
}


/////////////////////////////////////////////////////////////////////////
// DllRegisterServer - Adds entries to the system registry

STDAPI DllRegisterServer(void)
{
    AFX_MANAGE_STATE(_afxModuleAddrThis);

    if (!AfxOleRegisterTypeLib(AfxGetInstanceHandle(), _tlid))
        return ResultFromScode(SELFREG_E_TYPELIB);

    if (!COleObjectFactoryEx::UpdateRegistryAll(TRUE))
        return ResultFromScode(SELFREG_E_CLASS);

    return NOERROR;
}


/////////////////////////////////////////////////////////////////////////
// DllUnregisterServer - Removes entries from the system registry

STDAPI DllUnregisterServer(void)
{
    AFX_MANAGE_STATE(_afxModuleAddrThis);

    if (!AfxOleUnregisterTypeLib(_tlid))
        return ResultFromScode(SELFREG_E_TYPELIB);

    if (!COleObjectFactoryEx::UpdateRegistryAll(FALSE))
        return ResultFromScode(SELFREG_E_CLASS);

    return NOERROR;
}
```

The button.rc File

The button.rc file, in listing 11.3, contains the resource script for resources that are maintained with the AppStudio resource editor. This file defines your About dialog box and the string table used by the Button control.

Notice the differences in this script as compared to the ones you have seen in previous chapters. This script has a reference to only one bitmap, IDB_BUTTON, as opposed to two from the previous controls. In the previous controls, there were two bitmaps—one for a container's toolbar and one for visibility in the container's workspace. Since you will be utilizing the superclass' display functionality, you have no need for any additional bitmaps to display in the container. You need only the one that will appear in the toolbox. For this control, use the default bitmap shown in figure 11.7.

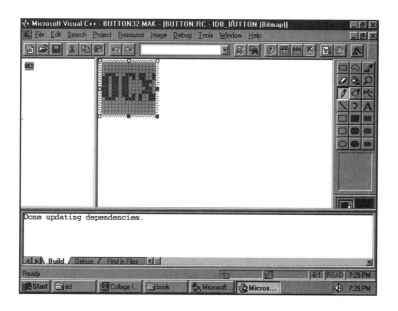

Fig. 11.7
The default Toolbox bitmap is displayed in the toolbar of the container in which the control is incorporated.

Listing 11.3   button.rc—The Button Control's Resource File

```
//Microsoft AppStudio generated resource script.
//
#include "resource.h"

#define APSTUDIO_READONLY_SYMBOLS
/////////////////////////////////////////////////////////////////////////////
//
// From TEXTINCLUDE 2
//
#include "afxres.h"

/////////////////////////////////////////////////////////////////////////////
#undef APSTUDIO_READONLY_SYMBOLS

#ifdef APSTUDIO_INVOKED

/////////////////////////////////////////////////////////////////////////////
//
// TEXTINCLUDE
//
```

(continues)

Listing 11.3 Continued

```
1 TEXTINCLUDE DISCARDABLE
BEGIN
    "resource.h\0"
END

2 TEXTINCLUDE DISCARDABLE
BEGIN
    "#include ""afxres.h""\r\n"
    "\0"
END

3 TEXTINCLUDE DISCARDABLE
BEGIN
    "#include ""afxres.rc""\r\n"
    "#include ""button.rc2""  // non-AppStudio edited
                              // resources\r\n"
    "#if 0\r\n"
    "#include "".\\tlb16\\button.tlb""  // 16-bit: force
                                        // dependency on
                                        // .TLB file\r\n"
    "#endif\r\n"
    "\0"
END


/////////////////////////////////////////////////////////////////
#endif    // APSTUDIO_INVOKED


/////////////////////////////////////////////////////////////////

IDI_ABOUTDLL    ICON    DISCARDABLE    button.ico

IDB_BUTTON    BITMAP DISCARDABLE  buttoctl.bmp
IDD_ABOUTBOX_BUTTON DIALOG DISCARDABLE  34, 22, 260, 55
CAPTION "About Button Control"
STYLE DS_MODALFRAME | WS_POPUP | WS_CAPTION | WS_SYSMENU
FONT 8, "MS Sans Serif"
BEGIN
    ICON            IDI_ABOUTDLL,IDC_STATIC,10,10,20,20
    LTEXT           "Button Control, Version 1.0",IDC_STATIC,
                        40,10,170,8
    LTEXT           "Copyright \251 1994, Edward B. Toupin",
                        IDC_STATIC,40,25,170,8
    DEFPUSHBUTTON   "OK",IDOK,220,10,32,14,WS_GROUP
END

IDD_PROPPAGE_BUTTON DIALOG DISCARDABLE  0, 0, 250, 62
STYLE WS_CHILD
FONT 8, "MS Sans Serif"
BEGIN
END
```

```
/////////////////////////////////////////////////////////////
//
// String Table
//

STRINGTABLE DISCARDABLE
BEGIN
    IDS_BUTTON              "Button Control"
    IDS_BUTTON_PPG          "Button Property Page"
    IDS_BUTTON_PPG_CAPTION  "General"

END

#ifndef APSTUDIO_INVOKED
/////////////////////////////////////////////////////////////
//
// From TEXTINCLUDE 3
//

#include "afxres.rc"
#include "button.rc2"  // non-AppStudio edited resources
#if 0
#include ".\tlb16\button.tlb"  // 16-bit: force dependency
                               // on .TLB file
#endif


/////////////////////////////////////////////////////////////

#endif    // not APSTUDIO_INVOKED
```

The button.rc2 File

The button.rc2 file in listing 11.4 contains the resource script for resources
that can only be changed manually. This information is specifically for copyright and version information to be incorporated into your application.
When working with this resource script, you will want to change the copyright and legal information for your specific purposes.

Listing 11.4 button.rc2—The Button Control's Resource File

```
//
// BUTTON.RC2 - resources AppStudio does not edit directly
//

#ifdef APSTUDIO_INVOKED
    #error this file is not editable by AppStudio
#endif //APSTUDIO_INVOKED
```

(continues)

Listing 11.4   Continued

```
//////////////////////////////////////////////////////////////
// Version stamp for this DLL

#ifdef _WIN32
#include "winver.h"
#else
#include "ver.h"
#endif

VS_VERSION_INFO      VERSIONINFO
  FILEVERSION        1,0,0,1
  PRODUCTVERSION     1,0,0,1
  FILEFLAGSMASK      VS_FFI_FILEFLAGSMASK
#ifdef _DEBUG
  FILEFLAGS          VS_FF_DEBUG|VS_FF_PRIVATEBUILD|VS_FF_PRERELEASE
#else
  FILEFLAGS          0 // final version
#endif
#ifdef _WIN32
  FILEOS             VOS__WINDOWS32
#else
  FILEOS             VOS__WINDOWS16
#endif
  FILETYPE           VFT_DLL
  FILESUBTYPE        0   // not used
BEGIN
    BLOCK "StringFileInfo"
    BEGIN
#ifdef _WIN32
        BLOCK "040904B0" // Lang=US English, CharSet=Unicode
#else
        BLOCK "040904E4" // Lang=US English,
                         // CharSet=Windows Multilingual
#endif
        BEGIN
            VALUE "CompanyName",      "\0"
            VALUE "FileDescription", "BUTTON OLE Control DLL\0"
            VALUE "FileVersion",      "1.0.001\0"
            VALUE "InternalName",     "BUTTON\0"
            VALUE "LegalCopyright",
                "Copyright \251 1994, Edward B. Toupin\0"
            VALUE "LegalTrademarks", "\0"
            VALUE "OriginalFilename","BUTTON.DLL\0"
            VALUE "ProductName",      "BUTTON\0"
            VALUE "ProductVersion",   "1.0.001\0"
            VALUE "OLESelfRegister", "\0"
        END
    END
    BLOCK "VarFileInfo"
    BEGIN
#ifdef _WIN32
        VALUE "Translation", 0x409, 1200
```

```
                    // English language (0x409) and the Unicode
                    // codepage (1200)
#else
            VALUE "Translation", 0x409, 1252
                    // English language (0x409) and the Windows ANSI
                    // codepage (1252)
#endif
        END
END


/////////////////////////////////////////////////////////////////
// Type library for controls in this DLL

1 TYPELIB button.tlb


/////////////////////////////////////////////////////////////////
// Add additional manually edited resources here...
/////////////////////////////////////////////////////////////////
```

The button.def File

The button.def file in listing 11.5 contains the definition for the 16-bit Button control. As with other controls, the exports are functions of the control made visible to Windows so that Windows can call them as required. In this file, you are exporting five functions for access by the Windows operating system. Each exported function is accessible for calling by the operating system and other applications.

The WEP export is the Windows exit procedure and is used as a destructor for the 16-bit DLL. This function allows you to perform any cleanup and housekeeping required before the DLL is unloaded from memory. The remaining exported functions provide a means of loading, unloading, and managing interfaces for the DLL.

Listing 11.5 button.def—The Button Control's 16-bit Definition File

```
; button.def : Declares the module parameters.

LIBRARY      'BUTTON'
DESCRIPTION  'BUTTON OLE Custom Control module'
EXETYPE      WINDOWS

CODE         PRELOAD MOVEABLE DISCARDABLE
DATA         PRELOAD MOVEABLE SINGLE

HEAPSIZE     1024   ; initial heap size
```

(continues)

```
Listing 11.5   Continued

EXPORTS
      WEP                 @1   RESIDENTNAME
      DLLCANUNLOADNOW     @2   RESIDENTNAME
      DLLGETCLASSOBJECT   @3   RESIDENTNAME
      DLLREGISTERSERVER   @4   RESIDENTNAME
      DLLUNREGISTERSERVER @5   RESIDENTNAME

SEGMENTS
      WEP_TEXT FIXED
```

The button32.def File

The button32.def file in listing 11.6 contains the definitions for the 32-bit
Button control. The difference between this definition and the 16-bit definition is that the EXETYPE and the SEGMENTS clauses are not included in this definition. The primary reason for the missing parameters is that you do not
need to be concerned about defining segments and executable types under
the flat memory model of 32-bit Windows.

```
Listing 11.6   button32.def—The Button Control's 32-bit
Definition File

   ; button32.def : Declares the module parameters.

   LIBRARY      BUTTON.OCX

   EXPORTS
         DllCanUnloadNow     @1  RESIDENTNAME
         DllGetClassObject   @2  RESIDENTNAME
         DllRegisterServer   @3  RESIDENTNAME
         DllUnregisterServer @4  RESIDENTNAME
```

The buttoctl.h File

Listing 11.7 shows the contents of the buttoctl.h header file that contains
the class definition for the CButtonCtl class. CButtonCtrl is derived from the
COleObject base class that provides much of the functionality required by the
Button control. The derived class contains a public constructor, a protected
destructor, the message-handling function OnDraw(), and the control reset
function OnResetState().

Listing 11.7 buttoctl.def—The Declaration of the OLE Control Class

```
// buttoctl.h : Declaration of the CButtonCtrl OLE control class.

/////////////////////////////////////////////////////////////////
// CButtonCtrl : See buttoctl.cpp for implementation.

class CButtonCtrl : public COleControl
{
    DECLARE_DYNCREATE(CButtonCtrl)

// Constructor
public:
    CButtonCtrl();

// Overrides

    // Drawing function
    virtual void OnDraw(
                    CDC* pdc, const CRect& rcBounds,
                    const CRect& rcInvalid);

    // Persistence
    virtual void DoPropExchange(CPropExchange* pPX);

    // Reset control state
    virtual void OnResetState();

// Implementation
protected:
    ~CButtonCtrl();

    DECLARE_OLECREATE_EX(CButtonCtrl) // Class factory and guid
    DECLARE_OLETYPELIB(CButtonCtrl)   // GetTypeInfo
    DECLARE_PROPPAGEIDS(CButtonCtr    // Property page IDs
    DECLARE_OLECTLTYPE(CButtonCtrl    // Type name and misc status

    // Subclassed control support
    BOOL PreCreateWindow(CREATESTRUCT& cs);
    WNDPROC* GetSuperWndProcAddr(void);
    LRESULT OnOcmCommand(WPARAM wParam, LPARAM lParam);

// Message maps
    //{{AFX_MSG(CButtonCtrl)
        // NOTE - ClassWizard will add and remove member
        // functions here.
        //    DO NOT EDIT what you see in these blocks of
        //    generated code !
    //}}AFX_MSG
    DECLARE_MESSAGE_MAP()

// Dispatch maps
    //{{AFX_DISPATCH(CButtonCtrl)
        // NOTE - ClassWizard will add and remove member
        // functions here.
```

(continues)

```
Listing 11.7   Continued
                    //     DO NOT EDIT what you see in these blocks of
                    //     generated code !
          //}}AFX_DISPATCH
          DECLARE_DISPATCH_MAP()

          afx_msg void AboutBox();

      // Event maps
          //{{AFX_EVENT(CButtonCtrl)
               // NOTE - ClassWizard will add and remove member
               // functions here.
               //     DO NOT EDIT what you see in these blocks of
               //     generated code !
          //}}AFX_EVENT
          DECLARE_EVENT_MAP()

      // Dispatch and event IDs
      public:
          enum {
          //{{AFX_DISP_ID(CButtonCtrl)
               // NOTE: ClassWizard will add and remove enumeration
               // elements here.
               //     DO NOT EDIT what you see in these blocks of
               //     generated code !
          //}}AFX_DISP_ID
          };
      };
```

In addition to the public constructor, a protected destructor, the message handling function OnDraw(), and the control reset function OnResetState(), you are overriding the functions PreCreateWindow() and GetSuperWndProcAddr(). PreCreateWindow() is called when the window for the superclass is created while GetSuperWndProcAddr() creates storage for the subclass window procedure OnOcmCommand().

The OnOcmCommand() function is the subclass window procedure that is used to modify the functionality of the superclass. This function is fired whenever a message is received by the superclass, which in this control is a Button control. You are not handling any other messages, so the message map itself is empty. As you can see, the message map macro DECLARE_MESSAGE_MAP() is preceded by no messages.

The buttoctl.cpp File

Listing 11.8 contains the code for the implementation file, buttoctl.cpp, of the Button control. This file contains the primary code for the functionality of the control itself, and is also where your code will reside to provide customized features for the control, such as the following:

- The *message map* for the Button control contains the assignment of a function, OnOcmCommand(), to the OCM_COMMAND message. This function will execute anytime a specific notification message is sent for the Button superclass.

- The *dispatch map* exposes the AboutBox() member for use by external applications.

- The OnDraw() function for a subclassed control will, by default, call the paint procedure of the superclass. In this control, you will be painting a button on the container's workspace. You can also modify this function in order to paint your own control, but it is best to use the paint functions of the subclassed control.

Listing 11.8   buttoctl.cpp—The Implementation File for the OLE Control Class

```
// buttoctl.cpp : Implementation of the CButtonCtrl OLE
// control class.

#include "stdafx.h"
#include "button.h"
#include "buttoctl.h"
#include "buttoppg.h"


#ifdef _DEBUG
#undef THIS_FILE
static char BASED_CODE THIS_FILE[] = __FILE__;
#endif


IMPLEMENT_DYNCREATE(CButtonCtrl, COleControl)


/////////////////////////////////////////////////////////////////////
// Message map

BEGIN_MESSAGE_MAP(CButtonCtrl, COleControl)
    //{{AFX_MSG_MAP(CButtonCtrl)
    // NOTE - ClassWizard will add and remove message map entries
    //    DO NOT EDIT what you see in these blocks of
    //    generated code !
    ON_MESSAGE(OCM_COMMAND, OnOcmCommand)
    //}}AFX_MSG_MAP
    ON_OLEVERB(AFX_IDS_VERB_EDIT, OnEdit)
    ON_OLEVERB(AFX_IDS_VERB_PROPERTIES, OnProperties)
END_MESSAGE_MAP()
```

(continues)

Listing 11.8   Continued

```
/////////////////////////////////////////////////////////////////
// Dispatch map

BEGIN_DISPATCH_MAP(CButtonCtrl, COleControl)
    //{{AFX_DISPATCH_MAP(CButtonCtrl)
    // NOTE - ClassWizard will add and remove dispatch map entries
    //    DO NOT EDIT what you see in these blocks of
    //    generated code !
    //}}AFX_DISPATCH_MAP
    DISP_FUNCTION_ID(CButtonCtrl, "AboutBox", DISPID_ABOUTBOX,
                     AboutBox, VT_EMPTY, VTS_NONE)
END_DISPATCH_MAP()


/////////////////////////////////////////////////////////////////
// Event map

BEGIN_EVENT_MAP(CButtonCtrl, COleControl)
    //{{AFX_EVENT_MAP(CButtonCtrl)
    // NOTE - ClassWizard will add and remove event map entries
    //    DO NOT EDIT what you see in these blocks of
    //    generated code !
    //}}AFX_EVENT_MAP
END_EVENT_MAP()


/////////////////////////////////////////////////////////////////
// Property pages

// TODO: Add more property pages as needed. Remember to increase
// the count!
BEGIN_PROPPAGEIDS(CButtonCtrl, 1)
    PROPPAGEID(CButtonPropPage::guid)
END_PROPPAGEIDS(CButtonCtrl)


/////////////////////////////////////////////////////////////////
// Initialize class factory and guid

IMPLEMENT_OLECREATE_EX(CButtonCtrl, "BUTTON.ButtonCtrl.1",
    0x56a2c5a0, 0x240a, 0x11ce, 0x96, 0xf, 0x52, 0x41, 0x53,
    0x48, 0x0, 0x5)


/////////////////////////////////////////////////////////////////
// Type library ID and version

IMPLEMENT_OLETYPELIB(CButtonCtrl, _tlid, _wVerMajor, _wVerMinor)


/////////////////////////////////////////////////////////////////
// Interface IDs
```

```
const IID BASED_CODE IID_DButton =
        { 0x56a2c5a1, 0x240a, 0x11ce, { 0x96, 0xf, 0x52, 0x41,
        0x53, 0x48, 0x0, 0x5 } };
const IID BASED_CODE IID_DButtonEvents =
        { 0x56a2c5a2, 0x240a, 0x11ce, { 0x96, 0xf, 0x52, 0x41,
        0x53, 0x48, 0x0, 0x5 } };


/////////////////////////////////////////////////////////////////////
// Control type information

static const DWORD BASED_CODE _dwButtonOleMisc =
    OLEMISC_ACTIVATEWHENVISIBLE ¦
    OLEMISC_SETCLIENTSITEFIRST ¦
    OLEMISC_INSIDEOUT ¦
    OLEMISC_CANTLINKINSIDE ¦
    OLEMISC_RECOMPOSEONRESIZE;

IMPLEMENT_OLECTLTYPE(CButtonCtrl, IDS_BUTTON, _dwButtonOleMisc)


/////////////////////////////////////////////////////////////////////
// CButtonCtrl::CButtonCtrlFactory::UpdateRegistry -
// Adds or removes system registry entries for CButtonCtrl

BOOL CButtonCtrl::CButtonCtrlFactory::UpdateRegistry(BOOL
   bRegister)
{
    if (bRegister)
        return AfxOleRegisterControlClass(
            AfxGetInstanceHandle(),
            m_clsid,
            m_lpszProgID,
            IDS_BUTTON,
            IDB_BUTTON,
            TRUE,                          //  Insertable
            _dwButtonOleMisc,
            _tlid,
            _wVerMajor,
            _wVerMinor);
    else
        return AfxOleUnregisterClass(m_clsid, m_lpszProgID);
}


/////////////////////////////////////////////////////////////////////
// CButtonCtrl::CButtonCtrl - Constructor

CButtonCtrl::CButtonCtrl()
{
    InitializeIIDs(&IID_DButton, &IID_DButtonEvents);

    // TODO: Initialize your control's instance data here.
}
```

(continues)

Listing 11.8   Continued

```
/////////////////////////////////////////////////////////////////////
// CButtonCtrl::~CButtonCtrl - Destructor

CButtonCtrl::~CButtonCtrl()
{
    // TODO: Cleanup your control's instance data here.
}


/////////////////////////////////////////////////////////////////////
// CButtonCtrl::OnDraw - Drawing function

void CButtonCtrl::OnDraw(
                CDC* pdc, const CRect& rcBounds,
                    const CRect& rcInvalid)
{
    DoSuperclassPaint(pdc, rcBounds);
}


/////////////////////////////////////////////////////////////////////
// CButtonCtrl::DoPropExchange - Persistence support

void CButtonCtrl::DoPropExchange(CPropExchange* pPX)
{
    ExchangeVersion(pPX, MAKELONG(_wVerMinor, _wVerMajor));
    COleControl::DoPropExchange(pPX);

    // TODO: Call PX_ functions for each persistent custom
    // property.

}


/////////////////////////////////////////////////////////////////////
// CButtonCtrl::OnResetState - Reset control to default state

void CButtonCtrl::OnResetState()
{
    COleControl::OnResetState();   // Resets defaults found in
                                   // DoPropExchange

    // TODO: Reset any other control state here.
}


/////////////////////////////////////////////////////////////////////
// CButtonCtrl::AboutBox - Display an "About" box to the user

void CButtonCtrl::AboutBox()
{
    CDialog dlgAbout(IDD_ABOUTBOX_BUTTON);
    dlgAbout.DoModal();
}
```

```
///////////////////////////////////////////////////////////////////
// CButtonCtrl::PreCreateWindow - Modify parameters for
// CreateWindowEx

BOOL CButtonCtrl::PreCreateWindow(CREATESTRUCT& cs)
{
    cs.lpszClass = _T("BUTTON");
    return COleControl::PreCreateWindow(cs);
}


///////////////////////////////////////////////////////////////////
// CButtonCtrl::GetSuperWndProcAddr - Provide storage for
// window proc

WNDPROC* CButtonCtrl::GetSuperWndProcAddr(void)
{
    static WNDPROC NEAR pfnSuper;
    return &pfnSuper;
}


///////////////////////////////////////////////////////////////////
// CButtonCtrl::OnOcmCommand - Handle command messages

LRESULT CButtonCtrl::OnOcmCommand(WPARAM wParam, LPARAM lParam)
{
#ifdef _WIN32
    WORD wNotifyCode = HIWORD(wParam);
#else
    WORD wNotifyCode = HIWORD(lParam);
#endif

    // TODO: Switch on wNotifyCode here.

    return 0;
}


///////////////////////////////////////////////////////////////////
// CButtonCtrl message handlers
```

The PreCreateWindow() function is called immediately before you create an instance of the Button control within a container. This function specifies a superclass, BUTTON, that is used for the subclass control. You also can specify other control classes here such as EDIT, COMBOBOX, LISTBOX, and so on.

The GetSuperWndProcAddr() function allocates a static instance for the subclass window procedure. The window procedure is the OnOcmCommand() function, which is the subclass' function for the Button superclass. This function is passed the word (WPARAM) and long (LPARAM) parameters of a notification message issued by the Button control. Within this function, you can add functionality with the `switch()` case block as follows:

```
switch (wNotifyCode)
{
    // Issue a message when the button is clicked
    case BN_CLICKED :    MessageBox("Button Clicked");
                    break;
}
```

In the preceding code, a `BN_CLICKED` notification message is sent whenever you click the button. A `MessageBox()` function is called to display the message "Button Clicked" when you click on the button. You can also process any of the standard notification messages sent by the superclass. Within the code for this control, you are able to capture any of the `BN_XXXX` messages and process them in a `switch()` case block.

The buttoppg.h File

Listing 11.9 shows the contents of the buttoppg.h header file. This file contains the class definition for `CButtonPropPage`. This class provides the definition of the class required for the `General` property page and is derived from the `CDialog` MFC class. This header file is created and maintained by the ControlWizard.

Listing 11.9 buttoppg.h—The Header File for the Class

```
// buttoppg.h : Declaration of the CButtonPropPage property page
// class.

/////////////////////////////////////////////////////////////////
// CButtonPropPage : See buttoppg.cpp for implementation.

class CButtonPropPage : public COlePropertyPage
{
    DECLARE_DYNCREATE(CButtonPropPage)
    DECLARE_OLECREATE_EX(CButtonPropPage)

// Constructor
public:
    CButtonPropPage();

// Dialog Data
    //{{AFX_DATA(CButtonPropPage)
    enum { IDD = IDD_PROPPAGE_BUTTON };
        // NOTE - ClassWizard will add data members here.
        //    DO NOT EDIT what you see in these blocks of
        //    generated code !
    //}}AFX_DATA
```

```
// Implementation
protected:
    virtual void DoDataExchange(CDataExchange* pDX);    // DDX/DDV
                                                        // support

// Message maps
protected:
    //{{AFX_MSG(CButtonPropPage)
        // NOTE - ClassWizard will add and remove member
        // functions here.
        //    DO NOT EDIT what you see in these blocks of
        //    generated code !
    //}}AFX_MSG
    DECLARE_MESSAGE_MAP()

};
```

The buttoppg.cpp File

Listing 11.10 shows the contents of the buttoppg.h header file. This file contains the class definition for `CButtonPropPage`. This class provides the functionality for the `General` property page based on the class defined in the respective header file. For this control, you are not going to perform any type of modifications to the code. You will leave the property pages empty and use the standard properties of the superclass.

The sections of the property page implementation file for the control are as follows:

- The *message map* is a shell for modifications to be made later. This message map contains no message handlers since you are not utilizing the property page for this control.

- The `IMPLEMENT_OLECREATE_EX` macro declares the class factory for the control and the `GetClassID()` function. Since `CButtonPropPage` is an OLE class, it is registered in the system registry using the class factory.

- The `CButtonPropPageFactory::UpdateRegistry()` function registers and deregisters the `CButtonPropPage` class.

- The *constructor* is included so that you can add your own initialization code for the instantiation of the control's property pages as required.

- The `DoDataExchange()` function overrides the standard `CHWnd::DoDataExchange()` function to provide data transfer between the control and the property pages.

Listing 11.10   buttoppg.cpp—The Implementation File for the
***CButtonPropPage* Class**

```cpp
// buttoppg.cpp : Implementation of the CButtonPropPage property
// page class.

#include "stdafx.h"
#include "button.h"
#include "buttoppg.h"

#ifdef _DEBUG
#undef THIS_FILE
static char BASED_CODE THIS_FILE[] = __FILE__;
#endif


IMPLEMENT_DYNCREATE(CButtonPropPage, COlePropertyPage)


/////////////////////////////////////////////////////////////////
// Message map

BEGIN_MESSAGE_MAP(CButtonPropPage, COlePropertyPage)
    //{{AFX_MSG_MAP(CButtonPropPage)
    // NOTE - ClassWizard will add and remove message map entries
    //     DO NOT EDIT what you see in these blocks of
    //     generated code!
    //}}AFX_MSG_MAP
END_MESSAGE_MAP()


/////////////////////////////////////////////////////////////////
// Initialize class factory and guid

IMPLEMENT_OLECREATE_EX(CButtonPropPage, "BUTTON.ButtonPropPage.1",
    0x56a2c5a4, 0x240a, 0x11ce, 0x96, 0xf, 0x52, 0x41, 0x53,
    0x48, 0x0, 0x5)


/////////////////////////////////////////////////////////////////
// CButtonPropPage::CButtonPropPageFactory::UpdateRegistry -
// Adds or removes system registry entries for CButtonPropPage

BOOL CButtonPropPage::CButtonPropPageFactory::UpdateRegistry(
    BOOL bRegister)
{
    if (bRegister)
        return AfxOleRegisterPropertyPageClass(
            AfxGetInstanceHandle(), m_clsid, IDS_BUTTON_PPG);
    else
        return AfxOleUnregisterClass(m_clsid, NULL);
}


/////////////////////////////////////////////////////////////////
// CButtonPropPage::CButtonPropPage - Constructor
```

```
CButtonPropPage::CButtonPropPage() :
    COlePropertyPage(IDD, IDS_BUTTON_PPG_CAPTION)
{
    //{{AFX_DATA_INIT(CButtonPropPage)
    // NOTE: ClassWizard will add member initialization here
    //     DO NOT EDIT what you see in these blocks of
    //     generated code!
    //}}AFX_DATA_INIT
}


/////////////////////////////////////////////////////////////////////
// CButtonPropPage::DoDataExchange - Moves data between page and
// properties

void CButtonPropPage::DoDataExchange(CDataExchange* pDX)
{
    //{{AFX_DATA_MAP(CButtonPropPage)
    // NOTE: ClassWizard will add DDP, DDX, and DDV calls here
    //     DO NOT EDIT what you see in these blocks of
    //     generated code!
    //}}AFX_DATA_MAP
    DDP_PostProcessing(pDX);
}


/////////////////////////////////////////////////////////////////////
// CButtonPropPage message handlers
```

The stdafx.h File

Listing 11.11 shows the stdafx.h file, which contains a single `#include` statement. This `#include` statement provides MFC support for OLE controls.

Listing 11.11   stdafx.h—The Standard System Include File

```
// stdafx.h : include file for standard system include files,
//      or project specific include files that are used frequently,
//      but are changed infrequently

#include <afxctl.h>          // MFC support for OLE Custom Controls
```

The stdafx.cpp File

Listing 11.12 shows the stdafx.cpp file, which is the implementation file for MFC OLE control support. This file, as with the Comm and Timer control, provides the resources necessary to create precompiled headers when compiling the Button control.

Listing 11.12 stdafx.cpp—The Standard System Implementation File

```
// stdafx.cpp : source file that includes just the
// standard includes
//   stdafx.pch will be the precompiled header
//   stdafx.obj will contain the precompiled type information

#include "stdafx.h"
```

The resource.h File

Listing 11.13 shows the resource.h file for use with AppStudio. You should recognize these names as identifiers for the various resources you can edit.

The #define statements correspond to the following:

IDS_?????	Strings in a string table
IDS_?????	Dialog box identifiers
IDB_?????	Bitmap identifiers
IDI_?????	Icon identifiers

When you load the button.rc file in the AppStudio, these names will also be loaded and used when you view the properties for the resources edited in the resource file. You should recognize these names as identifiers for the various resources you can edit.

Listing 11.13 resource.h—The Resource Header File

```
//{{NO_DEPENDENCIES}}
// AppStudio generated include file.
// Used by BUTTON.RC
//
#define IDS_BUTTON                 1
#define IDS_BUTTON_PPG             2
#define IDS_BUTTON_PPG_CAPTION    101

#define IDD_ABOUTBOX_BUTTON       100
#define IDD_PROPPAGE_BUTTON       101
#define IDB_BUTTON                 1
#define IDI_ABOUTDLL              10

#define _APS_NEXT_RESOURCE_VALUE      201
#define _APS_NEXT_CONTROL_VALUE       201
#define _APS_NEXT_SYMED_VALUE         101
#define _APS_NEXT_COMMAND_VALUE     32768
```

The button.odl File

The Button control's type library information is stored in the button.odl file shown in listing 11.14. The ClassWizard maintains the information stored in this file; however, you should be aware of the information in this file to understand how the control is registered and accessed by container applications.

Listing 11.14 button.odl—The Type Library File

```
// button.odl : type library source for OLE Custom Control project.

// This file will be processed by the Make Type Library (mktyplib)
// tool to produce the type library (button.tlb) that will become
// a resource in button.ocx.

#include <olectl.h>

[ uuid(56A2C5A3-240A-11CE-960F-524153480005), version(1.0),
  helpstring("Button OLE Custom Control module") ]
library ButtonLib
{
    importlib(STDOLE_TLB);
    importlib(STDTYPE_TLB);

    //  Primary dispatch interface for CButtonCtrl

    [ uuid(56A2C5A1-240A-11CE-960F-524153480005),
      helpstring("Dispatch interface for Button Control") ]
    dispinterface _DButton
    {
        properties:
            // NOTE - ClassWizard will maintain property
            // information here.
            //   Use extreme caution when editing this section.
            //{{AFX_ODL_PROP(CButtonCtrl)
            //}}AFX_ODL_PROP

        methods:
            // NOTE - ClassWizard will maintain method
            // information here.
            //   Use extreme caution when editing this section.
            //{{AFX_ODL_METHOD(CButtonCtrl)
            //}}AFX_ODL_METHOD

            [id(DISPID_ABOUTBOX)] void AboutBox();
    };

    //  Event dispatch interface for CButtonCtrl

    [ uuid(56A2C5A2-240A-11CE-960F-524153480005),
      helpstring("Event interface for Button Control") ]
    dispinterface _DButtonEvents
    {
```

(continues)

```
Listing 11.14  Continued

         properties:
               //  Event interface has no properties

         methods:
               // NOTE - ClassWizard will maintain event
               // information here.
               //   Use extreme caution when editing this section.
               //{{AFX_ODL_EVENT(CButtonCtrl)
               //}}AFX_ODL_EVENT
      };

      //  Class information for CButtonCtrl

      [ uuid(56A2C5A0-240A-11CE-960F-524153480005),
        helpstring("Button Control") ]
      coclass Button
      {
           [default] dispinterface _DButton;
           [default, source] dispinterface _DButtonEvents;
      };


           //{{AFX_APPEND_ODL}}
      };
```

Modifying the Control

As it is, the control will not perform the clicking operation that is normally
required of a button. For this application, you want the user to be able to
click on the button and have a certain operation occur. You have seen that
you can use the OnOcmCommand() function to capture notification messages
whenever a specific operation occurs on the superclass button control; however, you need a way to relay this event to a container application. To do
this, you need to add an event to the subclassed button that will fire when
the user clicks on the button. This event will, for instance, be utilized within
a container application so that user-specific code can be executed when the
button is clicked.

In figure 11.8, you are adding a stock click event to the control so that any
click event that occurs to the button will utilize a stock operation. Once the
stock click event is added through the ClassWizard, the stock click event
function is added to the event map (see listing 11.15). This function is fired
whenever the button is clicked and provides a means of interfacing to the
container.

Fig. 11.8
Adding a Click
event to the
Button control
allows the control
to capture mouse
click events on the
control within
a container
application.

Listing 11.15   The Modified Event Map for the Click Event in buttoctl.cpp

```
//////////////////////////////////////////////////////////////////
// Event map

BEGIN_EVENT_MAP(CButtonCtrl, COleControl)
    //{{AFX_EVENT_MAP(CButtonCtrl)
    EVENT_STOCK_CLICK()
    //}}AFX_EVENT_MAP
END_EVENT_MAP()
```

Within container applications, this stock click event is passed from the control to the container in order to perform event-based operations. For instance, if this control is incorporated into a development environment, such as Microsoft Access 2.0 or Visual Basic, event-based code can be added to the control, as is done with the environments standard controls. Anytime the control is selected, the code for that control within the container is executed whenever the custom control is selected.

Building and Registering the Control

The new control now has to be built and registered with the system registry before it can be used. This build operation is accomplished easily by selecting the Project, Build option from the Visual Workbench menu. During this operation, Visual C++ compiles all of the code for the control and links the resulting object files and MFC libraries together. The resulting 32-bit OCX is placed into the OBJD32 subdirectory and is ready for use by a container application.

To register the control, select Tools, Register Control from the Visual Workbench menu. This selection invokes REGSVR32.EXE, which loads the OCX as a DLL and calls the DLLRegisterServer() function. Once the control is successfully registered, REGSVR32.EXE displays the dialog box shown in figure 11.9. Once registered, you will be able to see the registration entry in the system registry by loading the registration editor, REGEDIT, application (see fig. 11.10).

Fig. 11.9
Once the
REGSVR32.EXE
application has
registered the
OCX, it displays
this dialog box.

Fig. 11.10
Once registered by
REGSVR32.EXE,
the Button control
is visible in the
system registry
by way of the
registration editor
REGEDIT.

Using the Control

To get a feel for the operation of a subclassed control, load the control into the Test Container application and experiment with the control's methods and members.

To load the Test Container, select Tools, Test Container from the Visual Workbench menu. Once the control is loaded, select Edit, Insert OLE Control to access the Insert OLE Control dialog box. From this dialog box, select the Button control from the list and click OK to load the control into the container application (see fig. 11.11).

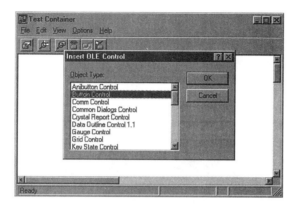

Fig. 11.11
From the Insert OLE Control dialog box, a custom control can be selected for insertion from the system registry.

As shown in figure 11.12, you can click on the Button control in the Test Container. Clicking issues a BN_CLICKED notification message, which is processed by the modified OnOcmCommand() function of the control. The message box you added to the control will be displayed as shown in the figure.

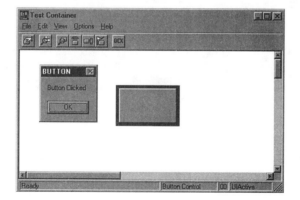

Fig. 11.12
Clicking on the Button control in the Test Container issues a **BN_CLICKED** message, which is processed by the OnOcmCommand() function.

To load the property sheet, select Edit, Button Control Object, Properties. As shown in figure 11.13, the property sheet will be blank because you added no code to perform property-specific operations for the control.

Selecting Edit, Invoke Methods enables you to view all of the available methods of the control. For this control, the only method that you see is the AboutBox method. Selecting the Invoke button invokes the AboutBox method and displays the About box for the Button control (see fig. 11.14).

Fig. 11.13
From the Test Container, the Button control's property page is displayed; however, there are no properties added to the page for editing.

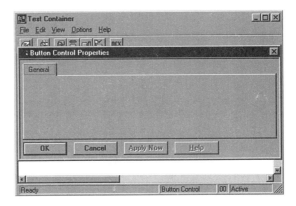

Fig. 11.14
Invoking the AboutBox method displays the About dialog box of the Button control.

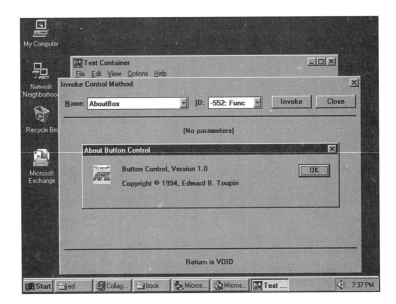

From Here...

In this chapter, you learned how to develop a subclassed control, install it, and use it in a container. You also learned more of the intricacies of coding with MFC in conjunction with the ControlWizard and ClassWizard. For further information, see the following:

■ Chapter 5, "The OLE Controls SDK," helps you understand how MFC is incorporated into OLE custom controls.

■ Chapter 12, "Data Binding," provides information on incorporating persistent objects into your control.

Chapter 12

Data Binding

by Edward B. Toupin

A powerful use of an OLE control involves binding a property of a control to a specific field in a database—also known as *data binding*. Whenever the contents of the control's bound property are changed, the control notifies the database that the value has changed and makes a request to have the field in the database record updated. The database then notifies the control of the success or failure of the request. Data bound controls also have the ability to view several different records in a database by scrolling through the database using a *cursor object* provided by the database.

This chapter explores the following topics:

- How data binding works
- Defining a bindable property
- Advanced data binding
- Open Database Connectivity (ODBC)
- The cursor object and library

How Data Binding Works

Data binding allows a database entry, such as a record field, to be linked to a property of an OLE control. The control can be used in the form of a container application, such as Visual Basic, and provides a visual interface to the current record state. Figure 12.1 shows a conceptual representation of controls bound to database record fields. In the figure, the OLE controls are represented by edit controls, and their bound properties are Text properties. These controls are linked to the database fields—Name and Address—of a record.

Fig. 12.1

Data binding
involves the
association of
control properties
with persistent
objects.

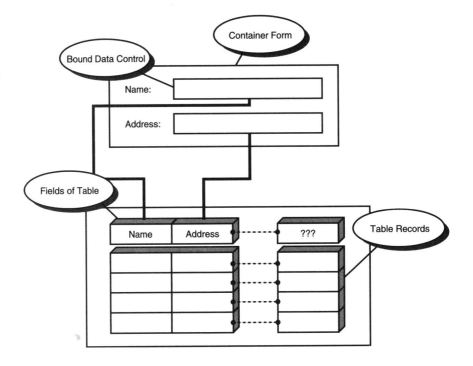

Whenever a bound property is changed, the control notifies the container by
calling the BoundPropertyChanged() function. This level of data binding is
called *optimistic data binding* because the control assumes that changes can be
made to the bound property. In *pessimistic data binding*, it is assumed that
changes cannot be made to a bound property. The control must first request
permission from the container by calling the BoundPropertyRequestEdit()
function. If the BoundPropertyRequestEdit() function returns True, the control may change the bound property as it would for optimistic data binding.
If the BoundPropertyRequestEdit() function returns False, the control must
not change the bound property.

Defining a Bindable Property

Data binding is automatically enabled by a call to EnableDataBinding(),
which is located in your control's constructor. Once compiled, an OLE control can incorporate data binding using the ClassWizard, where you can
choose which properties to make bindable.

The following steps outline the procedure for adding a text property to an
existing control. The control used in this outline subclasses an edit control;

and, you are going to bind a text property for that subclassed control to a field in a database. To add a bound property using ClassWizard, follow these steps:

1. Load a control project to what you want to add a data bound property.

2. Open ClassWizard.

3. Choose the OLE Automation tab.

4. Choose the Add Property button (see fig. 12.2).

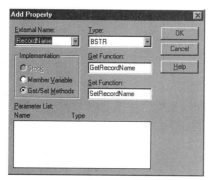

Fig. 12.2
The ClassWizard OLE automation Add Property dialog box allows you to add methods for use in managing Get and Set properties.

5. In the External Name box, type the external name of the property. For this example, use RecordName.

6. In the Implementation frame, select the Get/Set Methods radio button.

7. In the Return Type box, select the property's type. For this example, select BSTR.

8. Type unique function names for the Get and Set Functions, or accept the default names.

9. Choose the OK button to confirm your choices and close the Add Property dialog box (see fig. 12.3).

10. Choose the Data Binding button (see fig. 12.4).

11. Select the Bindable Property checkbox and any other data binding options you want.

12. Choose the OK button to confirm your choices and close the Data Binding dialog box.

13. Choose the OK button to confirm your choices and close ClassWizard.

Fig. 12.3

Once the new property is added, data binding options can be selected by pressing the Data Binding button control.

Fig. 12.4

The Data Binding dialog box allows you to select the functional characteristics of data binding with the custom control.

 Data binding is not supported for properties implemented as member variables of the control. Binding is only available for OLE automation properties.

In figure 12.4, you can see that the Data Binding dialog box contains several options for you to select for your control. The selections allow the container to determine what level of data binding the OLE control supports. The data binding notifications made available based on your selections in this dialog box are used to maintain connection between a control and a data source.

Options available for the Data Binding dialog box are as follows:

- **Bindable Property** specifies that this is a bindable property. The control will send an OnChanged notification after this property is changed.

- **Sends OnRequestEdit** specifies that the selected control sends an OnRequestEdit() notification before the property is changed.

■ **<u>V</u>isible to End User** specifies that the container should display this property to the end-user in a property binding dialog box.

■ **<u>D</u>efault Bindable Property** specifies that this property is the default bindable property choice for the control's container.

After completing this process, you will have a property called `RecordName` that can be bound to a string-valued field in a database. To provide a mechanism to bind your property to the database, the following code will be placed in your control's declaration file between the dispatch map comments:

```
afx_msg BSTR GetRecordName( );
afx_msg void SetRecordName( LPCTSTR lpszNewValue );
```

In addition to the previous changes, the following code will be added to your implementation file based on the previous procedure:

```
BSTR CSampleCtrl::GetRecordName()
{
    // TODO: Add your property handler here
    CString s;
    return s.AllocSysString();
}

void CSampleCtrl::SetRecordName(LPCTSTR lpszNewValue)
{
    SetModifiedFlag( );
}
```

To fully implement data binding for a control's property, you will have to modify the `GetRecordName()` and `SetRecordName()` functions. For example, in the `SetRecordName()` function, the code would first make a call to `BoundPropertyRequestEdit()` to request that a change be made to the database with the value of the bound property. If successful, the code would then save the property's new value and handle any other actions needed, before notifying the container that the property has changed. This notification would be done by making a call to the `BoundPropertyChanged()` function. The following code sample demonstrates these calls for data binding:

```
void CSampleCtrl::SetRecordName( LPCTSTR lpszNewValue )
{
    if( !BoundPropertyRequestEdit( dispidRecordName) )
        SetNotPermitted( );
    //TODO: Actually set property value.
    BoundPropertyChanged( dispidRecordName);
    SetModifiedFlag( );
}
```

The Cursor Library

A data bound control requests changes to a record field which the container accesses using an object known as a *cursor*. A cursor is so named because it indicates the current position in a result set, just as the cursor on a CRT screen indicates current position on the screen. Each time an application fetches new data from a data source, the database driver moves the cursor to the next row and returns that row.

 A *set* or *result set* are collections of records, rows, or items that meet a criteria specified in an SQL statement.

A control is unable to navigate by itself in the database because it does not manipulate the cursor directly; therefore, the OLE control has a limited capability with regard to database manipulation. The COleControl base class provides the functionality that allows the implementation of more advanced features of data binding in conjunction with ODBC.

ODBC

Open Database Connectivity (ODBC) allows applications to access data in database management systems (DBMS) using Structured Query Language (SQL). ODBC permits a single application access to different database management systems, thus allowing the development of an application without targeting a specific DBMS. Users can then easily add modules called database drivers that link the application to their choice of database management systems.

The ODBC architecture has five components, outlined as follows and depicted in figure 12.5:

- **Application** performs processing and calls ODBC functions in the ODBC API to submit SQL statements and retrieve results.

- **ODBC API** provides an interface between the functional level of the ODBC hierarchy and the application.

- **Driver Manager** loads drivers on behalf of an application.

- **Driver** processes ODBC function calls, submits SQL requests to a specific data source, and returns results to the application. If necessary, the driver modifies an application's request so that the request conforms to syntax supported by the associated DBMS.

■ **Data source** consists of the actual data the user wants to access, its associated database management system, and the network platform (if any) used to access the database management system.

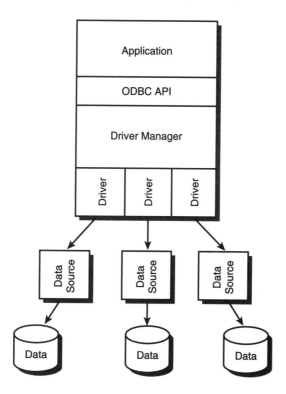

Fig. 12.5
The ODBC
Architecture
allows transparent
access to data
sources from
an application.

The following list outlines the primary steps required to allow an application to interact with a data source:

1. The application connects to the data source by specifying the data source name and any additional information needed to complete the connection.

2. The application places an SQL statement, as a text string, in a buffer and sets the parameter values required for the statement.

3. If the SQL statement returns a result set, the application or driver assigns a cursor to a member of the result set for the statement.

4. An application can submit an SQL statement for prepared or immediate execution.

5. If the SQL statement creates a result set, the application can inquire about the attributes of the result set, such as the number of columns and the name and type of a specific column. ODBC assigns storage for each column in the result set and fetches the results—thus creating *bound columns*.

6. If the SQL statement causes an error, the application retrieves error information from the driver and takes appropriate action.

7. The application ends each transaction by committing it or rolling it back.

 To *commit* an SQL statement means to execute the statement to its completion. To *roll back* an SQL statement means to *roll* the SQL statement *back* to its beginning.

8. The application terminates the connection when it has finished interacting with the data source.

The Driver Manager exists as a dynamic-link library (DLL) whose primary purpose is to load ODBC drivers for use with a specific data source. In addition, the Driver Manager does the following:

- Processes several ODBC initialization and information calls.

- Passes ODBC function calls from application to driver.

- Performs error and state checking.

- Logs function calls made by applications.

A driver is a DLL that implements ODBC function calls and interacts with a data source. The Driver Manager loads a driver when the application calls the `SQLBrowseConnect()`, `SQLConnect()`, or `SQLDriverConnect()` function.

A driver performs the following tasks in response to ODBC function calls from an application:

- Establishes a connection to a data source.

- Submits requests to the data source.

- Translates data to or from other formats if requested by the application.

- Returns results to the application.

- Formats errors into standard error codes and returns them to the application.

■ Declares and manipulates cursors if necessary.

The operation of declaring and manipulating cursors is invisible to the application unless there is a request for access to a cursor name.

■ Initiates transactions if the data source requires explicit transaction initiation.

A data source consists of the data a user wants to access, its associated DBMS, the platform on which the DBMS resides, and the network used to access that platform. Data sources require that a driver provide certain information—including the name of the data source, a user ID, and a password—in order to connect to it. ODBC extensions allow drivers to specify additional information, such as a network address or additional passwords as required. The data source is responsible for the following:

■ Processing SQL requests received from a driver.

■ Returning results to a driver.

■ Performing all other functions normally associated with a DBMS (concurrency control, transactions, and so on).

The ODBC cursor library is also a DLL, and it resides between the Driver Manager and a driver. When an application calls a function, the Driver Manager calls the function in the cursor library, which either executes the function or calls it in the specified data source's driver.

The ODBC cursor library passes all SQL statements directly to the driver except the following, which are passed to the cursor library:

■ Positioned update and delete statements.

■ SELECT FOR UPDATE statements.

■ Batched SQL statements.

Cache

The cursor library caches data in memory and in temporary files (see fig. 12.6 and 12.7). This limits the size of result sets that the cursor library can handle only by available disk space. If the cursor library terminates abnormally, such as when the power fails, it may leave Windows' temporary files named ~CTTnnnn.TMP in the TEMP directory on the disk. The files will be numbered sequentially with the file numbers replacing the *nnnn* in the filename.

Fig. 12.6
The cursor library operates at a level immediately above the drivers and below the Driver Manager in the ODBC hierarchy.

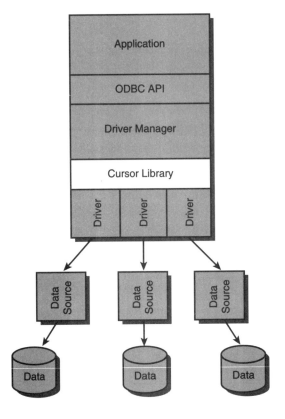

Using the Cursor Library

To use the ODBC cursor library, an application must perform the following steps in order to connect to and access ODBC:

1. The application calls SQLSetConnectOption() to specify how the cursor library should be used with a particular connection—always used, used only if driver does not support scrollable cursors, or never used.

2. It calls SQLConnect(), SQLDriverConnect(), or SQLBrowseConnect() to connect to the data source.

3. It then calls SQLSetStmtOptions() to specify the cursor type, concurrency, and rowset size. The cursor library supports forward-only and static cursors. Forward-only cursors must be read-only, while static cursors may be read-only or use optimistic concurrency control comparing values.

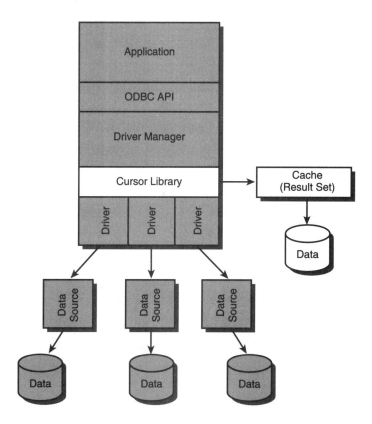

Fig. 12.7
The result set, produced by the cursor library, resides in a memory and is swapped to a disk file located in the TEMP directory.

NOTE

Cursor *concurrency* is the ability for more than one user to access the same data in a database at the same time.

A *rowset* or *keyset* are collections of rows or database keys that meet a specific criteria specified in an SQL statement.

4. Then, the application allocates one or more rowset buffers, and calls SQLBindCol() one or more times to bind these buffers to result set columns.

5. It generates a result set by executing a SELECT statement or a procedure, or by calling a function. If the application executes positioned update statements, it should execute a SELECT FOR UPDATE statement to generate the result set.

6. Finally, the application calls SQLExtendedFetch() one or more times to scroll through the result set.

NOTE   *Positioned update* or *delete* performs operations on the current position of the cursor within a result set.

> **Caution**
>
> If the application does not correctly update the rowset buffers before executing a positioned update statement, the data in the cache will be incorrect after the statement is executed.

> **Caution**
>
> The WHERE clause, constructed by the cursor library to identify the current row, can fail to identify any rows, can identify a different row than desired, or can identify more than one row.

All positioned update and delete statements require a cursor name. To specify the cursor name, an application calls SQLSetCursorName() before the cursor is opened. To use the cursor name generated by the driver, an application calls SQLGetCursorName() after the cursor is opened. After the cursor library executes a positioned update or delete statement, the status array, rowset buffers, and cache maintained by the cursor library contain the values shown in table 12.1.

Table 12.1 Cache Values Stored in Buffers			
Statement	**Row Status**	**Rowset buffers**	**Cache buffers**
Update	SQL_ROW_UPDATED	New values	New values
Delete	SQL_ROW_DELETED	Old values	Old values

The application must update the values in the rowset buffers before executing the positioned update statement. After executing the positioned update statement, the cursor library copies the values in the rowset buffers to its cache.

Sample Application

The following example uses the cursor library to retrieve each employee's name, age, and birthday from the EMPLOYEE table. It then displays 20 rows of data. If the user updates this data, the code updates the rowset buffers and executes a positioned update statement. Finally, it prompts the user for the direction to scroll and repeats the process.

You first want to allocate variables for use in managing the databases, cursor, and data for the application. The variables henv, hdbc, hstmt1, and hstmt2 are all handles to specific objects for the application. The remaining variables are used to maintain position within the database, flags, and data. Notice that the variables for name, birthday, and age are all declared for 20 rows. This information is where you store information entered by the user:

```
#define ROWS 20
#define NAME_LEN 30
#define BDAY_LEN 11
#define DONE -1

HENV     henv;                    /*Environment handle*/
HDBC     hdbc;                    /*Database connection handle*/
HSTMT    hstmt1, hstmt2;          /*SQL statement handle*/
RETCODE  retcode;
UCHAR    szName[ROWS][NAME_LEN], szBirthday[ROWS][BDAY_LEN];
UCHAR    szNewName[NAME_LEN], szNewBday[BDAY_LEN];
SWORD    sAge[ROWS], sNewAge[ROS];
SDWORD   cbName[ROWS], cbAge[ROWS], cbBirthday[ROWS];
UDWORD   fFetchType, crow, irow, irowUpdt;
UWORD    rgfRowStatus[ROWS];
```

Next, you need to allocate handles for the environment and database connection. These handles are used to connect to the database in which you will be managing your data. You then connect to the ODBC cursors library with a call to SQLSetConnectOption() using the SQL_ODBC_CURSORS parameter. Finally, you connect to the database using a call to SQLConnect():

```
SQLAllocEnv(&henv);
SQLAllocConnect(henv, &hdbc);

/* Specify that the ODBC Cursor Library is always used, */
/* then connect. */
SQLSetConnectOption(hdbc, SQL_ODBC_CURSORS, SQL_CUR_USE_ODBC);
SQLConnect(hdbc, "EmpData", SQL_NTS, "JohnS", SQL_NTS,
           "Sesame", SQL_NTS);
```

If you were successful in connecting to the database, you then allocate handles for your SQL statements that will be submitted to the cursor library:

```
if (retcode == SQL_SUCCESS || retcode == SQL_SUCCESS_WITH_INFO)
{

    /* Allocate a statement handle for the result set and a   */
    /* statement handle for positioned update statements.  */
    SQLAllocStmt(hdbc, &hstmt1);
    SQLAllocStmt(hdbc, &hstmt2);
```

The allocated handles are used to build statements to establish options for the cursor library. In this application, you will have a static cursor with concurrency and a cursor named EMPCURSOR: (Cursor types and concurrency are discussed in more detail in the next section.)

```
/* Updateable static cursor with 20 rows of data. Set cursor */
/* name, execute the SELECT statement, and bind the rowset  */
/* buffers to result set columns. */
SQLSetStmtOption(hstmt1, SQL_CONCURRENCY, SQL_CONCUR_VALUES);
SQLSetStmtOption(hstmt1, SQL_CURSOR_TYPE, SQL_SCROLL_STATIC);
SQLSetStmtOption(hstmt1, SQL_ROWSET_SIZE, ROWS);
SQLSetCursorName(hstmt1, "EMPCURSOR", SQL_NTS);
```

To build a result set, submit an SQL statement for execution. In this statement, you are merely collecting all of the columns in the table. The result set is then bound to the rowset buffers. In essence, you are using the arrays that you declared earlier in the program and associating the arrays with the buffers, thus binding the columns of the database to variables within your application:

```
/* Immediate execution of the SQL statement in hstmt1  */
SQLExecDirect(hstmt1,
             "SELECT NAME, AGE, BIRTHDAY FROM EMPLOYEE\
              FOR UPDATE OF NAME, AGE, BIRTHDAY",
             SQL_NTS);
SQLBindCol(hstmt1, 1, SQL_C_CHAR, szName, NAME_LEN, cbName);
SQLBindCol(hstmt1, 2, SQL_C_SSHORT, sAge, 0, cbAge);
SQLBindCol(hstmt1, 3, SQL_C_CHAR, szBirthday, BDAY_LEN,
           cbBirthday);
```

The remainder of the application, in listing 12.1, loops through the data to load and display the information to the user. The user is then prompted for input so that information may be stored into the rowset and eventually stored into the database.

Listing 12.1   A Program Selecting a Printer

```
/* Fetch the first block of data and display it, then prompt */
/* user for new data. If new values are supplied, update the */
/* rowset buffers, Bind them to the parameters in the update  */
/* statement, and execute a positioned update on another      */
/* hstmt. Prompt for scrolling. Fetch and redisplay data as   */
/* needed.                                                     */
fFetchType = SQL_FETCH_FIRST;
irow = 0;
do {
    SQLExtendedFetch(hstmt1, fFetchType, irow, &crow,
        rgfRowStatus);
    DisplayRows(szName, sAge, szBirthday, rgfStatus);
```

```
            if (PromptUpdate(&irowUpdt,szNewName,&sNewAge,
               szNewBday)==TRUE)
   {

            strcpy(szName[irowUpdt], szNewName);
            cbName[irowUpdt] = SQL_NTS;
            sAge[irowUpdt] = sNewAge;
            cbAge[irowUpdt] = 0;
            strcpy(szBirthday[irowUpdt], szNewBday);
            cbBirthday[irowUpdt] = SQL_NTS;
            SQLBindParameter(hstmt2, 1, SQL_PARAM_INPUT,
                  SQL_C_CHAR, SQL_CHAR, NAME_LEN, 0,
                  szName[irowUpdt], NAME_LEN, &cbName[irowUpdt]);
            SQLBindParameter(hstmt2, 2, SQL_PARAM_INPUT,
                  SQL_C_SSHORT, SQL_SMALLINT, 0, 0,
                  &sAge[irowUpdt], 0, &cbAge[irowUpdt]);
            SQLBindParameter(hstmt2, 3, SQL_PARAM_INPUT,
                  SQL_C_CHAR, SQL_DATE, 0, 0,
                  szBirthday[irowUpdt], BDAY_LEN,
                  &cbBirthday[irowUpdt]);
```

The application performs a positioned update of the data entered by the user. The `hstmt2` handle is used as a handle for the SQL statement passed for immediate execution.

```
            SQLExecDirect(hstmt2,
                          "UPDATE EMPLOYEE\
                          SET (NAME = ?, AGE = ?, BIRTHDAY =
   ?)\
                          WHERE CURRENT OF EMPCURSOR",
                          SQL_NTS);
        }

      while (PromptScroll(&fFetchType, &irow) != DONE)
   }
```

For each row of data in the result set, the cursor library caches the data for each bound column, the length of the data in each bound column, and the status of the row. The cursor library uses the values in the cache both to return through `SQLExtendedFetch()` and to construct searched statements for positioned operations.

> A bound column is one which has had storage allocated for it through a call to the `SQLBindCol()` function, while an unbound column is one which has no available allocated storage.

Specifying the Cursor Type

Depending on the application, there may be a need to dynamically update a result set by determining, or sensing, changes that occur to the tables or databases underlying the result set. For example, when managing accounting information, an accountant needs data that appears static. It is impossible to balance books when the data is continually changing. When selling concert tickets, a clerk needs real-time, or up-to-the-minute, data on ticket availability. Various cursor models are designed to meet these needs, each of which requires different sensitivities to changes in the tables underlying the result set.

To specify the cursor type, an application calls `SQLSetStmtOption()` with the `SQL_CURSOR_TYPE` option. The application can specify a cursor that only scrolls forward, a static cursor, a dynamic cursor, a keyset-driven cursor, or a mixed cursor. If the application specifies a mixed cursor, it also specifies the size of the keyset used by the cursor.

 NOTE

To use the ODBC cursor library, an application calls `SQLSetConnectOption()` with the `SQL_ODBC_CURSORS` option before it connects to the data source. The cursor library supports block scrollable cursors, and positioned update and delete statements.

Block Cursors

A block cursor is a pointer to a block of data established when the application calls `SQLSetStmtOption()` with the `SQL_ROWSET_SIZE` option to specify the rowset size. Each time the application calls `SQLExtendedFetch()`, the driver returns the next rowset size rows of data. After the data is returned, the cursor points to the first row in the rowset. By default, the rowset size is equal to one.

Static Cursors

Static cursors cause the data in the underlying tables to appear to be static or unchanging. The membership, order, and values in the result set used by a static cursor are generally fixed when the cursor is opened. Rows updated, deleted, or inserted are not detected by the cursor until the cursor is closed and then reopened. Static cursors are commonly implemented by notifying the cursor library to take a snapshot of the data or locking the result set. In the first case, the cursor diverges from the underlying tables as other users make changes. In the latter case, other users are prohibited from changing the data.

Dynamic Cursors

Dynamic cursors allow the data to appear to be dynamic. The membership, order, and values in the result set used by a dynamic cursor are constantly changing. Rows updated, deleted, or inserted are detected by the cursor when data is next retrieved or fetched. Even though these cursors are ideal for real-time situations to provide up-to-the-minute information, they are extremely difficult to implement.

Keyset-Driven Cursors

Keyset-driven cursors have attributes of both static and dynamic cursor types. Like static cursors, the membership and ordering of the result set of a keyset-driven cursor are generally fixed when the cursor is opened. Like dynamic cursors, most changes to the values in the underlying result set are visible to the cursor when data is next fetched.

When a keyset-driven cursor is opened, the driver saves the keys for the entire result set, thus fixing the membership and order of the result set. As the cursor scrolls through the result set, the driver uses the keys in this keyset to retrieve the current data values for each row in the rowset. Since data values are retrieved only when the cursor scrolls to a given row, updates to that row by other users after the cursor was opened are visible to the cursor.

If the cursor scrolls to a row of data that has been deleted, the row appears empty in the result set, since the key is still in the keyset but the row is no longer in the result set. Note that updating the key values in a row is considered to be deleting an existing row and inserting a new row. Rows of data for which the key values have been changed also appear as holes when cursors access these keys. To remedy this situation, drivers that encounter a hole in the result set return a status code of SQL_ROW_DELETED for the row on which the cursor currently resides. Likewise, rows of data inserted into the result set by users after the cursor was opened are not visible to the cursor, since the keys for those rows are not in the keyset.

Mixed (Keyset/Dynamic) Cursors

If a result set is large, it may be impractical for the driver to save the keys for the entire result set. In such a situation, the application can use a mixed cursor, which has a keyset that is smaller than the result set but larger than the rowset.

In the keyset, a mixed cursor is keyset-driven, meaning the driver uses keys to retrieve the current data values for each row in the rowset. When a mixed cursor scrolls beyond the boundaries of the keyset, it becomes dynamic, simply retrieving the next rowset size rows of data. The driver then constructs a new keyset, which contains the new rowset.

Assume a result set has 10,000 rows, and uses a mixed cursor with a keyset size of 1,000 and a rowset size of 100. When the cursor is opened, the driver saves keys for the first 1,000 rows and retrieves data for the first 100 rows. If another user deletes row 11 and the cursor then scrolls to row 11, the cursor will detect a hole in the result set, since the key for row 11 is in the keyset but the data is no longer in the result set. This is the same behavior as a keyset-driven cursor.

If, however, another user should delete row 1,001 and the cursor scrolls to row 1,001, the cursor will not detect a hole, since the key for the row 1,001 is not currently in the keyset. Instead, the cursor will retrieve the data for the row that was originally row 1,002. This is the same behavior as that of a dynamic cursor.

Specifying Cursor Concurrency

Cursor concurrency is the ability for more than one user to access the same data in a database at the same time. Serialized transactions on data appear as singular operations, such that no other transactions operate on the same data at the same time. For example, assume one transaction doubles data values and another adds 1 to data values. If the transactions are serialized and both attempt to operate on the values 0 and 10 at the same time, the final values will be 1 and 21 or 2 and 22, depending on which transaction is performed first. If the transactions are not serialized, the final values will be 1 and 21, 2 and 22, 1 and 22, or 2 and 21. The sets of values 1 and 22, and 2 and 21, are the result of the transactions acting on each value in a different order.

Transaction serializability is necessary in order to maintain database integrity. For cursors, it is most easily implemented at the expense of concurrency by locking the result set. A compromise between serializability and concurrency is *optimistic concurrency control*. In a cursor using optimistic concurrency control, the driver does not lock rows when it retrieves them. Instead, when the application requests an update or delete operation, the driver or data source checks if the row has changed. If the row has not changed, the driver or data source prevents other transactions from changing the row until the operation is complete. If the row has changed, the transaction containing the update or delete operation fails.

To specify the concurrency used by a cursor, an application calls SQLSetStmtOption() with the SQL_CONCURRENCY option. The application can specify that the cursor is read-only, locks the result set, or uses optimistic concurrency control. The application calls SQLSetPos() to lock the row currently pointed to by the cursor regardless of the specified cursor concurrency.

Some data sources close the cursors when a transaction is committed or rolled back. Transactions may be committed or rolled back with SQLTransact() or automatically committed with the SQL_AUTOCOMMIT connection option. A driver reports this behavior with the SQL_CURSOR_COMMIT_BEHAVIOR and SQL_CURSOR_ROLLBACK_BEHAVIOR information types in SQLGetInfo() function.

Column Data

The cursor library creates a buffer in the cache for each buffer bound to the result set with SQLBindCol(). It uses the values in these buffers to perform positioned update or delete statements. It updates these buffers from the rowset buffers when it fetches data from the data source and when it executes positioned update statements.

Row Status

The cursor library creates a buffer in the cache for the row status. The cursor library retrieves values for the rgfRowStatus array in SQLExtendedFetch() from this buffer. For each row, the cursor library sets this buffer to the following:

- SQL_ROW_DELETED, when it executes a positioned delete statement on the row.

- SQL_ROW_ERROR, when it encounters an error retrieving the row from the data source with SQLFetch().

- SQL_ROW_SUCCESS, when it successfully fetches the row from the data source with SQLFetch().

- SQL_ROW_UPDATED, when it executes a positioned update statement on the row.

Positioned Update and Delete Statements

The cursor library supports positioned update and delete statements by enumerating the values stored in its cache for each bound column. The cursor library passes the newly constructed SQL UPDATE and DELETE statements to the driver for execution. For positioned update statements, it then updates its cache from the values in the rowset buffers and sets the corresponding value in the rgfRowStatus array in SQLExtendedFetch() to SQL_ROW_UPDATED. For positioned delete statements, the cursor library sets the corresponding value in the rgfRowStatus array to SQL_ROW_DELETED.

Positioned update and delete statements are subject to the following restrictions:

- Positioned update and delete statements can only be used when a SE-LECT statement generated the result set; the SELECT statement did not contain a join, a UNION clause, or a GROUP BY clause; and any columns that used an alias or expression in the select list were not bound with SQLBindCol().

- If an application prepares a positioned update or delete statement, it must do so after it has called SQLExtendedFetch(). Although the cursor library submits the statement to the driver for preparation, it closes the statement and executes it directly when the application calls SQLExecute().

- If the driver only supports one active SQL statement handle, the cursor library fetches the rest of the result set and then refetches the current rowset from its cache before it executes a positioned update or delete statement.

SELECT FOR UPDATE Statements

Applications should generate result sets that will be updated with a positioned update statement. This is done by executing a SELECT FOR UPDATE statement. Although the cursor library does not require this, it is required by most data sources that support positioned update statements.

The cursor library ignores the columns in the FOR UPDATE clause of a SELECT FOR UPDATE statement and it removes this clause before passing the statement to the driver. In the cursor library, the SQL_CONCURRENCY statement option, along with the restrictions mentioned in the previous section, controls whether the columns in a result set can be updated.

Batched SQL Statements

The cursor library does not support batched SQL statements, including SQL statements for which SQLParamOptions() has been called with crow greater than 1. If an application submits a batched SQL statement to the cursor library, the results of the operation are not defined.

Constructing Searched Statements

To support positioned update and delete statements, the cursor library constructs a searched UPDATE or DELETE statement from the positioned statement. To support calls to SQLGetData() in a block of data, the cursor library constructs a SELECT statement to create a result set containing the current row of data. In each of these statements, the WHERE clause enumerates the values stored in the cache for each bound column that returns SQL_SEARCHABLE or

SQL_ALL_EXCEPT_LIKE for the SQL_COLUMN_SEARCHABLE descriptor type in
SQLColAttributes().

If a positioned update or delete statement affects more than one row, the
cursor library updates the rgfRowStatus array only for the row on which the
cursor is positioned. Once the update is completed, the cursor library returns
SQL_SUCCESS_WITH_INFO and SQLSTATE 01S04, meaning that more than one row
has been updated or deleted. If the statement does not identify any rows, the
cursor library does not update the rgfRowStatusArray. The return from the
cursor library in this situation is SQL_SUCCESS_WITH_INFO and SQLSTATE 01S03,
meaning that no rows have been updated or deleted. An application can call
SQLRowCount() to determine the number of rows that were updated or deleted.

If the SELECT clause used to position the cursor for a call to SQLGetData() identifies more than one row, SQLGetData() is not guaranteed to return the correct
data. If it does not identify any rows, SQLGetData() returns SQL_NO_DATA_FOUND.

If an application conforms to a specific set of guidelines, the WHERE clause
constructed by the cursor library should uniquely identify the current row,
except when this is impossible, such as when the data source contains dupli-
cate rows.

The guidelines required to be met so that the cursor library uniquely identifies the current row are as follows:

- Bind columns that uniquely identify the row. If the bound columns do
  not uniquely identify the row, the WHERE clause constructed by the cursor library might identify more than one row. In a positioned update or
  delete statement, such a clause might cause more than one row to be
  updated or deleted. In a call to SQLGetData(), such a clause might cause
  the driver to return data for the wrong row. Binding all the columns in
  a unique key guarantees that each row is uniquely identified.

- Allocate data buffers large enough that no truncation occurs. The cursor
  library's cache is a copy of the values in the rgbValue buffers bound to
  the result set with SQLBindCol(). If data is truncated when it is placed in
  these buffers, it will also be truncated in the cache. A WHERE clause constructed from truncated values might not correctly identify the underlying row in the data source.

- Specify non-null, or non-zero, length buffers for binary data. The
  cursor library allocates length buffers in its cache only if the pcbValue
  argument in SQLBindCol() is non-null. When the fCType argument is
  SQL_C_BINARY, the cursor library requires the length of the binary data to

construct a WHERE clause from the data. If there is no length buffer for an SQL_C_BINARY column and the application calls SQLGetData() or executes a positioned update or delete statement, the cursor library returns SQL_ERROR and SQLSTATE SL014. This error means that a positioned request was issued and not all columns were buffered.

■ Specify non-null length buffers for nullable columns. The cursor library allocates length buffers in its cache only if the pcbValue argument in SQLBindCol() is non-null. Since SQL_NULL_DATA is stored in the length buffer, the cursor library assumes that any column for which no length buffer is specified is non-nullable. If no length column is specified for a nullable column, the cursor library constructs a WHERE clause that uses the data value for the column.

SQLBindCol

An application allocates one or more buffers in which the cursor library returns the current rowset and it calls SQLBindCol() one or more times to bind these buffers to the result set.

On Windows 3.1, buffers bound with SQLBindCol() cannot cross segment boundaries, and the cursor library restricts their size. These restrictions do not exist on Windows NT.

When column-wise binding is used, the size of each buffer cannot exceed 65,500 bytes; the size of each pcbValue buffer cannot exceed 65,500 bytes; and the total size of the data and length-of-data fields for a single row of data cannot exceed 65,500 bytes.

When row-wise binding is used, the size of the entire rowset buffer, including data and length-of-data fields for each row of each bound column, cannot exceed 65,500 bytes.

If the application calls SQLBindCol() to rebind result set columns after it has called SQLExtendedFetch(), the cursor library returns an error. Before it can rebind result set columns, the application must close the cursor.

SQLExtendedFetch

The cursor library implements SQLExtendedFetch() by repeatedly calling SQLFetch(). An application must call SQLExtendedFetch() before it prepares or executes any positioned update or delete statements. It transfers the data it retrieves from the driver to the rowset buffers provided by the application.

It also caches the data in memory and disk files. When an application requests a new rowset, the cursor library retrieves it as necessary from the driver or the cache. Finally, the cursor library maintains the status of the cached data and returns this information to the application in the buffer.

Rowset Buffers

The cursor library optimizes the transfer of data from the driver to the rowset buffer provided by the application, if the following are true:

- The application uses row-wise binding.

- There are no unused bytes between fields in the structure that the application declares to hold a row of data.

- The fields in which SQLExtendedFetch() returns the number of available bytes for a column follows the buffer for that column and precedes the buffer for the next column.

When the application requests a new rowset, the cursor library retrieves data from its cache and from the driver as necessary. If the new and old rowsets overlap, the cursor library may optimize its performance by reusing the data from the overlapping sections of the rowset buffers. Unsaved changes to the rowset buffers are lost unless the new and old rowsets overlap and the changes are in the overlapping sections of the rowset buffers. To save the changes, an application submits a positioned update statement.

The cursor library always refreshes the rowset buffers with data from the cache when an application calls SQLExtendedFetch() with the fFetchType argument set to SQL_FETCH_RELATIVE and the current row, irow, argument set to 0.

Result Set Membership

The cursor library retrieves data from the driver only as the application requests it. Depending on the data source and the setting of the SQL_CONCURRENCY statement option, this has the following consequences:

- The data retrieved by the cursor library may differ from the data that was available at the time the statement was executed. For example, after the cursor was opened, rows inserted at a point outside of the cursor position can be retrieved by some drivers.

- The data in the result set may be locked by the data source for the cursor library and unavailable to other users.

Once the cursor library has cached a row of data, it cannot detect changes to that row in the underlying data source. This occurs because calls to SQLExtendedFetch() never allow the cursor library to refetch data from the data source. Instead, it refetches data from its cache.

Scrolling

The cursor library supports certain fetch types in SQLExtendedFetch(). Forward-only cursor types support the SQL_FETCH_NEXT type. Static cursor types support the fetch types listed in table 12.2.

Table 12.2 Scrolling Options	
Fetch Type	**Description**
SQL_FETCH_NEXT	Fetch the next row
SQL_FETCH_PRIOR	Fetch the previous row
SQL_FETCH_FIRST	Fetch the first row
SQL_FETCH_LAST	Fetch the last row
SQL_FETCH_RELATIVE	Fetch the row number relative to the current
SQL_FETCH_ABSOLUTE	Fetch the row number relative to the beginning

Errors

If the driver returns SQL_SUCCESS_WITH_INFO to the cursor library from SQLFetch(), the cursor library ignores the warning. For SQLExtendedFetch(), it retrieves the rest of the rowset from the driver and returns SQL_SUCCESS_WITH_INFO. The application cannot call SQLError() to retrieve the warning information unless the warning occurred the last time the cursor library called SQLFetch().

Other Cursor Functions

The cursor library also supports numerous other functions for allowing a property to interface to a data source. Each of the following functions are accessible through ODBC as are the functions previously outlined in this chapter.

SQLGetData

The cursor library implements SQLGetData() by first constructing a SELECT statement with a WHERE clause that enumerates the values stored in its cache for each bound column in the current row. It then executes the SELECT statement to reselect the row and calls SQLGetData() in the driver to retrieve the data from the data source—as opposed to the cache.

Calls to SQLGetData() are subject to the following restrictions:

- SQLGetData() cannot be called for forward-only cursors.

- SQLGetData() can only be called when a SELECT statement generated the result set; the SELECT statement did not contain a join, a UNION clause, or a GROUP BY clause; and any columns that used an alias or expression in the select list were not bound with SQLBindCol().

- If the driver only supports one active hstmt, the cursor library fetches the rest of the result set before executing the SELECT statement and calling SQLGetData().

SQLGetInfo

The cursor library returns values for the values of fInfoType (¦ represents a bitwise OR) that are listed in table 12.3. For all other values of fInfoType, it calls SQLGetInfo() in the driver.

Table 12.3 *fInfoType* **Options**

fInfoType	Returned Value
SQL_BOOKMARK_PERSISTENCE	0
SQL_FETCH_DIRECTION	SQL_FD_FETCH_ABSOLUTE ¦SQL_FD_FETCH_FIRST ¦SQL_FD_FETCH_LAST ¦SQL_FD_FETCH_NEXT ¦SQL_FD_FETCH_PRIOR ¦SQL_FD_FETCH_RELATIVE
SQL_GETDATA_EXTENSIONS	SQL_GD_BLOCK ¦any values returned by the driver
SQL_LOCK_TYPES	SQL_LCK_NO_CHANGE
SQL_POS_OPERATIONS	SQL_POS_POSITION
SQL_POSITIONED_STATEMENTS	SQL_PS_POSITIONED_DELETE ¦SQL_PS_POSITIONED_UPDATE ¦SQL_PS_SELECT_FOR_UPDATE
SQL_ROW_UPDATES	Y

(continued)

Table 12.3 Continued	
fInfoType	**Returned Value**
SQL_SCROLL_CONCURRENCY	SQL_SCCO_READ_ONLY ¦SQL_SCCO_OPT_VALUES
SQL_SCROLL_OPTIONS	SQL_SO_FORWARD_ONLY ¦SQL_SO_STATIC
SQL_STATIC_SENSITIVITY	SQL_SS_UPDATES

NOTE

The cursor library implements the same cursor behavior when transactions are committed or rolled back as the data source. That is, committing or rolling back a transaction—either by calling SQLTransact or by using the SQL_AUTOCOMMIT connection option—can cause the data source to delete the access plans and close the cursors for all hstmts on an hdbc. For more information, see the SQL_CURSOR_COMMIT_BEHAVIOR and SQL_CURSOR_ROLLBACK_BEHAVIOR information types in SQLGetInfo.

SQLSetStmtOption

The cursor library supports the SQL_BIND_TYPE, SQL_CONCURRENCY, SQL_CURSOR_TYPE, SQL_ROWSET_SIZE, and SQL_SIMULATE_CURSOR statements options with SQLSetStmtOption(). The cursor library supports only the SQL_CURSOR_FORWARD_ONLY and SQL_CURSOR_STATIC values of the SQL_CURSOR_TYPE statement option.

For forward-only cursors, the cursor library supports the SQL_CONCUR_READ_ONLY value of the SQL_CONCURRENCY statement option. For static cursors, the cursor library supports the SQL_CONCUR_READ_ONLY and SQL_CONCUR_VALUES values of the SQL_CONCURRENCY statement option.

Although the ODBC 2.0 specification supports calls to SQLSetStmtOption() with the SQL_BIND_TYPE or SQL_ROWSET_SIZE options after SQLExtendedFetch() has been called, the cursor library does not. Before it can change the binding type or rowset size in the cursor library, the application must close the cursor.

SQLGetStmtOption

The SQLSetStmtOption() allows you to set the characteristics of a cursor, while SQLGetStmtOption() allows you to retrieve the characteristics. The cursor library supports the SQL_BIND_TYPE, SQL_CONCURRENCY, SQL_CURSOR_TYPE, SQL_ROW_NUMBER, SQL_ROWSET_SIZE, and SQL_SIMULATE_CURSOR statement options with SQLGetStmtOption().

SQLNativeSql

If the driver supports this function, the cursor library calls `SQLNativeSql()` in the driver and passes the SQL statement. For positioned update, positioned delete, and `SELECT FOR UPDATE` statements, the cursor library modifies the statement before passing it to the driver.

SQLRowCount

When an application calls `SQLRowCount()` with a handle associated with the cursor, the cursor library returns the number of rows of data it has retrieved from the driver. If called with a positioned update or delete statement, the cursor library returns the number of rows affected by the statement.

SQLSetConnectOption

An application calls `SQLSetConnectOption()` with the `SQL_ODBC_CURSORS` option to specify whether the cursor library is always used, used if the driver does not support scrollable cursors, or never used. The cursor library assumes that a driver supports scrollable cursors if it returns `SQL_FD_FETCH_PRIOR` for the `SQL_FETCH_DIRECTION` option in `SQLGetInfo`.

The application must call `SQLSetConnectOption()` to specify the cursor library usage after it calls `SQLAllocConnect()` and before it connects to the data source. If an application calls `SQLSetConnectOption()` with the `SQL_ODBC_CURSORS` option while the connection is still active, the cursor library returns an error.

To set a statement option supported by the cursor library for all SQL statement handles associated with a database connection handle, an application must call `SQLSetConnectOption()` for that statement option after it connects to the data source and before it opens the cursor. If an application calls `SQLSetConnectOption()` with a statement option and a cursor is open on an SQL statement handle associated with the database connection handle, the statement option will not be applied to that SQL statement handle until the cursor is closed and reopened.

SQLSetPos

The cursor library only supports the `SQL_POSITION` operation for the `fOption` argument in `SQLSetPos()`. It only supports the `SQL_LOCK_NO_CHANGE` value for the `fLock` argument.

SQLSetScrollOptions

The cursor library supports `SQLSetScrollOptions()` only for backwards compatibility. Applications should use the `SQL_CONCURRENCY`, `SQL_CURSOR_TYPE`, and `SQL_ROWSET_SIZE` statement options instead.

SQLTransact

The cursor library does not support transactions, and passes calls to `SQLTransact()` directly to the driver. The cursor library does support the cursor commit and rollback behaviors as returned by the data source with the `SQL_CURSOR_ROLLBACK_BEHAVIOR` and `SQL_CURSOR_COMMIT_BEHAVIOR` information types.

- For data sources that preserve cursors across transactions, changes that are rolled back in the data source are not rolled back in the cursor library's cache. To make the cache match the data in the data source, the application must close and reopen the cursor.

- For data sources that close cursors at transaction boundaries, the cursor library closes the cursors and deletes the caches for all `hstmts` on the `hdbc`.

- For data sources that delete prepared statements at transaction boundaries, the application must re-prepare all prepared `hstmts` on the `hdbc` before re-executing them.

Testing the Control

The Test Container's Notification Log dialog box helps you test bound properties which use either optimistic or pessimistic data binding. Whenever the `BoundPropertyChanged()` function is called, a notification is logged in the dialog box. You are also allowed to choose the response to each call to the `BoundPropertyRequestEdit()` function. A different container might update a field in a database record whenever the `BoundPropertyChanged()` function was called. It might also return `False` from a call to the `BoundPropertyRequestEdit()` function if the field or record was in use.

To test data binding with the Test Container, follow these steps:

1. From the Tools menu, choose Test Container.

2. From the View menu, choose Notification Log to access the Notification Log dialog box. The option buttons at the bottom of the Notification Log dialog box can be used to test control properties which use pessimistic data binding.

3. From the Edit menu, choose Insert OLE Control to access the Insert OLE Control dialog box.

4. From the Control Class list box, select the control to test.

5. Choose the OK button to close the Insert OLE Object dialog box and insert a control into Test Container. Notice that there is no notification in the Notification Log dialog box when a control is first created.

6. From the Edit Menu, choose Control Object and then Properties. The Properties dialog box for the control appears.

7. Enter a new value for a bound property of the control and choose the Apply button. Information about the change to the bound property is displayed in the Notification Log dialog box. The line in the Notification Log dialog box looks like the following:

    00_XXXX_Control: property 'YYYY' changed

    This kind of information is displayed in the Notification Log dialog box every time the `BoundPropertyChanged()` function is called for a bound property. The line shows the control number, control type, and property name, and states that the property changed. In the previous Notification Log entry, XXXX is the name of the control that is in the Test Container and YYYY is the name of the bound property that was changed.

8. Change the bound property a few more times, watch the Notification Log dialog box, and exit Test Container when the control test is complete.

Using the `BoundPropertyChanged()` function to notify the container of changes to bound properties provides the simplest level of data binding.

From Here...

In this chapter, you learned about data binding for custom controls and how properties of controls can be tied to data via ODBC. You also learned about the ODBC Cursor Library and some of the functionality of the library for tying your custom controls to databases. For further information see the following chapters:

- Chapter 3, "OLE Controls," provides information on control properties and events.

- Chapter 7, "Control Containers," helps you learn more about control containers and how they affect data binding.

Index

CD-ROM Contents Page

The CD-ROM in the back of this book contains all of the source code used throughout this book. In addition, there are several OCX custom controls, so that you can get up to speed with them. Also included are two VBX custom controls so that you can try converting them to OCXs as you read Chapter 8, "Converting VBXs to OLE Custom Controls."

All of the files on the CD-ROM are uncompressed, so that you can easily copy them to a file on your hard drive for quick and easy use.

Here is an overview of the information contained on the CD-ROM:

The Source Code

/CODE

This directory contains subdirectories for each chapter. These subdirectories contain the uncompressed programming source code for each chapter.

The OCX Custom Controls

> The code included on this CD-ROM for the OCXs will compile correctly under Windows NT, but will not compile under Windows 95 without some slight changes. The modified code for Windows 95 is available from the Macmillan Computer Publishing CompuServe forum (GO QUEBOOKS) and the Macmillan Computer Publishing Information SuperLibrary Internet Site (http://www.mcp.com).

/GETHOST/

The **GETHOST** control is actually two controls in one. The first control, *GETNAME*, allows you to resolve the name of a network host from an address you provide. Conversely, the second control, *GETADRS*, allows you to retrieve the address of a network host from a given name. The purpose of these controls is to provide a means of address and name resolution for Internet connectivity in 32-bit container/controlling applications.

/MAIL/

Like **GETHOST**, the **MAIL** custom control module actually contains two independent controls for managing e-mail over the Internet. The *SMTP (Simple Mail Transfer Protocol) Control* sends e-mail to a destination address that you provide. The *POP (Post Office Protocol v3) Control* allows you to log on to your e-mail server and retrieve e-mail sent to you by other Net'ers.

/FINGER/

FINGER allows you to retrieve information about a user from a selected host. By selecting a host and a user on that host, you can retrieve information from the user's *finger-file*, that is, information specific to the user's account.

/WHOIS/

The **WHOIS** control allows you to retrieve information about hosts or users from a selected supporting host such as InterNIC. This control is essentially your electronic *white pages* for the Internet.

The VBX Custom Controls

/PUMP/

The **PUMP** control provides a graphical representation of a pump device used to pump fluids in a pipe. As part of a test control system, this VBX is a first-pass prototype; however, the resulting final control is in use as part of a real-time control system. This control may be used to practice porting VBXs to OCXs.

/VALVE/

As with the **PUMP** control, the **VALVE** control provides a graphical representation of a valve for use in a control system. This VBX is also a first-pass prototype for a control and can be used for practicing VBX porting methods.

Licensing Agreement

By opening this package, you are agreeing to be bound by the following:

This software product is copyrighted, and all rights are reserved by the publisher and author. You are licensed to use this software on a single computer. You may copy and/or modify the software as needed to facilitate your use of it on a single computer. Making copies of the software for any other purpose is a violation of the United States copyright laws.

This software is sold *as is* without warranty of any kind, either expressed or implied, including but not limited to the implied warranties of merchantability and fitness for a particular purpose. Neither the publisher nor its dealers or distributors assumes any liability for any alleged or actual damages arising from the use of this program. (Some states do not allow for the exclusion of implied warranties, so the exclusion may not apply to you.)

PLUG YOURSELF INTO...

THE MACMILLAN INFORMATION SUPERLIBRARY™

Free information and vast computer resources from the world's leading computer book publisher—online!

FIND THE BOOKS THAT ARE RIGHT FOR YOU!

A complete online catalog, plus sample chapters and tables of contents give you an in-depth look at *all* of our books, including hard-to-find titles. It's the best way to find the books you need!

- **STAY INFORMED** with the latest computer industry news through our online newsletter, press releases, and customized Information SuperLibrary Reports.

- **GET FAST ANSWERS** to your questions about MCP books and software.

- **VISIT** our online bookstore for the latest information and editions!

- **COMMUNICATE** with our expert authors through e-mail and conferences.

- **DOWNLOAD SOFTWARE** from the immense MCP library:
    - Source code and files from MCP books
    - The best shareware, freeware, and demos

- **DISCOVER HOT SPOTS** on other parts of the Internet.

- **WIN BOOKS** in ongoing contests and giveaways!

TO PLUG INTO MCP: ➤ WORLD WIDE WEB: **http://www.mcp.com**

GOPHER: gopher.mcp.com
FTP: ftp.mcp.com